Studies in Renaissance Literature

Volume 16

THE MAKING OF RESTORATION POETRY

This book explores the complex ways in which authors, publishers, and readers contributed to the making of Restoration poetry. The essays in Part I map some principal aspects of Restoration poetic culture: how poetic canons were established through both print and manuscript; how censorship operated within the manuscript transmission of erotic and politically sensitive poems; the poetic functions of authorial anonymity; the work of allusion and intertextual reference; the translation and adaptation of classical poetry; and the poetic representations of Charles II. Part II turns to individual poets, and charts the making of Dryden's canon; the ways in which *Mac Flecknoe* operates through intertextual allusions; the relationship of the variant texts of Marvell's 'To his Coy Mistress'; and the treatment of Rochester's canon and text by his modern editors. The discussions are complemented by illustrations drawn from both printed books and manuscripts.

PAUL HAMMOND is Professor of Seventeenth-Century English Literature at the University of Leeds.

Studies in Renaissance Literature

ISSN 1465–6310

General Editors
David Colclough
Raphael Lyne

Studies in Renaissance Literature offers investigations of topics in English literature focussed in the sixteenth and seventeenth centuries; its scope extends from early Tudor writing, including works reflecting medieval concerns, to the Restoration period. Studies exploring the interplay between the literature of the English Renaissance and its cultural history are particularly welcomed.

Proposals or queries should be sent in the first instance to the editors, or to the publisher, at the addresses given below; all submissions receive prompt and informed consideration.

Dr David Colclough, School of English and Drama, Queen Mary, University of London, Mile End Road, London, E1 4NS

Dr Raphael Lyne, New Hall, Cambridge, CB3 0DF

Boydell & Brewer Limited, PO Box 9, Woodbridge, Suffolk, IP12 3DF

Previously published volumes in this series are listed at the back of this volume.

The beehive from the title-page of Edward Wotton's *Insectorum sive Minimorum Animalium Theatrum* (1634) is reproduced by kind permission of the Syndics of Cambridge University Library

THE MAKING OF RESTORATION POETRY

Paul Hammond

D. S. BREWER

First published 2006
D. S. Brewer, Cambridge

ISBN 1 84384 074 X

D. S. Brewer is an imprint of Boydell & Brewer Ltd
PO Box 9, Woodbridge, Suffolk IP12 3DF, UK
and of Boydell & Brewer Inc.
668 Mt Hope Avenue, Rochester, NY 14620, USA
website: www.boydellandbrewer.com

A catalogue record for this title is available
from the British Library

This publication is printed on acid-free paper

Typeset by Pru Harrison, Hacheston, Suffolk
Printed in Great Britain by
MPG Books Ltd, Bodmin, Cornwall

CONTENTS

LIST OF ILLUSTRATIONS

All the illustrations are reproduced from books and manuscripts in the Department of Special Collections, Leeds University Library, by kind permission of the Librarian.

Plate 1 (p. 19)
Poems, &c. on Several Occasions: with Valentinian, a Tragedy. Written by the Right Honourable John Late Earl of Rochester (London, 1691), pp. 44–5.

Plate 2 (p. 22)
Poems. By the Incomparable, Mrs. K. P. (London, 1664), imprimatur and title page; and *Poems* By the most deservedly Admired Mrs. Katherine Philips The matchless Orinda (London, 1667), frontispiece portrait and title page.

Plate 3 (p. 23)
Miscellaneous Poems By Andrew Marvell, Esq; Late Member of the Honourable House of Commons (London, 1681), frontispiece portrait and title page.

Plate 4 (p. 25)
Title page of *Poems on Affairs of State* (1697), with the signature 'A. Pope'.

Plate 5 (p. 35)
Brotherton Collection MS Lt 55, fols. 36ᵛ–37ʳ, Rochester's satire on Charles II.

Plate 6 (p. 46)
Brotherton Collection MS Lt 110, fols. 11ᵛ–12ʳ, a poetical miscellany compiled in 1726, showing a previously unrecorded text of Rochester's *Satyre against Reason and Mankind.*

Plate 7 (p. 52)
Brotherton Collection MS Lt 54, p. 1, a richly bound and calligraphically written scriptorium manuscript originally compiled *circa* 1680, showing the opening of Dryden's *Mac Flecknoe.*

Plate 8 (p. 58)
[John Oldham], *Garnets Ghost, Addressing to the Jesuits, met in private Caball, just after the Murther of Sir Edmund-Bury Godfrey* [London, 1679], p. 1, and the opening of the same poem in Brotherton Collection MS Lt 87, fol. 18ʳ, a collection of satires mostly from the 1680s.

Plate 9 (p. 63)
Brotherton Collection MS Lt q 52, fols. 25ʳ–26ᵛ, a manuscript separate of Rochester's 'Upon Nothing' in a loose collection of verses compiled by John Gibson (1630–1711).

Plate 10 (p. 99)
John Dryden, *The Works of Virgil* (London, 1697), one of the plates illustrating *Aeneid* Book II.

Plate 11 (p. 149)
[John Dryden], *Absalom and Achitophel* (London, 1681), title page and p. 2.

Plate 12 (p. 164)
Brotherton Collection MS Lt 54, p. 448 (cp. Plate 7), a portion of the manuscript written in a later hand *circa* 1691, showing a text of Dryden's 'The Lady's Song', here entitled 'The Queen of May'.

ACKNOWLEDGEMENTS

Earlier versions of the following chapters originally appeared elsewhere, and I am grateful to the respective editors and publishers for permission to reprint them:

Chapter 1: The Restoration Poetic Canon
Revised from 'The Restoration Poetic and Dramatic Canon' in *The Cambridge History of the Book in Britain, Volume 4: 1557–1695*, edited by John Barnard and D. F. McKenzie (Cambridge: Cambridge University Press, 2002), pp. 388–409.

Chapter 2: Censorship and the Manuscript Transmission of Restoration Poetry
Revised from 'Censorship in the Manuscript Transmission of Restoration Poetry' in *Literature and Censorship* (Essays and Studies 1993), edited by Nigel Smith (Cambridge: D.S. Brewer for The English Association, 1993), pp. 39–62.

Chapter 3: Anonymity in Restoration Poetry
Revised from 'Anonymity in Restoration Poetry', in *The Seventeenth Century*, 8 (1993) 123–42.

Chapter 5: Classical Texts: Translations and Transformations
Revised from 'Classical Texts: Translations and Transformations' in *The Cambridge Companion to English Literature, 1650–1740*, edited by Steven N. Zwicker (Cambridge: Cambridge University Press, 1998), pp. 143–61.

Chapter 6: The King's Two Bodies: Representations of Charles II
Revised from 'The King's Two Bodies: Representations of Charles II' in *Culture, Politics and Society in Britain, 1660–1800*, edited by Jeremy Black and Jeremy Gregory (Manchester: Manchester University Press, 1991), pp. 13–48.

Chapter 7: The Circulation of Dryden's Poetry
Revised from 'The Circulation of Dryden's Poetry' in *Papers of the Bibliographical Society of America*, 86 (1992) 379–409.

Chapter 8: Flecknoe and *Mac Flecknoe*
Revised from 'Flecknoe and *Mac Flecknoe*' in *Essays in Criticism*, 35 (1985) 315–29.

Chapter 9: Marvell's Coy Mistresses
Revised from 'Marvell's Coy Mistresses' in *Literary Texts in Transmission*, edited by Maureen Bell et al. (Aldershot: Ashgate, 2001), pp. 22–33.

Acknowledgements

I have revised each essay, adding new material, correcting errors, and updating the references, and have also cut and rewritten passages in order to minimize repetition between the essays. There remain some repetitions which have been left in order to reduce the need for the reader to break off and refer to other chapters for essential information; in particular, the creation of Dryden's canon which is outlined briefly in chapter 1 is discussed more fully in chapter 7. I hope that the reader will find these occasional repetitions helpful rather than irritating.

I must also thank two members of the clerical staff in the School of English, University of Leeds, Louise Ward and Zoe Thompson, for producing electronic files by scanning texts of some of these articles.

I am grateful to Dr Nicholas Fisher for his kind permission to cite his thesis 'The Publication of the Earl of Rochester's Works, 1660–1779', unpublished PhD thesis, University of Leeds, 2004, which I had the pleasure of supervising.

ABBREVIATIONS

The following works are cited throughout by abbreviations. Other works are cited in full on their first appearance in each chapter, and thereafter by author or short title.

Beal, *Index*	Peter Beal, *Index of English Literary Manuscripts*, vol. 2, parts i–ii (London, 1987–93)
Diary of Samuel Pepys	*The Diary of Samuel Pepys*, edited by Robert Latham and William Matthews, 11 vols (London, 1970–83)
Fisher, 'Publication'	Nicholas Fisher, 'The Publication of the Earl of Rochester's Works, 1660–1779', unpublished PhD thesis, University of Leeds, 2004. [This includes a bibliography of early editions of Rochester.]
Gyldenstolpe	*The Gyldenstolpe Manuscript Miscellany of Poems by John Wilmot, Earl of Rochester, and other Restoration Authors*, edited by Bror Danielsson and David M. Vieth, Stockholm Studies in English 17 (Stockholm, 1967)
Hammond, *Traces*	Paul Hammond, *Dryden and the Traces of Classical Rome* (Oxford, 1999)
Macdonald, *Bibliography*	Hugh Macdonald, *John Dryden: A Bibliography of Early Editions and of Drydeniana* (Oxford, 1939)
PBSA	*Papers of the Bibliographical Society of America*
POAS	*Poems on Affairs of State*, edited by George De F. Lord et al., 7 vols (New Haven, 1963–75)
Poems of Andrew Marvell	*The Poems of Andrew Marvell*, edited by Nigel Smith (London, 2003)
Poems of John Dryden	*The Poems of John Dryden*, edited by Paul Hammond and David Hopkins, 5 vols (London, 1995–2005) [Quotations from Dryden are taken from this edition unless otherwise stated.]
Works of John Dryden	*The Works of John Dryden*, edited by H. T. Swedenberg et al., 20 vols (Berkeley, Calif., 1956–2000)
Works of John Wilmot	*The Works of John Wilmot, Earl of Rochester*, edited by Harold Love (Oxford, 1999)

Other abbreviations:

BL   The British Library
OED   *The Oxford English Dictionary*, second edition, CD-rom version
        2002

INTRODUCTION
POETRY, THE PUBLIC, AND THE PRIVATE

I

Like many binary oppositions, the antithesis between the 'public' and the 'private' is conceptually crude, and tends to obscure more than it illuminates. Yet if we keep in view the instability of these terms, they can be useful in identifying the ways in which Restoration poetry shapes complex forms of public discourse and of private reflection. When the restored Charles II saw the crowds which greeted him in May 1660 as he rode into London, he remarked that it was evidently his own fault that he had been away so long, since he had not met anyone who did not wish for his return. The irony in the king's remark shows that he was well aware that public opinion was not unanimous; indeed, the very notion of public opinion, in the singular, is dubious in this context. In 1660 there were many constituencies: principled republicans, pragmatic civil servants, opportunistic new royalists, long-suffering cavaliers, disappointed Nonconformists, triumphant Anglicans, unobtrusive Catholics – and any of these labels is liable to dissolve on contact with the complexities of individual beliefs and practices. But a study of Restoration poetry can map some of the ways in which forms of the public and the private were created.

The presentation of the new king was itself a public fiction – and one element in that fiction was the denial of the word 'new'. Charles dated his reign from 30 January 1649, the date of his father's execution, so according to official calculations his return in May 1660 fell in his twelfth regnal year. The time when Charles was in exile in France or in flight from his defeat at the Battle of Worcester was therefore presented as the first decade of his reign, so that a public fiction was laminated over what had actually been experienced. Poets began by celebrating his return through the imagery of Charles as Augustus or as David, which implied an imperial or providential narrative, but Dryden in *Astraea Redux*, while using both mythologies, pondered also the nature of the time and the implementation of the vocabulary.[1] The definition of mythology offered by Roland Barthes illuminates some of the modes through which poetry shaped a mythology for the public realm:

---

[1] Hammond, *Traces*, pp. 84–92.

Ce que le monde fournit au mythe c'est un réel historique. . . et ce que le mythe restitue, c'est une image naturelle de ce réel. . . le mythe est constitué par la déperdition de la qualité historique des choses: les choses perdent en lui le souvenir de leur fabrication. Le monde entre dans le langage comme un rapport dialectique d'activités, d'actes humains: il sort du mythe comme un tableau harmonieux d'essences.[2]

Though Barthes' definition is itself historically inflected – being a commentary particularly on the bourgeois and conservative myths of France in the 1950s – his analysis is suggestive. In many poems on the Restoration there is a loss of the historical quality of the time in so far as the complexities of human agency are elided. The poetic discourse of this period frequently invokes what Barthes called 'essences', or what Derrida would call the 'signifié transcendental',[3] that powerful term such as 'nature', 'truth', or 'God' which appears to give coherence to a discourse. Dryden, while seeing the hand of Providence in the king's Restoration, is attentive both to the making of events through the agency of particular historical actors – including General Monck and the king himself – and to the making of images through the work of the poet, so that *Astraea Redux* becomes a meditation on the relation of this particular piece of writing to the times which it addresses. The poem is aware of the status of the analogies which it makes for the understanding of public events, the process of 'fabrication'.

Dryden's *Annus Mirabilis*, written six years later at the time of the Second Dutch War, may at one level celebrate the heroism of the English sailors, but the poem keeps turning aside from its few images of national glory in order to attend to the courage and pain of individuals. The poem is a patchwork of human activities and philosophical vocabularies (Providence, Fortune, Fate) which is far from conjuring events into a harmonious plane of transhistorical essences. It concludes with the evocation of a new London, rebuilt after the Fire, which is explicitly presented as the poet's vision, quite clearly a myth:

> Methinks already from this chymic flame
>   I see a city of more precious mould:
> Rich as the town which gives the Indies name,
>   With silver paved, and all divine with gold.[4]

---

2 Roland Barthes, *Mythologies*, in *Œuvres complètes*, 5 vols (Paris, 2002), i 854: 'What the world provides to myth is an historical reality. . . and what myth provides in return is a natural image of this reality. . . myth is constituted by the loss of the historical character of things: in myth, things lose the memory of their making. The world enters language as a dialectical relationship between activities, between human actions: it comes out of myth as a harmonious picture of essences' (my translation).

3 'transcendental signified': Jacques Derrida, *L'Écriture et la différence* (Paris, 1967, new edition 1994), p. 411. I do not mean to imply that Barthes' term and Derrida's are synonymous or interchangeable.

4 Dryden, *Annus Mirabilis*, ll. 1169–72.

This is London transformed as by alchemy ('chymic flame') into the New Jerusalem from the Book of Revelation: London is cast in a 'precious' mould, like the holy city built from 'precious' stones, and it is 'all divine with gold' like the city which John the Divine saw that 'was pure gold'.[5] After describing this 'new deified'[6] London, Dryden introduces a series of first person plural pronouns which gather the nation into one. 'Already we have conquered half the war', says Dryden, drawing his readers (as a synecdoche for the country at large) into owning the battles which he has been describing, and he ends by moving from the activities of the single 'venturous merchant' to the venture upon which the whole nation is embarking, and for which trade is a metonymy:

> Thus to the eastern wealth through storms we go,
>   But now, the Cape once doubled, fear no more:
> A constant trade-wind will securely blow,
>   And gently lay us on the spicy shore.[7]

With a mythic title, *Annus Mirabilis*, and a subtitle claiming it to be 'An Historical Poem', it thoughtfully constructs myth from history without losing sight of the particularity of events.

But during the Second Dutch War there were other poetic voices, those of oppositional writers who linked the failure of English public policy with the venality of Charles's individual, named, courtiers, and his own preference for sexual rather than official business. According to the poems by Andrew Marvell and others which made up the series of 'Advice to a Painter' poems from 1667 onwards, it was the fracturing of the public sphere into a tawdry series of private pursuits, sexual and financial, which was responsible for the humiliation of the English navy and of the English capital. There was a dire symbolism in the destruction by the Dutch of a warship called the *Loyal London*, and the further loss of the *Royal Charles* and, ominously, the *Unity*. Such losses might seem to symbolize the loss or fragmentation of the public realm itself. In the oppositional poetry of the late 1660s and early 1670s, control over the voice of the public passes to individual poets who claim to be writing on behalf of the nation, for example by speaking in the persona of Britannia.

In reply, Dryden's narrative of the Exclusion Crisis in *Absalom and Achitophel* seeks to reconfigure the political sphere. It adroitly exploits the mixture of the divine and the mortal which was said to be combined in the king's person by admitting his sexual promiscuity at the beginning of the poem while asking readers to hear 'their maker in their master'[8] in the king's

---

5   Revelation xxi 18–19. The reference to the 'new foundations' of London (l. 1179) also echoes the emphasis on the 'foundations' of the New Jerusalem (Revelation xxi 14, 19).
6   Dryden, *Annus Mirabilis*, l. 1178.
7   Dryden, *Annus Mirabilis*, ll. 1197, 1209, 1213–16.

speech at the end. The poem's roll-call of individual opponents and supporters
was an implicit rejoinder to the series of portraits of corrupt courtiers which
had comprised the 'Advice to a Painter' poems, and suggested that in the
Exclusion Crisis individuals were playing roles which were at odds with their
publicly professed aims; moreover, each was participating in a transhistorical
narrative, with Shaftesbury, Monmouth, and Oates being turned by the allegory into archetypes of the scheming politician, the vain and malleable aristocrat, the venal demagogue. At the end of the poem the allegory delivers a
conclusion which is narrated in the past tense:

> Henceforth a series of new time began,
> The mighty years in long procession ran;
> Once more the godlike David was restored,
> And willing nations knew their lawful lord.[9]

But this is of course a pseudo-history, a myth in which there is no indication of
how the triumph of the king will be brought about. There is no trace of a 'rapport dialectique d'activités, d'actes humains', though earlier in the poem
Dryden had indeed engaged in a dialectical argument with Whig political
theory. For him, the Whigs were merely usurping the vocabulary of patriotism
and liberty,[10] pursuing private advantage under the cover of public good.

Meanwhile, what emerges in the poetry which treats cultural and social
pursuits is a series of distinct milieux:[11] besides the Court, there is the Town,
comprising the fashionable *beau monde*, often mapped and satirized on the
stage as Restoration comedy explores how individuals inhabit and manipulate
the social spaces of London, such as the Mall, St James's Park, and the
Exchange; and by contrast there is the City, where the more conservative citizens and their wives (much despised by the denizens of the Town) make and
spend their money. The satires of Rochester often explore how people inhabit
these social spaces, both the public spaces in the open air and the semi-private
spaces such as coffee houses and drawing rooms: all seem to be stages for the
performance of private acts, with the reader as implicit voyeur. By night St
James's Park becomes a space 'consecrate to *Prick* and *Cunt*', an 'All-sin-
sheltring *Grove*'.[12] The bore can transform a drawing room (in *Artemiza to
Chloe*) or the street itself (in *Timon*) into a place of embarrassment. The very
word 'embarrassed' appears in *Artemiza to Chloe* in its French form, when the
speaker declares that she is 'Embarassé with being out of Towne', and proceeds

---

8   Dryden, *Absalom and Achitophel*, l. 938.
9   Dryden, *Absalom and Achitophel*, ll. 1028–31.
10 Dryden, *Absalom and Achitophel*, ll. 51–2, 179.
11 See Harold Love, 'Dryden, Rochester, and the Invention of the "Town"', in *John Dryden
    (1631–1700): His Politics, His Plays, and His Poets*, edited by Claude Rawson and Aaron
    Santesso (Newark, N.J., 2004), pp. 36–51.
12 Rochester, 'A Ramble in St. *James's Park*', ll. 10, 25.

to use other French importations, 'a la mode' and its rhyming pair 'incommode'. The Town, then, defines what is *à la mode*, for example by prescribing the right kind of male partner: 'When I was marry'd, Fooles were a la mode, | The Men of Witt were then held incommode.'[13] There is a strong consciousness of the social geography of London, which is also a linguistic geography, since one's place is determined in part by use of the right terms: Melantha in Dryden's *Marriage A-la-Mode* learns her daily quota of French words, and is reluctant to spend them to no advantage: 'pray do not *embarrass* me' she says, and then regrets having spent part of her social capital: '*embarrass* me! what a delicious *French* word do you make me lose upon you too!'[14] The microsocieties within the broad divisions of fashionable London are intricately mapped through idiolects, often through the collision of idiolects.

The transgression of social and geographical boundaries is vividly portrayed when the Duchess of Cleveland, who had been the king's first *maîtresse en titre*, asks a confidante for advice:

> Quoth the *Dutchess* of *Cleveland*, to Counsellor *Knight*,
> I'd fain have a *Prick*, knew I how to come by't;
> I desire you'le be secret, and give your advice,
> Though Cunt be not coy, Reputation is nice.

and receives the following recommendation:

> To some *Cellar*, in *Sodom*, your *Grace* must retire,
> Where *Porters*, with Black Pots, sit round a *Coal-fire*,
> There open your *Case*, and your *Grace* cannot fail,
> Of a douzen of *Pricks* for a douzen of *Ale*.[15]

This supposedly private conversation is cast in the form of a song, which implies a performance to an audience, and the writer (perhaps Rochester, though the attribution is doubtful[16]) knows the frisson which can be created by the use of personal names in such coarse lampoons. Mary Knight, an actress who had played the roles of Peace and Daphne in the masque *Calisto* at Court, evidently knows her London geography, and directs the Duchess to an appropriate district. The song exploits the ironies inherent in the jarring of aristocratic forms of address with low vernacular speech. The Duchess claims to be fastidious ('nice') about her reputation, and desires to protect her privacy, but her reputation is being traduced by the very existence of this text, which was available to a small circle of readers in commercially produced scriptorium manuscripts in the 1670s, and subsequently in print in the clandestine 1680

---

13 Rochester, *Artemiza to Chloe*, ll. 98, 103–4.
14 Dryden, *Marriage A-la-Mode*, V i 100–2; *Works of John Dryden*, xi 300.
15 Rochester [?], 'Song', ll. 1–8.
16 *Works of John Wilmot*, pp. 421–2.

edition of *Poems on Several Occasions by the Right Honourable, The E. of R– – –*. She is advised that to obtain sexual satisfaction she has only to open her case to the working men, 'case' meaning 'circumstances, plight' (*OED sb.*[1] 5a), but also 'mask, disguise' (*OED sb.*[2] 4b), and also 'vagina'.[17] Multiple scenarios are built into this pun: the Duchess in a beer cellar explaining her plight to the working-class drinkers; the Duchess taking off her disguise to reveal her face to them; and the Duchess displaying her genitals to them. This is a deft denial by the poet of the dignity of the public space and the privacy of the private. Or rather, it is an exposure by the poet of how the stability of the civilized boundaries between public and private has been compromised by the Court's behaviour.

II

Ostensibly private worlds in Restoration poetry are in various ways opened out towards the reader, and offered as spaces into which we are invited to enter. Marvell's 'The Garden' celebrates 'delicious solitude', for 'Two Paradises 'twere in one | To live in Paradise alone'; but the rhetoric of the poem draws the reader in, as it opens with an exclamation which borders on being a rhetorical question: 'How vainly men themselves amaze | To win the palm, the oak, or bays', and the poem ends with another exclamation which again borders on a question: 'How could such sweet and wholesome hours | Be reckoned but with herbs and flow'rs!'[18] Rhetorically the reader is being invited to concur, though the pronouns remain singular, and the poem's spaces are singularities which do not invite easy sharing.[19] The private spaces of Rochester's erotic poetry are shared with a lover, but these addresses to a lover are often staged: 'Upon his Leaving his Mistress', for example, performs an argument to justify his own unfaithfulness which in its self-conscious wit seems to imply an audience and invite their admiration: though nominally addressing a woman, the male speaker is acting out the justification of his desire for change in front of an implicitly male readership, so that a private heterosexual conversation becomes an act of male homosocial display. And when the poetry imagines scenes of drinking and sexual boasting with male companions (in 'The Disabled Debauchee', for example, or 'Love a Woman! Th'rt an Ass') these worlds too are staged to be shared with readers, who are being teased into smothering embarrassment, challenged into emulation, or shocked into tearing the page from the book. The varied personae of Rochester's verse

---

[17] *Works of John Wilmot*, p. 422; Gordon Williams, *A Glossary of Shakespeare's Sexual Language* (London, 1997), p. 66.

[18] Marvell, 'The Garden', ll. 16, 63–4, 1–2, 71–2.

[19] See my 'Marvell's Pronouns', *Essays in Criticism*, 53 (2003) 225–40.

appear to be private individuals who are often defending their privacy or autonomy, but these too are literary constructions intended for circulation.

By contrast, Milton in *Paradise Lost* (offered to 'fit audience. . . though few'[20]) reflects on the spiritual grounds of the private, specifically on how the individual comes to embrace modes of autonomy which are, in the pejorative sense, selfish. In Book III we listen to the intricate colloquy between God the Father and God the Son, a shared speech which establishes a link between love and self-surrender; and then by contrast we move to Satan's solitary journey through Chaos to Mount Niphates. Here, at the beginning of Book IV, his soliloquy on Niphates' top is a form of self-dramatization in front of an audience of one – except that the reader overhears him, prompted by the poem's narrator, and one supposes that God does too. Puzzled angels notice his countenance disordered by emotion while he stands 'alone, | As he supposed, all unobserved, unseen'.[21] While Satan travels from Hell, through Chaos, and on to Earth, the crucial journey is the one which he cannot take, since he carries Hell within him:

> Which way shall I fly
> Infinite wrath, and infinite despair?
> Which way I fly is hell; myself am hell;
> And in the lowest deep a lower deep
> Still threatening to devour me opens wide. . .
>   is there no place
> Left for repentance, none for pardon left?[22]

Here the only form of space which signifies is the inner space, a singular private world from which he only half-yearns to escape.

Privacy in Eden is also troubled and troublesome, as Milton subtly delineates the shades of consciousness and behaviour which distinguish selfhood from selfishness. Adam and Eve's shared space, in which they walk naked, is enviously overlooked by Satan, and via Satan by the reader. The Fall is prepared for by Eve withdrawing her hand from Adam's hand, and insisting on working alone. After the Fall, the plural pronoun 'we' which had previously united her with Adam in one voice declines into the self-seeking 'I' which recoils from the prospect of her own annihilation and resolves that if she is to die, Adam will be made to share her destruction:

>   what if God have seen,
> And death ensue? Then I shall be no more,
> And Adam wedded to another Eve,
> Shall live with her enjoying, I extinct;

---

[20] Milton, *Paradise Lost*, vii 31.
[21] Milton, *Paradise Lost*, iv 129–30.
[22] Milton, *Paradise Lost*, iv 73–80.

A death to think. Confirmed then I resolve,
Adam shall share with me in bliss or woe:
So dear I love him, that with him all deaths
I could endure, without him live no life.[23]

The couple is reconstituted, not out of love but from the self-serving exploitation of one partner by the other.

Though the narratorial voice of *Paradise Lost* is generally impersonal, it occasionally modulates into tones which we recognize as nearly autobiographical – most notably in the invocation to light at the beginning of Book III, when the poet contemplates that wholly unwelcome mode of privacy which is the isolation caused by his blindness. By contrast, the kinds of private voice which we encounter in Dryden are more often alter egos than authorial personae.[24] Dialogue and translation are his preferred forms, so that an individual voice is merged in or played against others. Though there is what appears to be a passage of spiritual confession written in the first person in *The Hind and the Panther*, this is partly modelled on Tasso.[25] And Dryden's principal interest in this poem is in the play of voices, the exchange of argument between the two animals in his beast fable. What fascinates him is not his own voice, but how the speech of the Hind – as the Church of Rome – may be seen to be authoritative, so authoritative that at one point she quotes scripture, merging her voice with the voice of Jesus: '*She whom ye seek am I.*'[26]

In Dryden's *Fables Ancient and Modern* (1700) many of the characters find that their own individuality is compromised, and Dryden uses translation as a way of mapping the many forms of a person's dependence upon that which lies beyond him, be that society or superhuman forces. So in 'Palamon and Arcite' the two noble kinsmen who contend for the hand of Emily find themselves adrift in a world which eludes their understanding: they try to placate the powers beyond them by prayers to Mars and to Venus, but they are aware that Fate, or Chance, or Fortune, or Providence may also be at work.[27] In the translation from Ovid's *Metamorphoses* Book XV, which he called 'Of the Pythagorean Philosophy', Dryden ventured imaginatively into the realm of the transmigration of souls – without necessarily endorsing any of these ideas *in propria persona*, for such is the enticingly noncommittal art of translation – and explored the uncanny proximity between the human and the material worlds.[28]

---

23 Milton, *Paradise Lost*, ix 826–33.
24 See Cedric D. Reverand II, 'The Final "Memorial of my own Principles": Dryden's Alter Egos in his Later Career', in *John Dryden: Tercentenary Essays*, edited by Paul Hammond and David Hopkins (Oxford, 2000), pp. 282–307.
25 Dryden, *The Hind and the Panther*, iii 72–8; *Poems of John Dryden*, iii 54–5.
26 Dryden, *The Hind and the Panther*, ii 398.
27 See my 'The Interplay of Past and Present in Dryden's "Palamon and Arcite" ', in *The Age of Projects*, edited by Maximillian E. Novak (Toronto, forthcoming).
28 See Hammond, *Traces*, pp. 207–17.

A remarkable example of individual self-assertion occurs in 'Sigismonda and Guiscardo' translated from Boccaccio. Sigismonda, widowed and now back in the palace of her father King Tancred, chooses a lover from amongst his servants. She has taken considerable care to make her sexual relationship with Guiscardo private, but one afternoon her father falls asleep in her bedroom and is awoken by the sound of the couple's love-making. He has Guiscardo arrested and killed. Sigismonda's long speech of self-defence is an assertion of her autonomy, of her right to choose her own partner rather than be coerced by a parent's wishes – in this case, her possessive father's reluctance to countenance her remarriage. The speech reaches out beyond a defence of her private conduct into an attack upon the language by which, she assumes, Tancred would seek to justify his own attitude. Guiscardo's lowly birth is no reflection on his virtue or nobility, since virtue *is* true nobility.[29] Dryden's Sigismonda appropriates some of the key words of Restoration culture – nature, virtue, nobility – and insists upon her own individual right to define them. Language will not intimidate her or imprison her, for these public terms are made her own terms, defined and applied in ways which liberate and authorize her conduct.

III

Such modes of the public and the private are all poetic spaces which are made by writers, and which reach the reader as made objects; the reader then makes the poem afresh in his imagination. This book explores the 'making' of Restoration poetry in several senses. One theme is the way in which poetry in the period from 1660 to 1700 was created not only by writers, but also by scribes, publishers, and readers. The canon of major poets (discussed in Chapters 1 and 7) was fashioned partly by the decisions which those writers themselves made about how to publish their work – printed as single pieces, in collected editions, or in miscellanies; transcribed and circulated in commercially produced manuscripts or in privately made copies. But canons are also shaped by publishers, notably in this period by the influential and innovative Jacob Tonson. He commissioned work which might otherwise not have been undertaken, such as Dryden's Virgil, pioneered new modes of publication, including the poetical miscellany and publication by subscription, and also made sure that the texts of his poets were suitable for his particular market, so that his edition of Rochester excluded items which he or his editor thought inappropriate, while some poems which he did include were shorn of obscene or suggestive stanzas. (Nor did the editing of Rochester stop there, for

---

[29] *Virtus vera nobilitas,* as Dryden would have been reminded as an undergraduate every time he looked at the motto on his college's coat of arms.

twentieth-century editions too reflected a range of preconceptions about what should constitute Rochester's canon and text, as Chapter 10 shows.) Much of the erotic, libellous, or politically sensitive poetry from this period was circulated in manuscript, either in the form of the expensive products of commercial scriptoria, or as separates passed from hand to hand and subsequently transcribed into personal miscellanies. One might suppose this to have been a milieu of free expression, but these manuscript texts were actually often cut, expanded, anonymized, reattributed, and rewritten as they were transcribed (Chapters 2 and 9). Poetry which is published in various kinds of printed or manuscript text is aimed at different kinds of readership, and is accorded different kinds of authority, with the large illustrated folio of Dryden's Virgil at one end of the spectrum, and a grubby manuscript sheet of libellous verses at the other. But the libellous verses may adopt the voice of a culturally powerful speaker to voice political dissent; and there is a special cachet attached to the fugitive, oppositional manuscript, with its appearance of a hard-bought and dangerous freedom. The anonymity of such poems may be a creative rhetorical strategy rather than an accident which irritates scholars who are trying to construct authorially-based canons (Chapter 3). Such protective strategies are particularly deployed when the person of the king himself is being traduced (Chapter 6).

Another thread which runs through this book is the way in which poetry as a text is fashioned through intertextual allusion to other English poems, and to the classics (Chapters 4, 5, and 8). Here again, different readerships are envisaged, with some satires presupposing a knowledgeable interest in political or sexual intrigue at Court, while others address literary or theatrical cognoscenti, readers who know Shadwell's plays – even readers who know Flecknoe's letters. Classical allusion creates its own circle of understanders, and excludes the unlearned. Here again a rhetoric of authority is in play, for the Restoration poet may enlist the cultural standing of a Roman predecessor to license his own writing, especially if it is in some way oppositional. Many of these rhetorical strategies – anonymity, multiple personae, allegory, allusion – invite the reader to engage in a very active form of reading, making him in important respects a co-author, another maker of the text.

The book is divided into two parts, moving from essays on aspects of the poetic culture in Part I to studies of particular writers and poems in Part II. Part I explores how the literary culture of the period was shaped by the activities not only of writers, but of the copyists, printers, and booksellers who handled their work, and by the readers who annotated, replied to, and recomposed what they read. In this part I offer essays on the formation of the poetic canon around named authors, and by contrast the rhetorical uses of poetic anonymity; the vicissitudes which poems experienced through manuscript circulation; the ways in which intertextual allusion invited the reader to an active engagement in the construction of meaning, and particularly the uses which were made of allusions to and translations from classical Latin and

Greek poetry. Part I concludes with the rhetorical strategies which were deployed when poets wished to criticize the government of Charles II by depictions of his sacred monarchical body, a body which he himself had made into a sexual object of public interest.

Part II turns to case studies of individual writers, beginning with an analysis of the circulation of Dryden's poetry, and moving on to his intertextual uses of the work of one despised contemporary, Flecknoe, to discredit another, Shadwell. After an analysis of the remaking of one of Marvell's poems through its manuscript transmission, the book concludes with a critique of the handling of Rochester's texts by his modern editors.

The book is designed as a collection of essays which explore linked themes: it is not intended as a comprehensive study of either the Restoration publishing trade or Restoration poetics. But I hope that it will provide a varied, if necessarily partial, map of the complex material and intellectual factors which shaped the poetry of the period. Its chronological scope is approximately 1660 to 1700, from the Restoration of Charles II to the death of Dryden, with the occasional excursus back to Marvell's work in the 1650s and forward to Pope's in the early eighteenth century. The principal missing figure is, of course, Milton; but until the end of this period, when Tonson brought him into the English poetic canon, Dryden echoed him in his *Fables Ancient and Modern*, and the Whigs selectively appropriated him as their champion, his work was not a significant part of 'Restoration poetry' as it was perceived by the writers, readers, and booksellers of the metropolis who provide the principal material for this book. How Milton might be read within and against such a context, and how he came to be brought into the canon, is another story.[30]

---

[30] See, for example, George F. Sensabaugh, *That Grand Whig Milton* (Stanford, Calif., 1952); J. R. Mason, 'To Milton through Dryden and Pope', unpublished PhD thesis, University of Cambridge, 1987; Sharon Achinstein, *Milton and the Revolutionary Reader* (Princeton, 1994); Nicholas von Maltzahn, 'The First Reception of *Paradise Lost* (1667)', *Review of English Studies*, n.s. 47 (1996) 479–99; Stephen B. Dobranski, *Milton, Authorship, and the Book Trade* (Cambridge, 1999).

Part I

The Making of Restoration Poetic Culture

1

The Restoration Poetic Canon

I

When our great monarch into exile went,
Wit and religion suffered banishment . . .
At length the Muses stand restored again
To that great charge which Nature did ordain.[1]

THE IDEA, expressed here by Dryden, that the arts were restored in 1660 along with the Stuart monarchy was a commonplace of the day, and formed part of the mythological and ideological fashioning of this historical moment. The desire to represent the new king as a second Augustus, patron of poetry as well as bringer of peace and social order, was part of a movement by which this turning point in the nation's history was understood, by which the future was sketched out and the past rewritten. Retrospectively the republic is represented as a barbarous interlude, and Dryden himself quickly forgets that only a few months earlier he had written of Cromwell that 'in his praise no arts can liberal be'.[2]

During the early months of 1660, the presses poured out pamphlets of all kinds.[3] In January alone, George Thomason collected two dozen verse satires against the Rump Parliament, the army, and the leaders of the republic; in February there were a further dozen satires, now interspersed with panegyrics to General Monck; in March verses began to be published favouring the restoration of Charles II, and some satires took the form of miniature plays. By April it was possible to publish an elegy on Charles I. Charles II entered London on 29 May, and by the end of July Thomason had collected some thirty separate poems or collaborative volumes of verse celebrating the Restoration.

---

[1] John Dryden, *To My Lord Chancellor*, ll. 17–18, 23–4.
[2] John Dryden, *Heroic Stanzas*, l. 9.
[3] See *Catalogue of the Pamphlets, Books, Newspapers, and Manuscripts Relating to the Civil War, the Commonwealth, and Restoration, Collected by George Thomason, 1640–1661*, 2 vols (London, 1908).

The changing climate can be traced through the variety of bogus imprints used on these pamphlets, from the cautious 'Printed for Philo-Basileuticus Verax' on 6 March, to the bolder 'Printed for Charles King' on the 15th. Satirical imprints registered the decline of that republican and sectarian cause which had once flourished so vigorously when the printed media were opened to previously excluded political views and social classes: one pamphlet was ostensibly to be sold 'at the signe of the Roasted Rump', another claimed to be 'Printed for every body but the light-heel'd Apprentices and headstrong Masters of this wincing City of London', and a third was 'Printed at the Charge of John Lambert, Charles Fleetwood, Arthur Hesilrig and —— Hewson the Cobler, and are to be distributed to the fainting Brethren'.[4]

This is a moment at which ephemeral verses and quasi-dramatic texts are being rapidly produced for a wide readership in order to influence the emerging political settlement;[5] at the same time the more literary canon is being revised as established writers hastily reposition themselves, and newcomers seize the opportunity to initiate a career.[6] Dryden's poem to his friend and future brother-in-law Sir Robert Howard, prefixed to Howard's *Poems* (1660), admires Howard's politic relocation of himself through the publication of a volume which both praises the king and General Monck, and also sets out Howard's claim to be one of the poets of the new classical age through his translations from Virgil and Statius. By contrast, George Wither appealed to the nation to keep the faith, and in his *Fides-Anglicana* (1660) he included a list of his writings, a piece of self-canonization ostensibly offered in the national interest. Milton's position was much more precarious, but he saw the times as requiring a bold prose statement of his political views, the *Readie & Easie Way to Establish a Free Commonwealth* (late February 1660).[7] Such visibility was dangerous: Harrington replied a few weeks later with his *Censure of the Rota*, while Roger L'Estrange attacked him in *No Blind Guides*, published in April. In May the author of *Britains Triumph* gave an ominous foretaste of what might happen to prominent republican men of letters as the political tide

---

4 *Catalogue*, ii 290–5.
5 See *Poems of John Dryden*, i 36; Nicholas Jose, *Ideas of the Restoration in English Literature, 1660–71* (Basingstoke, 1984), pp. 1–66.
6 For the wider context of the publishing trade in this period, see *The Cambridge History of the Book in Britain: Volume IV: 1557–1695*, edited by John Barnard and D. F. McKenzie, with the assistance of Maureen Bell (Cambridge, 2002). There was also a flourishing Nonconformist literary culture, which was largely unconcerned with the literary milieux mapped in this chapter: see N. H. Keeble, *The Literary Culture of Nonconformity in Later Seventeenth-Century England* (Leicester, 1987), and Nigel Smith, 'Non-conformist voices and books' in Barnard and McKenzie, pp. 410–30.
7 For Milton's publication history in the Restoration see Stephen B. Dobranski, *Milton, Authorship, and the Book Trade* (Cambridge, 1999); Joad Raymond, 'Milton', in Barnard and McKenzie, pp. 376–87; Nicholas von Maltzahn, 'The First Reception of *Paradise Lost* (1667)', *Review of English Studies*, n.s. 47 (1996) 479–99.

turned: Milton, he said, should follow the example of Achitophel and hang himself; but in any case,

> stab'd, hang'd or drown'd,
> Will make all sure, and further good will bring,
> The wretch will rail no more against his *King*.[8]

In such circumstances Edmund Waller greeted the new king with as much fervour as he had mourned Cromwell. Marvell kept silent.

II

During the Restoration period the poetry of 'the last age', as it was now called, was selectively reprinted, and the canon of English literature was refashioned, both through the reprinting of works and, negatively, through what we would now regard as serious acts of oblivion. We need to integrate into any discussion of the Restoration poetic canon an awareness of how the literature of the earlier seventeenth century was regarded, because the culture of the Restoration period is too often treated as if it consisted solely of those works which were being published for the first time. For readers, of course, did not confine their attention to literature by their contemporaries, and might well be reading Donne one day and Dryden the next.[9] The frequency with which editions of earlier literature were issued during the Restoration period provides some indication of contemporary taste. The royalist poets maintained some popularity for a decade or so after 1660, but then declined: Cleveland enjoyed an intense but brief vogue;[10] Carew was reprinted in 1670 and 1671, but not thereafter; Lovelace not at all after 1659; Suckling in 1676 and 1696; Herrick not at all after 1648; Henry King in 1664 but not thereafter. As for poets from earlier generations, Chaucer was given a handsome folio in 1687, and Spenser in 1679. Donne was reprinted in 1669, but not subsequently. Herbert, however, remained consistently popular, perhaps because he affected the metaphysics less outrageously than Donne, but more probably because he had become established as a devotional classic: James Duport had told his students at Cambridge in the 1650s to regard 'the divine & heavenly book Herberts Poems' as second only to the Bible.[11] Herbert's *The Temple* was reprinted in 1660, 1667 (twice), 1674, 1678, 1679 and 1695. Quarles too remained popular

---

[8]   G. S., *Britains Triumph* (London, 1660), p. 15.

[9]   For one reader's view of the English poetic canon, see Paul Hammond, 'Sir Philip Wodehouse's Pantheon of Renaissance Poets', *The Seventeenth Century*, 18 (2003) 54–60. Written probably in the 1660s, Wodehouse's poem in praise of poetry lists many English and neo-Latin writers, but only from the Elizabethan and Jacobean periods.

[10] Brian Morris, *John Cleveland (1613–1658): A Bibliography of his Poems* (London, 1967).

[11] Trinity College, Cambridge, MS O. 10A. 33.

right through this period, the emblem evidently proving to be an enduringly appealing form for religious and moral reflection: there were seven editions of his *Emblemes* between 1660 and 1696.[12] Charles Hoole selected Herbert and Quarles as suitable reading for fourth-form schoolboys.[13] It was perhaps Catholic piety which provided a readership for Crashaw, with *Steps to the Temple* receiving three editions in 1670 and another *circa* 1685. But there was no demand for Henry Vaughan.

Two booksellers were particularly significant in shaping the canon of earlier poetry during the Restoration period, and in adding to this the work of select contemporary writers: the lists of Henry Herringman and Jacob Tonson are in themselves almost a late seventeenth-century canon. Herringman published poetry, drama, and classical translations, together with some prose romances, theology, and science.[14] His list was well established by the later 1650s, when he probably employed Dryden as an editorial assistant.[15] On the death of Cromwell he entered in the Stationers' Register his intention to publish a collection of three memorial poems by Marvell, Sprat, and Dryden, but (perhaps from political caution) never proceeded with the project.[16] At the Restoration he aligned himself with the new order by publishing welcome odes by Cowley, Davenant, Dryden, Higgons, Howard, and Waller. In subsequent years he signed up most of the leading contemporary poets and dramatists, publishing Cowley, Davenant, Denham, Dryden, Etherege, Fane, Howard, Killigrew, Orrery, Philips, Rochester, Roscommon, Sedley, Shadwell, Tuke, Waller, and Wycherley: a mixture of professionals and aristocratic amateurs, this list virtually defines contemporary literature. The works of some of these writers were collected into folio volumes, creating a highly visible and prestigious authorial canon. Cowley's *Poems* had been published in folio in 1656 by Humphrey Moseley; now in 1668 Herringman issued a folio *Works* which added Cowley's *Essays* and a preface by Thomas Sprat surveying Cowley's life and writing. This had reached its ninth edition by 1700, and there were also supplementary collections of his juvenilia and his Latin poems. A Davenant folio appeared from Herringman in 1673. But Herringman was also dominating the market for verse written in the early and mid-century: he published King and Waller in 1664, Donne in 1669, Carew and Crashaw in 1670, and Suckling in 1676; the absence of Milton from this list (in spite of the fact that like Waller and Crashaw he had been published by Moseley) is no doubt a sign of Herringman's political caution. This stable of authors, together with his share

---

[12] John Horden, *Francis Quarles (1592–1644): A Bibliography of his Works to the Year 1800* (Oxford, 1953).

[13] Charles Hoole, *A New Discovery of the Old Art of Teaching Schoole* (London, 1660), sig. A10ᵛ.

[14] C. W. Miller, *Henry Herringman Imprints: A Preliminary Checklist* (Charlottesville, Va., 1949).

[15] James M. Osborn, *John Dryden: Some Biographical Facts and Problems*, revised edition (Gainesville, Fla., 1965), pp. 184–99.

[16] Macdonald, *Bibliography*, pp. 3–4.

in the Beaumont and Fletcher folio and in the Shakespeare Fourth Folio, makes Herringman a dominant figure in early Restoration culture. Pepys visited Herringman's shop not only to buy books but also to hear literary gossip from him and to meet his other customers: it was from Herringman that he learned of the death of Cowley, and heard that Dryden himself called *An Evening's Love* 'but a fifth-rate play'; it was also Herringman's shop that Pepys appointed as the place for an illicit rendezvous with Mrs Willet – a scene (and, indeed, a name) which could have come straight out of the comedies which Herringman was selling.[17]

Herringman had in some respects been Moseley's successor as the principal publisher of English poetry, and in due course he was himself displaced by Jacob Tonson, who took over many of Herringman's writers.[18] Tonson's career had begun cautiously in 1675 with two conduct books, but in 1679 he published Dryden's *Troilus and Cressida*, marking the beginning of a long association between the two men. This provided Dryden with new opportunities, particularly for classical translation, and gave Tonson a prolific, popular, and controversial author of the first rank to act as the mainstay of his catalogue. Together they pioneered developments in literary publishing which would set precedents for a generation, including a new format for publishing verse in their miscellanies, and a new way of financing a major undertaking by inviting subscriptions for Dryden's Virgil.[19]

As well as cultivating Dryden (presenting him with melons, while paying him in clipped coin) Tonson added other major poets to his list. He published a *Second Part of the Works of Mr Abraham Cowley* in 1681, moving again into Herringman's territory. In 1691 he issued the poems of Rochester, including his adaptation of *Valentinian* which Herringman had published in 1685. He also made a momentous contribution to the emerging canonical status of Milton by publishing *Paradise Lost* in folio in 1688, following this with Milton's shorter poems in 1695, which together made up *The Poetical Works of Mr John Milton*. Prefaced with a handsome engraved portrait with verses by Dryden which cast Milton as the modern embodiment of Homer and Virgil, the 1688 edition was set in large clear type, and provided illustrations to each book of *Paradise Lost* which would have reminded readers of the cuts included in Ogilby's Virgil. Moreover, there are three hundred pages of annotation to *Paradise Lost* by Patrick Hume which expound the poem's vocabulary and

---

[17] *Diary of Samuel Pepys*, viii 380, 383; ix 248, 367.

[18] G. F. Papali, *Jacob Tonson, Publisher* (Auckland, 1968) includes a provisional checklist of Tonson's publications.

[19] For the financing of Dryden's Virgil see John Barnard, 'Dryden, Tonson, and Subscriptions for the 1697 Virgil', *PBSA*, 57 (1963) 129–51, and 'Dryden, Tonson, and the Patrons of *The Works of Virgil* (1697)' in *John Dryden: Tercentenary Essays*, edited by Paul Hammond and David Hopkins (Oxford, 2000), pp. 174–239.

theology, giving it a classical scholarly treatment which at that date had been accorded to no other English poem.

Tonson seems to have been especially interested in translations from the Greek and Latin classics, including Dryden's own version of Virgil (1697), and the translations by Dryden and others of *Ovid's Epistles* (1680), Plutarch (1683–6), and Juvenal and Persius (1693); there were also individual works such as Talbot's translation of Seneca's *Troades*, Higden's Juvenal XIII, and L'Estrange's rendering of Cicero's *De Officiis*. Tonson was evidently looking out for good translators, and signed up Thomas Creech after his Lucretius had been such a success for the Oxford bookseller Anthony Stephens,[20] publishing Creech's translations of Horace in 1684 and Manilius in 1697. He missed Oldham (published by Hindmarsh), but nevertheless found ways to associate him too with his list, printing his own memorial poem for Oldham anonymously in the miscellany *Sylvae* (1685), and including Oldham's elegy for Rochester in his 1691 edition of the earl's poetry. Tonson also published Roscommon's *An Essay on Translated Verse* (1684), whereas Herringman had published his translation of Horace's *Art of Poetry* in 1680. Dryden is once again a key figure in this story: he knew many of the contributors to the collaborative translations of Ovid, Plutarch, and Juvenal,[21] he had friendly relations with Creech, wrote a memorial poem for Oldham and a commendatory poem for Roscommon's *Essay*, and advised Tonson that he could safely venture to reprint the *Essay* in 1685.[22]

The collaboration of Dryden and Tonson was also crucial to the success of Tonson's miscellanies, which became a major influence upon Restoration and then on early eighteenth-century publishing: by providing a home for shorter poems and translations, and by collecting prologues, epilogues, epistles, and commendatory poems, these volumes shaped a literary world of mutual obligation and defined a canon of contemporary writers. The series began with *Miscellany Poems* in 1684, with a second part called *Sylvae* in 1685, followed by the third part under the title *Examen Poeticum* in 1693, the fourth in 1694, the fifth in 1704, and the sixth in 1709.[23] There are several indications that Tonson's ideas about this venture changed as he was putting the first two parts together:[24] *Miscellany Poems* reprints three of Dryden's major poems, *Absalom and Achitophel*, *The Medal*, and *Mac Flecknoe*, whereas subsequently the focus

---

20 D. G. Vaisey, 'Anthony Stephens: The Rise and Fall of an Oxford Bookseller', in *Studies in the Book Trade in Honour of Graham Pollard* (Oxford, 1975), pp. 91–117.

21 Arthur C. Sherbo, 'The Dryden-Cambridge Translation of Plutarch's Lives', *Études Anglaises*, 32 (1979) 177–84, and 'Dryden as a Cambridge Editor', *Studies in Bibliography*, 38 (1985) 251–61.

22 *The Letters of John Dryden*, edited by Charles E. Ward (Durham, N.C., 1941), pp. 22–3.

23 The pioneering study of the miscellanies is by W. J. Cameron, 'Miscellany Poems 1684–1716', unpublished PhD thesis, University of Reading, 1957.

24 Paul Hammond, 'The Printing of the Dryden-Tonson *Miscellany Poems* (1684) and *Sylvae* (1685)', *PBSA*, 84 (1990) 405–12.

was to be on new and shorter pieces;[25] this first volume also collects a large number of Dryden's prologues and epilogues, suggesting a connection with the earlier miscellanies which had centred around the theatre, smaller and cheaper volumes such as *Covent Garden Drolery* (1672).[26] Tonson's *Miscellany Poems* includes some translations from the classics, but by the time Tonson and Dryden brought out *Sylvae*, translation had become a feature of the collection: *Sylvae* started with a major critical preface by Dryden addressing the art of translation and the literary characteristics of the classical poets from whom he was working, and then offered his selections from Virgil, Lucretius, Horace, and Theocritus. Translations by other hands followed, so that purchasers who had their copies of these first two parts bound together (as many were) would have acquired a substantial selection from Ovid's *Elegies*, Horace's *Odes*, and Theocritus' *Idylls*, a complete set of Virgil's *Eclogues*, and samples of Lucretius, Catullus, Propertius, and of Virgil's *Georgics* and *Aeneid*. Tonson was thus providing his readers with a taste of the Greek and Roman poetic canon, appealing partly to a readership which had not had the benefit of a classical education (perhaps particularly to women, who were now influential in forming theatrical and poetic taste[27]) but also to connoisseurs of the classics and of the art of translation, since some classical poems were presented in more than one version. Later, Tonson would remember the interests of such a readership by making sure that the Latin accompanied Rochester's renderings of passages from Lucretius when he published his edition in 1691.

III

The formation of a contemporary canon was to some extent predicated upon the existence of a canon of classical Greek and Roman writing,[28] and the dispute between Dryden and Shadwell in the 1670s is in part an argument over which of them is properly the heir to the classical heritage, as Shadwell places himself in a lineage which includes Horace and Jonson.[29] But the classical canon was itself being reconfigured: a traditional canon had structured the grammar school curriculum,[30] and now translations increasingly brought this literature within the compass of the ordinary reader. Herringman had assisted in this by publishing Brome's *The Poems of Horace* in English in 1666, which

---

[25] Writing to Tonson in August or September 1684, Dryden says that 'since we are to have nothing but new' for *Sylvae*, 'I am resolvd we will have nothing but good' (*Letters*, p. 23).

[26] For the earlier printed miscellanies, see Adam Smyth, 'Printed Miscellanies in England, 1640–1682: "store-house[s] of wit."', *Criticism*, 42 (2000) 151–84.

[27] Women admirers of Dryden were responsible for a whole volume of elegies on his death, *The Nine Muses* (London, 1700): see Macdonald, *Bibliography*, p. 297.

[28] On translations and adaptations of the classics see chapter 5.

[29] See *Poems of John Dryden*, i 307–12.

[30] Hoole, *A New Discovery*.

collected translations by a variety of writers from the mid-century; this was sufficiently successful to be revised in 1671 and again in 1680, with new translations being added. Horace was a cornerstone of the classical canon and a *point de repère* for the contemporary canon, and writers such as Oldham and Roscommon, who were keen to promote modern translation themselves, translated the *Ars Poetica* both as a demonstration of what could be done and as a way of casting into contemporary English idiom the precepts which Horace offered.[31] Tonson in his miscellanies offered readers further examples of Horace by various hands, and published Thomas Creech's complete translation in 1684.

Ovid's *Metamorphoses* had been translated in the previous generation by George Sandys (1626, with subsequent revisions), and no one in the Restoration period succeeded in producing a new version of the complete text.[32] But several poets offered readers selected tales, often highlighting tales of sexual passion, with Oldham (1681) and Dennis (1692) both translating the story of Byblis, and Dryden rendering the tale of 'Cinyras and Myrrha' for his *Fables Ancient and Modern* (1700). Many writers gave readers versions of Ovid the witty poet of love through their selections from the *Amores* and *Heroides*. While such aspects of Ovid appealed strongly to Restoration sensibilities, Dryden responded to other elements in Ovid too, for he was attracted to tales of conjugal fidelity and reverence for the gods ('Baucis and Philemon', 'Ceyx and Alcyone'; both in *Fables*) and to the extended philosophical contemplation of nature's changes (*Metamorphoses* Book I, relating the creation of the world, in *Examen Poeticum* (1693); and 'Of the Pythagorean Philosophy' from Book XV in *Fables*).

Virgil had been translated by Ogilby in 1649 (re-issued with modifications 1650, 1654), and Dryden would translate the works again in 1697, but in between these two heroic ventures various poets published individual books: predictably Book IV, the story of Dido and Aeneas, was the most popular, with translations by Sir Richard Fanshawe (1652), James Harrington (1659), Sir Robert Howard (1660), and Sir John Denham (1668); but Denham and Harrington also translated the account of the fall of Troy in Book II (1656, 1658), with Harrington and Boys rendering Aeneas' journey to the underworld in Book VI (1659, 1660). The fact that many of these were written by Royalist sympathizers during the Interregnum points to the use of the *Aeneid* as a source for reflection on the destruction of an empire and the experience of exile.[33] Restoration taste also relished the burlesque versions of Books I and IV produced by Charles Cotton (1664–5, much reprinted).

---

31 Paul Hammond, *John Oldham and the Renewal of Classical Culture* (Cambridge, 1983).

32 David Hopkins, 'Dryden and the Garth-Tonson *Metamorphoses*', *Review of English Studies*, n.s. 39 (1988) 64–74.

33 Lawrence Venuti, '*The Destruction of Troy*: Translation and Royalist Cultural Politics in the Interregnum', *Journal of Medieval and Renaissance Studies*, 23 (1993) 197–219. Later,

Among those classical writers who appealed especially to Restoration taste was Anacreon: Thomas Stanley had published a complete translation of Anacreon in 1651, but in 1683 a volume called *Anacreon Done into English* collected versions by various hands (including Cowley and Oldham). It was issued by Anthony Stephens, the Oxford bookseller who also published Creech's Lucretius and Theocritus. The appearance of the latter in 1684 perhaps thwarted an attempt by Tonson to assemble an English Theocritus by various hands, relics of which may be traced in *Miscellany Poems* and *Sylvae*.[34] Creech's Lucretius was an extraordinarily successful translation, appearing in 1682 and being reprinted five times by 1700. It started life as an Oxford publication by an Oxford scholar, but quickly migrated into metropolitan literary circles, being taken up by Tonson, argued over in coffee houses (Dryden was asked to settle a dispute over Creech's grammar),[35] and accumulating commendatory poems from Behn, Otway, Tate and others. Prior remarked in his spiteful *Satire on the Modern Translators*,

> This pleas'd the genius of the vicious Town,
> The Wits confirm'd his Labours with Renown,
> And swear the early Atheist for their own.[36]

After Creech's death it became a canonical text in its own right, being issued in 1714 in two volumes with an extensive learned commentary in double columns elucidating the Epicurean philosophy and tracing parallels of thought and phrasing in Cowley, Milton, and Dryden.[37]

By 1700, readers without the classical languages, or those who were interested in translation as an art, would have had access to complete translations of Virgil and Persius by Dryden, and of Horace, Lucretius, and Theocritus by Creech; to volumes assembling translations by various hands from Horace, Ovid, and Juvenal; and to a large number of shorter translations from Latin and Greek scattered through the miscellanies. The classical and contemporary canons were each being reshaped by a process of interaction and reciprocal criticism.[38]

Dryden's translation of Virgil would also address the sense of exile and displacement, but from the experience of a Catholic and Jacobite in the England of William III: see Hammond, *Traces*, pp. 218–82.

[34] Hammond, 'The Printing of the Dryden-Tonson *Miscellany Poems*'.

[35] *Letters of John Dryden*, pp. 14–16.

[36] Lines 122–4, in *The Literary Works of Matthew Prior*, edited by H. Bunker Wright and Monroe K. Spears, 2 vols (Oxford, 1971).

[37] Paul Hammond, 'Milton, Dryden, and Lucretius', *The Seventeenth Century*, 16 (2001) 158–76.

[38] This is visible in Dryden's critical prefaces, which often compare classical and contemporary writers: see his 'Preface to *Sylvae*' and 'Preface to *Fables Ancient and Modern*' (*Poems* ii 234–57, v 47–90).

IV

But canons were not only shaped in print: throughout this period manuscript had a major impact on the creation of the literary culture, and on the experience, and indeed, the power, of individual readers.[39] Many readers kept notebooks in which they recorded details of their reading. Sometimes these are called 'commonplace books', which is the appropriate term if they are organized topically, with quotations assembled under subject headings and usually intended for later use in the reader's own compositions. Students were expected to make notes in this way, and the practice often survived into adult habits of reading. But alongside their notes, readers also transcribed extracts and often complete poems, and many manuscripts survive which are in effect 'personal miscellanies',[40] anthologies which represent an individual reader's taste but are also a reflection of his milieu: a provincial cathedral,[41] Oxford or Cambridge, the Inns of Court, the royal court in Whitehall. Such manuscripts are particularly rich sources of songs, theatrical prologues and epilogues, and satires. But also preserved among readers' papers are the 'separates' from which these notebook texts derive. Poems were typically handed round on separate sheets, often folded to make a booklet, and the purchase, reading, and exchange of such sheets were part of the entertainment in coffee houses.[42] The papers of John Oldham preserve amongst his own poetic drafts several separates of work by other writers, including his transcriptions of Rochester's *Satyre against Reason and Mankind* and Dryden's *Mac Flecknoe*.[43] From such loose texts, or from bundles of such texts assembled into micro-canons of related satirical or erotic poems, the scribes working for commercial scriptoria wrote out substantial manuscript volumes for sale to wealthy patrons. These manuscripts typically have a thematic rather than an authorial focus: they may be collections primarily of topical political satire, or of erotic material, or may be more wide-ranging, but containing thematic groups.[44] They are often

---

39 For the importance of MSS in this period see Beal, *Index*; Peter Beal, *In Praise of Scribes: Manuscripts and their Makers in Seventeenth-century England* (Oxford, 1998); Harold Love, *Scribal Publication in Seventeenth-Century England* (Oxford, 1993); Harold Love, 'Oral and Scribal Texts in Early Modern England' in Barnard and McKenzie, pp. 97–121; Harold Love, *English Clandestine Satire 1660–1702* (Oxford, 2004).

40 Harold Love's preferred term.

41 As in the MSS (such as Leeds University Library Brotherton Collection MS Lt q 5) which preserve the poems of Henry Hall, Jacobite satirist and organist of Hereford Cathedral: see Oliver Pickering, 'Henry Hall of Hereford's Poetical Tributes to Henry Purcell', *The Library*, 16 (1994) 18–29.

42 For a poem describing the hawking of MS poems in coffee houses, see Paul Hammond, ' "The Miseries of Visits": An Addition to the Literature on Robert Julian, Secretary to the Muses', *The Seventeenth Century*, 8 (1993) 161–3; the poem is reprinted in a modernized text in *Restoration Literature: An Anthology*, edited by Paul Hammond (Oxford, 2002), pp. 184–5.

43 Now all bound up together as Bodleian Library MS Rawl. poet. 123.

elegantly bound: the Gyldenstolpe manuscript is bound in red morocco with gilt tooling, and the texts are written calligraphically within ruled borders, with proper names picked out in bold lettering, and elegant flourishes around the titles. Characteristically, scriptorium texts tend to be presented anonymously, but many readers' own private miscellanies and many separates attribute the poems, often without any secure knowledge: hence a canon is assembled speculatively around such prominent figures as Rochester and Dryden.

There is here a whole culture which is only partially and intermittently visible in the print medium. Most of the personal lampoons and political satires from the period were never printed, but survive as separates, in scriptorium manuscripts, or in readers' personal miscellanies.[45] Individual reputations were made and destroyed through manuscript lampoons, while in the political sphere the oppositional *Advice to a Painter* poems had a considerable impact on public opinion during the Second Dutch War, and circulated both in print and in manuscript.[46] Attacks not only on the policies but also on the person of Charles II through this manuscript culture proved damaging to his credibility.[47] And this mode of publication empowered readers not only by making subversive texts available to them, but by making these readers into publishers and authors in their turn, since individuals not only selected texts for transcription but also altered the texts, censoring, adapting, and improving, not just transcribing.[48] Manuscript as an almost unpoliced medium played havoc with the stability of texts, canons, and reputations.

V

Poets who tried to control their own texts and canons through the medium of print found more, but not complete, success. It is notable that Dryden[49] himself never collected his poems into a single volume, and the early work such as *Astraea Redux* (1660) and *Annus Mirabilis* (1667) remained unobtainable by readers until Tonson began to reissue Dryden's poems in a uniform

---

44 For a facsimile of one such scriptorium MS see *Gyldenstolpe*; and for studies of other MSS see Paul Hammond, 'The Robinson Manuscript Miscellany of Restoration Verse in the Brotherton Collection, Leeds', *Proceedings of the Leeds Philosophical and Literary Society, Literary and Historical Section*, 18 (1982) 275–324; Michael Brennan and Paul Hammond, 'The Badminton Manuscript: A New Miscellany of Restoration Verse', *English Manuscript Studies 1100–1700*, 5 (1995) 171–207.

45 For a selection of personal lampoons see *Court Satires of the Restoration*, edited by John Harold Wilson (Columbus, Ohio, 1976), and for the political satires see *POAS*. The transmission of both categories is discussed by Love in *English Clandestine Satire*.

46 *Poems of Andrew Marvell*, pp. 321–6.

47 See chapter 6 below.

48 See chapter 2 below.

49 For a more detailed account, see chapter 7 below.

style late in his career: in 1688 several poems from the 1660s – *Annus Mirabilis*, *Astraea Redux*, *To his Sacred Majesty* and *To My Lord Chancellor* – were reprinted with continuous pagination, and in a quarto format which made them suitable for binding up with Dryden's later poems which were now published or reprinted in quarto: *Absalom and Achitophel*, *The Medal*, and *Mac Flecknoe* were reprinted in quarto in 1692 with continuous pagination, and Tonson also issued *Threnodia Augustalis*, *The Hind and the Panther*, and *Britannia Rediviva* in the same format.[50] Purchasers were therefore able to create their own version of Dryden's canon by having their personal selection of these works bound together. Though Dryden's conversion to Rome meant that *Religio Laici* was never reprinted after 1683, it is nevertheless found bound up with the other works, so readers could override any wishes which Dryden himself might have had about what should constitute his ideal canon. The canonization of Dryden in folio had to wait until the very end of his life: following on from the handsome folio Virgil of 1697, Tonson published Dryden's *Fables Ancient and Modern* in folio in 1700, and after the poet's death issued a folio collection of his *Poems on Various Occasions; and Translations from Several Authors* (1701): this collected the major political and religious poems (but not the *Heroic Stanzas*), the translations from *Ovid's Epistles* and *Sylvae* (but not from Juvenal, which Tonson no doubt wanted readers to buy as a separate volume), some of the commendatory poems (to Roscommon, Congreve and Kneller, but oddly not the elegy on Oldham), and some of the prologues and epilogues. This volume is often found bound together with the *Fables*. A two-volume folio set of the plays also appeared in 1701 to complete the œuvre.

One can perceive Dryden attaching a different status to his major poems through their differing modes of publication. In one group come the major public poems which he was happy to acknowledge: *Annus Mirabilis*, *Threnodia Augustalis*, *Religio Laici*; in another, those poems which he preferred to publish anonymously,[51] *Absalom and Achitophel*, *The Medal*, and *The Hind and the Panther*, where he seems to have wished for some distance between himself and the printed text – perhaps to protect himself from the repercussions of controversial material, perhaps to provide the poems themselves with a degree of autonomy and rhetorical objectivity. In a third category there is *Mac Flecknoe*, which circulated at first in manuscript and was never printed over Dryden's name in his lifetime. By circulating *Mac Flecknoe* in manuscript (and also, it would seem from the surviving copies, anonymously[52]) Dryden was restricting its impact, at least initially, to those metropolitan literary circles in which its literary and theatrical topics would be particularly appreciated.

---

[50] Macdonald, *Bibliography*, pp. 15–16.
[51] For the uses of anonymity see chapter 3.
[52] *Poems of John Dryden*, i 310.

Another special case is the *Heroic Stanzas* on the death of Cromwell: this poem exists in what is now the only surviving autograph manuscript of a substantial work by Dryden, seemingly a fair copy intended for presentation to someone in the circle around the late Protector in 1658.[53] The poem was first printed in 1659, and was reprinted by Dryden's enemies three times in 1681–2 (at the time of his defence of the king's interests during the Exclusion Crisis) and again in 1687 (with a rubric attributing it to 'the Author of *The H—d and the P—r*').[54] These were attempts to include within Dryden's canon a poem which clashed with his later political and religious convictions, and one which he might have preferred the public to forget. But he did not actually disown it, for it was re-issued *circa* 1692 by Tonson in quarto format so that readers could include it in their collections, and this looks like a brave and dignified attempt by Dryden to assert control over the canon of his work, to acknowledge his own history on his own terms at a time when, in the early years of William and Mary, he may have felt particularly vulnerable. In 1691, finding that several of his friends, 'in Buying my Plays, *&c.* Bound together, have been impos'd on by the Booksellers foisting in a Play which is not mine', he added to *King Arthur* a list of his plays and major poems, in chronological order, a canon which excludes *Heroic Stanzas* and (since Shadwell was still alive) *Mac Flecknoe*, but acknowledges *Absalom and Achitophel* and *The Medal*, includes *Religio Laici*, and proudly concludes with *The Hind and the Panther* and *Britannia Rediviva* on the birth of James II's son in 1688.[55]

Besides these major poems, Dryden wrote many occasional and commendatory pieces, and these he never collected: they include one of the finest poems in the language, 'To the Memory of Mr Oldham', which could be found only in Oldham's *Remains* (1684, frequently reprinted), and the prefatory poems which he wrote for works by Howard, Lee, Roscommon, and Congreve; like the prologues and epilogues which he contributed to plays by associates such as Etherege and Southerne, these too remained accessible only in the printed texts of the poems or plays which they introduced. Most of Dryden's prologues and epilogues for the King's Company in the 1670s and 1680s were gathered together in *Miscellany Poems*, but generally Dryden exhibited a singular unconcern about these many occasional pieces, short but significant works in which he not only cemented friendships but often defined the classical temper and status of Restoration poetry.

Meanwhile, the circulation of poetry in manuscript allowed readers to remake the canon of individual authors, including that of Dryden. The *Heroic Stanzas* were copied by readers into their personal commonplace books

---

[53] Now British Library MS Lansdowne 1045. See Paul Hammond, 'The Autograph Manuscript of Dryden's *Heroique Stanza's* and its Implications for Editors', *PBSA*, 76 (1982) 457–70.

[54] Macdonald, *Bibliography*, pp. 5–7.

[55] Macdonald, *Bibliography*, pp. 132–3.

throughout the Restoration period, thus keeping that poem alive;[56] similarly Dryden's verses to the Countess of Castlemaine, originally a private work for a patroness, were circulated through the medium of manuscript – no doubt more because of their addressee's notoriety than the lines' own literary merit.[57] In this milieu of manuscript circulation a writer's canon could be significantly reshaped by speculative or mischievous attributions. Thus several scurrilous verses were attributed to Dryden in manuscripts, and although we now doubt that he wrote verses on the Duchess of Portsmouth's picture, or a satire on Robert Julian, some of Dryden's contemporaries thought that he had done, and they had evidently acquired an impression of the Dryden canon which encouraged them to think of him as a likely author for topical satires and libellous lampoons.[58] Ironically, the only work attributed to Dryden which Locke owned was the spurious *Address of John Dryden, Laureat to His Highness the Prince of Orange* (1689).[59] After the Revolution the volumes of *Poems on Affairs of State* would remake Dryden's canon with more deliberate malice, as we shall see. Such reshaping of the canon by readers and copyists could be dangerous: it is quite likely that the attack on Dryden in Rose Alley in 1679 was occasioned by a speculative attribution assigning to him the *Essay upon Satire*, which was probably the work of the Earl of Mulgrave alone.[60]

Dryden was a professional writer for whom the status of his canon had vital commercial as well as artistic significance, but most of his contemporary poets did not depend on their writing for a living, and the fortunes of their œuvres show interesting variations.

John Wilmot, Earl of Rochester, did not collect his poems, and indeed very few appeared in print in his own lifetime.[61] A few love poems were printed anonymously in miscellanies, and a garbled version of *Tunbridge Wells* had been included in Richard Head's *Proteus Redivivus* (1675), but apart from this the only longer poems which had been printed were *Upon Nothing*, *Artemiza to Chloe*, and the *Satyre against Reason and Mankind*, each of which appeared as separate broadsides in 1679. There is no indication that these publications were authorized by Rochester, and none bears his name; they were probably

---

56 For a list of MS copies, see Beal, *Index*, i 403–4.

57 Paul Hammond, 'Dryden's Revision of *To the Lady Castlemain*', *PBSA*, 78 (1984) 81–90.

58 For a list of poems attributed to Dryden by contemporaries but rejected or doubted by modern scholars, see *Poems of John Dryden*, v 681–9.

59 J. P. Harrison and Peter Laslett, *The Library of John Locke*, second edition (Oxford, 1971), p. 126.

60 See *Poems of John Dryden*, v 684.

61 See David M. Vieth, *Attribution in Restoration Poetry* (New Haven, 1963); Beal, *Index*, ii 225–87; Love, *Scribal Publication*; Harold Love, 'Refining Rochester: Private Texts and Public Readers', *Harvard Library Bulletin*, n.s. 7 (1996) 40–9; Harold Love, 'The Scribal Transmission of Rochester's Songs', *Bibliographical Society of Australia and New Zealand Bulletin*, 20 (1996) 161–80; *Works of John Wilmot*; Fisher, 'Publication'.

opportunistic publications which took their texts from whatever manuscripts came to hand. At the time of Rochester's much-publicized death in 1680, the reading public would have known his lyrics and sexually explicit poems only through manuscript circulation.[62] Yet the substantial number of elegies for Rochester which appeared at his death[63] (some of which even generated complimentary poems in their turn) suggests that there was already a wide-spread sense in literary circles as to what constituted Rochester's canon. And in 1680 there began a process of canon formation which took strikingly different forms in manuscript and in print.

Several scriptorium manuscript miscellanies were compiled in 1680, or shortly thereafter, which contained a substantial selection of poems by Rochester, including his erotic poems and the longer poems which were already in print. Since all these poems were presented anonymously, there was no attempt to define a Rochester canon, even though a number of poems which we now attribute to Rochester were grouped together. Rather, the kind of canon which such manuscripts sought to present was topic-based, offering wealthy readers calligraphically written texts of erotic and satiric literature. A more deliberate attempt to define a canon for Rochester was made in the mid-1680s by the compiler of Yale University Library Osborn MS fb 334 (the 'Hartwell MS'); this manuscript has a title page announcing 'Poem's By The Right Honourable John Earle of Rochester', with an address to the reader, and texts of *Valentinian*, the *Satyre against Reason and Mankind*, *Artemiza to Chloe*, *An Allusion to Horace*, and some of Rochester's songs, but omits any sexually explicit pieces.[64]

This chaste selected canon contrasts markedly with the first printed collection of Rochester's poems, *Poems on Several Occasions by the Right Honourable, The E. of R–––* ('Antwerp', 1680).[65] This edition was evidently read to pieces, or destroyed in embarrassment or revulsion, for only two copies survive.[66] The volume contained sixty-one poems, of which only around a half are now accepted as his by Rochester's editors, the others being attributable with

---

[62] The obscene play *Sodom*, sometimes attributed to Rochester, appears to have circulated to some extent in MS, and there is some evidence that a printed edition was published in 1684 (*Works of John Wilmot*, pp. 674–6). The sole exemplar of a previously unknown printed edition from the early eighteenth century (the imprint is 'Hague: Printed in the Year 1000000') was sold at Sotheby's in 2004 (*English Literature, History, Children's Books and Illustrations: London Thursday 16 December 2004*, Lot 54).

[63] Printed in *Rochester: The Critical Heritage*, edited by David Farley-Hills (London, 1972), pp. 94–130; discussed by Fisher, 'Publication', pp. 18–27.

[64] For accounts of this MS see Harold Love, 'Rochester: A Tale of Two Manuscripts', *Yale University Library Gazette*, 72 (1997) 41–53; Fisher, 'Publication', pp. 36–8.

[65] Annotated facsimile edition published as *Rochester's Poems on Several Occasions*, edited by James Thorpe (Princeton, 1950).

[66] In the Huntington Library, San Marino, California, and the Pepys Library, Magdalene College, Cambridge.

varying degrees of certainty to a range of Rochester's contemporaries, including Oldham, Behn, Scroope, and Dorset. The collection capitalizes upon Rochester's notoriety to sell an anthology which is basically much the same as the manuscript anthologies which were circulating, but at a much lower price than those luxury items; and so what the purchaser acquired was not so much the Rochester œuvre as a canon of contemporary libertine verse: what makes it cohere is not the individual author but the persona, not John Wilmot but '*The E. of R– – –*' as a composite cultural fiction epitomizing the wit and the rake. Pepys made his copy the nucleus of a collection of material by and about Rochester by having it bound up with a manuscript supplement of additional poems, and with Gilbert Burnet's *Some Passages of the Life and Death of the Right Honourable John, Earl of Rochester* (1680), typically providing himself with a combination of the titillating and the edifying.[67]

This collection was reprinted through the early 1680s, though attempts were made to produce more socially respectable editions of Rochester. In 1685 a revised version of the 1680 edition appeared, with a text purged of some of the sexually explicit language.[68] In the same year Herringman published *Valentinian* with a preface by Robert Wolseley which defended Rochester's poetry (implicitly assuming an œuvre which had yet to be defined), and gave it a place in the canon by making comparisons not only with fashionable contemporary verses but also with classical Roman poetry. Then in 1691 Tonson published *Poems, &c. on Several Occasions: with Valentinian, a Tragedy*. This represented a significant step in the canonization of Rochester, and once again there was an important critical preface, this time by Thomas Rymer, where comparisons were again made with Latin poetry, and also on this occasion with Boileau, the principal classical poet of contemporary France. The volume itself started with an expensive rubricated title page, and offered spaciously printed texts of Rochester's more presentable poems. Though Rymer claimed that the publisher had been 'diligent out of Measure' to ensure that the volume was 'a Collection of such Pieces only, as may be received in a vertuous Court, and not unbecome the Cabinet of the Severest Matron',[69] it nevertheless includes some poems (such as '*Faire Chloris* in a Pigsty lay') which might raise eyebrows in the newly godly court of William and Mary, even though some lyrics (such as 'Love a Woman! Th'rt an Ass' and 'To A Lady, in A Letter') were edited to remove sexually explicit detail or homoerotic allusions (see Plate 1).[70]

---

67 Pepys Library, Magdalene College, Cambridge, 810.
68 Love, 'Refining Rochester'.
69 *Poems, &c. on Several Occasions: with Valentinian, a Tragedy*. Written by the Right Honourable John Late Earl of Rochester (London, 1691), sig. A6ᵛ.
70 David M. Vieth, 'A Textual Paradox: Rochester's "To a lady in a letter"', *PBSA*, 54 (1960) 147–62 and 55 (1961) 130–3; Paul Hammond, 'Rochester's Homoeroticism', in *That Second Bottle: Essays on John Wilmot, Earl of Rochester*, edited by Nicholas Fisher (Manchester, 2000), pp. 46–72, revised and reprinted as 'Rochester and Restoration Homoeroticism' in his *Figuring Sex between Men from Shakespeare to Rochester* (Oxford, 2002), pp. 226–54.

44   P O E M S

But whether Life, or Death, betide,
    In love 'tis equal Meaſure,
The Victor lives with empty Pride;
    The Vanquiſh'd die with Pleaſure.

A   S O N G.

1.

Love a Woman! you're an Aſs,
    'Tis a moſt inſipid Paſſion;
To chuſe out for your happineſs,
    The ſillieſt part of God's Creation.

2.

Let the Porter, and the Groom,
    Things deſign'd for dirty Slaves;
Drudge in fair *Aurelia's* Womb,
    To get Supplies for Age and Graves.

        3. Farewell

On ſeveral Occaſions.   45

3.

Farewell Woman, I intend,
    Henceforth, every night to ſit
With my lewd well natur'd Friend,
    Drinking to engender Wit.

A

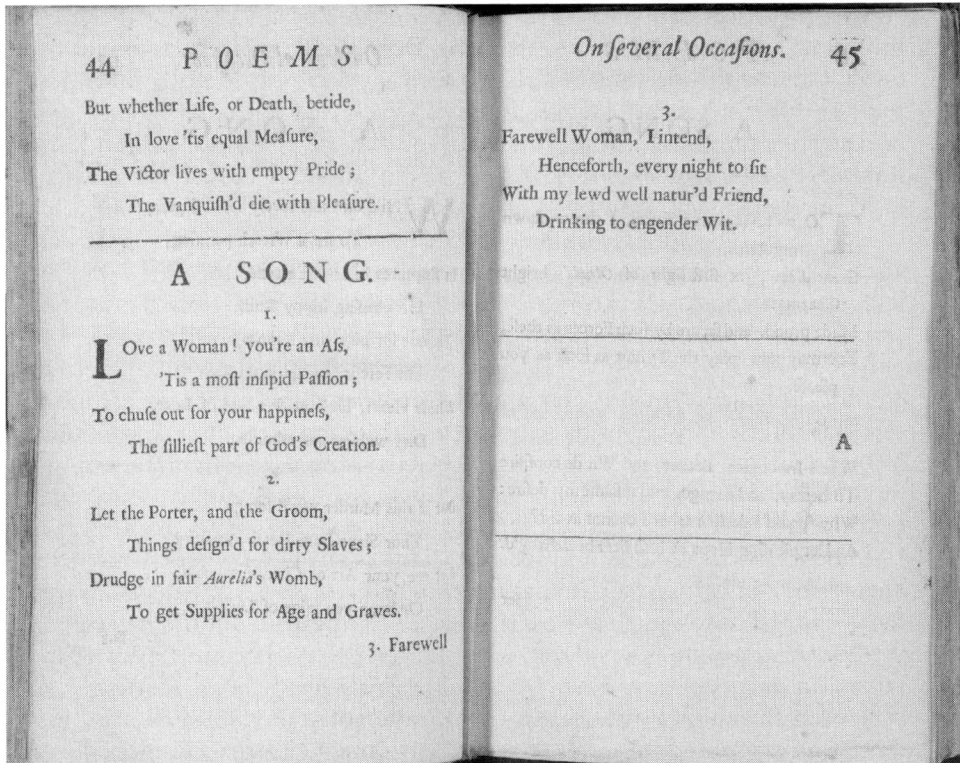

Plate 1. *Poems, &c. on Several Occasions: with Valentinian, a Tragedy.* Written by the Right Honourable John Late Earl of Rochester (London, 1691), pp. 44–5.
The right-hand page is a cancel leaf which was inserted late in the production process to replace the original ending of the poem, because stanza 4 had contained a reference to the male speaker enjoying sex with his page boy. The stub of the original leaf is still visible.

Some of Tonson's editorial work was undoubtedly concerned with establishing a text free from obscenity, either through such local textual alterations, or by the wholesale exclusion of poems such as 'A Ramble in St. *James's Park*' and 'The Imperfect Enjoyment', both of which had appeared in the 1680 edition; but there were also other motives shaping this reconfiguration of Rochester's canon. Some poems (such as *Tunbridge Wells* and *Timon*) may have been excluded because of doubts about their authorship, while *An Allusion to Horace* was perhaps omitted out of respect for Dryden, whom it criticizes. Some political poems by or attributed to Rochester (the 'sceptre' lampoon on Charles II (beginning 'In th' Isle of Brittain'), the 'History of Insipids', or 'On Rome's Pardons') would have been unacceptable on a combination of political, sexual, and religious grounds. The result is that this 1691 edition presents a Rochester canon which is not only purged of his more explicit erotic writing, but also distances him from the fierce literary and political squabbles of his day. He was to be replaced in a politically inflected canon by the *Poems on Affairs of State* in 1697, as a champion of the proto-Whig cause, as we shall see.

Though for rather different reasons, Katherine Philips was also hesitant about allowing her poetry to appear in print, and its principal readership was her own circle of friends and admirers who transcribed and exchanged her verse in manuscript.[71] She herself collected fifty-five poems into a manuscript volume of fair copies, and her friends frequently copied and circulated her verses to others: one of them transcribed ninety-six of her poems after her death and presented the volume to Mary Aubrey, who features in Philips's poems as Rosania – diplomatically excluding from this collection Philips's poem 'On Rosania's Apostacy'.[72] Philips insisted that she 'never writ any line in my life with an intention to have it printed',[73] and was (or affected to be) horrified when an edition of her poems was published by Richard Marriott in 1664. This volume, which half-concealed her identity under her initials,[74] is generally said to have been unauthorized, but it was not pirated: Marriott was a respectable publisher who had entered the book on the Stationers' Register and had it duly licensed. The volume was soon withdrawn because of pressure from Philips's friends, but after her death one of them put together a new edition, designed in several respects to eclipse Marriott's: titled rather

---

[71] *The Collected Works of Katherine Philips The Matchless Orinda*, edited by Patrick Thomas, G. Greer, and R. Little, 3 vols (Stump Cross, 1990–3), i 1–58; Beal, *Index*, ii 125–81; Elizabeth H. Hageman and Andrea Sununu, 'New Manuscript Texts of Katherine Philips, the "matchless Orinda" ', *English Manuscript Studies*, 4 (1993) 174–219, and ' "More copies of it abroad than I could have imagin'd": Further manuscript texts of Katherine Philips, "the matchless Orinda" ', *English Manuscript Studies*, 5 (1995) 127–69; Beal, *In Praise of Scribes*, pp. 147–91.
[72] National Library of Wales MSS 775 and 776.
[73] Philips, *Collected Works*, ii 128.
[74] *Poems. By the Incomparable, Mrs. K. P.* (London, 1664).

fulsomely *Poems By the most deservedly Admired Mrs. Katherine Philips The matchless Orinda* (1667), it was in folio rather than octavo, was published by Herringman, and included a frontispiece portrait of a bust of Orinda; it had a long preface denouncing Marriott's edition, followed by commendatory poems by the Earls of Orrery and Roscommon, Cowley and others (see Plate 2). The canon itself was expanded from 74 to 121 poems, and added her translations from Corneille.[75]

The story behind the shaping of Marvell's canon is as elusive as most other aspects of this man's life. *The First Anniversary of the Government Under His Highness the Lord Protector* was published anonymously in 1655 as a separate quarto; the anonymity is curious, given that Marvell was on the edges of the Protectoral government and perhaps seeking advancement, for in 1653 he had been recommended by Milton for appointment as assistant Latin Secretary to the Council of State, and would actually be appointed to that office in 1657: was he hedging his bets? In 1659 Herringman registered his intention to publish three poems on Cromwell's death by Dryden, Marvell, and Sprat, but when the volume eventually appeared from another bookseller Marvell's poem had been replaced by Waller's: was Marvell once more hedging his bets? At the very least he seems to have exercised considerable caution about allowing a poetic canon to emerge, a caution which is evident also in the remarkable absence of any evidence of manuscript circulation for most of the poems which Marvell wrote in the 1650s, including 'An Horatian Ode'. Even 'To his Coy Mistress' survives in only one Restoration copy, the anonymous, shortened, and probably corrupt version preserved in Bodleian MS Don. b. 8.[76]

It was more than two years after his death that Robert Boulter published in folio the *Miscellaneous Poems by Andrew Marvell, Esq; Late Member of the Honourable House of Commons* (1681) (see Plate 3).[77] Boulter was primarily a publisher of political and religious works rather than poetry, though he had been one of the booksellers for *Paradise Lost*. *Miscellaneous Poems* appeared at a time of great political tension, in the year of the Exclusion Crisis, and the reminder on the title page that Marvell had been an MP invites readers to expect a volume with some political significance. In fact, the book as actually published is principally a collection of lyrical and topographical poems, and is of little topical significance, for as the sheets were being assembled in the printer's shop 'An Horatian Ode upon Cromwell's Return from Ireland', 'The

---

[75] For the uses of manuscript and print by other notable women poets, see Kathryn R. King, *Jane Barker, Exile: A Literary Career 1675–1725* (Oxford, 2000), and *The Poems of Jane Barker: The Magdalen Manuscript*, Magdalen College Occasional Paper 3 (Oxford, 1998); *The Works of Aphra Behn*, edited by Janet Todd, 7 vols (London, 1992–6), i xxxvi–xlviii.

[76] See chapter 9.

[77] On Marvell's posthumously created canon, see Nicholas von Maltzahn, 'Marvell's Ghost', in *Marvell and Liberty*, edited by Warren Chernaik and Martin Dzelzainis (Basingstoke, 1999), pp. 50–74.

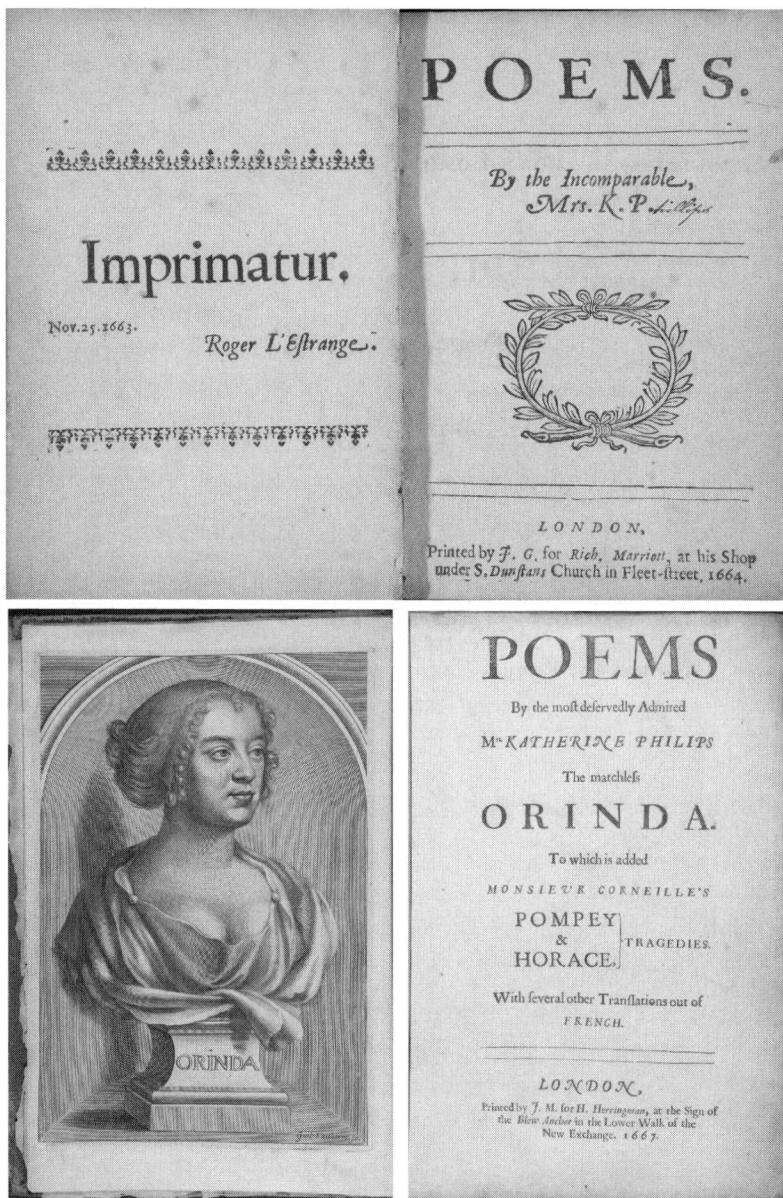

Plate 2. *Poems.* By the Incomparable, Mrs. K. P. (London, 1664), imprimatur and title page; and *Poems* By the most deservedly Admired Mrs. Katherine Philips The matchless Orinda (London, 1667), frontispiece portrait and title page.

The 1664 octavo edition published by Marriott seems to have been unauthorized (though, as the *imprimatur* shows, it was not pirated); the grander quarto edition of 1667, complete with portrait bust, was published by Herringman, whose list included most of the principal poets of the 1660s.

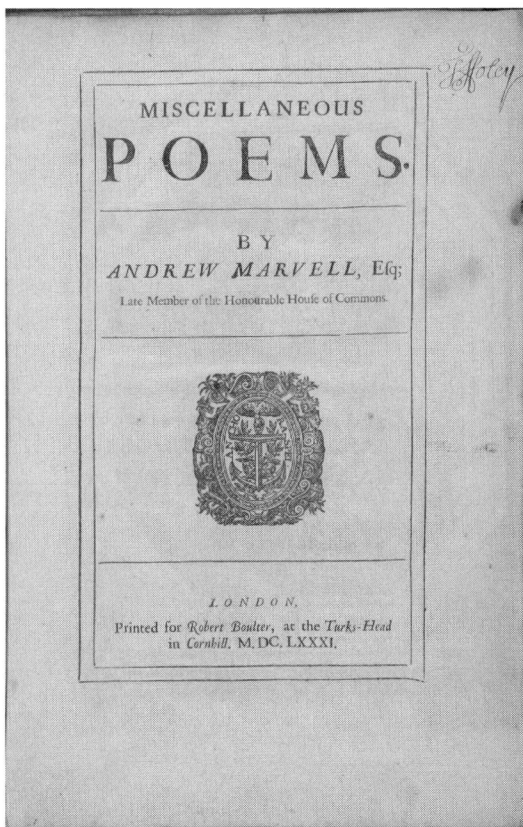

Plate 3. *Miscellaneous Poems.* By Andrew Marvell, Esq; Late Member of the Honourable House of Commons (London, 1681), frontispiece portrait and title page.
This copy, in the Fay and Geoffrey Elliott Collection, formerly owned by Lord Foley, lacks the 'Horatian Ode' and other Cromwellian poems, which were removed from the book as it was going through the press, probably to avoid the embarrassment of associating a prominent opposition champion with the Commonwealth.

First Anniversary of the Government under O.C.' and 'A Poem upon the Death of O.C.' were excised from all but two surviving copies.[78] Evidently the Marvell canon was being revised even as the book was going through the press. Though sometimes attributed to government intervention, it is more likely that this alteration was due to someone deciding that too overt a reminder of Marvell's association with the Cromwellian government would harm the opposition cause for which he had been such a prominent spokesman and pamphleteer. Any purchaser who expected to acquire texts of the political satires which Marvell had been writing in the late 1660s and 1670s would have been disappointed, for the *Miscellaneous Poems* omits the *Last Instructions to a Painter* and all the other Restoration satires which had been circulating in manuscript with more or less speculative attributions to Marvell.[79] One reader remedied this omission by adding a manuscript supplement of eighteen poems to a copy of the 1681 folio,[80] perhaps as the basis for a new edition. But the edition never materialized.

VI

All canon formation is to some degree politically inflected, and it may be instructive to conclude this introductory survey with a striking instance of this from the year 1697. The collection called *Poems on Affairs of State* draws principally upon the large body of satirical material which had circulated in manuscript in the reigns of Charles II and James II, providing (or so it claimed) 'a just and secret History of the former Times' (see Plate 4).[81] In order to promote a strongly Whiggish and Williamite view of recent history, this volume effected an adroit reconfiguration of the canon. Its title page offered poems 'Written by the greatest Wits of the Age', whom it identified as Buckingham, Rochester, Buckhurst, Denham, Marvell, Milton, Dryden, Sprat, Waller, and Ayloffe. But as we read on, it soon becomes apparent that this canon is highly tendentious.

On the one hand, *Poems on Affairs of State* sets out to canonize in print those satirists whose manuscript verses had advanced the Whig cause in the previous reigns. It invokes the example of Greek and Roman writers who had defended liberty, and promises 'the best Patriots, as well as Poets',[82] 'Patriots' being a favourite Whig self-description.[83] Milton is enlisted in this cause firstly

---

[78] The copies in the Huntington Library and the British Library are the only complete ones known.

[79] See Beal, *Index*, ii 17–67; *Poems of Andrew Marvell*.

[80] Now Bodleian Library MS Eng. poet. d. 49.

[81] *Poems on Affairs of State* (London, 1697), sig. A3r.

[82] *Poems on Affairs of State*, sig. A2r.

[83] *Poems of John Dryden*, i 471.

A. Pope

POEMS

ON

Affairs of State:

FROM

The Time of *Oliver Cromwell*, to the Abdication of K. *James* the Second.

Written by the greateſt Wits of the Age.

VIZ.

Duke of *Buckingham*,	Mr. *Milton*,
Earl of *Rocheſter*,	Mr. *Dryden*,
Lord *Buckhurſt*,	Mr. *Sprat*,
Sir *John Denham*,	Mr. *Waller*.
Andrew Marvell, Eſq;	Mr. *Ayloffe*, &c.

With ſome Miſcellany Poems by the ſame: Moſt whereof never before Printed.

Now carefully examined with the Originals, and Publiſhed without any Caſtration.

Printed in the Year 1697.

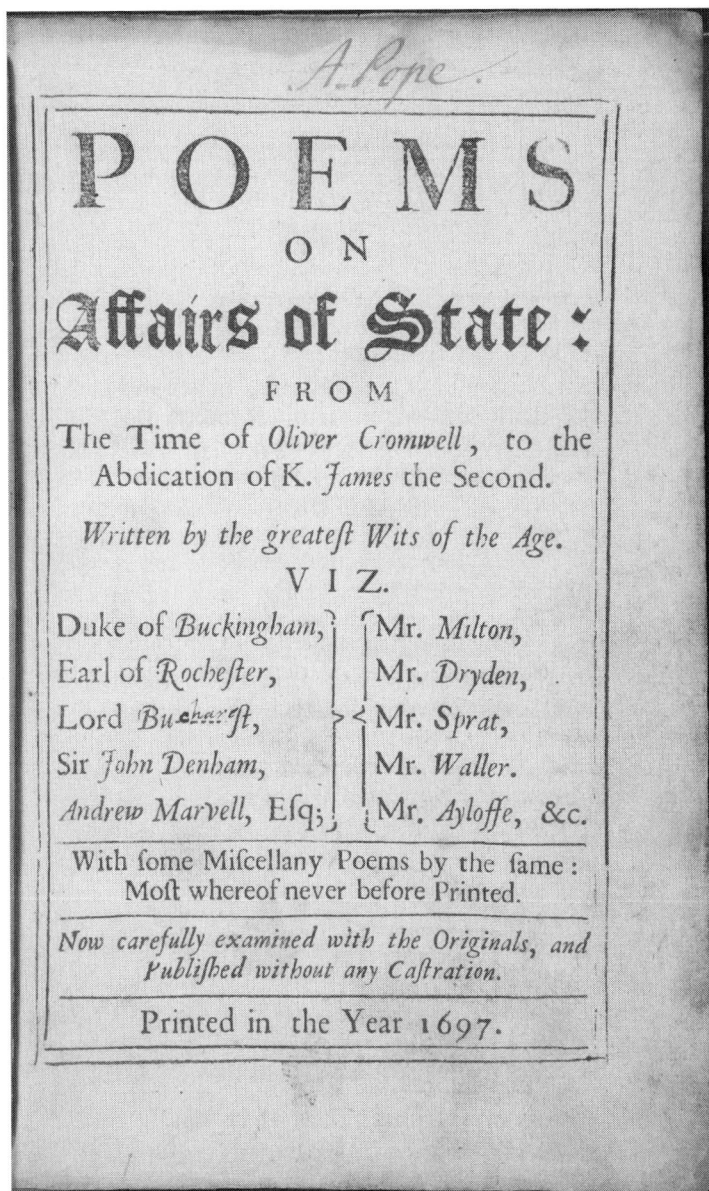

Plate 4. Title page of *Poems on Affairs of State* (1697), with the signature 'A. Pope'.

The title page lists the poets whose work is allegedly contained in this collection (mostly of poems from the reign of Charles II). Many oppositional poems which had circulated only in manuscript were collected here in printed form, providing a Whig retrospect on the period preceding the Revolution of 1688–9.

through a brief defence of the prosody of *Paradise Lost*, but more bizarrely by the claim that 'Directions to a Painter' is 'said to be written by Sir *John Denham*, but believed to be writ by Mr *Milton*'.[84] The various 'Directions' are grouped together, consolidating them into a substantial attack on the misgovernment of Charles II. A clear image of a politically committed Marvell is established by the attribution to him of sixteen satires, thus correcting the impression of his œuvre which had been created by the 1681 folio. His stature as a Whig hero is further confirmed by the inclusion of the poem 'Marvell's Ghost', and of an anonymous elegy which hails him as 'this Islands watchful Centinel'.[85] Rochester is accorded similar treatment, for five poems are attributed to him (including the notorious satire on Charles II), and the volume also includes 'Rochester's Farewell to the Court'. In the second part of *Poems on Affairs of State*, published in the same year, there are further pieces attributed to Rochester, and one writer laments: 'Had the late fam'd Lord *Rochester* surviv'd, | We'd been inform'd who all our Plots contriv'd'.[86] The virtually apolitical (and almost polite) image of Rochester presented in Tonson's 1691 edition is drastically revised.

On the other side, the collection mischievously reconfigures the canon of several royalist writers, notably Dryden. The preface to the first part quotes a couplet from *Absalom and Achitophel* (which had referred to the Civil War) and applies it to the editor's own retrospective view of the turmoil of the last two reigns:

> And looking backward with a wise Affright,
> See Seams of Wounds dishonest to the Sight.[87]

The poems themselves begin (ostensibly to provide a chronologically organized documentation of recent history) with the verses on Cromwell by Waller, Sprat, and Dryden; yet there is no trace of any of Marvell's three Cromwellian pieces: his reputation is being carefully managed. The anthology also attributes to Dryden the satire 'On the Young Statesmen' as well as the 'Essay upon Satire'. Special care is taken to include much material derogatory of Dryden. In part one, the speaker of 'The Town Life' rapidly surveys the Dryden canon with haughty moral disdain:

> I cannot vere with ev'ry change of State,
> Nor flatter Villains, tho' at Court they're great:
> Nor will I prostitute my Pen for Hire,
> Praise *Cromwell*, damn him, write the *Spanish Fryar*.

---

84 *Poems on Affairs of State*, sig. A4ʳ.
85 *Poems on Affairs of State*, p. 123.
86 *Poems on Affairs of State*, p. 159.
87 *Poems on Affairs of State*, sig. A3ʳ.

A Papist now, if next the Turk should reign,
Then piously transverse the Alcoran.[88]

The second part adds a further half-dozen poems which are equally derogatory of him.

As *Poems on Affairs of State* was being published, Dryden was putting the finishing touches to *The Works of Virgil* (1697). These two contrasting projects stand at the end of our period. The one assembles in print verses which had, for the most part, previously existed only in manuscript, circulating anonymously from hand to hand, being censored or improved upon as the transcribers thought fit: these were poems of the moment, poems shaped communally for a particular political cause. As the political climate changed after the revolution of 1688–9 it became possible to put these poems into print in an act of partisan historiography, conserving them for posterity as a highly selective archive of the Whig struggle, and bringing their putative authors out of the shadows. The other project is also affected by the winds of political change, as Dryden turned to translation to provide himself with the living which he could no longer expect from the government. This great folio associates Dryden and Virgil in a transcultural canon, and its title page carries the words of Aeneas, turned now into a claim which is at once modest and proud: *Sequiturque patrem non passibus aequis* ('and he follows his father with steps not equal to his'). Here we have two appropriations of Roman poetry to define one's freedom, two kinds of historiography, two contrasting pieces of book production, two different concepts of the canon, both competing for readers in the same year.

---

[88] *Poems on Affairs of State*, p. 190.

2

Censorship and the Manuscript Transmission of Restoration Poetry

I

Tory. But ha'ye no *Manuscripts?*
Whig. Yes I have Three cases there beyond the Chimny, that I wou'd not change for *Bodlies Library* three times over.
To. What do they treat of?
Wh. Two of 'em are altogether upon the *Art of Government*, and the *Third* is Cramm'd with *Lampoon* and *Satyr*. You sha'not name me any one Copy that has scap'd me; nor any Exigent of State; but I'le furnish ye out of these Papers with an Expedient for't.[1]

IN THIS episode from Sir Roger L'Estrange's Tory propaganda sheet *The Observator*, 'Whig' is showing 'Tory' around his library. The very existence of Whig's cache of manuscripts testifies to his seditious purposes: two whole bookcases are full of papers which allow Whig to campaign against the principles of government expounded in the officially licensed tracts, while the collection of satires preserves the work of the dissident literary imagination. L'Estrange is clearly suspicious of such a private, unofficial archive, a repository which both preserves and enables oppositional thought.[2]

As Surveyor of the Press, L'Estrange had devoted much of the previous twenty years to an onslaught on oppositional[3] publishing, searching the

---

1 *The Observator*, 110; 11 March 1682.
2 For L'Estrange see George Kitchin, *Sir Roger L'Estrange: A Contribution to the History of the Press in the Seventeenth Century* (London, 1913). For the circumstances in which political poetry circulated in the Restoration see *POAS*, i xxv–lvi; Brice Harris, 'Captain Robert Julian, Secretary to the Muses', *ELH*, 10 (1943) 294–309; Timothy Crist, 'Government Control of the Press after the Expiration of the Printing Act in 1679', *Publishing History*, 5 (1979) 49–77; Harold Love, *Scribal Publication in Seventeenth-Century England* (Oxford, 1993); Harold Love, 'Oral and Scribal Texts in Early Modern England' in Barnard and McKenzie, pp. 97–121; Harold Love, *English Clandestine Satire 1660–1702* (Oxford, 2004). Unless otherwise stated, the following discussion of political poetry draws upon the texts and collations printed in *POAS*, vols i–ii.
3 The terms 'oppositional' and 'dissident' are necessarily vague, since opposition to Charles and

premises of writers, printers and booksellers, using spies and informers, and instigating prosecutions. The licensing of books before publication may have ensured that some dissident material never reached print, though printers and booksellers were probably more deterred by the laws of sedition and libel. Attempts to police the world of printing were never wholly successful, and after the lapsing of the Printing Act in 1679 at the height of the Popish Plot scare, there was a deluge of pamphlets opposing the policies of Charles II and his ministers. Nevertheless, the obvious dangers of printing oppositional material did promote a flourishing manuscript culture, in which scribes produced copies of the latest political and erotic poems which no printer would risk handling, but which readers who wanted to be *au courant* with public affairs were happy to lock away in their desks or transcribe into their own notebooks.

Various literary and linguistic strategies were evolved in this world of manuscript circulation. Names of authors disappear,[4] or are attached speculatively or mischievously. Titles vary from copy to copy. Official tropes, the images of royal power, are parodically appropriated to oppositional causes. A non-literary language of slang, jargon, and obscenity is deployed, along with a repertoire of names, initials, and pseudonyms to designate public figures, a vocabulary which it is easy for scribes to alter at will. Obscurity and allegory proliferate, inviting readers to bring their own interpretations to bear upon elusive texts. Many poems highlight the acts of speaking and writing, giving themselves a licence to criticize: authoritative names such as 'Britannia' are given to the speakers of the poems; dialogues, debates, and prophetic voices are common; inscriptions of a riddling or satirical kind replace the formal inscriptions of royal power.[5] That writers are not to be silenced becomes a major part of their subject matter. A strongly intertextual awareness was built up among readers, who became alert to the charged usage of political vocabulary (like the Whigs' claims to stand for 'liberty' and 'property') and the reusing of literary forms such as the 'Advice to a Painter' mode or 'News from Hell'. Poets like Marvell and Rochester return as ghosts to comment on the new times. In this network of poems which pass from hand to hand in the

---

his policies came from several quarters. Ministers moved between government and 'opposition' both from principle and opportunism, and *ad hoc* alliances dominated politics until the coalescing of 'Whig' and 'Tory' groupings during the Exclusion Crisis. Most of the oppositional poems printed in *POAS* criticize Charles for tending towards Catholicism and absolutism, and for debasing the monarchy through his sexual promiscuity (see further chapter 6 below). In the poems of the 1660s and early 1670s there is sometimes a vigorous republicanism which is alien to (or tactically absent from) most Whig poems of the Exclusion Crisis.

4   See chapter 3 below.

5   Examples include the dialogue 'Britannia and Raleigh' (*POAS*, i 228–36), 'A Dialogue between the Two Horses' (*POAS*, i 274–83); 'Marvell's Ghost' (*POAS*, i 284–6); 'Hodge' (*POAS*, ii 145–53); 'A Bill on the House of Commons' Door' (*POAS*, ii 344–6).

coffee houses, there is a loss of authorially sanctioned meaning, which is replaced by a network of meanings generated by readers and scribes: hence multiple political significations become possible, and yet every interpretation is elusive, deniable.

The model which seems appropriate for the understanding of censorship in these circumstances, therefore, is not that of a central power which promotes orthodoxy and proscribes dissent (a model more appropriate to France under Louis XIV), but rather a network of power in which authors, scribes, and readers have considerable freedom to write and circulate material, no matter how scandalous or offensive, and in which various parties struggle for rhetorical mastery, for control over both writing and reading. The scribal culture was in effect produced by the government's attempts to control printing, and it may seem to be an arena of freedom, a site of unfettered production and exchange. Yet within this system of manuscript circulation, forms of control still operated. Both readers who were making copies for their own use, and professional copyists who were transcribing to commission, exercised their own taste and judgement, producing some striking textual alterations. Readings are conflated from different texts; lines and whole passages are inserted or omitted; marginal glosses to explain the identities of the poems' targets are added or changed; attributions are attached with varying degrees of plausibility. The scribes are thus not only transmitting texts but creating new texts, and new frameworks for their interpretation.[6] In such conditions one should think of the copyist as being also an editor, or even in some cases a second author, of the poems which he was transcribing. To these roles we can add that of censor. At this distance we cannot know who was responsible for these textual variants, and to attribute them to 'copyists' is a shorthand which probably conflates several distinct interventions which are now beyond recall. While it is unlikely that professional copyists actually composed variant passages, they certainly had considerable discretion in clarifying obscurities in their copytexts, and private readers making their own copies could vary the texts at will. As for censorship on moral and political grounds, it is clear that words, passages, and whole poems which were acceptable to some compilers (or their employers) proved unacceptable to others; conversely, poems could also become more explicit as they were transcribed and improved.

But, more broadly, censorship in these circumstances could be thought of as the ignoring of any claims to autonomy and authority which might be made

---

6   This also happens in a more limited but still effective way when printed texts are annotated. For contemporary readers' comments on *Absalom and Achitophel*, for example, see Paul Hammond, 'Some Contemporary References to Dryden', in *John Dryden: Tercentenary Essays*, edited by Paul Hammond and David Hopkins (Oxford, 2000), pp. 359–400, at pp. 368–9; Alan Roper, 'Who's Who in *Absalom and Achitophel?*', in *John Dryden: A Tercentenary Miscellany*, edited by Susan Green and Steven N. Zwicker (San Marino, Calif., 2001; also published as *Huntington Library Quarterly*, vol. 63, nos. 1–2), pp. 98–138.

for the original text and its author. Original intentions and meanings are over-written by scribes who produce texts to serve the reader's purposes, whether these purposes might be political opposition or erotic stimulation. The texts often have their marks of authorial origin removed, and are prepared for their place not in the author's *Works* but in the reader's archive. It is the aim of this chapter to explore the kinds of censorship which operated within this manuscript circulation, first in the case of political poetry, and then in the erotic and satirical work of Rochester.

II

Some of the most damaging oppositional poetry did find its way into print: several of the *Advice to a Painter* poems which satirized the conduct of the naval war against the Dutch in 1667 circulated in printed form as well as in manuscript.[7] Even the king's bookseller, Richard Royston, had these poems on his shelves, and they were read by that loyal civil servant Samuel Pepys.[8] The more openly republican and more sexually explicit oppositional poems of the 1670s circulated only in manuscript, though it is noticeable that during the years 1679 to 1681 Whig printers and booksellers became much bolder in what they were prepared to publish: this may be due partly to the demise of the Printing Act, but also to the intense commitment of writers who thought the nation to be in danger from popery and arbitrary government. Whig poems which appeared in print at this period included the notorious denunciation of the king and his policies called 'A Raree Show', which had an engraving depicting Charles as a travelling showman carrying Parliament around in a box.[9] For this and other satires Stephen College was executed.

Some poetry critical of Charles appeared more safely in print because its target was disguised. *A Poem to the Charming Fair One* from *circa* 1675 is an attack on the king's sexual enslavement to his French mistress the Duchess of Portsmouth, which is seen as a political enslavement to France. Her charms have defeated the English king, and so avenged England's military conquest of France. But the language of the poem is ostensibly that of a simple sexual lyric, and it has a style and rhythm which are remarkably close to Rochester's idiom:

---

7 See *Poems of Andrew Marvell*, pp. 321–6.
8 Kitchin, pp. 167–8; *Diary of Samuel Pepys*, vii 407 (he is sent a MS copy 'sealed up'), 421, viii 21 (he is lent a MS and decides to copy it), 313 (he reads several of the poems with his friends), 439 (he finds a copy when dining at a friend's house).
9 Text only in *POAS*, ii 426–31, which wrongly says that the engraving does not survive; there are illustrations of the two versions of the engraving reproduced in B. J. Rahn, '*A Ra-ree Show* – A Rare Cartoon: Revolutionary Propaganda in the Treason Trial of Stephen College' in *Studies in Change and Revolution: Aspects of English Intellectual History 1640–1800*, edited by Paul J. Korshin (Menston, 1972), pp. 77–98.

> Yet in her pomp this wretched Fair
>   Is despicably vain;
> A shrine so bright without, did ne're
>   Inclose a soul so mean.

Her lover exhausts Nature's store to adorn her:

> Thus Natures Treasuries unlock,
>   This Idoll to adorn:
> And from the glittering Diamond-Rock,
>   The crusted Jems are torn. . .

> Be frankly kinde, and pay Loves Debt!
>   Think thou'hast a King insnared:
> The Glory of a prize so great,
>   Does bring its own Reward.[10]

The trope of love as a kingdom, and lovers as royalty, is so common in Restoration erotic poetry that these verses could easily pass without a reader noticing their political charge; yet read in the light of contemporary anxiety and resentment about the duchess's conspicuous consumption of taxes and her political influence over the king, the ostensibly innocuous verses have a disturbing force, mobilizing for political purposes the rhetorical resources of the period's frightened fascination with sexually powerful women. In this case censorship has curtailed explicit speech, but promoted more complex modes of writing and interpretation.

Censorship in a different form affected some of the most outspoken manuscript poems which attack Charles directly, for several compilers evidently demurred about the terms in which the king was represented. Towards the end of the 'Fourth Advice to a Painter' (1667) there is a passage on Charles whose tone is more sarcastic and sexually explicit than the rest of the poem:

> As Nero once, with harp in hand, survey'd
> His flaming Rome and, as that burn'd, he play'd,
> So our great Prince, when the Dutch fleet arriv'd,
> Saw his ships burn'd and, as they burn'd, he swiv'd.
> So kind he was in our extremest need,
> He would those flames extinguish with his seed.
> But against Fate all human aid is vain:
> His pr— then prov'd as useless as his chain.[11]

This is the text as printed in the modern Yale edition of *Poems on Affairs of State* from Bodleian MS Eng. poet. e. 4, but other early witnesses tell a different story. The complete passage is omitted from three manuscripts, while the last

---

10 *A Poem to the Charming Fair One* [1675], pp. 1–2; not in *POAS*.
11 *POAS*, i 146, ll. 129–36; textual notes i 454.

four lines, the most sexually explicit ones, are omitted from the contemporary printed text, *Directions to a Painter* (1667). Other manuscripts illustrate the freedom with which sexual vocabulary was altered, as they replace 'prick' with 'swiving' or 'fucking'. Similarly, a manuscript of 'A Ballad called the Haymarket Hectors' cuts out a reference to Charles 'consulting his cazzo', and substitutes a comment on his liking 'for sweet variety'.[12]

Notable amongst the variations for reasons of sexual decorum is a tendency to eliminate references to sodomy (whether homosexual or heterosexual). 'Further Advice to a Painter' begins with a comparison of Charles II and the Roman emperor Commodus, which says that at night they repair 'One to his pathic, the other to his play'r'. One manuscript changes 'pathic' to 'punk', even though the reference here is to Commodus, not to Charles.[13] A line in 'Nostradamus' Prophecy' claiming that 'sodomy is the Prime Minister's sport' (referring to the Duke of Buckingham) is changed from 'sodomy' to 'so doing', a variant which can be explained both as a misreading of the handwriting in the copy which the scribe was working from, and as a rewriting on grounds of taste.[14] And in 'Last Instructions to a Painter' the line 'Bugger'd in incest with the mongrel beast' was too strong for the copyist who changed 'Bugger'd' to 'Proceeds'.[15] (Incest and bestiality apparently caused him no problem.)

Blasphemy was another reason for scribes censoring the poems that they copied. 'The Downfall of the Chancellor' has a couplet which one manuscript omits, probably because of its invocation of God:

> God is reveng'd too for the stones he took
> From aged Paul's to make a nest for th' rook.[16]

In 'Britannia and Raleigh' the line attacking the Duke of York's adherence to Roman Catholicism:

> Mac James the Irish pagod does adore:[17]

appears in many texts with 'pagod' changed to 'bigots': this is plausible palaeographically, but it also removes the suggestion that the Catholics' God is a pagan idol. 'The Royal Buss' comments that as in ancient times there was a struggle between the gods and the giants, so now there is a struggle between Parliament and the Court:

> But, bless'd be Jove, the gods of ours
> Are greater in their guilt than pow'rs.

---

12 *POAS*, i 169–71; textual notes i 457.
13 *POAS*, i 164–7, l. 10; textual notes i 456–7.
14 *POAS*, i 186–9, l. 17; textual notes i 459.
15 *POAS*, i 99–139, l. 146; textual notes i 452–3; see also *Poems of Andrew Marvell*, p. 450.
16 *POAS*, i 158, ll. 11–12; textual notes i 455.
17 *POAS*, i 233, l. 125; textual notes i 465.

> Though then the heathens were such fools,
> Yet they made gods of better tools.[18]

One manuscript omits the last two lines, perhaps from a sensitivity about the idea of making gods. Though one can never confidently assign motives for such misreading (or creative rereading), it does seem as if sexual and religious sensibilities prompted the production of textual variants which were in effect small acts of censorship within this arena which was specifically devoted to free speech.

Of all the political poems from the reign of Charles II, one of the most notorious (and one of the most unstable textually) was the Earl of Rochester's lampoon on Charles II (see Plate 5).[19] This was subjected to considerable alteration in transmission, with the order of the lines being changed, some of the more explicit sexual details omitted, and some passages being rewritten: indeed, so radical are the differences between the extant manuscripts that it is impossible to reconstruct the original text with any confidence. This makes comment on the direction of scribal revision hazardous, but some revealing features of the transmission can nevertheless be illustrated. Several variants suggest a nervousness about the poem. The title is sometimes given as 'On the King', sometimes simply as 'A Satyr'; other titles take an anecdotal form ('On K: C: IId by the E of Roch—r; For which he was banish'd the Court, and turn'd Mountebank') or they pass a judgement: 'A base Copy'. In Bodleian MS Rawl. D. 924 the poem is clearly set in the present:

> Their Reigns (&. oh Long May hee Reigne . . .

But other texts awkwardly try to disguise the contemporaneity:

> Not long since reign'd oh may he long survive.[20]

Some versions put the king's lament to his mistress in reported speech:

> To Carwell y^e. Most Deare of all his Deares
> The Best Releiffe of his Declining yeares
> Offt he Bewayles his fortune & her fate[21]

whereas others more boldly cast this into direct speech, showing no qualms about usurping the king's voice:

---

[18] *POAS*, i 263, ll. 5–8; textual notes i 468.

[19] Love in *Works of John Wilmot*, pp. 85–90, 596–9 identifies six major variant versions of the poem, and prints five different complete texts. For an account of the textual complexities see Harold Love, 'Rochester's "I' th' isle of Britain": decoding a textual tradition', *English Manuscript Studies 1100–1700*, 6 (1997) 175–223.

[20] BL MS Harley 7317.

[21] Bodleian MS Rawl. D. 924.

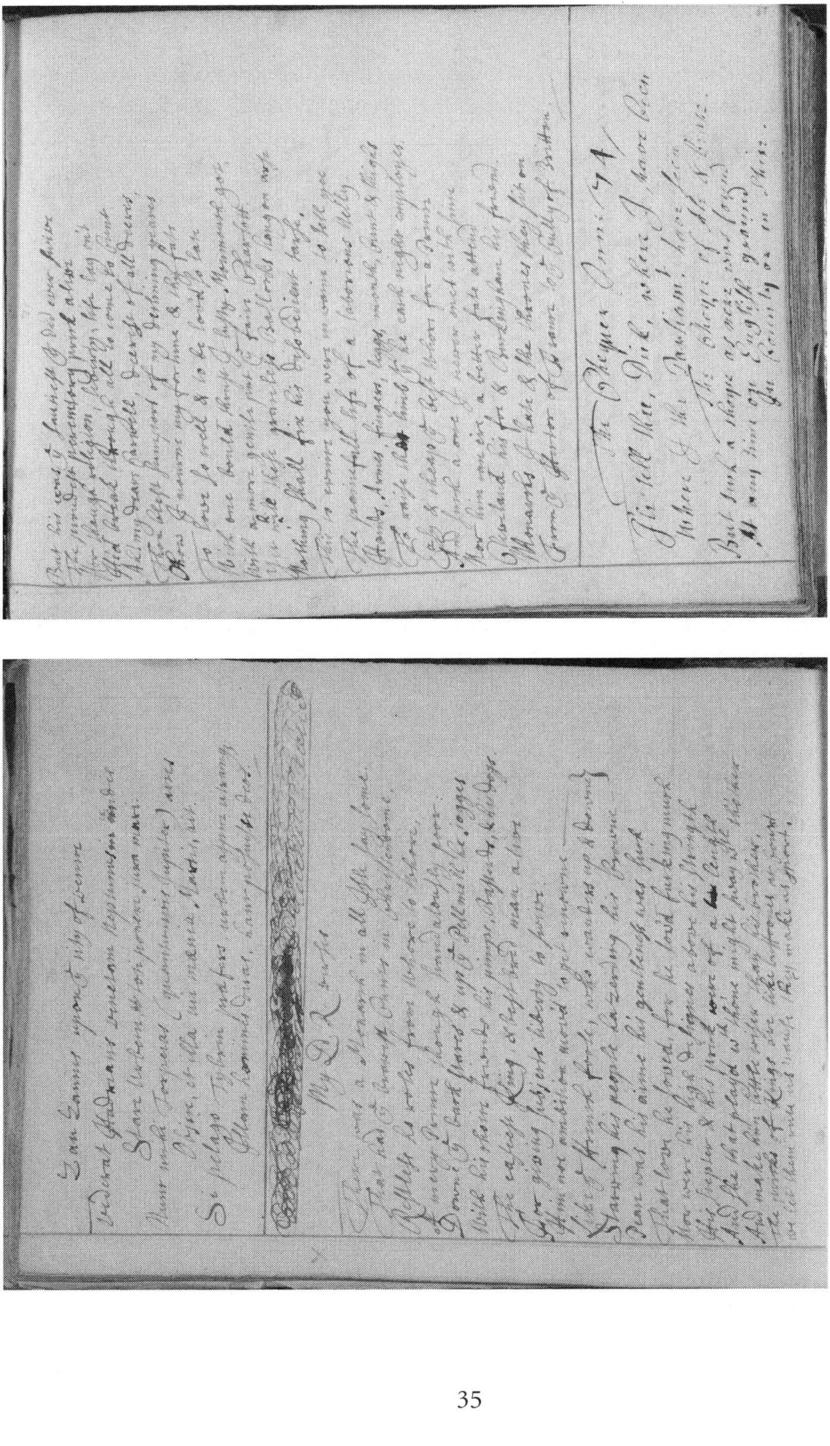

Plate 5. Brotherton Collection MS Lt 55, fols. 36v–37r, Rochester's satire on Charles II. The text of this outspoken attack on the king varies considerably in the extant manuscript sources: the opening words of this version ('There was a Monarch in all Isle say some') differ significantly from the more usual 'In th' isle of Britain, long since famous known', and are notably more cautious.

> Ah my deare Carwell, dearest of my Deares!
> Thou best Releife of my declineing yeares!
> O How I mourne thy Fortune & My Fate.[22]

Rochester's account of the king's liking for ease above all (and one kind of ease in particular) has a sharp epigrammatic force in some texts:

> Peace was his Aime, his gentleness was such
> And love, he lov'd, for he lou'd fucking much.[23]

But other texts (through anxiety, perhaps, about their very audacity) scramble the second line in various ways:

> That as his Loue is Great, he swiues as much[24]

> And's Loue, for he lou'd fucking much.[25]

> Oh how he lov'd, Oh he lov'd fucking much[26]

> And those he Loves, he loves for f— much[27]

The couplet which so vividly encapsulates the king's degeneracy:

> Who restless rowles ab⟨t⟩. from whore to whore,
> Grown impotent & scandalously poor.[28]

is also found as a triplet:

> Restlesse he Rowles about from Whore to Whore
> With Dogg & Bastard, always going before,
> A merry Monarch, scandalous & poore[29]

(where the tone is nicely complex in that third line); and in yet another version as four lines:

> Restlesse he roues from whore to whore,
> An easy Monarch, scandalous, &. poore.
> With a damn'd crue to whores he joggs
> Of Bastards, Pimps, Buffoones, & Dogs.[30]

Here the phrasing is cruder, the tone more cruel. This version is a more

---

22 BL MS Harley 7315.
23 Leeds University Library Brotherton Collection MS Lt 54.
24 Bodleian MS Rawl. D. 924.
25 Bodleian MS Don. b. 8.
26 BL MS Harley 7317.
27 Yale MS Osborn Chest II, Number 1.
28 BL MS Add. 23722.
29 BL MS Harley 7315.
30 Bodleian MS Don. b. 8.

outspoken piece of political opposition. The political character of the poem is also shifted by the different positions assigned to this explicitly republican couplet:

> I hate all Monarchs & the Thrones they sitt on,
> From yᵉ Hector of France to yᵉ Cully of Brittain[31]

which is sometimes placed in the middle of the poem, sometimes more emphatically at the end.

Without being able to reconstruct Rochester's original text, we cannot give a precise account of the way in which the poem was rewritten in transmission; but it is clear that many scribes, readers, and would-be satirists tried their hands at improving the piece as it was passed around, changing its tone, its sexual explicitness, and its political charge. The very fact that the original text is lost and replaced by a bewildering array of versions is a striking example of scribal censorship: censorship here is not simply the removing or rephrasing of offensive material (though that is clearly happening) but the recasting of the poem, its appropriation to a variety of new emphases. It is significant that the most outrageous satire on Charles II should be a locus of special textual difficulty, for this extraordinarily transgressive writing seems to have inhibited some of the copyists, while for others it liberated their own imaginations to extend and rework what they had set out simply to transcribe.[32] Indeed, so radical are the changes which were made to this poem that in some cases the text is likely to have been produced not by transcription from a written copy, but by memorial reconstruction. The memory easily retains couplets, but not always in their original order – particularly when a poem's structure is so slight – and couplets may be changed to triplets, or *vice versa*, in the act of writing down what is half-remembered. Typical of memorial reconstruction too is the ability to recall the main point of a line, but not its precise phrasing. This poem was probably too transgressive for some people to be comfortable about handling written copies, and so it would have been committed to memory and only later confided to paper in moments of privacy. Thus the fear of authority drove readers to guard this poem in that most secret of archives, their memories, where it was metamorphosed into whatever form most suited the readers by whom it was half-recalled, half-created.

---

[31] BL MS Add. 23722.

[32] It is worth repeating here that 'copyist' is an abbreviated way of referring to those involved in the reshaping of the text as it was circulated. Some changes are no doubt attributable to an individual scribe's lapses in concentration, or to his own taste (for example in spelling out or softening obscenities), but others should be thought of as editorial decisions which were not necessarily taken by the person doing the copying. In the case of this particular poem, Love suggests that different texts were prepared for different kinds of readership (*Works of John Wilmot*, p. 598).

III

After the revolution of 1688 many of the political poems which had circulated only in manuscript during the reigns of Charles II and James II appeared in printed collections of poems on affairs of state, several of which advertised on their title pages that they contained poems 'against popery and tyranny'. Ostensibly the tyranny of official censorship which had kept such pieces from being printed and published freely had now been broken. But an examination of the variants between the texts as printed in these anthologies and those from the original manuscript circulation shows that many of these poems were censored to remove sensitive material, presumably by compilers responding to the criteria of political correctness under the new regime. This amounts to a rewriting of the oppositional poetry from the time of Charles II in the light of what the Whig cause had subsequently become. Though the parliamentary Whig opposition to Charles's government had sought only to modify the constitutional arrangement for the succession so as to preserve protestant liberties, there had been a strong republican element in the Whig coalition which made its voice heard with particular force in manuscript poetry. It is striking that this radical component of early Whiggism is removed from the poems which are collected to create a Whig canon after 1688.

'The History of Insipids', from 1674, is a catalogue of the king's misman-agement which makes Charles personally responsible for the errors and disas-ters of his reign, and yet the printed texts of 1689 and 1697 tone down the poem in an effort to spare Charles (and by extension other English kings) some of the more damaging charges. One stanza, which in early manuscript sources appears as:

> The wolf of France and British goat,
>   One Europe's scorn, t'other her curse
> (This fool, that knave, by public vote,
>   Yet hard to say which is the worse),
> To think such kings, Lord, reign by thee
> Were most prodigious blasphemy.[33]

is rewritten to exclude Charles and make Louis XIV the sole example of bad kingship, for in these printed texts the first four lines become:

> That false, rapacious wolf of France,
>   The scourge of Europe and its curse,
> Who at his subjects' cry does dance,
>   And study how to make them worse.[34]

---

[33] *POAS*, i 250, ll. 145–50, from Yale MS Osborn Chest II no. 13.
[34] *POAS*, i 466, from *A Second Collection* (1689) and *Poems on Affairs of State* (1697).

The same late printed texts change 'Charles' to 'James' (l. 34), 'Charles and Louis' to 'treacherous Louis' (l. 141), and remove the republican threat in 'Turn'd commonwealth, we will abhor you' (l. 138) by changing it to the innocuous 'Grown wise by wrongs we shall abhor you'. Some of the more explicit lines on the king's sexual behaviour in 'Colin', 'The King's Answer', and 'Hodge' were also removed when the poems were printed, though present in the previous manuscripts.[35]

'A Dialogue between the Two Horses' (the horses from the equestrian statues of Charles I and Charles II) comes to a climax in these lines:

> Then England rejoice, thy redemption draws nigh:
> Thy oppression together with kingship shall die!
> A commonwealth! a commonwealth! we proclaim to the nation,
> For the gods have repented the King's Restoration.[36]

Though present in the manuscripts which preserve the poem as it first circulated in 1676, these lines are omitted by the printed texts from the reign of William III. Other alterations similarly remove republican sentiment: the prospect of 'monarchy's downfall' (l. 169) is changed to 'tyranny's downfall', while a reference to the 'crimes' of tyrants is softened into 'faults' (l. 176). Also omitted is the couplet which concludes the discussion in which monarchs are characterized as either cruel like Nero or lecherous and lazy like Sardanapalus:

> One of the two tyrants must still be our case
> Under all that shall reign of the false Scottish race.[37]

Since one member of that false Scottish race of Stuarts was currently on the throne as Mary II, these lines were cut from the printed edition of 1689 (but not, curiously, from that of 1697, after her death). Similar censorship cut out the discussion of the Stuarts in 'Britannia and Raleigh'. Britannia makes a powerful denunciation of Stuart tyranny:

> Raleigh, no more; too long in vain I've tried
> The Stuart from the tyrant to divide . . .
> And shall this stinking Scottish brood evade
> Eternal laws, by God for mankind made?[38]

These lines are cut out in the 1689 edition.

A bizarre allegation in 'Hodge' (1679) that Mary was married to William of Orange in order to introduce popery to the Netherlands was removed from the poem as printed in 1689, depriving readers of these choice lines:

---

[35] *POAS*, ii 522–4, 532.
[36] *POAS*, i 282, ll. 159–62; textual notes i 470.
[37] 'A Dialogue between the Two Horses', ll. 135–6.
[38] *POAS*, i 234, ll. 141–2; textual notes i 465.

> His pocky brat, got on adult'rous Nan,
> With Orange join'd the Belgians to trepan,
> Goes to The Hague for the same holy end
> As Rome to us does spurious Este send.[39]

It is understandable that a publisher in 1689 might think it unwise to describe Queen Mary in print as a 'pocky brat' and her mother as an adulteress. Similar sensitivities caused alterations in the text of 'An Historical Poem' from 1680. An uncomplimentary reference to Mary, Princess of Orange (mother of William III) is removed from the 1689 text:

> And his Dutch sister quickly after di'd,
> Soft in her nature and of wanton pride.[40]

These lines are followed by the allegation that Anne Hyde (mother of Mary II) was pregnant by the Earl of Falmouth when she married James Duke of York:

> Bold James survives, no dangers make him flinch,
> He marri'd Mynheer Falmouth's pregnant wench.[41]

In the 1689 edition these lines are replaced by the politically safer reflection on James's political role:

> Bold Y—k survives to be the nation's curse
> Resolv'd to ruin it by deceit or force.

The same text then omits the following passage on Queen Henrietta Maria, who as grandmother of Mary II was evidently also an unsuitable target for abuse in the new reign. A later reference to 'the ill-got race of Stuarts' (l. 57) is altered to omit 'ill-got', while the 1697 edition prudently changes 'ill-got' to 'royal'.

The rewriting of Whiggism which these texts offer is also seen in their treatment of the first generation of Whig heroes. 'A Charge to the Grand Inquest of England, 1674' is a piece of pro-government satire which blames the parliamentary opposition for encroaching on the royal prerogative. Many members of the opposition are named, but in the 1697 edition two names are changed: in the line

> Temple and Marvell, who yet wears his ears

the name 'Marvell' is changed to 'S__', while in the line

> Ransack your writers, Milton, Needham, Prynne;

---

[39] *POAS*, ii 148, ll. 68–71; textual notes ii 522.
[40] *POAS*, ii 155–6, ll. 19–20; textual notes ii 523.
[41] 'An Historical Poem', ll. 21–2.

'Milton' is replaced by 'Selden'.[42] It looks as if the reputations of these two major champions of the Whig cause are being protected by careful censorship.

IV

Censorship of the erotic and sexually explicit poems of the Earl of Rochester occurred in both manuscript and print.[43] One might expect Tonson, who was the leading literary publisher of his age, to issue a printed text which had been made verbally decent and visually sober, and was clearly distanced from both the scruffy 'Antwerp' editions of Rochester and the connoisseurs' luxury manuscripts. But the scribes who produced those manuscripts had their own moral and aesthetic criteria which often affected the process of transcription.

The selection of material for inclusion in manuscript miscellanies might not seem to merit the description of 'censorship', but the process of assembly determined which poems were read together as a group, and therefore suggested a framework of interpretation for individual poems, as well as fashioning a canon, and therefore an image, for Rochester. A substantial group of his erotic poems is found together in the Gyldenstolpe manuscript (a richly bound collection written by a professional scribe for a wealthy reader around 1680),[44] and in virtually the same order in other similar manuscripts from the same date. The inclusion of Rochester's translation fron Seneca's *Troades* ('After Death nothing is, and nothing Death . . .') between 'The Disabled Debauchee' and 'The Imperfect Enjoyment' implies that this should be read as a libertine poem, thus reducing its philosophical seriousness and turning it into a piece of fashionable sceptical posturing. Conversely, the quotations from Rochester in the writings of Charles Blount give the poetry a more serious philosophical status.[45] Because poems by (or associated with) Rochester often circulated in small groups, variations in the composition of the groups clearly reveal editorial intervention: a case in point is the unpleasant and crudely explicit poem 'Advice to a Cunt Monger' which appears in Badminton MS FmE 3/12 as part of a sequence of poems which is replicated exactly in the Gyldenstolpe manuscript except for the omission of this one piece.[46]

The structural alteration of these small canons of erotic poetry is one instance of the taste and sensibilities of the compilers, but the structure of

---

42 *POAS*, i 222, ll. 10, 42; textual notes i 464.
43 This section draws extensively on the collations in Harold Love's edition, *Works of John Wilmot*.
44 For a facsimile see *Gyldenstolpe*.
45 See Gillian Manning, 'Some Quotations from Rochester in Charles Blount's *Philostratus*', *Notes and Queries*, 231 (1986) 38–40.
46 Michael Brennan and Paul Hammond, 'The Badminton Manuscript: A New Miscellany of Restoration Verse', *English Manuscript Studies 1100–1700*, 5 (1995) 171–207, at p. 177.

individual poems is also manipulated. The song '*Fair Chloris* in a Pigsty lay' evidently disturbed some scribes. Chloris dreams first that one of her pigs is stuck in the entrance to a cave, and then that she is being penetrated by a local swain:

> Now peirced is her Vergins *zone*
> Shee feeles the foe within itt:
> She heares an Amourous broaken groane,
> The strieving *Lovers* fainting moane
> Just in the happy *Minute*.
>
> Frighted shee wakes, and wakeing friggs:
> Nature thus kindly eas'd
> In dreames raisd by her grunting Piggs
> And her owne thumb betwixt her Leggs,
> Shees Innocent and pleas'd.[47]

Tonson's edition of 1691 omits the last stanza, but prints the previous one; Yale MS Osborn PB, VI/88 omits both, along with the preceding stanza. In the case of 'To A Lady, in A Letter', Tonson's edition originally printed a full text of the poem, but this was subsequently cancelled and replaced by a shorter text.[48] Other poems are contained and made respectable not by excision but by addition: the yielding of Chloris to the shepherd in the song 'As *Chloris* full of harmless thought' is enclosed within a new narrative framework when the poem is printed in the broadside *Corydon and Cloris* [1676].[49] But structural alteration is not always carried out in the interests of decorum: indeed, the use of stanzas or couplets in most Restoration poems, together with their often casual design, seems to have encouraged other writers to add material of their own which extends rather than constrains the original. The verses on 'Signior Dildo', which describe the reactions of various court ladies to the arrival of this useful implement, appear in a different order in different manuscripts, and acquire additional stanzas in Bodleian MS Don. b. 8 which introduce further characters into the satire. In BL MS Harley 7312 Rochester's self-dramatizing poem 'To the Postboy' is joined to the poem usually called 'One writing against his prick', to produce not only a new version of Rochester's poem but a new version of his persona.[50]

It is again at the level of verbal variants that one can see the operation of the scribe as censor, for some of those who copied out Rochester's most explicit poems would at some points decide to intervene and tone down the text. In the

---

47 *Works of John Wilmot*, p. 40, ll. 31–40.
48 See David M. Vieth, 'A Textual Paradox: Rochester's "To a Lady in a Letter" ', *PBSA*, 54 (1960) 147–62, and 'An Unsuspected Cancel in Tonson's 1691 "Rochester" ', *PBSA*, 55 (1961) 130–3.
49 *Works of John Wilmot*, p. 532.
50 See John D. Patterson, 'Another Text of Rochester's "To the Post Boy" ', *Restoration*, 4 (1980) 14–16.

case of 'The Disabled Debauchee'[51] the manuscripts omit various stanzas, but the stanza which caused most concern was the following, where the male speaker recalls his contest with Cloris over which of them would bed the servant boy:[52]

> Nor shall our Love-fits *Cloris* be forgot,
> When each the well-look'd Linkboy strove t'enjoy;
> And the best Kiss was the deciding Lot,
> Whether the Boy Fuck'd you, or I the Boy.[53]

This is the text which appears in Harold Love's edition. Tonson's 1691 edition originally printed the stanza, but it was removed as the book was going through the press, and the poem's remaining verses were renumbered. Three of the twenty-two manuscripts recorded in Love's edition also omit it (one actually has the stanza number followed by a gap),[54] while others leave out a group of four stanzas of which this is one. Moreover, several of those manuscripts which do include the stanza alter the wording: two manuscripts change 'well-look'd' to 'best Lov'd'; four omit 'boy' altogether; three tone down the sexual contest by changing 'strove' to 'sought'. In the last line two manuscripts and *Poems on Several Occasions* (1680) read 'us'd' for 'fucked', another manuscript prefers 'kiss'd', while Bodleian MS Don. b. 8 makes a muddled attempt to remove the homosexual element altogether by replacing 'I' with 'you' in the last line.

This embarrassment about homosexual intercourse is found elsewhere in the textual transmission of Rochester's poems. The song which begins 'Love a Woman? Th'rt an Ass!' ends with the lines:

> And if buizy Love intrenches
> There's a sweet soft Page of mine
> Can doe the Trick worth Forty wenches.[55]

This stanza was omitted in the 1691 edition, but only after the page on which the full text had been printed was cancelled, and a replacement leaf substituted which removed the offending lines.[56] The entire poem is scribbled out in

---

51 *Works of John Wilmot*, pp. 44–5, 538–41.

52 For the homoerotic content of Rochester's poems, and attempts to neutralize it, see Paul Hammond, 'Rochester's Homoeroticism', in *That Second Bottle: Essays on John Wilmot, Earl of Rochester*, edited by Nicholas Fisher (Manchester, 2000), pp. 46–72, revised and reprinted as 'Rochester and Restoration Homoeroticism' in my *Figuring Sex between Men from Shakespeare to Rochester* (Oxford, 2002), pp. 226–54.

53 'The Disabled Debauchee', ll. 37–40, in *Works of John Wilmot*, p. 45.

54 In addition, BL MS Add. 73540, not collated by Love, also omits it (Hammond, *Figuring Sex*, p. 244).

55 *Works of John Wilmot*, p. 38, ll. 14–16.

56 See Vieth, 'An Unsuspected Cancel', p. 131 n. 2.

Pierre Danchin's manuscript.[57] 'The Imperfect Enjoyment' is an explicit poem which generally suffers little interference from scribal censorship,[58] and yet a couple of lines from Rochester's denunciation of his wayward penis did prompt some alteration:

> Stiffly Resolv'd t'would Carelesly invade
> Woman, nor man, nor ought its fury stayd –
> Where ere it pierc'd a Cunt it found or made –[59]

The compilers of two manuscripts seem to have found 'pierced' too explicit, and changed it to 'pressed'. The 1680 edition and two manuscripts change 'man' to 'boy', altering the homosexual encounter from that of two adults to that of adult and boy, apparently a more acceptable (perhaps because more classical) form of homosexual relationship.

In 'An Allusion to Horace' some copyists were offended by Rochester's obscene remarks on Dryden. This is how the lines appear in Love's edition:

> Dryden in vain tryd this nice way of Witt,
> For he to be a tearing Blade thought fitt.
> But when he would be sharp he still was blunt:
> To frisk his frolic fancy hee'd cry Cunt;
> Wou'd give the Ladyes a drye bawdy bobb,
> And thus he gott the name of Poet Squobb.[60]

Several scribes recoil from this denigration of Dryden: two manuscripts omit lines 73–4, while two more omit lines 73–6; most manuscripts replace 'Cunt' with a dash; and Bodleian MS Add. B 106 substitutes 'coy modest' for 'dry bawdy'. However, copyists are still capable of adding their own crudity to Rochester's: BL MS Sloane 1504 reads 'frig' for 'frisk'.

The fear of blasphemy also prompted some acts of censorship. Scribes who happily copied out the explicit sexual details of 'A Ramble in St. *James's Park*' balked at lines which used religious language in an irreverent context:

> But though *St. James* has the honor on 't,
> 'Tis consecrate to *Prick* and *Cunt*.[61]

These lines are omitted from BL MS Harley 6057, while Edinburgh University Library MS DC.1.3 omits the later lines which describe the impossible things which will come to pass before the poet ceases to seek revenge on his unfaithful mistress:

---

[57] *Works of John Wilmot*, p. 533.
[58] Though it is partly excised in one MS. Love suggests that all the surviving texts derive from commercial scriptoria (*Works of John Wilmot*, pp. 517–18).
[59] *Works of John Wilmot*, p. 15, ll. 41–3; textual notes pp. 517–19.
[60] *Works of John Wilmot*, p. 73, ll. 71–6; textual notes p. 589.
[61] *Works of John Wilmot*, p. 76, ll. 9–10; textual notes pp. 591–4.

> *Crab-Lowse*, inspir'd with Grace Divine,
> From Earthly *Cod* to *Heav'n* shall climb;
> *Physicians*, shall believe in *Jesus*,
> And disobedience cease to please us.[62]

Curiously, this same scribe had no qualms about including the *adynaton* which immediately precedes line 147:

> The *Jesuits fraternity*,
> Shall leave the use of *Buggery*;[63]

Was this because the allegation belonged to the repertoire of contemporary political jibes rather than to a primarily religious discourse?

V

If political and erotic poetry prompted most of the scribes' anxious rewritings, there were nevertheless other poems by Rochester which attracted intervention. *Tunbridge Wells*, with its loose structure and unfocussed satire, is one of the most chaotic of Rochester's poems textually, and seems to have lent itself to the addition, removal, and rearrangement of material *ad libitum*.[64] Philosophical argument caused problems for copyists of Rochester's *Satyre against Reason and Mankind* (see Plate 6).[65] Some manuscripts predictably omit lines which satirize the clergy, for example:

> that Sensual Tribe, whose Talents ly
> In Avarice, Pride, Sloth and Gluttony,
> Who hunt good Livings, but abhor good Lives. . .[66]

But more interesting is the problem which copyists have with the paradoxes which are typical of the poem's ironic style of argument, and its deployment of a speaker whom we do not know whether to trust. The difficult, compact argument in the line 'And therefore what they fear, at heart they hate' (l. 45) proved too difficult for the scribe of BL MS Harley 7312, who simply left it out, while relics of other struggles with the line can be seen in the variant readings 'least' and 'last' for 'heart'. The bold paradox 'For all men would be Cowards if they durst' (l. 158) defeated the copyist of BL MS Sloane 1458, who changed 'Cowards' into 'noble'. Similarly, the line 'Most men are Cowards, all men should be Knaves' (l. 169) puzzled the copyist of the Illinois manuscript, who left it out,

---

62 'A Ramble in St. *James's Park*', ll. 147–50.
63 'A Ramble in St. *James's Park*', ll. 145–6.
64 *Works of John Wilmot*, pp. 548–56.
65 See also the discussion in Fisher, 'Publication', pp. 60–1.
66 *Works of John Wilmot*, pp. 57–63, ll. 202–4; textual notes pp. 556–74.

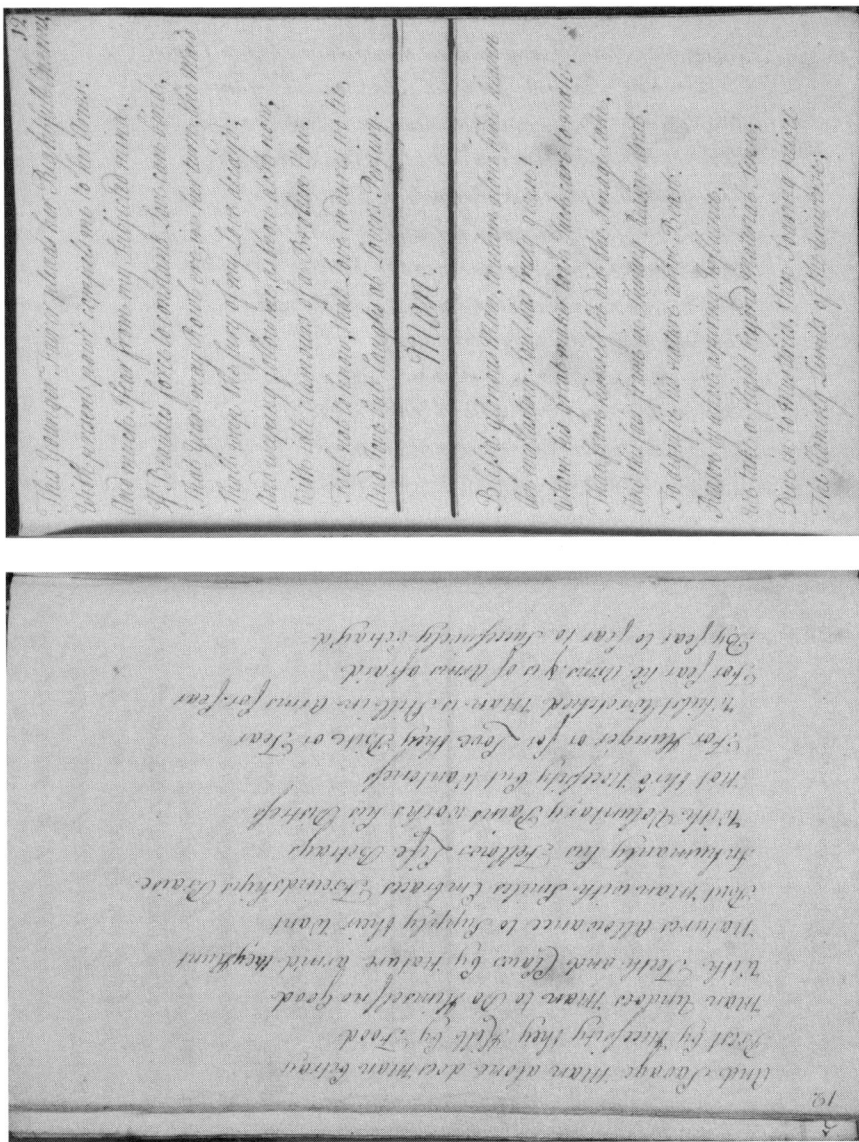

Plate 6. Brotherton Collection MS Lt 110, fols. 11v–12r, a poetical miscellany compiled in 1726, showing a previously unrecorded text of Rochester's *Satyre against Reason and Mankind*. The left-hand page shows part of the complete text of the *Satyre* (except for the 'Addition'), which is written sideways on the versos of the book; the right-hand page shows an extract from the *Satyre* under the heading 'Man' which forms part of an anthology of mostly moralizing verses written on the rectos. The lines from Rochester are given a moralizing continuation not found in other texts.

and the scribe of National Library of Scotland MS 2201, who turned it back towards the familiar association of knaves and fools by changing 'cowards' to 'fools'; others tried to make sense of the line by changing 'should' to 'would'. The philosophical vocabulary of the poem was similarly altered throughout by scribes who found Rochester's style and diction too demanding, and could not follow his argument or tone. A few examples will illustrate the point: 'instinct' becomes 'instance' (l. 10); 'doubts' becomes 'thoughts' (l. 19); 'profess' becomes 'suppose' or 'confess' or 'protest' (l. 53); 'aspiring' becomes 'inspiring' (l. 66); 'bounds' becomes 'binds' (l. 102); 'reforming' becomes 'performing' (l. 102); 'distinction' becomes 'discretion' (l. 110); 'true' becomes 'right' (l. 111); 'best' becomes 'lost' or 'base' (l. 143); 'passion' becomes 'actions' (l. 143). And there is one small but telling case of Rochester's sceptical argument being appropriated for orthodox religion when the line 'Hudled in dirt the reasoning Engine lies' (l. 29) is given a conventional biblical resonance by the alteration of 'dirt' to 'dust'.

Several passages in which the argument is particularly condensed or paradoxical are abbreviated or rewritten; one example is the comparison of man and dog:

> For all his Pride and his Philosophy,
> 'Tis evident Beasts are in their degree,   [115]
> As wise at least, and better farr than he.
> Those Creatures are the wisest who attain
> By surest means, the ends at which they aime:
> If therefore *Jowler* finds and kills his Hares,
> Better than *Meeres* supplies Committee chaires;   [120]
> Though one's a Statesman, th' other but a Hound,
> *Jowler* in justice would be wiser found.
> You see how farr Mans wisedome here extends;
> Look next if humane nature makes amends:
> Whose Principles most generous are and just,   [125]
> And to whose Morals you would sooner trust.
> Be Judge your self, I'le bring it to the test,
> Which is the Basest Creature, Man or Beast?[67]

This passage caused a considerable amount of confusion. BL MS Sloane 1458 omits the first line and lines 119–26; Bodleian MS Add. B. 106 transposes lines 121–2; the Illinois manuscript omits line 126. In the last line 'basest' appears in various witnesses as 'baser', 'noblest', 'better', 'vilest', 'wisest' or 'bravest', or is omitted altogether: evidently both the logic and the tone of Rochester's argument defeated many of these early readers. Indeed, so disconcerting was Rochester's argument that eight lines which try to explain it are added after line 122 in BL MS Harley 7312:

---

[67] *A Satyre against Reason and Mankind*, ll. 114–28.

> For Jowler finds, and kills; *Reason*'s his Cause
> But States men's reason's grounded upon Laws
> Which Contradict right reason in us hence
> Hee fondly makes the Senses Clash with sence
> For ask from whence the Lawes, do take their rise
> T'is answ'd Sence right reasons Paradice
> Jowler you see dispatch't, but you must Tarry
> Till the Greek Kalends, for the States man's Quarry.

What we see here is not simply perplexity in the face of a difficult and some-times slackly argued poem (though that is part of the problem) but an attempt to contain the poem's challenge to a complacent orthodoxy by spoiling its sharp paradoxes and uncomfortable ironies. The rebuttal of Rochester's poem was not conducted only in the formal rejoinders which were published: it began in the very transmission of the poem itself.

The archives which readers built up made these manuscript poems into their own property: the Gyldenstolpe manuscript became a luxury item in the Royal Library in Stockholm; the Badminton manuscript linked the poems with other material useful in a nobleman's study – details of the royal household, consti-tutional notes, and legal memoranda on the New Forest.[68] John Oldham's transcripts of Rochester (Bodleian MS Rawl. poet. 123) were shuffled in amongst working drafts of his own poetry, forming a physical symbol of the unresolved engagement with Rochester which characterized his work. The political circumstances which forced writers to resort to manuscript circula-tion enabled them to speak more forcefully than they could ever have done in print: censorship empowered writers. But the conditions of transmission also empowered readers, who selected, edited, and rewrote the material which interested them: manuscript circulation unlocked the creativity of readers by removing poetry from the fixity and dignity of print, with its claims for defini-tive authority. Virtually none of this poetry survives in authorial autograph manuscripts: this is a world without originals but full of multiple copies, every one unique; there are no authors but many redactors; no single controlling royal power, but a multitude of fractious and irreverent citizens. The death of the author is the birth of many censors.

---

[68] Brennan and Hammond.

3

Anonymity in Restoration Poetry

I

IN 1963 David M. Vieth published his magisterial book *Attribution in Restoration Poetry*,[1] in which he investigated the tangled web of attribution, misattribution, and anonymity in the works associated with the Earl of Rochester. Vieth saw anonymity and dubious attribution as problems to be solved, and his aim was to establish as far as possible the answer to the question, 'What did Rochester actually write?', and to the secondary question, 'Who then actually wrote the poems which were wrongly attributed to Rochester?' These are important questions, and Vieth's book laid secure foundations for the scholarship and criticism of Restoration poetry in subsequent years by providing the most judicious account of the boundaries of the Rochester canon. But there are other ways of understanding the uses of anonymity in the Restoration period: instead of regarding anonymity as a problem, can we not see it as a functional device, as a resource which enabled certain kinds of writing and reading, rather than a tiresome puzzle which obscures the real canon of those named poets in whom we are primarily interested?

The influence of modern editions of Restoration works is so powerful that it often takes a special effort both of scholarship and of imagination to undo the neat packages into which editors have assembled the poetry of Rochester or Dryden or Etherege, and instead to envisage that poetry as it was encountered by its first readers: circulating in the form of separate printed pamphlets or in manuscript, often anonymously or with conjectural attributions. Editors who carefully assemble a canon under the name of a major poet do something which was not only rarely attempted in the period, but which may actually run counter to Restoration habits of reading and assumptions about authorship and the function of poetry. Many writers did not show that concern for the creation of a personal œuvre under their own name which modern editors and critics display on their behalf. Marvell's canon was assembled after his death, and was shaped at least partly by the political concerns of his editor and

---

[1]   David M. Vieth, *Attribution in Restoration Poetry: A Study of Rochester's 'Poems' of 1680* (New Haven, 1963).

publisher. Rochester allowed his poems to circulate separately, and for the most part anonymously, in manuscript, and it was not until 1691, eleven years after his death, that a collection of his poems appeared which was free from spurious attributions (though it was not free from bowdlerizations). Dryden published some of his most important works anonymously, and never assembled a collected edition of his poetry.

When so much poetry circulates anonymously, and when readers as copyists are responsible for the preservation and publication of so many poems, the role of the reader is more active, more interventionist, than we commonly recognize. Readers may omit or add attributions when copying poems in manuscript, and may add their conjectural attributions to the title pages of anonymous printed pamphlets. When *The Medal of John Bayes*, a nasty satirical poem on Dryden, was printed anonymously in 1682, Narcissus Luttrell wrote on his copy: '6d By Thomas Shadwell. Agt Mr Dryden. very severe. 15 May',[2] while another reader inscribed the title page of his copy: 'Shadwell is Run Mad'.[3] Readers had considerable influence over the reputation of contemporary poets through their allocation of attributions, and through the choices which they made when compiling anthologies, constructing new contexts within which poems could be interpreted. They were also well used to interpreting poems within canons which were based not around authors, but on topics, as when reading scriptorium manuscripts which anthologized political or erotic verse.

Although we might expect professional writers to have built up a canon attached to their own names, while amateurs preferred to remain anonymous, the picture is actually more complex. Margaret Cavendish, Duchess of Newcastle, was an indefatigable promoter of her poetical effusions in folio volumes complete with her name, titles, and portrait. Some of the most forceful poetic voices of the Restoration – Marvell, Rochester, Oldham – were not professional writers, in that they did not earn their living from poetry or the theatre. To them, poetry may have been a way of intervening in the life of the nation, but that intervention did not entail the construction of a personal œuvre: their public persona was more complex than modern editions of their work might suggest.

II

The dominant professional writer of the period, John Dryden, generally signed his work, and yet he found subtle and important uses for anonymity within his œuvre.[4] When *Mac Flecknoe*, his satire on Thomas Shadwell, was released into

---

[2] Macdonald, *Bibliography*, p. 232.
[3] Trinity College Library, Cambridge, H. 6. 93.
[4] Since the original version of this essay appeared, two articles have discussed Dryden's uses of

circulation in manuscript in 1676 it was almost certainly anonymous (to judge by the evidence of the extant manuscripts).[5] This form of publication was perhaps arranged so as not to force an open breach with Shadwell, and, if so, it was a gesture which on the surface maintained the rhetoric of politeness and even amity which the two men had deployed throughout the argument which they had conducted in their prologues and prefaces over the previous ten years: they never referred to each other by name, but always by a polite formula such as 'my particular friend for whom I have a very great respect'.[6] It is this form of decorum which is shattered in *Mac Flecknoe*, however, by the insistent use of names: Shadwell is named ten times in the 217-line poem. Although the authoritative text of *Mac Flecknoe* printed in the Dryden-Tonson *Miscellany Poems* (1684) gives the name as 'Sh—', the manuscripts which predate this text spell the name out in full – so those modern critics who comment on the poem's association of 'Sh—' with shit are basing their inter- pretation on a typographical convention not encountered by the poem's first readers, and almost certainly not in the original manuscript;[7] moreover, many manuscripts (particularly scribal miscellanies) highlight proper names by using bold script, so there is no doubt that early readers would have found the name both rhetorically and visually prominent (see Plate 7). The naming of Shadwell brings the poem (and Shadwell himself) out of respectable literary discourse into the twilight world of literary satire. Flecknoe too is named, and renamed as Augustus and John the Baptist, which is a just retribution for his incessant self-promotion in his many volumes of verses, letters, and essays.[8]

In this period, literary lampoons such as the *Sessions of the Poets* or Roches- ter's *An Allusion to Horace* make free use of writers' names and nicknames: Mr Bayes, Poet Squab, Poet Ninny, Lord All-Pride. Formal literary essays, however, often eschew names altogether, preferring to use some polite periph- rasis, even if the politeness is merely a suavely turned insult. Dryden avoids naming the Earl of Rochester, or his brother-in-law Sir Robert Howard, when he is sharply disagreeing with them: instead, he calls Howard '*The Author of The Duke of* Lerma',[9] while Rochester is alluded to through a safe plural form: 'those who are allow'd for witty men'.[10] The latter phrase, in the Preface to *All for Love*, is part of Dryden's rejoinder to Rochester's attack on him in *An Allusion to Horace*. Rochester's poem, circulated sometimes anonymously,

anonymity: Randy Robertson, 'The Delicate Art of Anonymity; The Case of *Absalom and Achitophel*', *Restoration*, 27 (2003) 41–60; John Mullan, 'Dryden's Anonymity', in *The Cambridge Companion to John Dryden*, edited by Steven N. Zwicker (Cambridge, 2004), pp. 156–80.

5   Only two of the MSS attribute the poem to Dryden: see *Poems of John Dryden*, i 310.
6   See Paul Hammond, *John Dryden: A Literary Life* (Basingstoke, 1991), pp. 78–9.
7   *Poems of John Dryden*, i 315.
8   See chapter 8.
9   'A Defence of an Essay of Dramatique Poesie', in *Works of John Dryden*, ix 5.
10 *Works of John Dryden*, xiii 13.

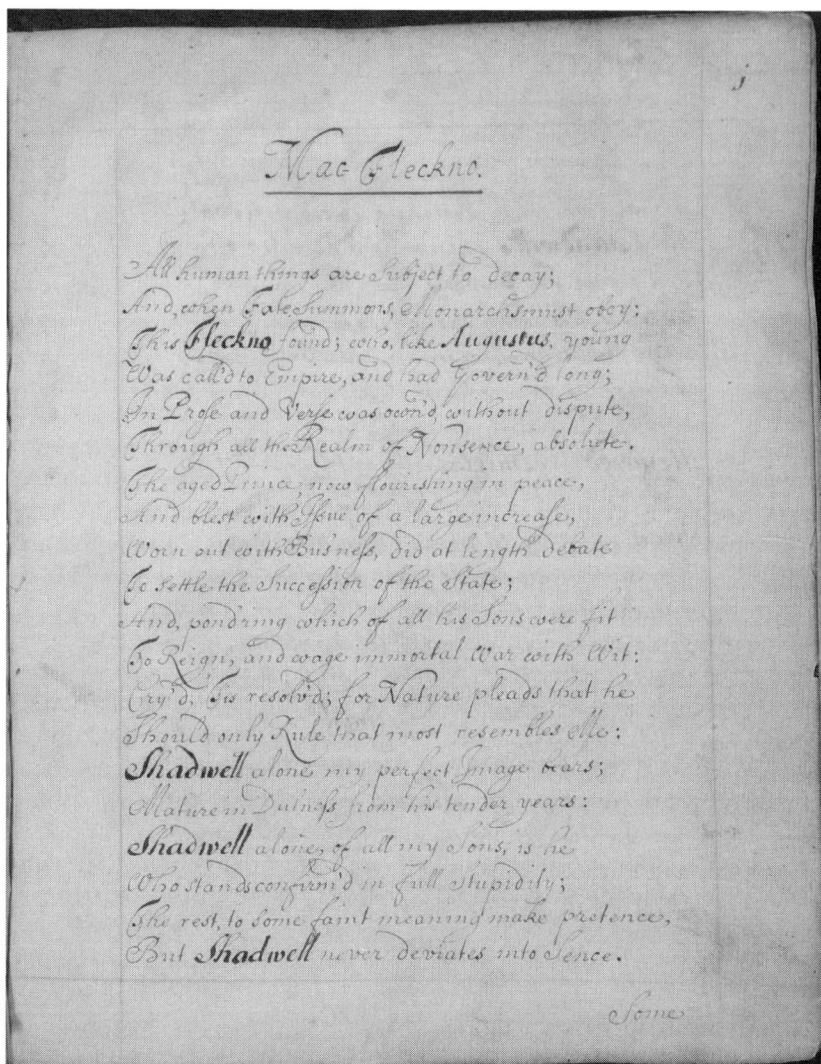

Plate 7. Brotherton Collection MS Lt 54, p. 1, a richly bound and calligraphically written scriptorium manuscript originally compiled *circa* 1680, showing the opening of Dryden's *Mac Flecknoe.*

The poem was written in 1676 and circulated in manuscript before being printed in a pirated edition in 1682, and then in an authorized text in the Dryden-Tonson *Miscellany Poems* (1684). The scribe has emphasized the names, whereas the 1684 printed text substitutes initials and dashes.

sometimes attributed,[11] had named Dryden as a crass dramatist and an unprincipled critic; Dryden's Preface, which was of course signed, avoids naming Rochester, but through various allusions and half-quotations makes his target clear.[12] (The names which he does use are Nero and Dionysius, translations of Rochester into classical tyrants.) Moreover, Dryden challenges the author of *An Allusion* to sign his work:

> I would wish no other revenge ... than that he would subscribe his Name to his censure, or (not to tax him beyond his learning) set his Mark: for shou'd he own himself publickly, and come from behind the Lyons Skin, they whom he condemns wou'd be thankful to him, they whom he praises wou'd chuse to be condemned.[13]

Dryden has carefully devised a rhetoric which makes a general point about vain aristocrats for the general public, while allowing those who knew the authorship of *An Allusion* to appreciate the full force of his reply. In using a signed, printed essay to reply to an unsigned manuscript poem, Dryden has had to fashion a mode of writing which is critically effective but still socially acceptable, and one which simultaneously engages different groups of readers.

But even Dryden's compliments are delivered without names: commending Aphra Behn for her skill in translating Ovid without knowing any Latin, Dryden refers to her as 'the authour, who is of the fair sex':[14] her sex is cited to explain her ignorance and to enhance her skill, but her actual name is evidently unimportant to Dryden's purposes. Wycherley is praised under the title of 'the Author of the *Plain Dealer*, whom I am proud to call my Friend.'[15] Thomas Creech is commended in the Preface to *Sylvae* as 'the ingenious and learned translator of Lucretius', though not named: Dryden's reference to 'that commendation which he has so justly acquired' by the translation, and 'his reputation [which] is already established in this poet', shows that he expected readers to know Creech's identity well enough.[16] There is no actual concealment here, but it seems that it is mainly dead authors whom Dryden feels it proper to name: Cowley, Denham, Hobbes, Spenser, and Suckling are named freely. The kind of literary criticism which Dryden pioneered in England sought to define the individual characteristics of named writers, and the great writers of the past are evaluated and memorialized in his essays by having their

---

[11] Nine of the extant MSS listed by Harold Love attribute the poem to Rochester (*Works of John Wilmot*, pp. 586, 590), as does the MS separate sold at Sotheby's in 2004 (*The Library of John R. B. Brett-Smith: London Thursday 27 May 2004*, lot 492).

[12] *Works of John Dryden*, xiii 403–10; Paul Hammond, 'Two Echoes of Rochester's *A Satire Against Reason and Mankind* in Dryden', *Notes and Queries*, 233 (1988) 170–1.

[13] *Works of John Dryden*, xiii 17.

[14] 'Preface to *Ovid's Epistles*', in *Poems of John Dryden*, i 390.

[15] 'The Authors Apology for Heroique Poetry; and Poetique Licence' prefixed to *The State of Innocence* (1677), in *Works of John Dryden*, xii 89.

[16] *Poems of John Dryden*, ii 253–4.

names woven into an elaborate comparative and genealogical narrative of European poetry: 'Milton was the poetical son of Spenser', Chaucer is the father of English poetry as Boccaccio was of Italian.[17] To Dryden, the naming of writers was often a way of admitting them to the canon: accordingly the occasional compliments to named contemporaries (such as the Earl of Roscommon, whose *Essay on Translated Verse* is praised in the Preface to *Sylvae*) stand out all the more prominently; on the other hand, his contemporaries of uncertain worth were generally discussed anonymously, or had their names twisted into puns and pseudonyms: Shadwell becomes Mac Flecknoe, Sh—, and Og.[18]

It is a significant move, then, whenever Dryden decides not to put his name to his own work. *Mac Flecknoe* was evidently not a work for the laureate to sign. The reasons for publishing *Absalom and Achitophel* anonymously are clearly ones of political prudence: as an outspoken partisan work it risked violent retribution. Dryden draws attention to the poem's anonymity in the prefatory 'Epistle to the Whigs': 'You cannot be so unconscionable as to charge me for not subscribing of my name, for that would reflect too grossly upon your own party, who never dare, though they have the advantage of a jury to secure them.'[19] Here Dryden is claiming that although he is writing on behalf of the king's interests, he is actually less secure than opposition writers, since the Whig party has been able to manipulate the law by packing juries: anonymity in this case is not only a protection, but ostensibly the protection needed by the weaker party. Dryden was keen not to risk any repetition of the incident in 1679 when he was beaten up in Rose Alley, almost certainly because he was suspected of having written the anonymous *Essay on Satire*.[20] This poem is now thought to be the work of the Earl of Mulgrave, who as an aristocrat was too grand to acknowledge poems, or to be beaten up in alleys. But it is interesting that when Dryden reprinted his three satires at the beginning of Tonson's collection *Miscellany Poems* in 1684, after the political battle had been won, they still appeared anonymously:[21] it seems as if Dryden wanted them to be read together as a group, and in uncorrupt texts, but did not wish to insert them formally into his œuvre over his own name. Editors, of course, have decided that they know better, but how many students whose first encounter with Dryden's work is with these poems are told of their equivocal

---

[17] 'Preface to *Fables Ancient and Modern*' in *Poems of John Dryden*, v 49–50.

[18] For Shadwell as Og see *The Second Part of Absalom and Achitophel*, ll. 459–509 in *Poems of John Dryden*, ii 54–7.

[19] *Poems of John Dryden*, i 451.

[20] See p. 16 above.

[21] *Absalom and Achitophel*, *The Medal*, and *Mac Flecknoe* were attributed to Dryden on the contents page of the second edition of *Miscellany Poems* (1692), though not in the text. Dryden did not personally acknowledge the authorship of *Mac Flecknoe* until 1693, after Shadwell's death, when he cited it along with *Absalom* as an example of Varronian satire in his 'Discourse Concerning Satire' (*Poems of John Dryden*, iii 389).

status in Dryden's canon? Much as they may now seem to transcend their original circumstances, they evidently seemed to Dryden to be properly and necessarily anonymous works.

There is also a notable self-consciousness from Dryden about the uses of his own name. *Religio Laici*, which is both a personal apologia and a public treatise, appeared with his name on the title page, but Dryden opens the preface by saying that 'A poem with so bold a title, and a name prefixed from which the handling of so serious a subject would not be expected',[22] needs some explanation. By drawing attention to the signing of the work with a name which was chiefly associated with plays and political writing, Dryden is seeking to redefine the significance of his public name. Unlike *Mac Flecknoe* or *Absalom and Achitophel*, *Religio Laici* has Dryden speaking in his own voice, both in the poem and the preface, deploying a rhetoric which is at once modest and self-assured, and which thus associates a wholly new tone of voice with the name 'John Dryden'. When he writes that he has consulted a theologian for advice, the man is referred to as 'a judicious and learned friend, a man indefatigably zealous in the service of the church and state, and whose writings have highly deserved of both.'[23] This is handsome praise, but the theologian is not named; modern scholars have agreed that he is probably John Tillotson, but contemporary readers are unlikely to have reached the same conclusion, with so many possible candidates. Unlike the transparent allusion to Creech, this reference to Tillotson is not meant to be decoded: rather, it thanks a friend without embarrassing him with the public connection of their two names, invokes an authority which authenticates Dryden's venture into theological discussion, and gives it the imprimatur of church and state; at the same time, it is the unofficial imprimatur of friendship, and one which Dryden feels happy to set aside when he wishes to pursue his own path:

> 'Tis true he had too good a taste to like it all, and amongst some other faults recommended to my second view what I have written, perhaps too boldly, on St Athanasius, which he advised me wholly to omit. I am sensible enough that I had done more prudently to have followed his opinion, but then I could not have satisfied myself that I had done honestly not to have written what was my own.[24]

The satisfaction of the self, and the creation of a kind of public religious poetry to which Dryden can honestly put his name, requires this deft invocation and evasion of authority, before he goes on to take issue with Athanasius himself.

Elsewhere Dryden explores the possibilities of merging or associating his identity with classical writers: in his criticism he often identifies himself with

---

22 *Poems of John Dryden*, ii 86.
23 *Poems of John Dryden*, ii 87.
24 *Poems of John Dryden*, ii 88.

Horace,[25] while his misfortunes bring out parallels with Virgil.[26] It is beyond the scope of this essay to explore Dryden's intricate revoicings of himself through his classical translations,[27] but it is worth recalling one tellingly ambiguous renaming of himself which invokes the *Aeneid*. In 'To the Memory of Mr Oldham' the comparison of the young poet with the unfortunate Nisus (who slips and loses a race) and himself with the successful Euryalus (Nisus' friend who goes on to win) is unstable, reversing itself into the opposite association, and so opening up a tragic sense of his own mortality and perhaps his wasted gifts.[28] Such subtle and fluid remakings of his public identity include and draw upon those significant moments of silence when Dryden refuses to sign works which would compromise his professional standing – or which would be compromised by their association with him.

III

One writer who avoided any public name was John Oldham himself,[29] whose three volumes of poetry were all published anonymously. *Satyrs upon the Jesuits* (1681) was a polemical and in places almost obscene collection which perhaps Oldham did not think it prudent to sign, as he was earning his living as a schoolmaster and tutor. His subsequent volumes *Some New Pieces* (1681) and *Poems, and Translations* (1683) are both described on the title pages as being 'By the Author of the *Satyrs upon the Jesuits*',[30] so that Oldham ties his work together into an œuvre, even while remaining anonymous. Only with the posthumous *Remains* (1684) does Oldham's name come before the public. The four volumes are bound together with the title page *The Works of Mr. John Oldham*, so that familiar poems now appear under this unfamiliar name, with a new identity for the author created by a collection of memorial poems from a group of well-known writers, headed by Dryden's description of Oldham as 'too little and too lately known'. Later, in the 1710 edition, an engraved frontispiece portrait was added. However, in various ways Oldham's identity

---

25 See Paul Hammond, 'Figures of Horace in Dryden's Literary Criticism', in *Horace Made New: Horatian Influences on British Writing from the Renaissance to the Twentieth Century*, edited by Charles Martindale and David Hopkins (Cambridge, 1993), pp. 127–47.

26 In his translation of Virgil's *Eclogue* IX contributed to *Miscellany Poems* (1684); *Poems of John Dryden*, ii 208–13.

27 See Hammond, *Traces*.

28 Dustin Griffin, 'Dryden's "Oldham" and the Perils of Writing', *Modern Language Quarterly*, 37 (1976) 133–50; Paul Hammond, *John Dryden: A Literary Life*, pp. 83–5, 146–7.

29 See Paul Hammond, *John Oldham and the Renewal of Classical Culture* (Cambridge, 1983).

30 Though not noted by Harold F. Brooks ('A Bibliography of John Oldham the Restoration Satirist', *Oxford Bibliographical Society Proceedings and Papers*, 5 (1936–9) 1–38) some copies of *Poems, and Translations* have a variant title page with Oldham's name. This edition appears to be printed from a completely different setting of type, which is a puzzle (see *The Library of John R. B. Brett-Smith*, p. 209).

had been known to the connoisseurs: Thomas Wood in 1683 referred to him as 'Auldram',[31] which suggests that he had heard the name, but had never seen it written down. Sir William Soame in his poem of rebuke 'To the author of *Sardanapalus* upon that and his other writings'[32] does not name Oldham, but knows that he is a schoolmaster, and while Soame is prompted by the one poem which he cites, he has evidently seen more, knows of Oldham's interest in Horace and Boileau, and has some sense of an embryonic Oldham canon. The compiler of Yale MS Osborn b. 105 of poems by Rochester and others knew enough to attribute several poems to Oldham in 1680:[33] evidently he was a privileged reader.

The anonymous circulation of Oldham's poetry during his lifetime provides examples of the complex and shifting relationships between author and persona which develop with this form of publication. In 1676 Oldham wrote an ironical attack on virtue in the form of a speech which, according to the poem's subtitle in Oldham's own manuscript, is 'Suppos'd to be spoken by a Court-Hector at Breaking of the Dial in Privy-Garden', referring to the occasion when Rochester and some friends returning from a drinking bout smashed the phallic glass sundials in the king's private garden. Oldham's poem circulated anonymously in manuscript under the spurious title *A Satire against Virtue*,[34] and without the explanatory subtitle, thus effacing the persona, the satirized speaker of the diatribe, and leading readers to mistake the poem's stance and attribute the sentiments directly to the author. In this way the pirated manuscript circulation created for Oldham an anonymous *succès de scandale* which was far from his intentions, and attributed libertine attitudes directly to the author, if not actually by name to the little-known 'John Oldham' himself. In 1679 the first of Oldham's *Satyrs upon the Jesuits*, called *Garnet's Ghost*, appeared in a pirated printed form with the attribution, 'Written by the Author of the *Satyr against Virtue*, (not yet Printed)' (see Plate 8),[35] which shows that the *Satire against Virtue* had achieved a sufficient reputation through its manuscript circulation for it to be used as a selling point for the new poem. An unauthorized canon for Oldham is being assembled here without the use of his name, and through the use of a misleading title which obscures the important distinction between author and persona. One effect of this was that Oldham wrote two explanatory poems: 'An Apology for the Foregoing Ode, by Way of Epilogue', in which he explains for the benefit of his less sophisticated readers that his Muse

---

[31] Thomas Wood, *Juvenalis Redivivus, or the First Satyr of Juvenal Taught to Speak Plain English* (London, 1683), p. 9.

[32] This poem circulated in manuscript in the early 1680s, and was first printed in *Examen Poeticum* (London, 1693), p. 328.

[33] Vieth, *Attribution*, pp. 98–9.

[34] *The Poems of John Oldham*, edited by Harold F. Brooks and Raman Selden (Oxford, 1987), pp. lxxix, cxi.

[35] Brooks, 'Bibliography', p. 18.

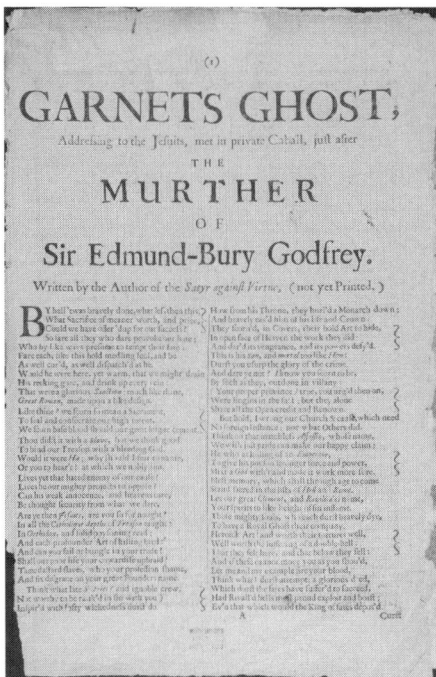

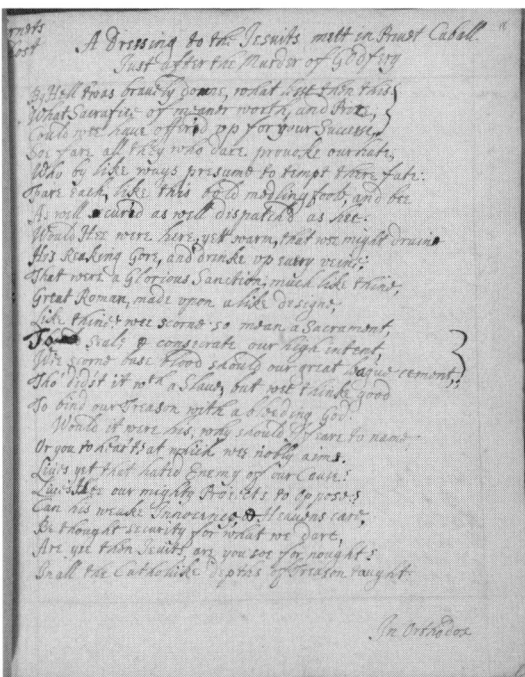

Plate 8. [John Oldham], *Garnets Ghost, Addressing to the Jesuits, met in private Caball, just after the Murther of Sir Edmund-Bury Godfrey* [London, 1679], p. 1, and the opening of the same poem in Brotherton Collection MS Lt 87, fol. 18r, a collection of satires mostly from the 1680s.

This poem, which became the first of Oldham's *Satyrs upon the Jesuits* (1681), exploits the terror created by the murder of the magistrate to whom Titus Oates had made the initial allegations about a Popish Plot. The poem is anonymous, but the attribution to the author of the *Satire against Virtue* indicates that the publisher expected readers to have heard of that other, rather scandalous, piece. There are a few manuscript copies of *Garnet's Ghost*, but curiosity seems mostly to have been satisfied by this printed edition, which was followed by the collection of four satires on the Jesuits in the autumn of 1680 (dated 1681).

> only acted here in Masquerade;
> And the slight Arguments, she did produce,
> Were not to Flatter Vice, but to Traduce;[36]

and another poem called 'Counterpart to the Satyr against Vertue', written, as the subtitle makes plain, 'In Person of the Author'.[37] Confusions persisted, however: one manuscript of the satire attributes it correctly to Oldham at the beginning, but at the end adds 'Ld Roch^r:' which is then crossed out.[38] One wonders whether this was a guess at the identity of the author or of the speaker, and whether the scribe reflected at all on the difference between the two. Three of Oldham's poems, the *Satire against Virtue* and its 'Apology', and 'Upon the Author of a Play called *Sodom*' (on the obscene play often attributed to Rochester) appeared in the 1680 edition of *Poems* by '*the E. of R– – –*' because of their thematic links with the Earl and his milieu.

Each of the three collections which Oldham himself published has a preface in which the anonymous author outlines an attitude to the writing and publishing of poetry. The Advertisement to *Satyrs upon the Jesuits* says that the 'Satyr against Vertue' was never given that title by its author, and was printed without his knowledge; now it is being reprinted in a correct text as 'a justice due to his own Reputation', since in its corrupt form it had been 'a worse Satyr upon himself, than upon what it was design'd'.[39] He has a reputation to guard, therefore, even when publishing anonymously. The Advertisement to *Poems, and Translations* says that the volume has been put together hastily, in no particular order, but if the poems win approval from readers, then they may appear in a revised, collected edition:

> By that time belike he means to have ready a very Sparkish Dedication, if he can but get himself known to some Great Man, that will give him a good parcel of Guinnies for being handsomly flatter'd. Then likewise the Reader (for his farther comfort) may expect to see him appear with all the Pomp and Trappings of an Author; his Head in the Front very finely cut, together with the Year of his Age, Commendatory Verses in abundance, and all the Hands of the Poets of *Quorum* to confirm his Book, and pass it for Authentick. This at present is content to come abroad naked, Undedicated, and Unprefac'd, without one kind Word to shelter it from Censure; and so let the Criticks take it amongst them.[40]

Here the anonymity is an element in Oldham's proud refusal to be part of a venal and sycophantic literary coterie, jostling to confirm the work's

---

36 *Poems of John Oldham*, pp. 68–70; ll. 4–6.
37 *Poems of John Oldham*, pp. 268–73. This poem was left in MS and was printed after Oldham's death in his *Remains* (1684).
38 British Library MS Add. 14047; Vieth, *Attribution*, p. 459.
39 *Poems of John Oldham*, p. 4. The unauthorized title was, however, used as a half-title in the printed collection *Satyrs upon the Jesuits* (London, 1681): see *Poems of John Oldham*, pp. 56–7.
40 *Poems of John Oldham*, p. 161.

authenticity as true poetry, and thus reassure the reader. This stance is all of a piece with the attitude which is adopted in several of the poems. In 'A Satyr Dissuading from Poetry' the ghost of Spenser rebukes him for thinking in terms of personal glory:

> *But is it nought* (thou'lt say) *in Front to stand,*
> *With Laurel crown'd by* White, *or* Loggan's *hand?*
> *Is it not great and glorious to be known,*
> *Mark'd out, and gaz'd at thro the wond'ring Town,*
> *By all the Rabble passing up and down?*
> So *Oats* and *Bedloe* have been pointed at,
> And every busie Coxcomb of the State:
> The meanest Felons who thro *Holborn* go,
> More eyes and looks than twenty Poets draw:
> If this be all, go, have thy posted Name
> Fix'd up with Bills of Quack, and publick Sham;[41]

It is significant that for Oldham the poet's 'name' rhymes with 'shame', with a pun on 'sham'. The ideal life, for Oldham, is a quiet country retreat which includes anonymity: in 'A Satyr Address'd to a Friend' he writes:

> 'T has ever been the top of my Desires,
> The utmost height to which my wish aspires,
> That Heav'n would bless me with a small Estate,
> Where I might find a close obscure retreat;
> There, free from Noise, and all ambitious ends,
> Enjoy a few choice Books, and fewer Friends,
> Lord of my self, accountable to none,
> But to my Conscience, and my God alone:
> There live unthought of, and unheard of, die,
> And grudg Mankind my very memory.[42]

It is not that Oldham lacks poetic personality: in 'A Letter from the Country' he writes a detailed account of the psychological process of poetic composition, while a strong and distinctive voice passes literary judgement in his imitation of Horace's *Ars Poetica,* and social judgement in his imitations of Juvenal and Boileau. The use of anonymity, and of translation from authoritative classical and neo-classical writers, gives a rhetorical power to the satirist's voice which it would not have if it could be clearly identified with John Oldham, grammar-school boy and household tutor. There is no doubting the individuality of this poet's voice, the vigour of his rhythms and vocabulary, or the thoughtfulness and passion of his self-analysis and social commentary. But for Oldham anonymity was his way of fashioning a freedom from the loss of

---

[41] *Poems of John Oldham*, pp. 240–1; ll. 69–79.
[42] *Poems of John Oldham*, p. 229; ll. 115–24.

personal and professional integrity which he saw as characteristic of the Restoration literary world.

IV

Almost the opposite might be said of Rochester, whose name was notorious, and whose literary persona shows a sharp awareness (now delighted, now troubled) of how unstable one's poetic and personal identity may be. Like most of the aristocratic writers of this period, he eschewed print, and those poems which circulated in manuscript or in pirated printings often carried no attribution. He kept a small collection of his own poems in his autograph, chiefly rough drafts of lyrics,[43] so he had at least that limited and private sense of his own œuvre. The edition of *Poems on Several Occasions By the Right Honourable, the E. of R– – –*, which appeared in 1680,[44] gathered together not only poems by Rochester but a bundle of material by other writers, including Oldham, Etherege, and Behn, thus immediately confusing the public's sense of Rochester's canon. It is difficult at this distance to reconstruct the notion which the reading public would have had as to what constituted Rochester's work before the publication of this misleading collection,[45] but the surviving manuscripts suggest that, amongst the major poems, the *Satyre against Reason and Mankind* was generally known to be his (though the 1679 broadside printing is anonymous); *Artemiza to Chloe* is attributed to him in half the extant manuscripts and is anonymous in the other half, while the two broadsides of 1679 are both anonymous; and there is a similar division in the extant witnesses for *An Allusion to Horace, Upon Nothing,* and the translation from Seneca's *Troades. Timon* is attributed variously to Rochester, Sedley, and Buckingham. Some of the songs appeared anonymously in printed miscellanies during his lifetime.[46]

The anonymity which attended much of Rochester's poetry had complex effects upon the ways in which the poetry might be read. It is well known that Rochester's poetry plays various games with personae, from the ostensibly autobiographical 'I' of the lyrics and 'To the Post-Boy', to the named speaker of *Artemiza to Chloe*, the implicit narrators of *Timon* and *An Allusion to Horace*, and the disputants of the *Satyre against Reason and Mankind*. But the circulation of this poetry either anonymously, or in circumstances where a scribe or reader takes responsibility for adding the attribution, creates new possibilities. The 'I' of *An Allusion to Horace* who is so jauntily rude about his

---

[43] Nottingham University Library MS Portland PwV 31.
[44] See Vieth, *Attribution, passim,* for this collection.
[45] But see Fisher, 'Publication', pp. 18–40.
[46] For the circulation of Rochester's poetry see chapter 1 above, and Vieth, *Attribution*; Fisher, 'Publication'; Beal, *Index*, ii 225–87; *Works of John Wilmot.*

contemporaries is a different kind of 'I' depending on the attribution and the context: when the poem is attributed to Rochester it makes an aristocratic judgement on the literary world; when circulated anonymously among other lampoons it is a less distinctive voice, competing for authority with many others. In the case of 'The Disabled Debauchee' (where most of the manuscripts attribute the poem to Rochester, but several are anonymous) one manuscript calls it 'The Lord Rochester uppon himselfe', while another entitles it 'Upon his lyeing in and cou'd not drinke'.[47] Whatever sophistication attached to Rochester's creation of a persona and his distanced exploration of a role may be removed by the copyist's simple equation of speaker and author. A striking example of the rewriting of the authorial persona which can take place in these conditions is the Leeds manuscript of *Upon Nothing*, a separate in which the poem has been recast as a dialogue between Buckingham, Rochester, and Fleetwood Shepherd (see Plate 9): here the scribe imports into this poem both an explicitly Rochesterian persona and a clash of voices which are absent from all other texts.

This last instance may seem extreme, but there are much more radical interventions in the text of poems by Rochester and his circle. *The Sessions of the Poets* gathers additional stanzas over the years;[48] the order of the lines in the notorious 'sceptre' lampoon on Charles II varies considerably;[49] and lines drop into and out of *Tunbridge Wells* in a perplexing way as the poem is passed from hand to hand in manuscript.[50] In some cases it becomes difficult to say who the author of a poem is, because copyists have added and rearranged material: authorship becomes collective, and it may be that one should see the circulation of poems in manuscript as an implicit invitation to readers to adapt them. Although a modern editor may wish to retrieve or reconstruct *Tunbridge Wells* as it left Rochester's hands, that would in some respects be no more 'authentic' a text than one which was arrived at by a process of accretion and opportunistic adaptation to new scandals. Anonymity facilitates this kind of adaptation by removing the signs of authorial origin and authorial ownership of the text, opening the way for a different mode of authorship and authenticity based on the tastes of the reader.

V

What, then, are the possibilities created for a reader by the publication of poetry anonymously? How might a reader approach an anonymous collection? A case in point is the Gyldenstolpe manuscript miscellany. It is a

---

[47] *Works of John Wilmot*, p. 539.
[48] See *POAS*, i 471–2.
[49] See pp. 34–7 above.
[50] *Works of John Wilmot*, pp. 548–56.

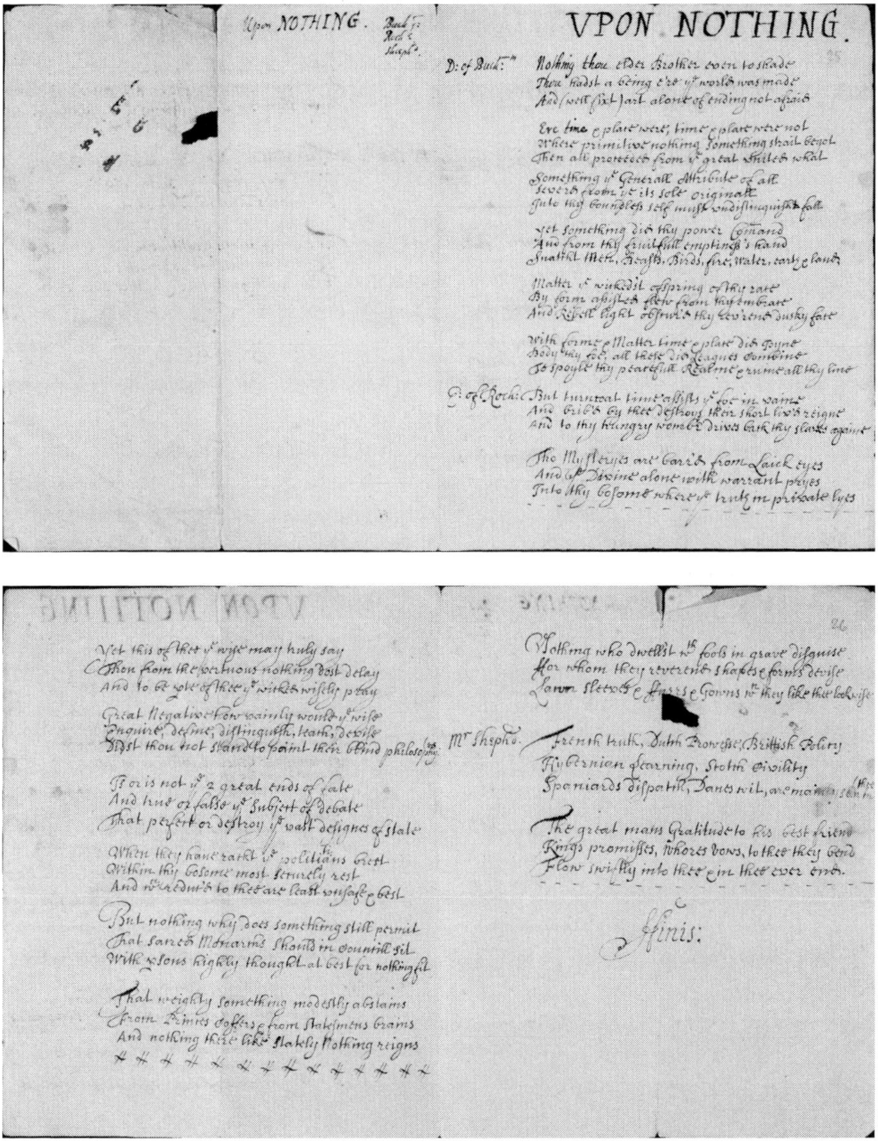

Upon NOTHING.

UPON NOTHING.

D: of Buck:

Nothing thou Elder Brother even to shade
Thou hadst a being e're ye world was made
And (well fixt) art alone of ending not afraid

Ere time & place were, time & place were not
When primitive nothing something strait begot
Then all proceeded from ye great united what.

Something ye Generall Attribute of all
Severd from thee its sole originall
Into thy boundless self must undistinguish't fall

Yet something did thy power Comand
And from thy fruitfull emptiness's hand
Snatcht Men, Beasts, Birds, fire, water, earth & land

Matter ye wickedst offspring of thy race
By form assisted flew from thy embrace
And Rebell light obscured thy reverend dusky face

With forme & Matter time & place did joyne
Body thy foe, all these did leagues combine
To spoyle thy peacefull Realme & ruine all thy line

E: of Roch: But turncoat time assists ye foe in vaine
And brib'd by thee destroys their short liv'd reigne
And to thy hungry womb drives back thy slaves againe

The Mysteryes are barr'd from Laick eyes
And ye Divine alone with warrant pryes
Into thy bosome where ye truth in private lyes

Yet this of thee ye wise may truly say
Thou from the vertuous nothing dost delay
And to be part of thee ye wicked wisely pray

Great Negative how vainly would ye wise
Enquire, define, distinguish, teach, devise
Didst thou not stand to point their blind philosophys

Is or is not ye 2 great ends of fate
And true or false ye Subject of debate
That perfect or destroy ye vast designes of state

When they have rackt ye politicians brest
Within thy bosome most securely rest
And when reduc'd to thee are least unsafe & best

But nothing why does something still permit
That sacred Monarchs should in councill sit
With persons highly thought at best for nothing fit

That weighty something modestly abstains
From Princes coffers & from Statesmens brains
And nothing there like stately Nothing reigns

Nothing who dwellst wth fools in grave disguise
For whom they reverend shapes & forms devise
Lawn sleeves & furrs & Gowns wn they like thee look wise

Mr Shephe: French truth, Dutch Prowess, British Policy
Hybernian learning, Scotch Civility
Spaniards dispatch, Danes wit, are mainly seen in thee

The great mans Gratitude to his best friend
Kings promisses, whores vows, to thee they bend
Flow swiftly into thee & in thee ever end.

Finis:

Plate 9. Brotherton Collection MS Lt q 52, fols. 25r–26v, a manuscript separate of Rochester's 'Upon Nothing' in a loose collection of verses compiled by John Gibson (1630–1711).
This is a single sheet which has been folded once to make a four-page booklet, with the poem being written on the first three pages, leaving the fourth page blank. The whole was then folded again vertically to form a tall narrow booklet which could easily be fitted into a pocket, and the title and speakers of the poem were added on what was now the outer cover. The poem has been set out as a dialogue between the Duke of Buckingham, the Earl of Rochester, and Fleetwood Shepherd.

substantial collection of poetry compiled around 1680 by a professional scribe, probably for a wealthy purchaser. The first group of poems relate to fashionable court and town life, pieces which exemplify or satirize a rakish ethos. Some are now known to be by Rochester, while others adopt or parody a Rochesterian voice, such as 'Regime d' viver', which begins:

> I Rise at Eleaven and I dine about Two,
> I gett drunk before seaven & the next thing I doe
> I send for my whore . . .[51]

Subsequently the reader comes across 'The Disabled Debauchee' and 'The Disappointment' ('Naked she lay clasp'd in my longing Armes . . .', often known as 'The Imperfect Enjoyment'), both by Rochester, and then the poem 'On Marriage' ('The Clogg of all pleasure The luggage of life . . .'), not by Rochester; 'Upon his leaving his Mistress', which is by Rochester; and 'The Imperfect Enjoyment' – a title used for poems by Rochester and Etherege, but this one is by Aphra Behn. The attributions which have just been given derive from David Vieth's work on this material, not from the manuscript itself, where all the poems are anonymous. It would take an unusually well-informed reader to know who actually wrote these poems, so the expectation must be that the recognition of authorship would play little part in the reading process. Without attributions, these poems relate not to named authors, to particular rakes, but to an ethos, a style of life, a group of attitudes and poses, a shared idiom. Much of this poetry describes and enacts role-playing, charting the precariousness of those forms of identity which are constructed and tested through sexual experimentation. Anonymity frees the persona from the author, and in so doing invites the reader to write himself into this play of social and erotic fantasy. There is a canon here, but it is not authorially-based so much as persona-based: the unifying interest is not in the author but in the pose. It is also a canon which the reader can remake, fashioning his own persona by choosing which poems to commission from a professional copyist, or by selecting pieces to transcribe into his own commonplace book. In the case of MS Lt 54 in the Brotherton Collection at the University of Leeds,[52] what begins as a professional, scribal miscellany becomes a personal anthology as the owner adds poems himself on the blank pages at the end of the book, and inserts bawdy verses into the gaps left by the copyist between poems. So Rochester's poem on marriage ('Out of Stark Love, and arrant Devotion') acquires these extra lines at the end, added by a later hand as his own commentary on the topic:

---

[51] *Gyldenstolpe*, p. 35.
[52] See Paul Hammond, 'The Robinson Manuscript Miscellany of Restoration Verse in the Brotherton Collection, Leeds', *Proceedings of the Leeds Philosophical and Literary Society: Literary and Historical Section*, 18 (1982) 275–324.

> For Mankind from Adam, have been Womens fools;
> Women from Eve, have been the Devil's Tools:
> Had but God gave us: one Blessing when we fell;
> Not left us Woman, or not Threatned Hell.[53]

This literal writing of the reader into the gaps in the text is perhaps emblematic of the activity of reading in this period, exemplifying the possibilities for appropriation which anonymity created.

The productive uncertainties generated by anonymity clearly affect the perception and construction of gender. When Rochester's *Artemiza to Chloe* appears anonymously, there is no immediate signal to the reader as to the gap between the male author and the female persona, so the reader may well take longer to evaluate the self-revealing narrator. In the case of Aphra Behn's 'The Imperfect Enjoyment',[54] anonymity is a valuable element in the strategy by which the poem disconcerts male readers. It begins in a familiar way, with 'the amorous *Lysander*' attempting to seduce Cloris. At first the poem seems to align itself with Lysander's impatience, and the erotic descriptions direct the reader's attention almost exclusively to Cloris, up to the point when she is lying in a trance on the ground, her 'loose thin Robes' revealing 'A shape design'd for Love and play'. The viewpoint of Lysander, narrator, and reader seem virtually identical. But when Lysander finds that he is unable to perform, the poem moves to an ironic distance from him:

> *Cloris* Returning from the Trance
> Which Love and soft desire had bred
> Her timerous hand she gently layd
> (Or guided by design or Chance)
> Upon that Fabulous *Priapus*
> That Potent God as Poets feign . . .
>
> Fair *Cloris* her fair hand withdrew
> Finding that God of her desires
> Dissarm'd of all his awfull fires . . .
> Who can the *Nymphs* confusion guess
> The blood forsook the kinder place
> And strew'd with blushes all her face
> Which both disdain *&* shame express

The deflation of masculine pretensions here implicates both male lovers and male poets – and the implicitly male readers of this connoisseur's manuscript. The narrator of this poem emerges directly at the end in a comment on Cloris' disappointment:

---

[53] Leeds University Library Brotherton Collection MS Lt 54, p. 133; Hammond, 'Robinson Manuscript', p. 308.

[54] *Gyldenstolpe*, pp. 89–96; for an edited text see *The Works of Aphra Behn*, edited by Janet Todd, 7 vols (London, 1992–6) i 65–9.

> The *Nymphs* Resentments none but I
> Can well imagine or Condole . . .

where the 'I' is suddenly by implication a woman who knows this story all too well herself. If the reader of this poem is a smug male, he will find himself caught in a trap which is nicely disguised by this late disclosure that the anonymous (and therefore, in this period, implicitly male) narrator is a woman.

VI

Although the anonymity which was frequently a feature of manuscript circulation empowered readers in particularly effective ways, the evidence from printed miscellanies confirms that reading was often free from any anxiety about, or even interest in, authorial identity. An early and influential example of the printed miscellany is *Covent Garden Drolery* (1672). The title page of the first edition informs us that the poems were collected by 'R.B. Servant to His Majestie'; in a reprint, this is altered simply to 'A.B.', an evasive formula which some modern critics have fancifully interpreted as standing for Aphra Behn:[55] such is the desire to create identities for anonymous writers, and to create canons for women writers. Although the title page entices the purchaser by describing the poems as 'Written by the refined'st Witts of the Age', all the poems are anonymous. Evidently readers were expected to take an interest in the poems for generic reasons: they are either prologues and epilogues, or songs. Though some are now known to be by Dryden, this is not mentioned, and instead reference is made to the plays to which the poems relate, or the actors who spoke them. As the book's title suggests, the theatrical connection is the chief focus of interest, and any indications of origin or signals of authenticity relate to the corporate world of the playhouses, not to individual authors.

In the playhouses themselves, many prologues and epilogues seem to have been presented anonymously, and there appears to be no evidence that the name of the writer of the verses was announced to the audience. Indeed, prologues and epilogues are written in a range of modes, some evidently being apologias by the dramatist (such as Dryden's Prologue to *Aureng-Zebe*), others excuses for a fledgling dramatist by a more experienced writer (Dryden's Prologue to Charles D'Avenant's *Circe*); others focus on the dramatic role which has just been performed by the actor who now speaks the epilogue while

---

[55] 'A.B.' is identified as 'Aphra Behn' by G. Thorn Drury in his edition of *Covent Garden Drollery* (London, 1928); the identification is accepted by Sara Heller Mendelson, *The Mental World of Stuart Women* (Brighton, 1987), p. 126, and James Anderson Winn, *"When Beauty Fires the Blood": Love and the Arts in the Age of Dryden* (Ann Arbor, 1992), p. 423. But I have offered bibliographical reasons for doubting the attribution in 'The Prologue and Epilogue to Dryden's *Marriage A-la-Mode* and the problem of *Covent Garden Drolery*', *PBSA*, 81 (1987) 155–72.

remaining in character (Mr Limberham in Dryden's *The Kind Keeper*); while in the case of Dryden's Epilogue to *Tyrannick Love* – spoken by Nell Gwyn, who has just rather improbably performed the role of the chaste princess Valeria – the verses exploit the disparity between her present role, her usual repertoire, and her life offstage. But in most cases the 'I'of the verses is the actor, not the poet or dramatist. Various alliances are half-jestingly set up in such pieces: actors and dramatist against audience; actors and audience against dramatist; actors, dramatist, and those intelligent judges amongst the audience against the boors who cannot appreciate true art; and all these games are facilitated by the removal of any interest in the actual writer of the prologue or epilogue: a form of communal art is being fashioned. It is entirely in keeping with this understanding of the function of prologues and epilogues that their texts should have been altered to include topical material, alterations that often seem to have been made without reference to the original author.[56]

Even when we turn from a cheap and ephemeral production like *Covent Garden Drolery,* which shared many of the assumptions about the status of texts which operated in the playhouses themselves, and examine the more substantial and prestigious *Miscellany Poems* issued by Tonson in 1684, we find that the names of the authors, though generally given, are not prominent. The title page is revealing in its emphasis:

> Miscellany Poems.
> Containing a New
> TRANSLATION
> OF
> *VIRGILLS* Eclogues,
> *OVID'S* Love Elegies,
> Odes of HORACE,
> And OTHER AUTHORS;
> WITH SEVERAL
> ORIGINAL POEMS.
> By the most Eminent Hands.

The primary attraction is clearly supposed to be a collection of translations from Virgil, Ovid, and Horace; the Restoration authors may be 'the most Eminent Hands', but they are not named here. On opening the book, the reader finds that Dryden's three satires which begin the volume are all anonymous, and in the section of translations which make up a large proportion of the collection, the pieces are arranged according to the classical author translated, not the translator. The reader's attention is thus drawn primarily to Virgil, Ovid, and Horace, rather than to the work of Thomas Creech or the

---

56 A number of Dryden's prologues and epilogues seem to have been altered in the playhouse to take account of topical events; see *Poems of John Dryden* i 246–8, and Hammond, 'Prologue and Epilogue to Dryden's *Marriage A-la-Mode*'.

Earl of Roscommon, and several of the translators are not named at all. In some cases alternative, anonymous translations of the same original are provided, with the implicit invitation to readers to compare and evaluate the versions: the focus is on the art of translation, not on the translator. A shift is perceptible in the sequel, *Sylvae*, where Dryden's translations from Virgil, Lucretius, Theocritus, and Horace are placed together at the beginning of the volume, following Dryden's critical preface. In that preface he shows that he is aware of the reputation which Creech and Roscommon have acquired from their translations, and the new arrangement which Dryden obtained from Tonson may indicate his desire to establish his name more prominently as a translator.

These varied examples suggest that Restoration readers were well used to interpreting poems without any reference to authorial intention or reputation; instead, the use of attributions such as 'eminent hands' and 'refined wits' points to a strong awareness of canons which derive from a community or coterie. The reader who engages with poetry on such terms is making himself part of such a group of wits, albeit joining the outer circle of those who do not have access to these poems in manuscript, and who therefore have to buy printed miscellanies as a supplement to their own commonplace books. The power of the coterie, and the embarrassment of those who were not quite in the know, can be imagined from the beginning of Etherege's *The Man of Mode*. Dorimant enters, quoting verses by Waller – though these are not attributed in the play. Apparently, contemporaries who saw Dorimant as in part a portrait of Rochester seized on this quoting of Waller as evidence for the identification.[57] But what about members of the audience who did not recognize that the verses were by Waller, or did not know that Rochester was in the habit of quoting him? The play divides its audience according to their skill in attribution, a skill which was as much a matter of social standing as of literary acumen.

VII

The implicit community fostered by anonymous publication is most apparent in the field of political poetry. The most obvious reason for concealing the authorship of political poetry was the safety of the writer. To write, or even to own, a satirical poem on the king or his ministers was hazardous. Sir Roger L'Estrange, who attempted to control the press, sought also to suppress the manuscript circulation of oppositional poems and tracts, and in 1675 he advised the House of Lords how possession of such a document should be punished: 'whoever shall receive, and Conceale any such Libell, without giving

---

[57] Sir George Etherege, *The Man of Mode*, edited by John Barnard (London, 1979), p. 9.

notice thereof, to some of his Matyes Justices, within a certain space of time after the receipt of it; let him suffer as an Abettour of it, & if he shall not produce ye person of whom he had it, let him suffer as ye Authour of it.'[58] According to this principle, the possessor of an oppositional document who will not name its author (or even its publisher) is deemed to *be* its author. Here the political machine attempts to deny both the power of communally authorized verse, and the rival form of political authority which such a group of writers and readers claims; for by limiting authorship to an individual, L'Estrange can attach the oppositional poem to a single dissident, and deny it the special power which accrues to a communal product. It is a neat example of Foucault's point that society produced authors when it needed someone to hold responsible for a piece of writing:[59] the author is invented in order to be punished. One example of this process is the fate of Stephen College, who was executed in 1681 on charges which included libelling the king in *A Raree Show*, a satirical poem and caricature attacking the absolutism of Charles II.[60] College denied writing it, but the crown brought in (or bought in) a witness to testify that College had acknowledged authorship of it in conversation, and that hearsay attribution was enough.

Not surprisingly, few of the oppositional poems on affairs of state which circulated in Charles's reign had names attached. When they did, the attributions were often not only misleading but positively mischievous or satirical, like the attribution of the series of *Advice to a Painter* poems to Sir John Denham, or the attempt to credit (or rather, discredit) Dryden with a number of satirical verses on public figures including the Duchess of Portsmouth.[61] But the original anonymity of these political poems should not be thought of as a lack: rather, anonymity had positive functions, besides the obvious one of protection. Poems which are circulated anonymously come to speak not with the voice of a single author, but with the voice of those who read them, copy them out, and pass them on to others – with the voice, in effect, of a community; they become corporate poems, particularly when the act of transcribing is a political act fraught with danger; the copyist literally becomes the writer of the poem, especially if he adds material or improves the piece as he goes along, as often happened. Anonymous authorship also helped to promote the use of authoritative personae, so that the criticism of the king and his ministers is voiced not by an individual but by a representative of the nation: these figures

---

58 MS in House of Lords Record Office, quoted from Harold Love, 'Scribal Texts and Literary Communities: The Rochester Circle and Osborn b. 105', *Studies in Bibliography*, 42 (1989) 219–35, at p. 230.

59 Michel Foucault, 'Qu'est-ce qu'un auteur?' in *Dits et Ecrits 1954–1988: I: 1954–1969* (Paris, 1994), pp. 789–821.

60 *POAS*, ii 425–31; B. J. Rahn, '*A Ra-ree Show* – A Rare Cartoon: Revolutionary Propaganda in the Treason Trial of Stephen College' in *Studies in Change and Revolution: Aspects of English Intellectual History 1640–1800*, edited by Paul J. Korshin (Menston, 1972), pp. 77–98.

61 See p. 16.

included Britannia, Raleigh, Hodge the countryman, Marvell's ghost, or in one poem the allegorical figure of England, who appears naked to Charles II one night in his bedchamber, only to have her intentions misinterpreted. In this corpus the anonymous voice of the poet is easily represented as being the collective voice of the nation, authorized and enabled to speak through a patriotic community of copyists and readers.

The positive rhetorical advantages of anonymity are deployed not only by oppositional poetry, but also by Dryden's *Absalom and Achitophel.* An important reason for the anonymous publication of this poem is to make it appear not as one man's partisan intervention in a factional squabble, but as a disinterested and definitive statement of the relationship between king and people. We hear the voice of the quasi-biblical narrator all the more strongly because of the author's anonymity, and this gives added force to the translation of names (Shaftesbury into Achitophel, Oates into Corah) through which the poem fixes unwelcome identities on to the king's opponents. The poem even claims the power to consign some noblemen to oblivion by refusing to give them any kind of name:

> Titles and names 'twere tedious to rehearse
> Of lords below the dignity of verse.

while it preserves Oates from the oblivion which he might have preferred:

> To speak the rest, who better are forgot,
> Would tire a well-breathed witness of the plot.
> Yet Corah, thou shalt from oblivion pass.[62]

The power of the unnamed author to name the opposition was crucial to the poem's strategy. It is significant that the commendatory verses in early editions are pointedly addressed to the 'unknown' author of the poem, even though the author's name was by then widely known: evidently it was important rhetorically to maintain the fiction that the poem could not be attributed simply to a nameable writer. Richard Duke in his prefatory verses 'To the Unknown Author of this Admirable Poem' wrote that:

> Here all consent in wonder and in praise,
> And to the unknown poet altars raise,
> Which thou must needs accept with equal joy
> As when Aeneas heard the wars of Troy,
> Wrapped up himself in darkness and unseen,
> Extolled with wonder by the Tyrian Queen.
> Sure thou already art secure of fame,
> Nor want'st new glories to exalt thy name:[63]

---

62 Dryden, *Absalom and Achitophel*, ll. 569–70, 630–2.
63 *Poems of John Dryden*, i 541–2.

This attempt to present the author of *Absalom and Achitophel* as an unknown god, or as Aeneas about to refound his country, is a touch absurd, but the rhetorical strategy is clear: the poet is without concern for his own fame. When *The Second Part of Absalom and Achitophel* appeared, written by Nahum Tate with some contributions by Dryden, it was not only anonymous but even included praise of Dryden (under the name Asaph), thus indicating that Dryden was not (or was not solely) its author. These fictions may have been transparent, but in a struggle over what rights the name of king was to carry with it, such rhetorical manoeuvres had their place: at stake – as Dryden put it in *The Medal* – was whether the Whigs would succeed in arrogating power to themselves, while Charles was left as a mere figurehead:

> Yet to consult his dignity and fame
> He should have leave to exercise the name,
> And hold the cards while Commons played the game.[64]

VIII

This survey of the functions of anonymity in Restoration poetry reminds us that writing and reading are acts of power, and that if we understand something of the intricate relationships between author, text, and reader in this period, we have understood part of the power relations within English society. The practices of naming and anonymity are part of the force field of social status, the way in which aristocrats and commoners, men and women, represented themselves to their readers. In a period when so much political debate was conducted through illicit publication, and was carried on amongst a comparatively small group of writers and readers, there is an intense awareness of the significance of names, pseudonyms, and anonymity, and a whole repertoire of rhetorical gestures is developed. We need to learn to read these signs of power, not to obscure them through the uniform conventions of modern editions. Thus we should ponder what Foucault called 'the author function'[65] rather than just the named authors themselves. The Restoration was a period which followed immediately upon a great upheaval in naming: during the Commonwealth it seemed as if everything and everyone was being renamed, from the state itself to ships, from the king to the individual radicals who sought new identities for themselves. This renaming was a refiguring of social and ideological relationships, and the renaming was itself revised in 1660. The Restoration establishment fostered the belief that the old names had been reinstated without stress, but this was hardly the case; and in a society where

---

[64] *Poems of John Dryden*, ii 28; ll. 232–4.
[65] Foucault, p. 798.

philosophers and libertines alike are toying with nominalism, the stability and authenticity of names becomes an issue of fundamental importance.[66]

Dryden was haunted by a line in Sir John Denham's translation of the *Aeneid*, where the body of King Priam is lying on the sea shore:

> A headless Carcass, and a nameless thing.[67]

In recent memory the source of the state's identity had been reduced to a 'nameless thing', the ultimate signified had been emptied of meaning. In the society which restored to his son 'the name and all th' addition to a king',[68] many readers and writers found that anonymity was not only a refuge from an intrusive power, but a source of power for themselves.

---

[66] For a discussion of this in Restoration drama see Derek Hughes, 'Naming and Entitlement in Wycherley, Etherege, and Dryden', *Comparative Drama*, 21 (1987) 259–89.

[67] 'The Second Book of the *Aeneis*' l. 763 lifts the whole line verbatim from Denham, as Dryden notes: *Works of John Dryden*, v 403.

4

Intertextuality in Restoration Poetry

I

ALL POETRY in some degree works intertextually, aware if only implicitly of the traditions within which it locates itself, using a vocabulary which is shaped by its predecessors and shared by its contemporaries; but the poetry of the Restoration is self-conscious and self-referential to an unusual degree. There are several reasons for this. The political upheavals of the period were profound, for the thirty years from 1658 to 1688 brought the death of England's first republican ruler, the restoration of the monarchy, an attempt to change the hereditary principle of succession, the accession of a Catholic king who was widely seen as a threat to his people's liberties, the deposing of that king, and the installation of new joint sovereigns chosen by the ruling elite to legitimize a peaceful conquest. All these political changes were debated in the public press, in prose pamphlets and in verse; therefore the vocabulary through which the nation argued over its political culture was subject to repeated revision: words such as 'arbitrary', 'liberty', 'patriot', 'prerogative', 'Protestant', 'tyranny', 'usurper', became counters which were used and reused. Within the textual communities formed by the circulation of letters, pamphlets, newspapers, and verses, there emerged an acute consciousness of the semantic field of such terms, and their emotive charge. In the literary world, too, an exchange of prologues, epilogues, satires, verse letters, critical essays, prefaces, and dedications created a self-aware literary milieu, often centred around the playhouses, and intersecting with the partisan world of politics in unpredictable and shifting ways. When Dryden's literary satire *Mac Flecknoe*, for instance, was put into print by an opportunistic pirate in 1682, six years after it had first circulated in manuscript, it was given the subtitle 'A Satyr upon the True-Blew-Protestant Poet, T. S. By the Author of Absalom & Achitophel', in order to make it appear to be another contribution by Dryden to the debate over Exclusion. Parody and rejoinder are common Restoration genres: *Absalom and Achitophel* attracted eight full-length responses,[1] many attempting to deploy the rhetoric of Dryden's poem against him; and *The Medal* similarly generated

---

[1] *Poems of John Dryden*, i 449; Macdonald, *Bibliography*, pp. 223–30.

four replies.[2] Dryden's *Mac Flecknoe* is an intricate web of allusions to the works of Shadwell and Flecknoe, and also draws upon Virgil, Cowley, Davenant, Waller, and Milton for the vocabulary of empire in order to establish a mock-heroic empire of dullness.[3] And the rhetoric which Dryden established in *Absalom and Achitophel* and *Mac Flecknoe* was borrowed by others.[4]

Poems work intertextually as they weave the threads which go to make up their texture.[5] Sometimes this may be by direct allusion, an unmistakable reference through naming; in such cases the reader must understand the allusion to grasp the full force of the poet's idea.[6] Sometimes this may be by quotation, either by the offset quotation of displayed text, as in an epigraph,[7] or by the inclusion within the body of the text of phrases which are taken from other poems, and which signal their presence – sometimes typographically through italicization or quotation marks, sometimes because their lexis differs markedly in tone or idiom from the surrounding text. Poems may also activate the roots of words through degrees of linguistic estrangement, signals to the reader that the words are not to be taken superficially, merely according to current usage, but are to be read afresh and questioned for their semantic fields. This following of traces may be thought of as happening along two axes: vertically or diachronically, by making the reader aware that a particular term ('nature', 'virtue', 'fortune') is one which has a rich and complex cultural history, a record of conceptual shading and changing sensibilities which may have been washed out of the word in current usage but can now be recovered and brought into play; and horizontally or synchronically, by referring the reader to the ways in which the word ('wit', 'dull', 'laurel') has acquired a set of contemporary resonances to which the present poem is contributing.

The textual field which is shaped by Dryden's poems is intricately intertextual. *Mac Flecknoe* presupposes in its readers a knowledge of Shadwell's plays and elements of contemporary theatrical gossip; of the poems and autobiographical writings of Flecknoe; and of *Paradise Lost*, which had been published in 1667, nine years before *Mac Flecknoe*, but had been slow to make its mark. *Absalom and Achitophel* quotes and reapplies terms from Exclusion Crisis pamphlets and speeches; *The Medal* assumes that readers will have seen the medal which supporters of the Earl of Shaftesbury coined to

---

2 *Poems of John Dryden*, ii 8; Macdonald, *Bibliography*, pp. 228–33.

3 See the notes in *Poems of John Dryden*, i 306–36.

4 See *Poems of John Dryden*, i 312, 449; *John Dryden: Tercentenary Essays*, edited by Paul Hammond and David Hopkins (Oxford, 2000), pp. 373–4, 382–3, 389.

5 I have explored the intertextual engagement of Dryden's poetry with Latin literature in *Traces*, and in 'Milton, Dryden, and Lucretius', *The Seventeenth Century*, 16 (2001) 158–76.

6 For pioneering studies of the uses of allusion see Reuben Arthur Brower, *Alexander Pope: The Poetry of Allusion* (Oxford, 1959); Christopher Ricks, *Allusion to the Poets* (Oxford, 2002).

7 See Gérard Genette, *Palimpsestes: la littérature au second degré* (Paris, 1982).

celebrate the verdict of *ignoramus* in his trial; *Religio Laici* and *The Hind and the Panther* both assume a fairly sophisticated knowledge of theology and ecclesiastical controversy.[8] And Dryden's classical translations frequently allude to contemporary affairs, so that his *Aeneis* (1697) is from time to time a meditation on the Revolution of 1688–9,[9] while many of the tales collected in *Fables Ancient and Modern* (1700) have contemporary references.[10]

It is sometimes impossible to be precise about the difference in particular cases between allusions (deliberate acts by the poet which expect conscious acts of recognition by the reader) and borrowings (conscious or unconscious uses of poetic idioms which may or may not be recognized by the reader). But whatever the authorial intention may be, intertextual poetry implies an intertextual readership, a readership which is itself situated between texts, knows its ancient and modern classics, is *au courant* with contemporary debates, and is sufficiently agile and alert to recognize and weigh the connotations of a poem's language. Intertextuality places considerable responsibilities upon the reader.

II

Let us consider first the intertextuality of political poetry. Here the poet is deliberatively fashioning a text which offers certain terms to the reader as elements which constitute that polity which poet and reader share – or perhaps that polity which the poet would like to call into being, and which the collaborative co-creation of a text by his reader may help to implement. At moments of political crisis the language of poetry is under special obligations, and receives unusual scrutiny. One such moment was the death of Oliver Cromwell. Edmund Waller's poem 'Upon the Late Storm, and Of the Death of His Highness Ensuing the Same' turned to the origins of classical Rome for an appropriate image:

> So Romulus was lost!
> New Rome in such a tempest missed her king,
> And from obeying fell to worshipping.[11]

At first the simile seems to work well enough, as Romulus, like Cromwell, had founded a new political order, and his passing, like Cromwell's, had been

---

[8] This is charted in the notes to these poems in *Poems of John Dryden*, ii and iii.
[9] Hammond, *Traces*, pp. 218–28.
[10] See the annotation in *Poems of John Dryden*, v *passim*; Paul Hammond, 'The Interplay of Past and Present in Dryden's "Palamon and Arcite" ', in *The Age of Projects*, edited by Maximillian E. Novak (Toronto, forthcoming).
[11] Edmund Waller, 'Upon the Late Storm, and Of the Death of His Highness Ensuing the Same', ll. 6–8, in *The Poems of Edmund Waller*, edited by G. Thorn Drury, 2 vols (London, 1901), ii 34.

attended by a storm. But the use of 'king' (awkwardly exposed here as a rhyme word) undoes the simile by inadvertently reminding us that Cromwell was not a king, that he had authorized the execution of the country's last king, and had himself refused the crown. It is also hard not to feel that word 'worshipping' as another *faux pas*, a gesture which can find no actual counterpart in the England of 1658. Waller's 'So' builds a bridge of allusion which unfortunately has no foot in the present. It was no doubt intended to be hortatory rather than descriptive, but its excess is embarrassing. Dryden at least seems to have thought so, for the opening of his own commemorative poem *Heroic Stanzas* takes up Waller's image, and seems to reply to – indeed, to rebuke – Waller's facile lines. Dryden writes:

> And now 'tis time; for their officious haste
> Who would before have borne him to the sky,
> Like eager Romans, ere all rites were past
> Did let too soon the sacred eagle fly.[12]

Though Dryden's starting point here is the ceremony for the deification of Romulus, the simile links not Cromwell and Romulus as Waller had tried to do, but the overeager poets and the overeager worshippers. Dryden's attention is directed to the predicament of those who commemorate Cromwell, to the difficulty of appropriate and timely speech; and his first person plural pronouns refer to the group of poets not the community of citizens.[13] Though Dryden goes on to suggest a series of classical parallels for Cromwell's career, this opening intertextual move draws attention primarily to the work of poetry, not only to the failure of Waller, but more broadly to the predicament of poetic language when faced with finding terms for Cromwell's unprecedented achievement.

Poems – both successful and unsuccessful – become implicated in later poems, answered, cited, raided, dismembered, parodied. Waller's earlier 'A Panegyric to My Lord Protector' attracted two stanza-by-stanza rebuttals, one royalist, one republican,[14] and his grandiose instruction to the Muses to celebrate Cromwell –

> Tell of towns stormed, of armies overrun,
> And mighty kingdoms by your conduct won.[15]

– would be wickedly transformed by Rochester into:

---

12 Dryden, *Heroic Stanzas*, ll. 1–4.
13 Dryden, *Heroic Stanzas*, ll. 5–15.
14 Timothy Raylor, 'Waller's Machiavellian Cromwell: The Imperial Argument of *A Panegyrick to My Lord Protector*', *Review of English Studies*, 56 (2005) 386–411, at p. 387; see also his 'Reading Machiavelli; Writing Cromwell', *Turnbull Library Record*, 35 (2002) 9–32.
15 Waller, 'A Panegyric to My Lord Protector', ll. 177–8, in *Poems of Edmund Waller*, ii 17.

I'll tell of Whores attack'd, their Lords at home;
Bauds Quarters beaten up, and Fortress won:[16]

Dryden's own *Heroic Stanzas* were republished later in his career in order to embarrass him, and several of his enemies quoted the line in which he refers to the execution of Charles I by saying that Cromwell tried 'To stanch the blood by breathing of the vein'.[17] But Dryden's poem also generated an odd echo for which it is hard to account. George Stepney's poem on the death of Queen Mary in 1695 says:

But whence shall we begin? Or whither steere?
Her Vertues like a perfect Round appeare.[18]

For readers who remembered Dryden's lines on Cromwell there is an unmistakable echo:

How shall I then begin, or where conclude,
 To draw a fame so truly circular?
For in a round what order can be shewed,
 Where all the parts so equal perfect are?[19]

Dryden did not write a poem on the death of Queen Mary: as a loyal Jacobite he would have regarded her as a usurper, and an undutiful daughter to her deposed father. But we know that Stepney sent a draft of his poem to Tonson with a request that he ask Dryden to correct it.[20] Did Stepney write these lines as a rebuke to Dryden's silence by reminding him of his past allegiance? As an ironic and covert way of associating two usurpers? Or was it an unconscious recollection of a helpful way of opening an elegy which Stepney remembered without, unfortunately, remembering its source? Or did Dryden insert the lines as a mischievous comment on Mary? Or did neither Stepney, Dryden, nor Tonson recognize the echo? At this distance we cannot say, and we cannot, in this case, know what readers thought. There is an intertextual link here of some kind, but whether it is an allusion or a borrowing, and how we are to read it, remains problematic.

For more controlled allusions let us turn to *Absalom and Achitophel*. This poem is deeply dyed in the political vocabulary of the Exclusion Crisis, and

---

[16] Rochester, 'The Disabled Debauchee', ll. 33–4, in *Works of John Wilmot*, p. 45.
[17] Dryden, *Heroic Stanzas*, l. 48; for the hostile recollections of this line see *Poems of John Dryden*, i 21.
[18] George Stepney, *A Poem Dedicated to the Blessed Memory of her late Gracious Majesty Queen Mary* (London, 1695), p. 2.
[19] Dryden, *Heroic Stanzas*, ll. 17–20.
[20] Macdonald, *Bibliography*, p. 281; Kathleen M. Lynch, *Jacob Tonson, Kit-Cat Publisher* (Knoxville, Tenn., 1971), pp. 106–7; James Anderson Winn, *John Dryden and his World* (New Haven, 1987), p. 477.

repeatedly reuses the terms and tropes which Dryden and his readers knew from pamphlets, letters, and speeches.[21] The character of Shaftesbury, for example, is informed by Dryden's wide and alert reading in the controversial literature of the Exclusion Crisis, and his own rhetoric takes over and redeploys terms which the Whigs had tried to make their own. The Earl of Shaftesbury, as Achitophel, is described as 'Restless, unfixed in principles and place', whereas Shaftesbury himself had claimed to be 'one that, in all these variety of changes of this last Age, was never known to be either bought or frighted out of his publick Principles'.[22] Shaftesbury thought of himself as 'a man daring but more able', but in Dryden's hands this becomes a recklessness which endangers the ship of state:

> A daring pilot in extremity:
> Pleased with the danger, when the waves went high
> He sought the storms;[23]

Shaftesbury 'Usurped a patriot's all-atoning name', 'patriot' being a common self-description of the Whigs and one commonly resented by their opponents.[24] Dryden appropriates his opponents' key terms, and redefines them for his own purposes, rhetorically correcting their semantic and ideological errors.

The poem also draws upon the Bible, upon Milton, particularly *Paradise Lost*, and upon classical literature, notably Virgil. One classical allusion among many illustrates the way in which Dryden draws a rich and complex set of connotations into his poem. In *Astraea Redux* (1660), Dryden's poem on the Restoration, the people of England were said to have created a form of society from which Justice had departed in disgust. The poem offers a narrative of the Civil War and Commonwealth which represents it as no more than a return to a state of nature:

> The rabble now such freedom did enjoy
> As winds at sea that use it to destroy:
> Blind as the Cyclops, and as wild as he,
> They owned a lawless salvage liberty,
> Like that our painted ancestors so prized
> Ere empire's arts their breasts had civilized.[25]

---

21 See the notes in *Poems of John Dryden*, i 444–532; Phillip Harth, *Pen for a Party: Dryden's Tory Propaganda in its Contexts* (Princeton, N.J., 1993).

22 Dryden, *Absalom and Achitophel*, l. 154; [Shaftesbury, perhaps directing John Locke], *A Letter from a Person of Quality, to his Friend in the Country* (London, 1675), p. 9, quoted from *Poems of John Dryden*, i 467.

23 Dryden, *Absalom and Achitophel*, ll. 159–61; *A Letter from a Person of Quality*, p. 3, quoted from *Poems of John Dryden*, i 469.

24 Dryden, *Absalom and Achitophel*, l. 179; *Poems of John Dryden*, i 471.

25 *Astraea Redux*, ll. 43–8.

This passage cites the vocabulary of 'freedom' and 'liberty' which had been so ubiquitous a rhetorical foundation of the republican cause, with its insistence on what Milton called 'the liberty and right of free born Men, to be govern'd as seems to them best'.[26] Dryden might more readily have agreed, however, with Milton's observation in the same treatise that 'none can love freedom heartilie, but good men; the rest love not freedom, but licence'.[27]

The qualification of 'liberty' by the adjective 'savage', especially in its common seventeenth-century spelling 'salvage', brings into play an etymological connection back to the Latin *silva*, wood, and beyond this particular word to Virgil's account of society before the reign of Saturn:

> haec nemore indigenae Fauni Nymphaeque tenebant
> gensque virum truncis et duro robore nata,
> quis neque mos neque cultus erat.[28]

In Dryden's translation:

> These Woods were once the Seat of *Silvan* Pow'rs,
> Of Nymphs, and Fauns, and salvage Men, who took
> Their Birth from Trunks of Trees, and stubborn Oak.
> No Laws they knew, nor Manners.[29]

In *Absalom and Achitophel* Dryden warns that the upheaval of the Exclusion Crisis risks a repetition of the Civil War, as if history threatens to be cyclical; in the 1640s, he reminds us,

> These Adam-wits, too fortunately free
> Began to dream they wanted liberty,
> And when no rule, no precedent was found
> Of men, by laws less circumscribed and bound
> They led their wild desires to woods and caves,
> And thought that all but savages were slaves.[30]

The opening line refers us not only to Genesis but to *Paradise Lost* – part of Dryden's appropriation in *Absalom and Achitophel* of Milton's rhetoric for a very unMiltonic political purpose.

But Dryden is also drawing upon Virgil. When reflecting on the state of the country before the Civil War from the vantage point of his exile in France during the Restoration, Edward Hyde, Earl of Clarendon, wrote that it was a period when 'those two miserable adjuncts, which *Nerva* was deified for

---

26 *The Tenure of Kings and Magistrates* (1649), in *The Complete Prose Works of John Milton*, edited by Don M. Wolfe et al., 8 vols (New Haven, 1953–82), iii 206.
27 *Complete Prose Works of John Milton*, iii 190.
28 Virgil, *Aeneid*, viii 314–17.
29 Dryden, 'The Eighth Book of the Aeneis', ll. 417–20, from *Works of John Dryden*, vi 620.
30 *Absalom and Achitophel*, ll. 52–6.

uniting, *imperium et libertas*, were as well reconciled as is possible.'[31] And yet Englishmen, especially the turbulent spirits whose agitation led to the Civil War, failed to see just how fortunate they were to be living in the England of Charles I: *O fortunati nimium, bona si sua norint!*[32] – 'O how exceptionally fortunate, if only they had known their good fortune!' Clarendon's quotation from Virgil applies to the people of England the words which the Roman poet had used of the farmers who have an ideal mode of life away from the pressures of the city and public affairs – ideal except only that they do not appreciate that it *is* ideal. The phrase 'too fortunately' in Dryden's passage is a literal translation of that same phrase *fortunati nimium*, thus invoking a lost paradise whose inhabitants failed to appreciate their good fortune. This image of an implicit golden age is countered by the shadow of other Latin texts, however. We hear echoes of Lucretius' myth of primitive man, who *nemora atque cavos montis silvasque colebant*, 'lived in woods, and mountain caves, and forests',[33] and also of Virgil's episode which tells of the women who madly burnt Aeneas' boats, and then *silvasque et sicubi concava furtim | saxa petunt*, 'sought the woods and the hollow rocks'.[34] The Adam-wits 'thought that all but savages were slaves', and if 'savages' were spelt 'salvages' again, the punning link 'salvages/slaves' would become even more apparent: the savages are indeed slaves to their own passions ('slaves within doors' in Milton's phrase[35]). Though Dryden was happy on occasions to imagine the state of nature as a Montaignian state of innocence (after all, it was Dryden who coined the phrase 'the noble savage'[36]), his imagination is haunted by the possibility of a return to the woods and caves: this is not something which happened mythically 'once upon a time', but is, it seems, a perpetual possibility. Rebels can destroy civil society, women can burn the ships which are their only hope of escape; Adam can dream that he lacks freedom. These classical allusions and miniature borrowings in Dryden's texts lead our imaginations to link up Milton's Fall, the Roman myths of life before civilization, and the anarchy of the Civil War. The images draw together different forms of history, reconfiguring our understanding of how one writes and how one inhabits history. And the purpose of these allusions is to redefine the past in order to avoid its repetition in the future.

---

31 *The Life of Edward Earl of Clarendon . . . written by himself*, 3 vols (Oxford, 1759), i 71.
32 Virgil, *Georgics*, ii 458.
33 Lucretius, *De Rerum Natura*, v 955.
34 Virgil, *Aeneid*, v 677–8; translated by Dryden as 'Dispers'd, to Woods and Caverns take their Flight' ('The Fifth Book of the Aeneis', l. 885 in *Works of John Dryden*, v 517).
35 *The Tenure of Kings and Magistrates*, in *Complete Prose Works of John Milton*, iii 190.
36 Dryden, *1 The Conquest of Granada*, I i 203–9.

III

In the poems which circulated in the late 1660s, particularly after the naval disasters which beset Charles II's government during the Second Dutch War, Marvell and other writers drew upon both classical and contemporary precedents as part of the rhetoric through which they fashioned an oppositional critique. Once again Waller inadvertently supplied the material upon which parodic variations were made, in his *Instructions to a Painter* (1665).[37] Waller allowed his royalist enthusiasm to carry him into some rather grandiose comparisons. The English and Dutch fleets meet like the two fleets which at Actium contended for mastery of the Roman world – but on the outcome of this battle depends the fate, he says, not of one empire but two, the old world and the new. The Duke of York is braver than Achilles, since Achilles waited for a shield before fighting, whereas James stands without such protection on his quarterdeck. The poem's Envoi to the king elevates him to divine status by saying that as Hercules has his club, Apollo his bow, and Jupiter his thunderbolts, so Charles has his navy. Charles instructs the shipwrights how to build ships, as Jove showed the Cyclops how to forge his thunder. But Crete, the birthplace of Jove, is outclassed by this other island ruled by another Thunderer.

This was an irresistible target for Marvell and whoever helped him with *The Second Advice to a Painter*.[38] The reference to Actium is turned into a vignette of James feasting his duchess like Anthony roistering effeminately with Cleopatra. The warship *London* burns like Nero's Rome – which slyly raises the question of Charles's ultimate responsibility for the disaster. And the Envoi of the *Second Advice* takes up Waller's comparison of Britain with Crete by casting Charles as Minos and Clarendon in the role of Daedalus, the inventor of labyrinths in which monsters may be hidden away. But as well as its topic-by-topic parody of Waller's poem, the *Second Advice* challenges Waller's claim to be writing heroic, classically authorized poetry, and institutes a different role for the morally and publicly responsible poet. Other forms of citation come into play which help to create an oppositional voice, for different manuscript copies supply a range of epigraphs from Latin literature.[39] Some texts quote Horace's *pictoribus atque poetis | quidlibet audendi semper fuit*[40] ('painters and poets have always been allowed to dare anything'), from the *Ars Poetica*, while another source cites Juvenal's *difficile est satyram non scribere*[41] ('it is difficult *not* to write satire'). The two principal Roman

[37] *Poems of Edmund Waller*, ii 48–60.
[38] *Poems of Andrew Marvell*, pp. 327–41.
[39] *Poems of Andrew Marvell*, p. 330.
[40] Horace, *Ars Poetica*, ll. 9–10.
[41] Juvenal, *Satire* i 30.

satirists therefore license this poem with their *imprimatur*, so that it proceeds as if in their voices, as if it were a continuation or elaboration of their work. In some manuscripts the poem is prefaced with an epigraph from Persius:

> navem si poscat sibi peronatus arator
> Luciferi rudis, exclamet Melicerta perisse
> frontem de rebus.[42]

Perhaps we should remind ourselves of the context of this quotation. Persius' fifth satire, according to Dryden's prefatory note to his own translation in 1692, 'excellently treats the paradox of the Stoics, which affirms that the wise or virtuous man is only free, and that all vicious men are naturally slaves'.[43] So the quotation both addresses the incompetence and absurd ambition of the naval commanders, and locates the *Second Advice* within a tradition of moral thought about true freedom and the threats to it. Persius maintains that true liberty has nothing to do with that so-called liberty which is handed down by governments; in Dryden's translation of *Satire* V:

> O freedom, first delight of human kind!
> Not that which bondmen from their masters find . . .
> 'What, since the Praetor did my fetters loose,
> And left me freely at my own dispose,
> May I not live without control or awe,
> Excepting still the letter of the law?'
>   'Hear me with patience, while thy mind I free
> From those fond notions of false liberty:
> 'Tis not the Praetor's province to bestow
> True freedom, nor to teach mankind to know
> What to ourselves or to our friends we owe.'[44]

False, deceptive, liberty is what governments bestow on their subjects, while telling them they are free; true freedom lies within our own minds.

Another epigraph to the *Second Advice*, found only in a few manuscripts, cites Tacitus:

> studia illi ut plena vaecordiae, ita inania et fluxa sunt; nec quicquam graue ac serium ex eo metuas qui suorum ipse flagitiorum proditor non virorum animis sed muliercularum adrepit. cedat tamen urbe et bonis amissis aqua et igni arceatur: quod perinde censeo ac si lege maiestatis teneretur.[45]

---

[42] Persius, *Satire* v 102–4: 'If a hobnailed countryman, who knows nothing of the morning star, were to ask for the command of a ship, Melicerta would declare that modesty had perished from off the earth.'

[43] *Poems of John Dryden*, iv 180.

[44] 'The Fifth Satire of Persius', ll. 100–1, 126–34.

[45] Tacitus, *Annales*, iii 50: 'His occupations are as futile and erratic as they are charged with folly; nor can any grave and considerable danger be expected from a person who by betraying his

The context of this passage from the *Annales* is that during the reign of Tiberius, one Clutorius Priscus had been paid by the emperor to write a poem about the death of Germanicus, who had been a renowned military leader, a popular favourite, and a man of republican principles, whose death was attributed by rumour to poison. Clutorius also received another commission to write about Tiberius' son Drusus which would bring him even more money if Drusus were to die. The senators demanded the death penalty for this outrageous treatment of two popular leaders, but Marcus Aemilius Lepidus delivered the speech quoted here, arguing that Clutorius Priscus should be exiled instead of executed. But he lost the argument, and the mercenary poet was imprisoned and put to death. When placed as an epigraph to the *Second Advice*, the quotation functions as a warning to Waller and his ilk that the opposition will not allow liberty and its champions to be denigrated by hired pens. This may seem a sufficiently incendiary sentiment, even when couched in the oblique form of a Latin epigraph; but the wording, with its reference to one whose occupations are futile and who courts the favour of women, could also be construed as an allusion to the king himself.

These political poems deploy intertextual references in two ways: by bringing into play contested political terms such as 'patriot' or 'liberty', and by invoking classical precedents to suggest other forms of political organization (a Roman republican model, for instance). They suggest an alternative authority to that which prevailed at Whitehall, an alternative way of organizing society, another set of values – in short, a world elsewhere.

IV

Worlds elsewhere, free alternative spaces shaped by intertexual play, were in effect kinds of paradise for the writer's and reader's imagination. Throughout the 1650s and into the Restoration, writers had turned to classical literature to fashion forms of retirement from the public world, and especially to Horace and Martial, and the contemporary Polish Horace, Kazimierz Sarbiewski. For many poets – Carew, Cowley, Fane, Fanshawe, Marvell, and others – the pastoral world, the country estate, and the garden, form spaces of retreat, or spaces where the writer might contemplate Nature and God.[46] This was not only a space of retreat from the Civil War, for Marvell's poem 'The Garden' was almost certainly written in 1668. The poem may be thought of as one of

---

own infamy insinuates himself into the favour not of men but of silly women. Expel him, however, from Rome, confiscate his property, ban him from fire and water: this is my proposal and I make it precisely as though he were guilty under the law of treason.'

[46] Maren-Sofie Røstvig, *The Happy Man: Studies in the Metamorphoses of a Classical Ideal*, second edition (Oslo, 1962); *The Country House Poem*, edited by Alastair Fowler (Edinburgh, 1994).

Marvell's responses to *Paradise Lost*: 'Two Paradises 'twere in one | To live in Paradise alone' (ll. 63–4): a community of one. For the speaker of this poem, 'Society is all but rude | To this delicious solitude' (ll. 15–16). The adjective 'rude', emphatically linked by rhyme to its contrasting 'solitude', is worth pondering. 'Rude' here means 'uncivilized, barbarous' (*OED* 3b), but also has strong Latin associations, notably recalling Ovid's line *rudis indigestaque molis*,[47] 'a rough, unordered mass', which is his description of the chaos before the world was created and order emerged. Compared to the solitude of the garden, then, society is almost uncivilized, indeed chaotic: society is pre-social.

But there is a another, complex form of community – a textual community – fashioned within this poem, as Marvell draws upon a wide range of poetic, philosophical, and theological ideas.[48] It is difficult to know whether to call this a dialogue or a distillation, but it is the shaping of an imaginatively complex space in response to the unsatisfactory complexities of the political world. The poem is full of words with Latin roots, whose Latinity is called into play in the text by the poem's generic classical ancestry: palm, uncessant, labours, crowned, herb, verged, prudently, quiet, innocence – these just from the first ten lines. And Virgil's *Ciris* provides some of the poem's turns of phrase,[49] notably the famous 'a green thought in a green shade' (l. 48), which elaborates upon Virgil's *florentis viridi Sophiae . . . umbra*[50] ('the green shade of flowering Wisdom'). Allusions to the classical myths turn out to be witty challenges to commonplace assumptions:

> Apollo hunted Daphne so
> Only that she might laurel grow:
> And Pan did after Syrinx speed,
> Not as a nymph, but for a reed.[51]

In the second line, 'that' remains temporarily suspended between result and purpose, until we realize as the argument continues that Marvell really does mean that Apollo chased Daphne in order that she might be turned into a tree, and Pan pursued Syrinx in order to obtain pipes. The disappearance of women from the scene is deeply gratifying to the poet, as they are magically transformed into beautiful trees and useful musical instruments.[52] Indeed, the erasure of women actually enables the production of the poet's song by

---

47 Ovid, *Metamorphoses*, i 7.
48 *Poems of Andrew Marvell*, pp. 152–9.
49 As Nigel Smith points out: *Poems of Andrew Marvell*, pp. 155, 157.
50 Virgil, *Ciris*, l. 4.
51 Marvell, 'The Garden', ll. 27–32.
52 For Marvell's evasions of heterosexuality see Paul Hammond, 'Marvell's Sexuality', *The Seventeenth Century*, 11 (1996) 87–123, revised and reprinted in my *Figuring Sex between Men from Shakespeare to Rochester* (Oxford, 2002), pp. 186–225.

providing his reed. And the poet implicitly changes the myth in another way, since in Ovid's handling of the story, the laurel which Daphne has become is made by Apollo into a symbol of military triumph:

> tu ducibus Latiis aderis, cum laeta Triumphum
> vox canet et visent longas Capitolia pompas;
> postibus Augustis eadem fidissima custos
> ante fores stabis mediamque tuebere quercum.[53]

There is a striking intertextual silence here, as the poem refuses to take over Ovid's glorification of Roman military power, maintaining that laurel is just laurel, prized for its own sake, not as a symbol.

The poem fashions an alternative space of solitude for the poet to inhabit away from the 'busy companies of men'; but if the poet has no companions, the poem does, for it is accompanied in the 1681 folio by the Latin verses called 'Hortus', and in this version of 'The Garden' the speaker casts himself as a citizen of a flowery society:

> Municipem servate novum, votoque potitum,
> Frondosae cives optate in florea regna.[54]

It is remarkable that Marvell could write about this garden in terms of citizenship and a kingdom in Latin but not in English, for the English poem has no such terminology. Perhaps the English political terms were too compromised to be used in this alternative space, and this kindgom of the mind could only freely be written in Latin.

Dryden does not write his paradises in Latin, but he writes a form of English which repeatedly calls into play the Latin roots of the language and Roman cultural precedents.[55] For Dryden paradise had three main textual sources besides the Bible: Horace's second *Epode*, Virgil's second *Georgic*, and Milton's *Paradise Lost*. Dryden's translation of Horace's *Epode* II had carefully rethought the Latin original and transposed it into a dimension which was at once classical and contemporary.[56] It continued to shape his vision of the ideal state of life, so that Horace's opening exclamation:

> Beatus ille qui procul negotiis,
> Ut prisca gens mortalium,

---

53 Ovid, *Metamorphoses*, i 560–3: 'With thee shall Roman generals wreathe their heads, when shouts of joy shall acclaim their triumph, and long processions climb the Capitol. Thou at Augustus' portals shalt stand a trusty guardian, and keep watch over the civic crown of oak which hangs between' (Loeb translation).

54 Marvell, 'Hortus', ll. 14–15: 'preserve your new citizen, and, having granted this wish, garlanded citizens, accept me in your flowery kingdom'.

55 See Hammond, *Traces*, *passim*.

56 See pp. 96–7 below, and *Poems of John Dryden*, ii 378–85.

Paterna rura bubus exercet suis,
Solutus omne faenore.[57]

inflects the opening of 'To my Honoured Kinsman, John Driden of Chesterton' (1700):

How blessed is he who leads a country life,
Unvexed with anxious cares, and void of strife![58]

'How blessed is he' is more than just a translation of *Beatus ille*, for it sets in motion in the mind of the reader a string of assumptions derived from Horace's poem: that the truly happy life is the one based in the countryside; that it does not require riches but only a modest competence; that it entails a deliberate rejection of the bustle and corruption of town and court. And that it is a state of mind, as the second line of 'To John Driden' indicates, which is 'Unvexed with anxious cares, and void of strife'. That line has its origins in Horace's *Solutus omne faenore* (literally, 'free from all interest/profit', so by synecdoche, free from business), which had already been given a psychological turn in Dryden's translation in *Sylvae*, where it became 'Discharged of business, void of strife'.[59] That last phrase reappears in the second line of 'To John Driden', along with two other terms which have intertextual resonance. 'Unvexed' appears to be a word which, for seventeenth-century writers, was a particular characterization of paradise, for John Donne writes of Elizabeth Drury as one 'in whom all white, and redde, and blue | (Beauties ingredients) voluntary grew, | As in an unvext Paradise',[60] while Dryden himself had described the happy farmer's life as 'Unvex'd with Quarrels, undisturb'd with Noise'.[61] As for the phrase 'anxious cares', that had been used by Dryden in 'Horace: *Epode* II',[62] but derived originally from Milton, who in *Paradise Lost* has Adam acknowledge that paradise is not only a place but a state of mind from which 'God has bid dwell far off all anxious cares'.[63] Though these words formed a network of associations in Dryden's mind, we need not suppose that he expected readers to trace 'anxious cares' to its Miltonic source; but he

---

57 Horace, *Epode* II, ll. 1–4: 'Happy is the man who, far from business, like the first race of mortals, cultivates his paternal acres with his own oxen, free from all money-lending'.

58 Dryden, 'To my Honoured Kinsman John Driden of Chesterton', ll. 1–2. My discussion of this poem and its sources is endebted to the annotations in *Poems of John Dryden*, v 188–201, which in this instance were drafted by Professor David Hopkins, and also to J. R. Mason, 'To Milton through Dryden and Pope', unpublished PhD thesis, University of Cambridge, 1987, which collects and analyses Dryden's borrowings from Milton.

59 Dryden, 'Horace: *Epode* II', l. 4.

60 John Donne, 'The Anatomy of the World', ll. 361–3, in *The Epithalamions, Anniversaries, and Epicedes*, edited by W. Milgate (Oxford, 1978).

61 Dryden, 'The Second Book of the Georgics', l. 659, in *Works of John Dryden*, v 202.

62 Line 55; and see the note in *Poems of John Dryden*, ii 370.

63 John Milton, *Paradise Lost*, edited by Alastair Fowler, second edition (London, 1998), viii 185.

would have expected them to hear the opening phrase of the poem as an allusion to Horace, an invitation to understand that 'To John Driden' was informed by the Latin lines and would in turn engage in a form of dialogue with them. For there are some surprises in store for the reader who expects 'To John Driden' just to replicate the tropes of Horace's poem.

The contented countryman of the *Epode* spends most of his time cultivating his crops, but Driden is engaged with his neighbours, settling disputes which they refer to him for arbitration. Unlike the Horatian farmer who was 'rich in humble poverty',[64] Driden is rich *tout court*, and gives generously to the poor. Unlike the farmer, who might have 'a chaste and pleasing wife | To ease the business of his life',[65] Driden is unmarried, and is congratulated on his wisdom in avoiding the tribulations of marriage. And unlike the farmer who distances himself from the town –

> The clamours of contentious law,
>   And court and state he wisely shuns,
> Nor bribed with hopes nor dared with awe
>   To servile salutations runs.[66]

– John Driden of Chesterton serves his country as an MP, and is a model patriot. That word had been prised away from the Whigs in *Absalom and Achitophel*, and in the Dedication to the *Georgics* Dryden had defined 'patriot' as one 'under whom we see their Country Flourish';[67] now Dryden defines it in his own terms, in quiet opposition to the adherents of William III:

> A patriot both the king and country serves;
> Prerogative and privilege preserves:
> Of each our laws the certain limit show;
> One must not ebb, not t' other overflow:
> Betwixt the prince and parliament we stand,
> The barriers of the state on either hand:
> May neither overflow, for then they drown the land.
> When both are full, they feed our blessed abode,
> Like those that watered once the paradise of God.[68]

This passage makes two intertextual gestures. One brings into play lines from Sir John Denham's *Cooper's Hill* (1642), the poem which used its meditation on part of the English landscape to figure the ideal balance within the

---

[64] Dryden, 'Horace: *Epode* II', l. 2, an addition to the Latin.

[65] Dryden, 'Horace: *Epode* II', ll. 58–9; the second line has no equivalent in the Latin.

[66] Dryden, 'Horace: *Epode* II', ll. 14–17; the first two lines are an expansion of *forumque vitat*, 'and he avoids the forum'.

[67] *Works of John Dryden*, v 141.

[68] Dryden, 'To my Honoured Kinsman John Driden of Chesterton', ll. 171–9. The two over-full lines (ll. 177 and 179 are alexandrines) mimic the fullness of the river.

constitution betwen king and people, for there are dangers if kingly power overflow its banks, or the people attempt to divert the stream into a new course. River, nation, and, indeed, poem, should be

> Though deep, yet clear, though gentle, yet not dull,
> Strong without rage, without ore-flowing full.[69]

This couplet was so well-known, and so frequently imitated,[70] that Dryden could expect his readers to see immediately that he was alluding to an ancient idea of the ideal, and necessary, balance between the powers of king and people: his vision is not that of the Jacobite who yearns nostalgically for absolute monarchy. The second gesture suggests that England may be a form of paradise. The last line of the passage explicitly recalls the garden of Eden watered by rivers: 'And a river went out of Eden to water the garden; and from thence it was parted, and became into four heads.'[71] But while the allusion is biblical, the borrowings are Miltonic: though Dryden's 'watered' is found in both the Bible and Milton, his 'feed' suggests that he looked at Milton's description of Eden where the rivers 'fed | Flowers worthy of Paradise',[72] while his phrase 'the paradise of God' seems to come from Milton's 'for blissful Paradise | Of God the garden was'.[73] And 'abode' – prominently placed as a rhyme word to catch the eye – is both biblical and Miltonic, a word used not just for a place to live, but for a secure dwelling, often a dwelling with God.[74] So in Dryden's lines there is an explicit invocation of Denham's vision of the ideal political community at harmony with itself, and also a vision of England as paradise which is shaped by both allusion and lexical connotations. Whether this is to be a paradise lost or a paradise regained seems to be left in the hands of the reader.

[69] Sir John Denham, *Cooper's Hill*, ll. 191–2, in *The Poetical Works of Sir John Denham*, edited by Theodore Howard Banks, second edition (n.p., 1969).

[70] Banks collects examples in *Poetical Works of Sir John Denham*, pp. 77, 343–51.

[71] Genesis ii 10 (AV).

[72] Milton, *Paradise Lost*, iv 240–1.

[73] Milton, *Paradise Lost*, iv 208–9.

[74] John xiv 23 (Jesus promising that he and his followers will 'make our abode' with God); Milton, *Paradise Lost*, iii 734 (describing Paradise), iv 939 (Satan seeking an alternative dwelling to hell), vii 553 (heaven as God's dwelling place).

5

Classical Texts: Translations and Transformations

I

IN WHAT respects is Andrew Marvell's 'Horatian Ode' an Horatian ode?[1] Marvell and his contemporaries gathered their ideas of Horace and of Horatian odes from a variety of sources. They would have read the Latin text of Horace's poetry in editions which surrounded it with glosses, notes, parallel passages, and perhaps a prose paraphrase;[2] they would have practised translating and imitating Horace's poetry at school; they would have read English translations and imitations of Horace by writers such as Jonson or Milton. Horace, therefore, was already a complex text for readers of Marvell's poem, a text which they fashioned for themselves out of all these interpretative materials. Horace's odes spoke of private and domestic experiences – love and desire, both homosexual and heterosexual; friendship and the pleasures of conviviality; the passage of time and the poignant delight which may attend an awareness of life's passing. The poetry also spoke of the great public events which were shaping Rome under Augustus, though often addressing such matters at a tangent, cautious about how a private citizen might speak to power or understand history, and jealous of the poet's precarious independence. It was perhaps with a teasingly deliberate naivety that Horace wrote:

> Integer vitae scelerisque purus
> Non eget Mauris iaculis, neque arcu

---

[1] For discussions of the classical hinterland of Marvell's poem see Nigel Smith's notes in *Poems of Andrew Marvell*; J. S. Coolidge, 'Marvell and Horace', *Modern Philology*, 63 (1965) 111–20; A. J. N. Wilson, 'Andrew Marvell: *An Horatian Ode Upon Cromwell's Return from Ireland*: The Thread of the Poem and its Use of Classical Allusion', *Critical Quarterly*, 11 (1969) 325–41. For Horace in the seventeenth century see *Horace Made New: Horatian Influences on British Writing from the Renaissance to the Twentieth Century*, edited by Charles Martindale and David Hopkins (Cambridge, 1993).

[2] The importance of the interpretative material in the editions available to seventeenth-century writers was pointed out by J. McG. Bottkol, 'Dryden's Latin Scholarship', *Modern Philology*, 40 (1943) 214–54.

Nec venenatis grauida sagittis
    Fusce pharetra.[3]

  Vertue, Dear Friend, needs no defence,
  The surest Guard is innocence;
  None knew till Guilt created Fear
  What Darts or poyson'd Arrows were.[4]

For many seventeenth-century poets and readers, virtue was to be sought in innocent pastoral retirement, and this ideal was often imagined through material taken from Horace, notably his *Epode* II on the delights of country life.[5] But virtue does need defence in a period of civil upheaval such as both Horace and Marvell experienced; and much as Horace might praise the delights of the retired life on his Sabine farm, there might be times when retirement itself was no longer a virtue. And so,

  The forward youth that would appear
  Must now forsake his Muses dear,
      Nor in the shadows sing
      His numbers languishing:

  'Tis time to leave the books in dust,
  And oil th'unusèd armour's rust;
      Removing from the wall
      The corslet of the hall.[6]

As readers pondered the significance of Marvell's invocation of Horace, they would recognize certain features of the ode as approximating to Horace's methods. The verse form mirrors one of Horace's meters, and there is a comparably adroit management of tone and voice through teasing shifts in subject matter and perspective which challenge readers to negotiate transitions and make connections, so allowing political implications to emerge obliquely rather than as directly authorial observations. Like some of Horace's odes, Marvell's poem addresses the movement of public affairs, and through the shifts in tone and contents it speaks of the precariousness of our powers of recognition and representation, the difficulty of turning our present experiences into an historical narrative.

But as we read further into the poem, its manipulation of Horatian motifs,

---

[3] *Carm.* I xxii, quoted from *In Horatium Flaccum, Dionysii Lambini . . . Commentarius locupletissimus* (Geneva, 1605), p. 46, one of the editions of Horace used by Dryden.

[4] Translated by the Earl of Roscommon, quoted from *Horace in English*, edited by D. S. Carne-Ross and Kenneth Haynes (Harmondsworth, 1996), p. 114.

[5] *Epode* II was translated by Jonson, Cowley, and Dryden, among others; for the tradition of Horatian meditation in rural retirement see Maren-Sofie Røstvig, *The Happy Man: Studies in the Metamorphoses of a Classical Ideal*, second edition (Oslo, 1962).

[6] Andrew Marvell, 'An Horatian Ode upon Cromwell's Return from Ireland', ll. 1–8.

and of other kinds of classical Roman material, becomes puzzling, teasing us in a way which is perhaps not too dissimilar to Horace's own style. The poem deploys a Latinate vocabulary and philosophical framework: we are in a world of temples (l. 22), Gods (l. 61), Fortune (l. 113), and Fate (l. 37), but this classicizing is problematic. Since some had thought that it was primarily Charles I's devout adherence to the Church of England which led him to the scaffold, to associate him with 'the Gods' is to traduce rather than translate, or is at best a tendentious translation. So too when Cromwell, who continually referred his military successes to divine Providence, is called 'the War's and Fortune's son' (l. 113) this translation of English history into a Roman idiom is more than an elegant classicizing gesture, it questions the very language through which Cromwell represented his motives to himself and to observers. Later we are told that Cromwell is 'still in the Republic's hand', but the word 'Republic' is also problematic. A Latinate term, from *res publica*, it used to mean in English simply 'the state' or 'the public sphere' (*OED* 1). After the execution of the king in 1649 England was a republic in the usual modern sense, but the word itself was not commonly used to describe the new state, which was instead officially called the 'Commonwealth and Free State'.[7] It was not clear, when Marvell was writing in 1650, who or what constituted 'the Republic': the Roman term does not quite pass into modern English speech. Because of the poem's Roman allusions, we are more sensitive than usual to the word's Roman history and its imperfect naturalization, and so we are led to hear a strangeness in its usage. Moreover, there are unsettling associations if we trace the word back to Horace's time, for Augustus had, in effect though not in name, abolished the Roman republic with its liberties and instituted a monarchy, even while avoiding the hated name of king.

Similarly, the poem's use of allusions to Julius Caesar is problematic. Cromwell's forceful rise unseated Charles,

> And Caesar's head at last
> Did through his laurels blast.[8]

Caesar here stands for Charles I, both rulers who were killed because they were thought to pose a threat to the people's liberties; but later in the poem Caesar is now Cromwell:

> A Caesar he ere long to Gaul,
> To Italy an Hannibal.[9]

Here Cromwell is the Caesar who expanded the Roman empire through his

---

7   *Milton and Republicanism*, edited by David Armitage, Armand Himy, and Quentin Skinner (Cambridge, 1995), pp. 15, 27–8.
8   Marvell, 'An Horatian Ode', ll. 23–4.
9   Marvell, 'An Horatian Ode', ll. 101–2.

foreign conquests, and yet since Caesar's untimely end has already been alluded to, it is difficult to expunge that part of his story from our memory as we ponder this image. But Cromwell is also aligned here with Hannibal, the foreigner who invaded Italy to destroy Rome, but was himself destroyed in the attempt. What does that suggest about Cromwell's future? These allusions appear at first to locate Cromwell in a clear narrative of military success, and yet if we remind ourselves of the original Roman contexts, they turn into narratives of hubris and nemesis.

These various allusions suggest parallels, both large-scale and local, between England in 1650 and Rome in the years after its civil wars had ended but before the triumph of Augustus was secure. But the parallels are fragmentary, inconsistent, and contradictory, suggestive (teasing, even) rather than definitive, disturbing us and through their interaction disturbing one another. The reader faces a complex interpretative problem, as no coherent narrative pattern is able to triumph. The experience of reading the 'Horatian Ode' with Horace's own odes in mind becomes a lesson in the complexities of reading history and reading the present.

The local and structural tensions in Marvell's use of classical precedent are paralleled on a larger scale in his contemporaries' political uses of Roman material. The Parliamentarian Thomas May translated Lucan's poem on the Roman civil war,[10] Edmund Waller celebrated Cromwell as Augustus,[11] and the Protectoral coinage depicted Cromwell as a Roman emperor,[12] but Roman history and iconography were not used with any consistency to forge a new civic idiom. Meanwhile, Royalist writers turned to the translation of Latin poetry as a way of making coded statements of their loyalty to the defeated cause.[13] And some distrusted the classics altogether: from contrasting ideological standpoints extreme Puritans condemned all classical learning as ungodly, while Hobbes blamed the discontent which led to the Civil War on too much reading of classical histories.[14] The reading of contemporary events via classical texts was as unsettled and unsettling as the times themselves.

[10] David Norbrook, *Writing the English Republic: Poetry, Rhetoric and Politics 1627–1660* (Cambridge, 1999), pp. 23–62.

[11] 'A Panegyric to My Lord Protector', ll. 169–72, in *The Poems of Edmund Waller*, edited by G. Thorn Drury, 2 vols (London, 1901), ii 17.

[12] Laura Lunger Knoppers, *Constructing Cromwell: Ceremony, Portrait, and Print, 1645–1661* (Cambridge, 2000).

[13] Lawrence Venuti, '*The Destruction of Troy*: Translation and Royalist Cultural Politics in the Interregnum', *Journal of Medieval and Renaissance Studies*, 23 (1993) 197–219; Timothy Raylor, *Cavaliers, Clubs, and Literary Culture* (Newark, N.J., 1994), pp. 183–8.

[14] Thomas Hobbes, *Behemoth, or The Long Parliament*, edited by Ferdinand Tönnies (London, 1889), p. 3.

II

John Dryden, too, pondered Roman examples as he wrote about Cromwell.[15] In his *Heroic Stanzas* Cromwell's funeral becomes a Roman rite, where the sacred eagle is released to fly over the pyre, and the hero's ashes rest in a sacred urn (lines 1–4; 145). Other allusions cast Cromwell as a quasi-Roman ruler:

> When past all offerings to Feretrian Jove
> He Mars deposed, and arms to gowns made yield,[16]

The first allusion associates Cromwell with Romulus, the founder of the Roman state, who dedicated arms which he had captured in battle to Jupiter Feretrius, while the phrase 'Arms to gowns made yield' echoes Cicero's description of his own consulship, *cedant arma togae* ('let arms yield to the toga', the toga being the dress of peace). The poem's allusions and vocabulary classicize Cromwell not by suggesting a single point of comparison with Roman history (which would link past and present in an allegorical or typological reading), but by suggesting that England might be able to fashion equivalent but idiomatic classical forms and structures. Dryden may be attempting to shape a classical republican aesthetic in these sober quatrains, but like the concurrent development of a Puritan classicism in architecture,[17] it was short-lived.

The association of England and Rome is rethought in *Astraea Redux*, the poem in which Dryden greets the return of Charles II, and with him the return of Astraea, goddess of justice. Here the association which Dryden develops (in common with many of his contemporaries, who found the analogy irresistible) is that of Charles and Augustus, and the Latin quotation which Dryden places as the epigraph to his poem – *iam redit et virgo, redeunt Saturnia regna* ('now the goddess returns, the reign of Saturn returns') – brings into play Virgil's fourth *Eclogue* and its promise of a golden age under Augustus. Time present is renewed by a recovery of time past.

But the past which is being recovered in this trope is not an historical moment but an already mythologized time, not Rome but Virgil's hopes for Rome. Dryden knew, of course, that such mythologies have only an hortatory force, no predictive or definitive power, and the actual poetry which establishes such parallels is apt to underline their fictive status. As Paul de Man observes, 'A literary text simultaneously asserts and denies the authority of its own rhetorical mode . . . Poetic writing is the most advanced and refined mode

---

[15] For a much expanded version of this discussion of Dryden and the classics see Hammond, *Traces*.

[16] Dryden, 'Heroic Stanzas', ll. 77–8.

[17] See Timothy Mowl and Brian Earnshaw, *Architecture without Kings* (Manchester, 1995).

of deconstruction.'[18] Dryden's uses of classical reference, like Marvell's in the 'Horatian Ode', tend to set to work in the text a semiotic movement which cannot be contained, for these invocations of Rome lead readers into a complex world, the imaginative world of a poem in which time and space are both English and Roman, and so not quite either, and where the English language is made to disclose its Latin roots: we hear another language resonating through Dryden's English.

Annus Mirabilis is a good example of a poem which uses Latin pre-texts both to construct an interpretation of the present and at the same time to set in motion (as all true poetic language must) a deconstruction of the authority of that interpretation. A Virgilian thread running through the fabric of Dryden's poem invites us to see a parallel between the burning of London in the Great Fire of 1666 and the destruction of Troy as told in the *Aeneid*. The allusion is present in the epigraph from *Aeneid* II, *urbs antiqua ruit, multos dominata per annos* ('The ancient city falls, having dominated for many years'), and in a series of tiny echoes which shape the texture of the work. For example, when Dryden writes that the homeless Londoners 'repeat what they would shun',[19] he is using 'repeat' in the Latin sense of 'encounter again', and recalling the moment when Aeneas says *urbem repeto*[20] ('I encounter the city again') in telling of his escape from the flames of Troy. But set alongside these Virgilian signals – which move the account toward epic, so dignifying subject, writer, and reader – there are other Latin texts drawn into the poem's imaginative world. Lines adapted from Ovid describing an exhausted hare pursued by a dog evoke our sympathy for the plight of the weary sailors in the Dutch war,[21] reminding us that military success has its human price; while verses adapted from Petronius speak of man wandering blindly in the dark empire of Fortune,[22] a philosophical vision which clearly works in tension with the poem's assertions that the hand of God is directly guiding the nation's history. What this mixing of classical material achieves is a complex texture (complex, that is, both linguistically and philosophically) which invites the reader to see parallels between his experience and Roman history, while at the same time setting to work a deconstructive movement between the various components which questions the stability of these conceptual structures. The result is neither a glib mystification of power nor a nihilistic destruction of meaning, but a responsibly complex meditation on the acts of representation and of reading. It is a poem written by a man whose study housed annotated editions of Virgil alongside newsbooks and manuscript satires, where Lucretius and St Paul inhabited the same space.

---

[18] Paul de Man, *Allegories of Reading* (New Haven, 1979), p. 17.

[19] Dryden, *Annus Mirabilis*, l. 1028.

[20] Virgil, *Aeneid* ii 749.

[21] Dryden, *Annus Mirabilis*, ll. 521–8.

[22] Dryden, *Annus Mirabilis*, ll. 125–40.

III

This deployment of allusion and quotation is one kind of translation between Roman and Restoration culture: another is the formal translation of complete poems into modern English. Dryden was the unrivalled master of translation in his age, and in the course of his career he turned increasingly to this mode of writing. This was partly for commercial reasons, since translations began to find a market (ably exploited by Dryden's publisher, Jacob Tonson) among both lovers of the classics and a growing reading public which lacked Latin and Greek (including women readers). It was partly also for political reasons, since the Revolution of 1688–9 displaced Dryden from his positions as Poet Laureate and Historiographer Royal, and compelled him to find new ways of writing poetry and history: translation offered an opportunity for oblique commentary on the times. But primarily there was throughout his later life a strong imaginative and philosophical necessity for Dryden to translate the classics, since he had a dramatist's fascination with the play of different voices, and a sceptic's reluctance to adhere to any single system.

Dryden's formal translations began with versions from the *Heroides* for *Ovid's Epistles* (1680), where he took on the voices of women embroiled in tragic love affairs; then he rendered portions of Virgil, Lucretius, Horace, and Theocritus for the first two of Tonson's anthologies, *Miscellany Poems* and *Sylvae* (1684–5); several of Juvenal's satires and all of Persius for a collected translation which he supervised and prefaced with a long essay on satire (1693); then the complete works of Virgil (1697); and finally tales from Homer and Ovid alongside Chaucer and Boccaccio in the crowning achievement of his career, *Fables Ancient and Modern* (1700).

In the Preface to *Ovid's Epistles* Dryden summarized the varied methods of translation current in his day. Some translators (like Ben Jonson with Horace's *Ars Poetica*) used metaphrase, a close word-by-word rendering which was liable to result in stilted, unidiomatic English; others (like Waller with the fourth book of the *Aeneid*) used paraphrase, translating with some latitude; while a third group practised imitation, a transposition of the original not only into the English language but into the contemporary social world, peopling the text with modern references. Dryden cites Cowley's versions of Pindar as examples of imitation, and this form of translation had been practised by Rochester in *An Allusion to Horace*, and would be developed with great verve by Oldham[23] and Pope. Dryden's own practice as a translator generally follows the middle path, with some diversions into imitation: he seems to have been concerned to produce neither a close crib for those who wanted the bones of the Latin poem, nor a virtuoso variation on classical themes to divert

---

[23] See Paul Hammond, *John Oldham and the Renewal of Classical Culture* (Cambridge, 1983).

contemporaries, but an imaginative recreation of the voice of the original, paying attention not only to the poet's ideas but to his persona and style.

The translations which Dryden produced in this middle way are poems which situate themselves between England and Rome. As an example we may take his translation of Horace's *Epode* II, which tells of the delights of a country life. Dryden does not consistently preserve Horace's references to the Italian countryside as Jonson had done in his version; neither does he simply transpose it into an English setting, as Oldham had chosen to do with Horace's *Ode* I xxxi, which he transferred to the Cotswolds. Instead, he fashions a poetic world in which Roman references can coexist with a plausibly English life. As a sample of his working methods, here is the opening:

> How happy in his low degree,
> How rich in humble poverty is he
>   Who leads a quiet country life!
>   Discharged of business, void of strife,
> And from the griping scrivener free.
> (Thus ere the seeds of vice were sown,
>   Lived men in better ages born,
> Who ploughed with oxen of their own
>   Their small paternal field of corn.)
> Nor trumpets summon him to war,
>   Nor drums disturb his morning sleep,
> Nor knows he merchants' gainful care,
>   Nor fears the dangers of the deep.
> The clamours of contentious law,
>   And court and state he wisely shuns,
> Nor bribed with hopes nor dared with awe
>   To servile salutations runs.[24]

This is neither metaphrase nor paraphrase nor imitation, but a version which is often close to the Latin while sometimes adding whole lines (lines 2–3, 7, and 11–12 are additions, while others are substantial expansions of single words or short phrases).[25] This world seems to belong recognizably to Horace's Italy, where men grow vines and plough with oxen, but also recognizably to Dryden's England, where men eat turbot and complain of scriveners. (A scrivener was a moneylender, and at the end of the poem we discover that this praise of country life has been spoken by a moneylender called Morecraft – a name from the English tradition of satirical comedy.) And many of the details of this imagined world are comfortably common to England and Italy (the sheep, the mead, the mallows). In lines 14–15 Dryden eliminates the

---

24 Dryden, 'Horace: *Epode* II', ll. 1–17.
25 For details of Dryden's treatment of Horace's original, see the notes in *Poems of John Dryden*, ii 378–85, and H. A. Mason, 'The Dream of Happiness', *Cambridge Quarterly*, 8 (1978) 11–55 and 9 (1980) 218–71.

specifically Roman reference in *forumque vitat* ('and he avoids the Forum'), and by choosing the word 'court' he allows the reader to see both the lawcourt and the king's court as oppressive places. Dryden has made the moral thought of the poem more explicit, adding the striking quasi-biblical paradox in line 2, while in line 16 he anticipates a reference later in the poem to larks who are caught by being 'dared' (dazzled with mirrors), using this as an image of men helplessly intimidated by power. Some of the vocabulary is taken from the seventeenth-century English tradition of writing about the joys of rural retirement: 'How happy' and 'quiet' and 'business' are part of this hallowed vocabulary, and help to evoke in the reader's mind that collection of morally informed meditations on the countryside. Some of the phrasing has been influenced by other Latin poets: line 7 comes not from Horace but from Virgil's *magnanimi heroes nati melioribus annis* ('great heroes born in better times') in *Aeneid* VI. Other ideas are prompted by the glosses in the editions which Dryden was using: from the 1605 commentary by Lubinus the phrase *lucri spe* ('hope of gain') seems to have suggested line 12, which has no equivalent in Horace. The vocabulary has occasionally resulted from a careful perusal of previous translations both in English and in French, for Dryden apparently noted down 'void of' from Alexander Brome's version and 'déchargé' from Otto van Veen's (which prompted 'discharged'). Other phrases have been shaped by recollections of Spenser, of Cowley's *Essays*, Virgil's *Eclogues* and *Georgics*, and other poems by Horace. So what Dryden is fashioning here is not only a translation of Horace's *Epode* II, but a concentrated meditation on the poem and the questions which it raises, with its vocabulary bringing into play a tradition of both classical and contemporary thought.

Dryden turned to classical translation particularly as a way of moving aside from the contingencies of the present to imagine other ways of living, and to manage the incoherence and instability of life. The sceptical sensibility which led him to weave together such different philosophical strands in *Annus Mirabilis* drew him also to translate parts of Lucretius' passionately argued account of the universe as a collection of atoms in random motion, a world in which the individual consciousness arises from and returns to chaos. But Lucretius' philosophy also encourages man to seek tranquillity of mind, and Dryden responded to this by selecting passages 'Against the Fear of Death' and 'Concerning the Nature of Love', where Lucretius urges us not to be anxiously possessed by the fear of death, or obsessed with the pursuit of sexual pleasure. Equanimity is the goal of this text, and indeed the goal of many of Dryden's translations: readers are brought to take possession of themselves more profoundly by making this detour through the philosophies of the ancient world. The movement away from contemporary England and the compromises of public life does not take us into a private world of untroubled communion with the classics, but into a variety of contrasting, competing textual worlds which challenge us to rethink ourselves.

The translation of Virgil which occupied much of Dryden's attention after the Revolution is the epic, the national poem, which the nation could not have, and did not, perhaps, deserve. While the supremacy of epic as a genre was widely acknowledged, and some writers, including Milton and Dryden, had aspired to write an epic on British history, the epics of this period all refuse, in some way, to be poems of nationhood: *Paradise Lost* meditates on the failure of the English nation to respond to its God-given freedom, while *The Rape of the Lock* and *The Dunciad* use epic strategies to reveal the impoverished values of social and literary coteries. The nation has no epic; the epic has no nation.

Dryden's *Aeneis* (1697) begins with lines which hover between Rome and England:

> Arms, and the Man I sing, who, forc'd by Fate,
> And haughty *Juno*'s unrelenting Hate,
> Expell'd and exil'd, left the *Trojan* Shoar:
> Long Labours, both by Sea and Land he bore,
> And in the doubtful War, before he won
> The *Latian* Realm, and built the destin'd Town:
> His banish'd Gods restor'd to Rites Divine,
> And setl'd sure Succession in his Line:
> From whence the Race of *Alban* Fathers come,
> And the long Glories of Majestick *Rome*.[26]

While Dryden preserves the Roman proper names, some of the phrasing here invites us to recall the recent political history of England as we read. The phrase 'Expell'd and exil'd' might prompt memories of the expelled and exiled James II, while line 7 is a curiously free translation of *inferretque deos* ('and brought in his gods'): the Latin verb does not mean 'brought *back*,' so the stress on return and restoration is Dryden's own. Line 8 is entirely Dryden's addition, and seems to recall the disturbed succession to the English throne. '*Alban* Fathers' is an exact translation of *Albanique patres*, but readers who have by now been alerted to undercurrents in the text may remember that James II had been Duke of Albany, and had been celebrated by Dryden under the allegorical title of Albanius in the opera *Albion and Albanius* (1685). Ironically, it is this absolutely faithful translation of *Albanique patres* which permits a reading which leaves faithful interpretation far behind. But then, keeping faith is exactly what both Virgil and Dryden, in their different ways, are concerned with. This teasingly unfaithful yet faithful opening to the *Aeneis* sets these issues working in the mind of the reader, and the irresolvable tensions of the initial paragraph initiate us into a complex mode of reading. Dryden is opening the poem out to include England, without making it an allegory of English history. The temporary association of Aeneas and James is quickly shown not to be allegorical as the poem itself rapidly deconstructs the

---

[26] 'The First Book of the Aeneis', ll. 1–10; quoted from *Works of John Dryden*, v 343.

Plate 10. John Dryden, *The Works of Virgil* (London, 1697), one of the plates illustrating *Aeneid* Book II.

Each of the plates in this translation was dedicated to one of the subscribers who had supported the project by paying five guineas in advance, and who received in return a copy which was printed on larger and better quality paper. This image represents Aeneas carrying his father Anchises on his shoulders and accompanied by his son Ascanius as they escape from the burning ruins of Troy; his wife Creüsa stands to one side, and will be lost in the mêlée. On the title page Dryden placed a quotation from *Aeneid* Book II, *Sequiturque Patrem non passibus Æquis*: 'and he [Ascanius] follows his father with steps not equal to his'. Through this quotation Dryden places himself in the same relation to Virgil that Ascanius had to Aeneas – not able to match his heroic steps, but nevertheless his true heir. So Dryden is at once modestly and proudly claiming to be the heir of Virgil, and is implicitly contrasting himself with Shadwell who was represented in *Mac Flecknoe* (l. 108) as 'our young Ascanius' in his role as heir to Flecknoe.

rhetorical scheme which it had appeared to offer: the present tense in 'come' takes the poem into a present in which the long-established glories of Rome are still flourishing. This present tense would be appropriate for Virgil, writing when Rome was indeed still glorious, though in fact the Latin lacks a verb here, and so does not specify any tense. It is Dryden's translation which, by creating this emphatic but impossible present – a time in which the Alban fathers and the glories of Rome are fully present – makes us recognize our own separation from such a time, and our displacement from such a rich kind of nationhood. It establishes for the duration of the poem a milieu which is neither Rome nor England, but a placing and displacing of both.

IV

It was also by the translation and imitation of classical texts that Alexander Pope shaped a world which he could control, a milieu in which his friends and enemies appeared translated, some like Bottom sporting an ass's head, others made into sometimes equally unrecognizable models of sophistication and generosity.[27] Underlying much of Pope's writing in this mode is a vision of the impossibility of Britain having an Augustan age, if that entailed taste and decency being promoted by rulers rather than flourishing in private enclaves of classical culture and embattled patriotism. *The Dunciad* is an epic not about the founding of empires, as the *Aeneid* had been, but about the displacement of literary achievements and civic values by a bizarre gallimaufry of tasteless entertainments and witless writing, presided over by a travesty king. In this empire of dullness, where 'Dunce the second reigns like Dunce the first',[28] the responsibilities of the poet can, it seems, only be exercised through travesty: the ironic distancing of the contemporary world from the classical past is both the appropriate tribute which the modern writer pays to his classic predecessors, and the necessary means by which he asserts his own taste and judgement and independence. In *The Dunciad* Pope fills a poem with scholars, writers, actors, clowns, and publishers, and surrounds it with a critical apparatus which mimics the variorum commentaries in Renaissance classical texts. Paradoxically, the lavish *mise-en-page* of this poetry proclaims its own value at the same time as it offers itself as a satire on the encrustation of classic texts by editorial secretions. The poem comes accompanied by a ready-made critical tradition, ostensibly saving readers the labour of thinking for themselves. And yet, of course, it is precisely in order to manoeuvre readers into shaping their own interpretative space and fashioning their own commentary on literary and political affairs, that Pope creates such an elaborate textual playground.

---

[27] Pope is quoted from *The Twickenham Edition of the Poems of Alexander Pope*, edited by John Butt et al., 10 vols (London, 1938–67).

[28] *The Dunciad*, i 6.

In the *Imitations of Horace* Pope invites the reader to make comparisons with Horace's own epistles and satires, and to see Pope himself as a second Horace.[29] In contrast with Oldham's imitations of Horace, where an anonymous voice spoke to the age, Pope's collection is an exercise in self-promotion which also delineates a Horatian circle of named friends, including Arbuthnot and Swift. Yet there is a problem with replicating Horace's recurring references to his patron Maecenas. Viscount Bolingbroke is paralleled with Maecenas in 'Epistles of Horace. Book 1. Epistle 1', but 'The Seventh Epistle of the First Book of Horace' (addressed in the original to Maecenas) is addressed by Pope to an unspecified lord, while in 'The Sixth Satire of the Second Book of Horace' (to which Swift and Pope both contributed) Maecenas is paralleled with Robert Harley, Earl of Oxford. The absence of a single, dominating Maecenas is partly a mark of Pope's independence, for he had had sufficient commercial success as a man of letters not to need the practical financial help of a patron. But it also suggests that the trio of ruler, patron, and poet represented classically by Augustus, Maecenas, and Horace cannot be replicated in early eighteenth-century England because there is no Augustus. Bolingbroke, who was probably the nearest equivalent to Maecenas in Pope's life, as a source of political and philosophical ideas if not of farms, was himself displaced and at odds with the country's rulers, for he was a Tory statesman whose public influence ended when the Hanoverian line succeeded, and he fled abroad to join the Pretender. When Pope was writing his imitation of Epistle 1. 1 in 1738, Bolingbroke was back in England, but only on a brief visit before returning to his retirement in France. Readers who register Pope's difficulty in establishing a convincing modern parallel for Maecenas thereby register much of his own displacement from public affairs. And yet these local tensions between past and present cumulatively work to suggest rather that it is the rule of the Georges which has displaced the country from its true culture and its true origin.

Pope's 'First Epistle of the Second Book of Horace, Imitated' defines this displacement through a teasing reworking of the Latin original which Horace had addressed to Augustus. Writing in 1737, Pope apparently addresses George II, who had been christened Augustus. At first, the coincidence looks even more heaven-sent than the Augustan parallel which delighted Dryden's contemporaries when Charles II returned in 1660. But for Pope nothing about the Hanoverians was heaven-sent. The very title warns the reader to be alert when interpreting the poem, for it includes an epigraph which comes (with disingenuous simplicity) from the Latin text: *Ne rubeam, pingui donatus munere!* ('I hope that I may not blush at having given such a stupid gift'). The gift was, in one sense, self-evidently stupid, because George II was notoriously insensitive to poetry; and so this apparent act of homage begins the work of its self-deconstruction before we have even read a line of Pope's English, simply through a straight quotation from Horace.

---

[29] On Pope's imitations of Horace see Frank Stack, *Pope and Horace* (Cambridge, 1985).

This imitation includes passages whose ironies even a Hanoverian might be thought capable of perceiving, but many of its deadliest effects derive from Pope's trust in the ability of his readers to compare the English with the Latin, to note subtle adjustments, and to register additions and omissions: even silence speaks. Both Horace and Pope begin with an address in the second person direct to the ruler, and Horace delays the moment when he names Augustus as the recipient of this poem until a suitably climactic moment at the end of the fourth line, when he calls him 'Caesar', a title which associated Augustus with his predecessor and adoptive father Julius Caesar, warrior, statesman, and god. Pope too delays, using in the first line an ostensibly grand (but on careful inspection, vacuous and ironic) phrase 'great Patron of Mankind'; but in this case there is no climactic name to follow. It is not simply that none of the names which Pope might have wished to call George II were printable, but that this refusal to implement a similarly powerful act of naming (which in Horace was an act of praise, an affirmation of Augustus's legitimacy and his place in history) deprives George II of a secure place in the poem and in the English language. This suspension places him in limbo, declining to define his relation to Augustus, as if the two names could not possibly appear together in the syntax of cultural history.

Among the various places where Pope's text diverges from that of Horace is the reference to servile writers who praise:

> some monster of a King,
> Or Virtue, or Religion turn to sport,
> To please a lewd, or un-believing Court.[30]

By consulting the Latin text which was conveniently placed alongside the English, readers could see that there is no justification for this in the original. Also added to Horace here is the reference to Swift as a poet whose writings defended Ireland and made good the deficiency of the laws; by noticing that there is no precedent in Horace for this, we take the point that in the reign of Augustus poets did not need to act to defend public interests which government and law neglected. In such places we note the absence of any Latin pretext for Pope's English; elsewhere we realize that there is, damningly, no English equivalent available for Horace's Latin when he praises Augustus for his discriminating critical judgement in favouring the poets Virgil and Varius. His gifts to them have redounded to the credit of the giver, says Horace.[31] Pope's silence tells us that no contemporary English equivalent is imaginable.

As silence speaks, so too does slyly inexact translation. A significant mismatch of English and Latin occurs at the point when Pope is describing the staging of the coronation scene from Shakespeare's *Henry VIII*. In his note to

---

[30] Pope, 'First Epistle of the Second Book of Horace, Imitated', ll. 210–12.
[31] Pope, 'First Epistle of the Second Book of Horace, Imitated', ll. 389–90; Horace, *Epist.* II i 245–7.

line 319, Pope observes that in a recent performance 'the Armour of one of the Kings of England was borrowed from the Tower, to dress the Champion', the champion being one of Pope's many *bêtes noires*, Colly Cibber. Whereas Horace is concerned only about the low Roman taste for spectacle, Pope's example extends beyond this point to suggest that in a world where the armour of the English kings can be borrowed and turned into stage props, the coronation of George II (which had taken place just two weeks before Cibber's performance) is a similarly empty charade, a borrowing of regalia and titles to which a Hanoverian has no better claim than any other actor.

Another mismatch invites interpretation when Horace's allusion to the library established by Augustus on the Palatine hill as part of the complex around the temple of Apollo is paralleled by a reference to Merlin's Cave.[32] This was a thatched house with gothic windows established in the royal gardens at Richmond, containing wax figures of Merlin and his secretary, two Tudor queens, and two characters out of Ariosto, a poet who had celebrated the Hanoverians' ancestors. As part of the decoration of this 'cave' the king ordered a collection of English books to be installed. The site is therefore an attempt to legitimize the Hanoverians by associating them with ancient British historical legend and with the Tudor monarchy. The contrast between this self-serving and grotesque fabrication and the Palatine library makes embarrassingly clear the gap between the two cultures.

If Horace helped Pope to define culture, Homer helped him to define nature.[33] What Pope said of Virgil might also be said of Pope himself: '*Nature and Homer* were, he found, the *same*'.[34] Homer was the primary genius, not simply the first poet but the originary poet.[35] In the Preface to his translation of the *Iliad*, Pope credits Homer with supreme powers of invention (principally in the Latin sense of *inventio*, the discovery of material), for he saw nature with such clarity and reported it with such force that 'no Man of a true Poetical Spirit is Master of himself while he reads him'.[36] Homer indeed saw the animation of the material world ('An Arrow is *impatient* to be on the Wing, a Weapon *thirsts* to drink the Blood of an Enemy'),[37] but by 'Nature' Pope primarily means 'how the world is' or 'how human beings behave': the basic nature of man is Homer's subject, and Pope's subject too.

In his translation of the *Iliad* Pope made his understanding of Homer as a moral writer explicit in notes which analyze Homer's conception of the principal characteristics of his heroes: 'he has plac'd Pride with Magnanimity in *Agamemnon*, and Craft with Prudence in *Ulysses*. And thus we must take his

---

32 Pope, 'First Epistle of the Second Book of Horace, Imitated', l. 355.
33 On Pope's Homer (and Dryden's) see H. A. Mason, *To Homer through Pope* (London, 1972).
34 Pope, *An Essay on Criticism*, l. 135.
35 See Kirsti Simonsuuri, *Homer's Original Genius* (Cambridge, 1979).
36 *Twickenham Edition*, vii 4.
37 *Twickenham Edition*, vii 10.

Achilles, not as a meer heroick dispassion'd Character, but as compounded of Courage and Anger'.[38] Whether or not this now seems a plausible account of ancient Greek psychology, it is a reading which neatly fits with Pope's own understanding of man as a creature driven by ruling passions, as set out in his *Epistle to Cobham*. And it is Pope's own mode of moral thought which often shapes the way he translates the Greek verse. Here he is at a moment in Book I which might have specially appealed to him, when Achilles confronts Agamemnon, the supreme commander of the Greek army, who has just tried to appropriate one of Achilles' prisoners. Pope shows us a man telling his ruler that he is behaving unjustly:

> O Tyrant, arm'd with Insolence and Pride!
> Inglorious Slave to Int'rest, ever join'd
> With Fraud, unworthy of a Royal Mind.
> What gen'rous *Greek* obedient to thy Word,
> Shall form an Ambush, or shall lift the Sword?
> What Cause have I to war at thy Decree?
> The distant Trojans never injur'd me.
> To *Pthia*'s Realms no hostile Troops they led;
> Safe in her Vales my warlike Coursers fed:
> Far hence remov'd, the hoarse-resounding Main
> And Walls of Rocks, secure my native Reign,
> Whose fruitful Soil luxuriant Harvests grace,
> Rich in her Fruits, and in her martial Race.
> Hither we sail'd, a voluntary Throng,
> T'avenge a private, not a publick Wrong:
> What else to *Troy* th'assembled Nations draws,
> But thine, Ungrateful, and thy Brother's Cause?[39]

Pope's reworking of Homer begins by translating Agamemnon from a military commander into a tyrant whose behaviour is paradoxically disturbing the natural hierarchy: though a ruler, he has made himself morally a slave. He is all the more servile, in fact, the more he deploys his power in the service of his self-interest, which is shown to be his ruling passion. It is not control so much as self-control that concerns Pope, a general moral lesson which he takes Homer to be illustrating. The Greek soldiers, by contrast with Agamemnon, are truly noble (the meaning of 'generous' here). All this moral placing of Agamemnon has been added by Pope to Homer's confrontation between the two generals, as has the distinction between private and public in line 208. Pope's habit of expounding the moral issues in a generalized vocabulary, however, can lead him away from the unsettling directness of Homer's Greek: Pope's Achilles cannot be allowed to call Agamemnon anything like Homer's

---

[38] Pope's note to *Iliad* i 155.
[39] Pope, *Iliad*, i 194–210.

κυνῶπα, metaphorically 'shameless' but literally 'dog-eyed'. For Pope the moral force of 'Ungrateful' is quite strong enough.

By way of comparison, here is Dryden's version of the same passage:

> O impudent, regardful of thy own,
> Whose thoughts are centred on thyself alone,
> Advanced to sovereign sway for better ends
> Than thus like abject slaves to treat thy friends!
> What Greek is he that, urged by thy command,
> Against the Trojan troops will lift his hand?
> Not I! Nor such enforced respect I owe;
> Nor Pergamus I hate, nor Priam is my foe.
> What wrong from Troy remote could I sustain,
> To leave my fruitful soil and happy reign,
> And plough the surges of the stormy main?
> Thee, frontless man, we followed from afar,
> Thy instruments of death, and tools of war.
> Thine is the triumph, ours the toil alone;
> We bear thee on our backs, and mount thee on the throne.
> For thee we fall in fight; for thee redress
> Thy baffled brother, not the wrongs of Greece.[40]

Dryden was a dramatist, as we can hear in these lines which ask to be declaimed, for his rhythms are more varied than Pope's, and the passage effectively combines swelling periods with terse phrases such as 'Not I'. We can see that Pope has taken some of his vocabulary from Dryden, but the two translators generally find quite different interests in the passage. For Dryden, what needs to be stressed is that Agamemnon, having been made a king for the sake of the public good, has now turned his subjects into slaves. Though Pope picks up Dryden's word 'slave', the moral issue for him primarily concerns the government of the passions. Dryden's Achilles harps on the theme of the Greeks being reduced to mere instruments and tools, even (in an image which makes Agamemnon into a barbarian monarch) reduced to being trodden on as the ruler ascends the throne. None of Dryden's emphasis on the individual being brutally subjected to the power of the ruler is present in Pope, or, indeed, in Homer. While these brief passages cannot be taken as representative of the two translations, they do illustrate that to translate is to transform.

V

The translator is, whether implicitly or explicitly, implicated in a myth of origins. He has an original text in front of him, but in only a limited sense could Pope's copy of Homer or Marvell's copy of Horace be thought of as

---

40 Dryden, 'The First Book of Homer's *Ilias*', ll. 225–41, from *Fables Ancient and Modern*.

supplying the 'original' text. The text is always already reconstructed. Nor was the trope of originality itself original: what Pope said of Homer's unrivalled proximity to Nature, Dryden had already said more eloquently of Shakespeare.[41] And Dryden had also reminded his readers that the Greeks were not the originators of European culture:

> Whether the fruitful Nile, or Tyrian shore,
> The seeds of arts and infant science bore,
> 'Tis sure the noble plant, translated first,
> Advanced its head in Grecian gardens nursed.[42]

The Greeks were only the first translators.

Translation reimagines the original according to the ideals of the present, while redescribing the present in terms of this irrecoverable past. Through translation, past and present are reciprocally mythologized. But they are not thereby confused: translation demanded of its practitioners and readers a comparative movement between past and present which enabled a sharper understanding of their difference. Through poetry's recurring marks of separation from its supposed origins – its many signs that the translation is not the original, that England is not Rome, that Pope's Homer is not Homer's Homer – the culture of the present is made legible. And the disappointments of the present are made bearable by the consolation that there is a world elsewhere – even if this is, inevitably, always a Rome recomposed in each reader's imagination.

---

41 Pope's praise of Homer's originality in his Preface to the *Iliad* echoes Dryden's praise of Shakespeare's originality in his *Essay of Dramatic Poesy* (*Works of John Dryden*, xvii 55), while '*Nature* and *Homer* were, he found, the *same*' is traced by the Twickenham editors to Dryden's lines on Shakespeare in his 'Prologue to *The Tempest*', ll. 7–8. For the terms in which Dryden thought of Shakespeare see Paul Hammond, 'The Janus Poet: Dryden's Critique of Shakespeare', in *John Dryden (1631–1700): His Politics, His Plays, and His Poets*, edited by Claude Rawson and Aaron Santesso (Newark, N.J., 2004), pp. 158–79.

42 Dryden, 'To the Earl of Roscommon, on his Excellent *Essay on Translated Verse*', ll. 1–4.

6

The King's Two Bodies: Representations of Charles II

I

WHEN THE English republic finally crumbled, and Charles Stuart returned to England in 1660 as king, great efforts were made to represent this as a restoration, the return to their rightful place of the people, the institutions and the habits of thought which had prevailed before the flood. And yet, however much the dominant rhetoric insisted upon this as a return to normality, the old customs and images could not be used in quite the same way again, for the whole basis of English sovereignty had been debated and remodelled. The language in which power is represented, and through which it is exercised, is necessarily different after 1660, no matter how much the iconography and political theory of the early Stuarts may be redeployed. This language is now assertive rather than simply declarative; it knows that there are alternatives. The discourse of sovereignty under the Tudors and the early Stuarts had centred upon the person of the monarch, and had developed the idea of the king's two bodies: the one public, sacred, and eternal, the other private, frail, and mortal.[1] After 1660 this was palpably a damaged and questionable theory, for any notion of sovereignty which was founded upon the royal body had to take account of two scandals: firstly the execution of Charles I, the literal dismemberment of the king's body as a deliberated judicial and symbolic act; secondly the sexual exploits of Charles II, the involvement of the king's body in highly publicized promiscuity. The object of the present essay is to explore the language of kingship during the reign of Charles II in the light of the trauma and embarrassment which thus afflicted the traditional theory of 'the king's two bodies'.

While the theory of the king's two bodies is medieval in origin, it acquired special iconographical power under Elizabeth I.[2] The queen's body was turned

---

[1] See Ernst H. Kantorowicz, *The King's Two Bodies: A Study in Medieval Political Theology* (Princeton, 1957); Marie Axton, *The Queen's Two Bodies: Drama and the Elizabethan Succession* (London, 1977).

[2] For Elizabethan iconography see Frances Yates, *Astraea: The Imperial Theme in the Sixteenth Century* (London, 1975), pp. 29–87; John N. King, *Tudor Royal Iconography: Literature and*

into an icon: her physical virginity was read as a sign of her special distinction, setting her apart as someone of almost supernatural power in a liminal state between the human and the divine. She is the Virgin Queen, the Faerie Queene, the goddess Astraea, the phoenix; with a significant blurring of gender, she is also Solomon. In her portraits, which were widely disseminated, her body is subsumed by the rich dresses which speak of her power and her stability. The physical body of Elizabeth is made into an image of separateness; it is not to be thought of as an active, individual body with its own private sexuality, let alone a sexuality which might interfere with the interests of government. Her own sexuality is strictly governed in the interests of political control.

James I used the body differently, creating a language of patriarchy through which he was seen as the father of his people and the husband of the realm; this exploitation of a familial rhetoric was no doubt a deliberate contrast to the cult of the Virgin Queen, and perhaps an attempt to deflect attention from his homosexual interests. In addition, it was James who promoted the idea of the divine right of kings, insisting that he held the throne directly as a gift from God, and this notion of kingship gave added emphasis to the sacredness of the king's person. Charles I promoted the cult of platonic love, and made his own marriage with Henrietta Maria a focus of attention in the court masques. But both James and Charles were reluctant to allow the ordinary people access to their physical presence: James endured his ceremonial entry into London with tetchy ill-humour, while Charles refused to hold one at all, and retreated from many public exercises of his monarchical role, replacing royal progresses with private hunting expeditions, and continually finding excuses for postponing the ceremonies at which he would touch for the King's Evil.[3] The authoritarian portraits and statues of Charles which seem so striking and poignant to us were not widely distributed at the time, and few of his subjects had any idea either of his physical appearance or of his symbolic code.[4]

These strategies of legitimation centred upon the body of the monarch, giving it a timelessness and a quasi-divine stability, but there was also a need to locate the present ruler within history, to construct a narrative which justified the ruler syntagmatically through a teleological history as well as para-digmatically through his participation in an eternal order. Such anxiety about historical legitimation is already seen in the founder of the Tudor dynasty, Henry VII, who traced his line back to King Arthur. There were difficulties in

---

Art in an Age of Religious Crisis (Princeton, 1989); Philippa Berry, *Of Chastity and Power: Eliza-bethan Literature and the Unmarried Queen* (London, 1989).

3 J. Richards, ' "His Nowe Majestie" and the English Monarchy: the Kingship of Charles I before 1640', *Past and Present*, 113 (1986) 70–96.

4 For Jacobean and Caroline iconography see Graham Parry, *The Golden Age Restor'd: The Culture of the Stuart Court, 1603–42* (Manchester, 1981); *The Royal Image: Representations of Charles I*, edited by Thomas N. Corns (Cambridge, 1999).

providing a genealogical lineage for Elizabeth, since she had been made illegiti-mate, but secular versions of the biblical Tree of Jesse were constructed which showed Elizabeth as the culminating flower on a tree whose roots go back to Edward III. More effective was the narrative which Foxe constructed in his *Acts and Monuments*, which told of a series of independent-minded, God-fearing monarchs from Alfred onwards who prefigured Elizabeth; she thus became the defender and embodiment of contemporary Protestantism and the point towards which English history had been striving. James too had difficulties with his genealogy, since his mother had been executed for plotting against his predecessor, and his family was barred from the succession under the will of Henry VIII. His narrative of legitimacy followed Henry VII's strategy in invoking a sense of British origins and enlisting King Arthur; the name 'Charles James Stuart' was discovered to be an anagram of 'Claimes Arthurs Seate'.[5] Thus Elizabeth compensated for weaknesses in her genealog-ical narrative by inhabiting a providentially given state outside heredity, and James by casting himself as a father figure, the author rather than the benefi-ciary of heredity. Charles promoted the idea of a Stuart line by having Rubens paint an extravagant apotheosis of his father on the ceiling of the Banqueting House, but plans for an elaborate monument to James fell victim to Charles's selective parsimony, while Inigo Jones's idea for a Stuart mausoleum likewise remained unfulfilled.

Both the doctrine of the king's two bodies and the narrative of historical legitimation were violently fractured by the Civil War. The new republic tried to dispense with the body as an image of sovereignty; the seal of the Common-wealth showed on one side the House of Commons as an assembly of equal individuals, and on the other a map of England, Wales and Ireland where the land itself is given prominence, free from any stamp of monarchical owner-ship.[6] Under the Protectorate, however, seals, coins, medals, and charters show Cromwell in royal robes, with a laurel wreath as if he were a Roman emperor, or on horseback dominating the landscape. The ruler is once more pictorially manifest, while land and people lack any independent symbolic representation.[7]

During the 1650s rival constructions of both the private and the political body flourished. Hobbes's *Leviathan* rethought the idea of sovereignty by arguing for a body politic in which the sovereign incorporates the individuals' rights (as is displayed visually on the title page) and this arrangement is

[5] *Ben Jonson*, edited by C. H. Herford, Percy and Evelyn Simpson, 11 vols (Oxford, 1925–52), vii 323, 509.

[6] For monarchical control expressed through maps see Richard Helgerson, 'The Land Speaks: Cartography, Chorography, and Subversion in Renaissance England', *Representations*, 16 (1986) 51–85.

[7] For the iconography of the Commonwealth and Cromwell see Laura Lunger Knoppers, *Constructing Cromwell: Ceremony, Portrait, and Print, 1645–1661* (Cambridge, 2000).

validated by ostensibly emerging from an analysis of the body's physical needs and fears. Nor does Hobbes neglect to provide a legitimizing narrative, for he describes in quasi-historical terms how men move from a state of nature into one of security under the sovereign. Among the radicals we find Winstanley's myth of the Norman yoke and his accounts of both the mystical and the economic role of the body, and the Quakers' narratives of their personal spiritual life and their attempts to thwart the constraining social and political system by using the body symbolically – refusing to raise their hats, keeping silence, going naked for a sign. Ordinary women and men who had previously had no part other than a passive one in the discourse of power are now telling their own narratives and asserting their political freedom by using their bodies in ways which they themselves choose – through co-operative economic activity, free sex, silence, and nakedness. The body is being used to fashion alternatives to the prevailing discourse of power, and even to refute such notions of power altogether, simultaneously refusing both the political and the symbolic order.

These narrative and semiotic revolutions showed that the discourse promoted by the Stuart monarchy was only one language amongst many; no longer could it be seen as normative and natural. The mythology of Stuart kingship is revealed as a mythology, an ideological assertion which seeks to persuade rather than a declarative discourse which reveals what God has ordained. But the process of demythologizing is not a once-for-all gain; a deliberately reconstructed mythology can be just as powerful in its new form as it was in the old. Recently invented 'traditions' can command as much loyalty as old ones, particularly if they provide the reassurance of continuity and stability after some trauma. Besides, many people would have seen real mystical and legal continuity where we may see reinvention. The fact that the monarchy had to be reconstructed after 1660 does not mean that its hold on the people was necessarily weaker, merely that it had to reinvent ceremonies, traditions and iconographies while representing that reconstruction as an act of recovery and restoration.

Yet there is inevitably an element of stress in the fabrication of the second Stuart monarchy, and as Dryden said, looking back in 1694 at the culture of Charles II's reign, 'The second temple was not like the first'.[8] The most awkward element in the new edifice was the person of the king himself. The inscription on one of the arches erected for his coronation in 1661 hailed him as 'most blessed and most pious, most worthy of all the human race',[9] yet by the time that a poet in 1674 began some verses with the words 'Chaste, pious,

---

8   'To my Dear Friend Mr Congreve, On his Comedy called *The Double-Dealer*', 1. 14. For the implications of the image see Hammond, *Traces*, pp. 9–16.
9   John Ogilby, *The Entertainment of His Most Excellent Majestie Charles II, in His Passage through the City of London to his Coronation* (London, 1662), p. 31; my translation from the Latin.

prudent Charles the Second,'[10] every reader would recognize the irony. Irony began to attend every monarchical image – Charles the father of his people was the father of fourteen of them outside wedlock:

> The truest *Pater Patriae* ere was yet,
> For all, or most of's subjects, does beget.[11]

It was the actual character and public behaviour of the king which did much to undermine the reconstructed edifice of Stuart monarchy which his propagandists were building.

II

The reinvention of the Stuart monarchy entailed a rewriting of the past. The trial and execution of Charles I were restaged with different actors when the bodies of Bradshaw, Cromwell, and Ireton were exhumed and hanged at Tyburn, and their heads impaled above Westminster Hall for the duration of Charles II's reign. Along with this went the executions of the surviving regicides, which Charles himself watched. It was evidently important that vengeance, or justice, should be carried out upon the bodies of the republicans in order to reassert the control of the king over the body politic. Contemporary history was also rewritten through the construction of a new liturgical calendar which included services for the anniversaries of Charles I's execution and Charles II's return. The attempt to manipulate time and control memory is also seen in the royalist histories of the Civil War which appeared in the early 1660s[12] and the mockery of puritans and republicans on the stage.[13] Writers of panegyrics on the Restoration contemplated the inauguration of a new time which would blot out the past. Dryden in *Astraea Redux* says:

> And now time's whiter series is begun
> Which in soft centuries shall smoothly run;[14]

As the poem's title and epigraph make clear, this is also the return of a golden age: '*Iam Redit & Virgo, Redeunt Saturnia Regna*'. The rewriting of history, the purging of sacred, monarchical time from the taint of republicanism,[15] is most evident in the creation of the cult of Charles King and Martyr, through which

---

[10] *The History of Insipids*, l. 1, in *POAS*, i 243.

[11] *A Satyr upon the Mistresses*, ll. 16–17, in *The Roxburghe Ballads*, vol. 5, edited by J. W. Ebsworth (Hertford, 1885), 130.

[12] See Royce Macgillivray, *Restoration Historians and the Civil War* (The Hague, 1974).

[13] Robert D. Hume, *The Development of English Drama in the Late Seventeenth Century* (Oxford, 1976), pp. 239–40.

[14] Dryden, *Astraea Redux*, ll. 292–30.

[15] See Dryden's 'To His Sacred Majesty, A Panegyric on his Coronation', ll. 17–32.

the fallible human being (a convicted traitor in many eyes) is removed from the unseemly messiness of history into the eternity of martyrdom.

As for Charles II, the new king was virtually unknown to his people. Even the author of *The History of His Sacred Majesty* (1660) knew little about Charles's life in exile or his qualities as an individual.[16] Royalist pamphleteers attempted to allay public ignorance or unease with assurances that he was 'meek, gentle, sweet of behavior, lovely, amiable, firm, constant, obliging, modest, patient', 'valiant, chaste, temperate', and 'Religiously Devout'. He was also credited with a 'Physiognomy . . . something extraordinary above vulgar countenances . . . A Majesty in his very looks'.[17] The only historical narrative which could usefully be told about Charles was the story of his escape from the Battle of Worcester, but there were difficulties in telling this tale to Charles's advantage.[18] Much of the writing which greeted the return of Charles preferred to work with one of two typologies. In one, Charles was likened to Augustus, restoring peace, prosperity, and culture to a land blighted by civil war;[19] in the other he was like King David, the young king protected by God through years of trouble and exile, but restored at last to his kingdom.[20] The former appealed particularly to poets looking for a golden age of artistic achievement under enlightened patronage, the latter to clerics for whom this was one way of wresting from the radicals the language of divine guidance which had been so characteristic an idiom of the 1650s. Both typologies glorified Charles without being too specific, and by rewriting already established images of monarchy they suggested continuity; both also stabilized and occluded recent history by imposing a pattern upon contingency.[21] There is a marked preference for narratives of preservation and restoration rather than the elaboration of an iconography which could serve for a whole reign. More time is spent defending the naturalness of monarchy than elaborating the specific virtues of Charles, and we do not see the beginnings of a personalized iconography such as pertained to Elizabeth and James.

This is illustrated by the entertainments staged for Charles's coronation, as described by John Ogilby.[22] The triumphal entry into London astutely

---

16 Macgillivray, *Restoration Historians*, p. 49.

17 Quoted from Caroline Edie, 'The Popular Idea of Monarchy on the Eve of the Stuart Restoration', *Huntington Library Quarterly*, 39 (1975–6) 343–73, at pp. 347–8.

18 Harold Weber, 'Representations of the King: Charles II and his Escape from Worcester', *Studies in Philology*, 85 (1988) 489–509.

19 H. T. Swedenberg, 'England's Joy: *Astraea Redux* in its Setting', *Studies in Philology*, 50 (1953) 30–44; Howard Erskine-Hill, *The Augustan Idea in English Literature* (London, 1983), pp. 213–22.

20 Caroline Edie, 'Right Rejoicing: Sermons on the Occasion of the Stuart Restoration, 1660', *Bulletin of the John Rylands University Library of Manchester*, 62 (1979–80) 61–86.

21 For the use of typology see Steven N. Zwicker, *Dryden's Political Poetry: The Typology of King and Nation* (Providence, R.I., 1972).

22 See also Gerard Reedy, 'Mystical Politics: The Imagery of Charles II's Coronation', in *Studies*

repaired the mistake of Charles I, who had kept his coronation as private as possible, and drew upon the genuine popular enthusiasm which existed for the new king at the beginning of his reign. The coronation entry for Charles II emphasized the hopes which the kingdom had for itself rather than any specific glorification of Charles. The first arch shows monarchy triumphing over rebellion, the second celebrates the navy, the third concord, and the fourth plenty. Charles himself is twice represented on the first arch, once when he is shown landing at Dover, and again when he puts Usurpation to flight:

> The Painting over the Middle Arch represents the *King*, mounted in calm Motion, *USURPATION* flying before him, a Figure with many ill-favoured Heads, some bigger, some lesser, and one particularly shooting out of his Shoulder, like *CROMWEL'S*; Another Head upon his Rump, or Tayl.[23]

Republicans are reduced to this grotesque version of their bodies, and to being part of a trophy of decollated heads.

From Ogilby's account it is clear that defence of monarchy itself is the main object of this exercise. Just as there is little religious content to the arches (unlike those for Elizabeth's coronation, which stressed godly Protestant government) so too Ogilby prefers to find his authorization of the English monarchy in the Roman empire, justifying the details of each arch through elaborate citations from the Latin poets. The designation 'Divus' is accorded to James I and Charles I on the first arch because: 'The Title of *DIVUS* was constantly attributed by the *Romans* to their *Emperours* after their Consecration, or Ἀποθέωσις'. We are even told that 'they questioned not the Ἀποθέωσις even of the worst of their *Emperours*, as we see in . . . Verses of *Lucan* on *Nero*, that Prodigie of Nature',[24] which neatly – though perhaps ominously – avoids the question of the king's personal merit. Ogilby does not discuss how we are to understand the divinity accorded to Roman emperors, and here borrowed unblushingly for the Stuart kings, compared with the sacredness attributed to Charles under the theories of early Stuart kingship and symbolized by the ceremony performed in Westminster Abbey. This implication that Roman and English vocabularies are interchangeable raises the possibility that sacredness is just a politically necessary trope, an idea which could benefit from the reinforcement of Roman idiom because in English it no longer passes unquestioned.

But was this iconography effective? Pepys when describing the procession says nothing about its significance, and reports it only as a spectacle; he uses the word 'show' five times, and is chiefly interested in the dress of the participants. Eventually, he says, 'So glorious was the show with gold and silver, that

---

in Change and Revolution: Aspects of English Intellectual History 1640–1800, edited by Paul J. Korshin (Menston, 1972), pp. 19–42.

23 Ogilby, *The Entertainment*, p. 28.
24 Ogilby, *The Entertainment*, pp. 32, 35.

we were not able to look at it – our eyes at last being so much overcome with it.'[25] Evidently the conspicuous display of wealth was itself an effective demonstration of the power of the new monarchy; it dazzled, and that was enough.

III

But such official royal spectacle was not to be the dominant manner of Charles's public appearances. He preferred an informal style, and was often to be seen around Whitehall, sauntering with his dogs and courtiers in the royal parks, and at the theatre.[26] Subject to his subjects' gaze, Charles showed little interest in controlling public opinion through forms of spectacle which would display an iconic majesty. Sometimes this informality was politically astute, as when he lounged by the fire in the House of Lords, theoretically invisible but silently coercive. Yet this policy did make him vulnerable to the dramas which his subjects performed around him. In the theatre unscripted plays sometimes occurred:

> Mr. Pierce . . . tells me . . . how the King, coming the other day to his Theatre to see *The Indian Queene* . . . my Lady Castlemaine was in the next box before he came; and leaning over other ladies a while to whisper with the King, she ris out of that box and went into the King's and sat herself on the King's right hand between the King and the Duke of Yorke – which he swears put the King himself, as well as everybody else, out of countenance.[27]

The openness with which Charles conducted his sexual affairs gave a new significance to the idea of the king's body as an object of public interest.

Pepys's diary records the observations of one who was a loyal servant of the monarchy – and no prude – but who was shocked at the way in which Charles behaved. On 1 February 1663 Pepys recorded:

> This day Creed and I, walking in White-hall garden, did see the King coming privately from my Lady Castlemaynes; which is a poor thing for a Prince to do. And I expressed my sense of it to Creed in termes which I should not have done, but that I believe he is trusty in that point.[28]

We do not know what the terms were in which Pepys spoke unguardedly about

---

[25] *Diary of Samuel Pepys*, ii 83.

[26] The contribution which the theatre made to public understanding of the links between royal sexuality and political power is beyond the scope of this chapter, but see Derek Hughes, *Dryden's Heroic Plays* (Basingstoke, 1981), Susan Staves, *Players' Scepters: Fictions of Authority in the Restoration* (Lincoln, Nebr., 1979), and Susan J. Owen, *Restoration Theatre and Crisis* (Oxford, 1996).

[27] *Diary of Samuel Pepys*, v 33.

[28] *Diary of Samuel Pepys*, iv 30–1.

Charles, but he evidently thought that Creed would concur. Most of the entries in which Pepys comments on Charles's sexual behaviour are reports of conversations, forming a partial record of the opinions of various disgruntled observers. Sir Thomas Crew told Pepys that 'the King doth mind nothing but pleasures and hates the very sight or thoughts of business. That my Lady Castlemayne rules him; who he says hath all the tricks of Aretin that are to be practised to give pleasure – in which he is too able, hav[ing] a large ———'.[29] Thomas Povey, the Treasurer for Tangier, told Pepys what Charles preferred doing in bed: 'The King doth spend most of his time in feeling and kissing them naked all over their bodies in bed – and contents himself, without doing the other thing but as he finds himself inclined'.[30]

It is in the crisis years of 1666–7 that Pepys's diary records the most damning criticisms of Charles. In 1666 he notes a conversation with the banker John Colvill about 'the viciousness of the Court' and 'the contempt the King brings himself into thereby', and how the king has begun to bed Frances Stuart. He also reports from the naval surgeon James Pearse an anecdote which was already second-hand via Abraham Cowley: Thomas Killigrew had told the king about a talented but lazy man called Charles Stuart 'who now spends his time in imploying his lips and his prick about the Court, and hath no other imployment'.[31] The following year Pepys again discussed with Povey the king's 'horrid effeminacy'[32] (that is, his enslavement to women), and on another occasion heard from him an account of a great row at court:

> It seems she [Castlemaine] is with child, and the King says he did not get it; with that, she made a slighting 'puh!' with her mouth and went out of the house, and never came in again till the King went to Sir Dan. Harvy's to pray her; and so she is come today – when one would think his mind should be full of some other cares, having but this morning broken up such a Parliament, with so much discontent and so many wants upon him, and but yesterday heard such a sermon against adultery. But it seems she hath told the King that whoever did get it, he should own it; and the bottom of the quarrel is this: she is fallen in love with young Jermin, who hath of late lain with her oftener then the King and is now going to marry my Lady Falmouth. The King, he is mad at her entertaining Jermin, and she is mad at Jermin's going to marry from her, so they are all mad; and thus the kingdom is governed.[33]

When, in the last weeks of Charles's life, Evelyn observed a 'scene of luxurious dallying and prophanesse' he recorded it retrospectively as an emblem of vanity:

---

29 *Diary of Samuel Pepys*, iv 136–7.
30 *Diary of Samuel Pepys*, vi 267.
31 *Diary of Samuel Pepys*, vii 323–4, 400.
32 *Diary of Samuel Pepys*, viii 288.
33 *Diary of Samuel Pepys*, viii 366; cp. 355.

the King, sitting & toying with his Concubines Portsmouth, Cleaveland, & Mazarine: &c: A french boy singing love songs, in that glorious Gallery, whilst about 20 of the greate Courtiers & other dissolute persons were at Basset round a large table, a bank of at least 2000 in Gold before them, upon which two Gent: that were with me made reflexions with astonishment, it being a sceane of uttmost vanity; and surely as they thought would never have an End: six days after was all in the dust.[34]

It is clear that Charles was content to display himself publicly as a sexually active male. There was no attempt to preserve dignity around the physical presence of the king, for Charles scorned the elaborate ceremonies of the French and Spanish courts which were designed to preserve a mystique around even the monarch's most mundane activities, as Pepys noted: 'the King did speak most in contempt of the ceremoniousnesse of the King of Spain, that he doth nothing but under some ridiculous form or other; and will not piss but another must hold the chamber-pot'.[35] This tended to dispel any aura which might have surrounded him, and also laid the king open to the commentary of others. Whether they saw his activities as material for gossip or for moralizing, the initiative, the control of the means of representation, passed from the monarch to his subjects. Pepys, Evelyn and their friends were conservative royalists whose comments are imbued with a sense of what should properly belong to the monarchy and to royal spectacle. Evelyn shapes his comment into an emblem of the vanity of human wishes, while Pepys maintains a verbal decorum even in the privacy of his diary through such polite evasions as 'a large ——' or 'doing the other thing'. But when those whose political beliefs made them suspicious of or hostile to the monarchy began to produce their representations of the king, all decorum was discarded.

Even if Charles and his ministers had wished to, they were unable to impose a totalizing discourse upon the country. The old republicanism survived, and religious dissent flourished. From the beginning of the reign dissenting voices were heard, and writers such as Milton and Bunyan developed their own coded ways of representing kingly power. Their readers accordingly became adept at ingenious interpretation, deploying an independent, radical, and sceptical hermeneutics which is skilled at irony and reversal. The sympathetic reader of *Paradise Lost* or *The Holy War* finds traditional images of monarchy made oppressive and even diabolical. Nor were such writers and readers only to be found skulking in rural conventicles; the radicalism of Londoners may have been in abeyance during the early 1660s, but it would not long lie dormant. It is several years before overt criticism of the king becomes widespread, but opposition to him couched in specifically personal terms is found even before the Restoration. Richard L. Greaves has collected some examples:

[34] *The Diary of John Evelyn*, edited by E. S. de Beer (Oxford, 1959), p. 791.
[35] *Diary of Samuel Pepys*, vii 201.

it was frequently alleged that Charles was a bastard, the son of Henrietta Maria ('the Great Whore of Babylon') and Henry Jermyn; he was also accused of incest with his mother. A Newcastle woman hoped to see his bones hanging from a horse's tail and the dogs running through his 'puddins'; one Londoner looked forward to washing his hands in the king's blood. An ex-Cromwellian officer boasted that 'he would have his head off, and cut him as small as herbs in a pot', while another man thought that Charles should be whipped to London where his skin should be 'pulled over his Eares'. One man demanded that Charles be hanged, and when a woman objected he retorted: 'Did you anoint him, did you take up your Coates & pisse upon his head to Anoynt him?'[36] This idiom is a popular appropriation and reversal of the two key elements in the royalist rhetoric of legitimation, the hereditary principle and the sacredness of the king's person.

IV

It seems to have been the sequence of disasters from 1665 to 1667 – the plague, the fire, and the Dutch War – which loosened the tongues of the disenchanted. A number of nonconformist tracts had prophesied that the year 1666 would bring about divine retribution on the court,[37] and this was the moment when verse satires on the government began to circulate. These poems are almost without parallel in England: though some manuscript satires had hinted at James I's homosexual interests,[38] there is no precedent for such a sustained attack on the person of the king. With only occasional exceptions these verses circulated in manuscript rather than in print, passing from hand to hand between friends, or around the so-called 'treason table' in the coffee houses. The composition and circulation of such poems was dangerous, so the authorship of most of them naturally remains obscure. The circulation of personal satires against Charles was a factor in the convictions of Robert Julian (fined one hundred marks and pilloried) and Stephen College (executed), while Sir John Coventry had his nose slit by the king's thugs for a much milder remark than anything found in these verses. The poems themselves show an awareness of such dangers: the *Last Instructions to a Painter* (1667) says, 'Blame not the

---

36 Richard L. Greaves, *Deliver Us from Evil: The Radical Underground in Britain, 1660–1663* (New York, 1986), pp. 22–4; see also Tim Harris, *London Crowds in the Reign of Charles II: Propaganda and Politics from the Restoration until the Exclusion Crisis* (Cambridge, 1987), pp. 50–1, 78–9, 162.

37 See Michael McKeon, *Politics and Poetry in Restoration England: The Case of Dryden's 'Annus Mirabilis'* (Cambridge, Mass., 1975), pp. 190–204.

38 For contemporary discussions of James's sexuality, including MSS poems, see Paul Hammond, *Figuring Sex between Men from Shakespeare to Rochester* (Oxford, 2002), pp. 128–50, and for the wider context of oppositional satire in the reigns of James I and Charles I see Andrew McRae, *Literature, Satire and the Early Stuart State* (Cambridge, 2004).

Muse that brought those spots to sight', while the author of the *Third Advice to a Painter* (1666) compares himself with Philomel, who was raped and had her tongue cut out to prevent her speaking of the crime.[39]

Besides facing the physical dangers of oppositional speech, each writer had to confront the question of whether the ordinary person had any authority to pass judgement on his king. Many of these poems are therefore concerned to find ways of legitimizing their speech, of empowering their own representation of Charles and their appropriation and travesty of the official symbolism. The first major oppositional poems take up the 'Advice to a Painter' form, which had begun in English with Waller's royalist celebration of the Dutch War in his *Instructions to a Painter* (1665).[40] Here a painter is being given directions for the representation of England's naval glory, and the form includes a series of portraits. This mode was easily adapted to the satirical portraiture of incompetent commanders and venal courtiers, but for a while writers held back from criticizing the king directly. Waller's poem ended with a direct address to the king which is imitated in many of the rejoinders. Initially we hear the voice of sober complaint to the king about the fools and parasites who are preventing his true glory from becoming apparent:

> Imperial Prince, King of the seas and isles,
> Dear object of our joys and Heaven's smiles:
> What boots it that thy light does gild our days
> And we lie basking in thy milder rays,
> While swarms of insects, from thy warmth begun,
> Our land devour and intercept our sun?[41]

The *Last Instructions to a Painter* makes its final portrait that of Charles, seen at dead of night in his bedchamber, haunted by the ghostly apparition of an England gagged and blindfolded. The poet's audacity in representing the king at all requires an explanation:

> So his bold tube man to the sun appli'd
> And spots unknown to the bright star descri'd,
> Show'd they obscure him while too near they prease,
> And seem his courtiers, but are his disease.[42]

Moreover, this is said to be the last occasion on which poet or painter will have

---

[39] *Last Instructions to a Painter*, l. 957, *POAS*, i 138; *Third Advice to a Painter*, ll. 451–6, *POAS*, i 87. Charles in *The King's Vows* threatens to cut off the nose of any opponent (l. 41, *POAS*, i 161), while the horses are aware of the dangers of speech in *A Dialogue Between the Two Horses* (ll. 97–105, *POAS*, i 280). Some MSS omit the more dangerous passages, e.g. ll. 129–36 of the *Fourth Advice to a Painter*, comparing Charles with Nero (*POAS*, i 146, 454).
[40] *POAS*, i 20–33.
[41] *Second Advice to a Painter*, ll. 345–50, *POAS*, i 52.
[42] *Last Instructions to a Painter*, ll. 949–52, *POAS*, i 138.

to carry the burden of representation, for the reformation of government on which the chastened king is embarking will demand no less than a royal hand to represent it:

> But this great work is for our Monarch fit,
> And henceforth Charles only to Charles shall sit.
> His master-hand the ancients shall outdo,
> Himself the painter and the poet too.[43]

The *Fifth Advice to a Painter* suggests that interpretation of Charles's political aims is a problem, and ends with a blank space in the picture which is implicitly reserved for the king:

> Stay, Painter! now look, here's below a space;
> I'th'bottom of all this, what shall we place?
> Shall it be Pope, or Turk, or prince, or nun?
> Let the resolve write *nescio*. So have done.[44]

Whatever hopes for reform these writers may have entertained (albeit, perhaps, only rhetorically), they were not realized, and the poems of the 1670s and early 1680s become much more outspoken. Accordingly their strategies of empowerment are more prominent and less apologetic. Authoritative speakers are introduced to voice the protests – Britannia, Raleigh, Marvell's ghost, Sir Edmund Berry Godfrey's ghost, and the two horses from the equestrian statues of Charles I and Charles II. The king himself is made the speaker of some of these poems (*The King's Vows, A New Ballad, A Raree Show*, and *Old Rowley the King*),[45] which is the ultimate appropriation of royal authority. In these ways the Englishman is trying to assert his own voice and avoid being reduced to the condition of the ducks who quack Charles's praise in *The King's Vows*:

> I will have a fine pond and a pretty decoy
> Where the ducks and the drakes may their freedoms enjoy
> And quack in their language still, "Vive le Roy!"[46]

So how could Charles appropriately be represented? Several writers turned to the unfortunate statue of Charles II on horseback which had been erected by Sir Robert Viner; it had originally represented Jan Sobieski, King of Poland, trampling a Turk, and had been converted to show Charles trampling Cromwell.[47] It seems exemplary of the predicament of Carolean iconography that

---

[43] *Last Instructions to a Painter*, ll. 945–8, *POAS*, i 138.
[44] *Fifth Advice to a Painter*, ll. 143–6, *POAS*, i 152.
[45] *POAS*, i 159–62; *POAS*, ii 176–9; *POAS*, ii 425–31; *POAS*, iii 478–83.
[46] *The King's Vows*, ll. 52–4, *POAS*, i 162.
[47] *POAS*, i 266–83.

this image of imperial authority should be second-hand, and so botched in the making that the fissures in its construction and the ungainliness of the resulting image invited ridicule rather than respect. A number of poems tackle the problem of the king's identity by casting him as some kind of player:

> No tumbling play'r so oft e'er changed his shape
> As this goat, fox, wolf, timorous French ape.[48]

One compares him with the actor who was currently playing Scaramouche at Whitehall; another has him cuckolding a scrivener in masquerade.[49] In another Charles confesses that he is Sir Martin Mar-all, the conceited and incompetent figure in Dryden's play whose folly spoils all the strategems devised on his behalf by his cleverer servants.[50] He is a changeling Louis; he acts Agathocles the Sicilian tyrant;[51] he acts the Turk:

> I will have a fine tunic, a sash, and a vest,
> Though not rule like a Turk, yet I will be so dress'd,
> And who knows but the mode may soon bring in the rest?[52]

Charles's actorly assumption of Turkish costume may lead to a Turkish tyranny. And by his side players like Nell Gwyn act the part of queens.[53]

In these images of the king as actor the poets show Charles not as a masquer taking part in the carefully scripted drama of state power, but as a private man whose inscrutable political aims and overt promiscuity are rewriting the king's traditional role.[54] The poems are full of examples of the confusion of public and private. The only heroic exploits which interest him are those of the bedchamber, as we see from the Latin inscription said to have been written there:

> Bella fugis, bellas sequeris, belloque repugnas,
>   et bellatori sunt tibi bella tori;
> imbelles imbellis amas, audaxque videris
>   Mars ad opus Veneris, Martis ad arma Venus.[55]

---

48 *Oceana and Britannia*, ll. 19–20, POAS, ii 396.
49 *The Statue at Charing Cross*, ll. 5–8, POAS, i 270; *A Dialogue Between the Two Horses*, ll. 110–14, POAS, i 280.
50 *A New Ballad*, l. 44, POAS, ii 178.
51 *Oceana and Britannia*, ll. 26, POAS, ii 397.
52 *The King's Vows*, ll. 49–51, POAS, i 162.
53 *Nostradamus' Prophecy*, ll. 15–16, POAS, i 187.
54 For a wider discussion of the links between sexuality and politics in this period see James Grantham Turner, *Libertines and Radicals in Early Modern London: Sexuality, Politics and Literary Culture, 1630–1685* (Cambridge, 2002).
55 'You shun battles and chase beauties, hate what is warlike and make your wars in bed. Being fond of peace you love the weak. You seem like bold Mars only in the works of Venus, but like Venus in the arms of Mars'; *Fifth Advice to a Painter*, ll. 153–6, POAS, i 152.

When the nude allegorical figure of England appears one night to reproach him, he assumes that she is there for his sexual pleasure.[56] The king's own sexual body is exhibited by these poets to indicate how the private body has tyrannized over the body politic. Rochester, notoriously, wrote that:

> His scepter and his p—k are of a length;
> And she may sway the one who plays with t'other.[57]

Another writer concurred:

> —— and Scepter are about a length,
> In thy hot —— lies thy wit and strength.[58]

Others wrote of his impotence,[59] added innuendoes of homosexual behaviour,[60] and commented on how he was reduced to sharing his mistresses with other men:

> Alas! I never got one brat alone,
> My bitches are by ev'ry fop well known,
> And I still willing all their whelps to own.[61]

Charles was said to squander his semen, fathering a degenerate line:

> How poorly squander'st thou thy seed away,
> Which should get kings for nations to obey!
> But thou, poor Prince, so uselessly hast sown it,
> That the Creation is asham'd to own it.
> Witness the royal line sprung from the belly
> Of thine anointed Princess, Madam Nelly.[62]

As well as creating a grotesque parody of hereditary kingship, Charles swears parodic oaths; he

> . . . would swear by Carwell's c— he'd do it,
> And by the contents of the oath he took,
> Kneel down in zeal and kiss the book.[63]

---

[56] *Last Instructions to a Painter*, ll. 889–904, *POAS*, i 136.

[57] *The Earl of Rochester's Verses for which he was Banished*, ll. 11–12, *POAS*, i 424.

[58] *A Satyr upon the Mistresses*, ll. 18–19, *Roxburghe Ballads*, v 130.

[59] *Fourth Advice to a Painter*, l. 136, *POAS*, i 146.

[60] *A Song*, l. 14, *POAS*, ii 110, on Danby lying with Charles. Evidence was given in court in 1680 that Titus Oates had said that 'the King had kissed Mr. *Cheffins* his Tool' (*An Exact and Faithful Narrative of the Horrid Conspiracy of Thomas Knox, William Osborne, and John Lane* (London, 1680), p. 8).

[61] *The King's Answer*, ll. 23–5, *POAS*, i 256; cp. *A Satire in Answer to a Friend*, l. 89, *POAS*, iii 32.

[62] *Satire*, ll. 19–24, *POAS*, i 426.

[63] *The Royal Buss*, ll. 14–16, *POAS*, i 264; cp. *Posted upon the House of Commons' Door*, ll. 1–4, *POAS*, ii 344.

Charles himself travesties the principles of the king's sacred person and the hereditary succession.

These writers even envisage an alternative kind of royal spectacle. Sexual intercourse becomes a public royal performance. In *Colin* there is a competition to find a successor to the Duchess of Portsmouth,[64] while the *Satyr on the Court Mistresses* seems to envisage a public exhibition of intercourse between Charles and Portsmouth,

> Where all stood by, as on a Bridal night,
> Spectators of this present dear delight;
> And swore by ——— that he had passed the Test
> Of all his Empire to have swived the best.[65]

The two most notorious depictions of royal sex as public spectacle do not refer directly to Charles, but cannot avoid alluding to his behaviour. In *Sardanapalus* John Oldham depicts the Assyrian monarch choosing to die in an unusual form of royal ceremonial:

> . . . on glorious Bed of State,
> A Princely Maid for thy approach did wait:
>   Stretch'd out the willing Virgin lay, unbound,
> Ready from thy kind Stroke to meet the gentle Wound.
> An hundred more on the Surrounding Beds lay by,
>   All gallant Vent'rers in thy Destiny:
>   And of thy Race as many Princes too,
> T'attend thy Fate, their Loyalty and Duty show.
>   By Order now, at the loud Trumpet's call,
>   The starting Pr—ks at once strive for the Goal;
> All press, all act, what ever mortal Strength can do,
>   But none their mighty Soveraign outgo.[66]

Sardanapalus then gives the order for the palace to be fired. In the play *Sodom* King Bolloxinian rules his country entirely according to sexual whims, and his court engages in all manner of erotic display. The king makes clear the principles upon which he governs:

> Thus in the Zenith of my lust I reigne:
> I eat to swiue & Swiue to eat againe.
> Let other Monarchs who their Scepters beare
> To keepe their subjects lesse in loue then feare
> Bee slaues to Crownes, my nation shall be free:
> My Pintle onely shall my scepter bee.

---

[64] *POAS*, ii 167–75.

[65] *A Satyr upon the Mistresses*, ll. 36–9, *Roxburghe Ballads*, v 130.

[66] *Sardanapalus*, ll. 152–63, in *The Poems of John Oldham*, edited by Harold F. Brooks and Raman Selden (Oxford, 1987), pp. 349–50.

> My laws shall Act more pleasures then Comand
> And with my Prick I'le gouerne all the land.[67]

But no nation can be free which is governed in this way, as we see when the king commands his subjects to engage in sodomy. One could not extract a very sophisticated political message from this particular work,[68] but it is at least symptomatic of a general concern in the 1670s that Charles's private sexual obsessions are becoming a form of tyranny over the body politic.

The travestying of the king's body is a deliberate and calculated strategy which goes along with denunciations of the idea that the king is godlike or rules by divine right. There are ironic inflations of the Stuart claim to be God's deputy on earth when Charles is called 'his godship', and 'a god incarnate'.[69] He is vicegerent to Moloch.[70] To him no oaths or sacraments are sacred,[71] and far from having a divine gift to cure the King's Evil, Charles is himself the author of a disease in the body politic:

> The royal evil so malignant grows,
> Nothing the dire contagion can oppose.[72]

The two horses from the equestrian statues are outraged

> To see *Dei Gratia* writ on the Throne,
> And the King's wicked life say, God there is none.
> That he should be styl'd Defender o' th' Faith,
> Who believes not a word the word of God saith.[73]

The writer of *The History of Insipids* explicitly attacks the idea that kings like Charles and Louis reign by divine right:

> To think such kings, Lord, reign by thee
> Were most prodigious blasphemy. . . .
> If such kings be by God appointed,
> The Devil is then the Lord's annointed.[74]

The idea of divine right is, according to several writers, merely something devised by priests in the pay of the monarchy.[75] In place of Christian worship,

---

[67] *Works of John Wilmot*, p. 303.
[68] For the politics of *Sodom* see *Works of John Wilmot*, p. 497.
[69] *Flatfoot the Gudgeon Taker*, ll. 5–9, *POAS*, ii 190; *An Ironical Satire*, l. 4, *POAS*, ii 200.
[70] *An Historical Poem*, l. 81, *POAS*, ii 159.
[71] *Marvell's Ghost*, l. 29, *POAS*, i 286.
[72] *An Historical Poem*, ll. 130–1, *POAS*, ii 161.
[73] *A Dialogue Between the Two Horses*, ll. 43–6, *POAS*, i 277.
[74] *The History of Insipids*, ll. 149–56, *POAS*, i 250–1.
[75] *Britannia and Raleigh*, ll. 85–93, *POAS*, i 232; *Sir Edmund Berry Godfrey's Ghost*, ll. 92–5, *POAS*, ii 11; and, most outspokenly, *An Historical Poem*, ll. 82–111, *POAS*, ii 159–60.

Charles and his court indulge in the cult of Priapus;[76] this is how the court appears to a visiting countryman:

> 'Behold,' says he, 'the fountain of our woe,
> From whence our vices and our ruins flow.
> Here parents their own offspring prostitute,
> By such vile arts t'obtain some viler suit.
> Here blooming youth adore Priapus' shrine,
> And priests pronounce him sacred and divine.
> The goatish god behold in his alcove,
> The secret scene of damn'd incestuous love;
> Melting in lust, and drunk like Lot he lies
> Between two bright daughter divinities.'[77]

Charles's behaviour has become a travesty of the very idea of a divinely instituted monarchy, a blasphemous parody of its own legitimizing rhetoric.

It is clear that the kind of government which Charles practises is thought of as tyrannical. In *Britannia and Raleigh* a figure representing absolutist France advises Charles that

> 'Tis royal game whole kingdoms to deflower,
> Three spotless virgins to your bed I bring,
> A sacrifice to you, their god and King.

Absolutist monarchy performs a rape of three virgin kingdoms.[78] The body politic is corrupted by tyranny:

> If this imperial oil once taint the blood,
> It's by no potent antidote withstood,
> Tyrants, like lep'rous kings, for public weal
> Must be immur'd, lest their contagion steal
> Over the whole.

The poem goes on to question the other main element in Stuart rhetoric, the claim to historical continuity:

> Th' elect of Jessean line
> To this firm law their scepter did resign.
> And shall this stinking Scottish brood evade
> Eternal laws, by God for mankind made?[79]

---

[76] *A Satyr upon the Mistresses*, ll. 48–9, *Roxburghe Ballads*, v 131; *An Historical Poem*, l. 64, *POAS*, ii 158.

[77] *Hodge*, ll. 36–45, *POAS*, ii 147.

[78] For rape as a political trope in the drama, see Owen, *Restoration Theatre and Crisis*, pp. 174–6, 231–2.

[79] *Britannia and Raleigh*, ll. 99–101, 147–54, *POAS*, i 232, 234.

This is not the only poem to denounce the whole line of Stuarts, and several invoke Elizabeth as a lost ideal of Protestant monarchy. *Marvell's Ghost* alleges that the Stuart kings come from an illicit sexual union anyway, and relates this prophecy which the ghost has seen in the book of fate:

> A wanton fiddler shall be led
> By Fate to stain his master's bed,
> From whence a spurious race shall grow
> Design'd for Britain's overthrow.[80]

The poem concludes with the warning that England must take decisive action to rid herself of the Stuarts; eventually she will

> to those resentments come
> That drove the Tarquins out of Rome,
> Or such as did in fury turn
> Th' Assyrian's palace to his urn.[81]

As this illustrates, these oppositional poems deploy many examples from Roman history which replace the Augustan myth of stability and culture with an alternative one of tyranny and decadence. Tarquin was a particularly apposite example,[82] since he was the last of the Roman kings and was expelled for his murderous lust, but Charles is also compared to Nero:

> As Nero once, with harp in hand, survey'd
> His flaming Rome and, as that burn'd, he play'd,
> So our great Prince, when the Dutch fleet arriv'd,
> Saw his ships burn'd and, as they burn'd, he swiv'd.
> So kind he was in our extremest need,
> He would those flames extinguish with his seed.
> But against Fate all human aid is vain:
> His pr— then prov'd as useless as his chain.[83]

Other poems compare Charles with Commodus, Heliogabalus, Tiberius and Domitian. He is like Caesar, but only in the fate which he deserves. Several writers besides Oldham saw Charles as Sardanapalus, made weak and ridiculous by his abject pursuit of women.[84]

---

[80] *A Dialogue Between the Two Horses*, ll. 149–50, *POAS*, i 281; cp. *Britannia and Raleigh*, ll. 42–7, *POAS*, i 231.

[81] *Marvell's Ghost*, ll. 9–12, 43–6, *POAS*, i 285–6.

[82] For Tarquin see *Britannia and Raleigh*, l. 180, *POAS*, i 236; *Sir Edmund Berry Godfrey's Ghost*, ll. 84–9, *POAS*, ii 10–11; *A Satyr upon the Mistresses*, ll. 20–1, *Roxburghe Ballads*, v 130.

[83] *Fourth Advice to a Painter*, ll. 129–36, *POAS*, i 146; for Nero cp. *Britannia and Raleigh*, l. 172, *POAS*, i 235; *Marvell's Ghost*, l. 28, *POAS*, i 286; *Satire*, l. 74, *POAS*, i 428; *Oceana and Britannia*, l. 25, *POAS*, ii 397.

[84] Commodus: *Further Advice to a Painter*, ll. 3–4, *POAS*, i 164; Heliogabalus: *Satire*, l. 71, *POAS*, i 427; Tiberius: *An Historical Poem*, l. 67, *POAS*, i 158; Domitian: *Flatfoot the Gudgeon Taker*, ll.

The Making of Restoration Poetic Culture

There was also a flourishing strain of animal imagery. No longer the British lion, Charles is merely a goat, and provides no protection for the country against the predatory ambitions of Louis XIV, who is variously figured as a lion or wolf.[85] The fable of the frogs and the crane is often employed; the English people who once prayed to God for a king now regret it:

> Too late the frogs, grown weary of their crane,
> Shall beg of Jove to take him back again.[86]

Sometimes Charles is the inert log in this fable, while his brother James is the devouring crane.

Of all these poems the one which caused the greatest stir was *A Raree Show*, attributed to Stephen College, which analyses the aims and machinations of Charles the politician more directly than most other pieces.[87] The ballad is accompanied by an engraving which seems to be the only surviving satirical representation of Charles in visual form.[88] In it he is depicted as a travelling showman, dressed in a coat which is embroidered with faces, alluding to the image of the sovereign in the frontispiece to *Leviathan*; on his back is a box in which he carries parliament around – in this case to Oxford. Charles has two faces: one says 'A Ra-ree Showe' and the other 'Ra-ree Shite's'; the second face is blowing bubbles, signifying the emptiness of his words. In the second half of the image Charles is stuck in the mire and pulled down by three officers of parliament, while parliament is rescued from the box and the Church of England stuffed in instead. Part of the ballad is spoken by the king himself as 'Leviathan', who confesses jauntily to his absolutist aims:

> Two states in blind house pent
> Make brave strong government.

7–8, *POAS*, ii 190; Caesar: *Britannia and Raleigh*, l. 180, *POAS*, i 236; Sardanapalus: *Britannia and Raleigh*, ll. 119–20, *POAS*, i 233; *A Dialogue Between the Two Horses*, l. 134, *POAS*, i 281; *Marvell's Ghost*, l. 46, *POAS*, i 286; *Sir Edmund Berry Godfrey's Ghost*, ll. 76–83, *POAS*, ii 10; and see J. H. O'Neill, 'Oldham's "Sardanapalus": a Restoration Mock-encomium and its Topical Implications', *Clio*, 5 (1976) 193–210.

85 *The History of Insipids*, l. 145, *POAS*, i 250; *A Dialogue Between the Two Horses*, ll. 131–2, *POAS*, i 281; *Oceana and Britannia*, l. 20, *POAS*, ii 396.

86 *Nostradamus' Prophecy*, ll. 49–50, *POAS*, i 189; cp. *The History of Insipids*, ll. 167–8, *POAS*, i 251; *A Dialogue Between the Two Horses*, l. 144, *POAS*, i 281; *The Rabble*, ll. 14–16, *POAS*, ii 343.

87 *POAS*, ii 425–31; see also B. J. Rahn, '*A Ra-ree Show* – A Rare Cartoon: Revolutionary Propaganda in the Treason Trial of Stephen College', in Korshin (ed.), *Studies in Change*, pp. 78–98; and M. D. George, *English Political Caricature to 1792* (Oxford, 1959), pp. 56–7.

88 The Dutch published caricatures of Charles, but apparently none have survived. Pepys was told 'how in Holland publicly they have pictured our King with reproach. One way is with his pockets turned the wrong side outward, hanging out empty – another, with two courtiers picking of his pocket – and a third, leading of two ladies, while others abuse him' (*Diary of Samuel Pepys*, iv 400).

126

The other speaker is the Sargeant-at-Arms, Topham, who refers to Charles as 'child of heathen Hobbes' and warns him:

> And popularity, with a hey, with a hey,
> Adds power to majesty, with a ho;
> But Dom. Com. in little ease
> Will all the world displease.

But by the time that this ballad was circulated in 1681 there was little prospect of Charles courting popularity, and all too many signs that he would rely upon power alone.

In these poems the mythology and iconography of the Stuart monarchy are clearly seen as something which is an ideological construct, a politically convenient fiction propagated by the king's priests and poets which must be appropriated and rewritten in the interest of English freedoms. It is not altogether possible to categorize these pieces as 'Whig': some, notably the 'Advice to a Painter' poems, predate the coalescing of the Whig opposition by up to a decade, while others seem to be outraged by Charles's desecration of their own cherished ideal of kingship. But the arguments and rhetorical strategies of these poems do relate to those of the prose pamphlets which the Whigs were producing in the late 1670s and early 1680s.[89] Most of those tracts tend to avoid the problem of the person of the king, and concentrate instead upon the rights of the subject, employing the vocabulary of law, liberty, and property. This establishes a countervailing position from which to speak, insisting that the subject has rights over his body and his property, and that his relations with his sovereign are governed by law. The king's authority is conferred by and subject to the law, rather than mystically donated by God himself.

Shaftesbury made a specific rebuttal of the theory of divine right in a speech to the House of Lords in 1675:

> there is another Principle got into the World, my Lords, that hath not been long there; for Arch-Bishop *Laud* was the first Author that I remember of it: And I cannot find, that the Jesuits, or indeed the Popish Clergy hath ever own'd it, but some of the Episcopal Clergy of our *British Isles*; and 'tis withal, as 'tis new, so the most dangerous destructive Doctrine to our Government and Law, that ever was. 'Tis the first of the Cannons published by the Convocation, 1640, *That Monarchy is of Divine Right*. This Doctrine was then preached up, and maintained by Sibthorp, *Manwaring*, and others; and of later years, by a Book published by Dr. *Sanderson, Bishop of Lincoln*, under the name of *Arch-Bishop Usher*; and how much it is spread amongst our Dignified Clergy, is very easily known. We all agree, *That the King and His Government, is to be obeyed for Conscience sake*; and that the Divine Precepts, require not only here, but in all parts of the World, *Obedience to Lawful Governours*. But that this Family are our

---

[89] Whig propaganda is analysed best in Harris, *London Crowds*, and in Richard Ashcraft, *Revolutionary Politics and Locke's 'Two Treatises of Government'* (Princeton, 1986).

Kings, and this particular frame of Government, is our lawful Constitution, and obliges us, is owing only to the particular Laws of our Country.[90]

Here the mythologizing activity of the Stuart monarchy is laid bare. God may have ordained obedience to our rulers, but he has not prescribed who those rulers should be: that England is ruled by the Stuarts depends on English law, not divine decree. It is self-interest which has promoted that doctrine, and the origin and development of the idea can be traced to named individuals and a particular historical moment. By showing how, when, and why the idea of divine right was constructed, Shaftesbury has made a deft and effective deconstruction of the ideology through which the Stuarts governed.

V

The response which Charles's ideologues made to these challenges was to reassert the mythology all the more vigorously. In the late 1670s and the early 1680s a large number of sermons, pamphlets, and treatises repeat in uncompromising terms the main elements in the Stuart theory of divine right.

First, the power of patriarchy was reasserted. The publication of Filmer's *Patriarcha* in 1680 exemplifies the reactionary invention of a tradition, for not only is Filmer's treatise disinterred some forty years after its composition, but the version of patriarchy which it offers is peculiarly literal-minded. Since Adam had control over his children, all succeeding parents have authority over theirs:

> creation made man Prince of his posterity. And indeed not only Adam, but the succeeding Patriarchs had, by right of fatherhood, royal authority over their children . . . For as Adam was lord of his children, so his children under him had a command over their own children, but still with subordination to the first parent . . . And this subordination of children is the fountain of all royal authority, by the ordination of God himself.[91]

Even Filmer realizes that there are possible objections to this:

> It may seem absurd to maintain that Kings now are the fathers of their people, since experience shows the contrary. It is true, all Kings be not the natural parents of their subjects, yet they all either are, or are to be reputed, as the next heirs of those progenitors who were at first the natural parents of the whole people, and in their right succeed to the exercise of supreme jurisdiction.[92]

---

90 *Two Speeches. I. The Earl of Shaftsbury's Speech in the House of Lords, the 20th of October, 1675* . . . (Amsterdam, 1675), pp. 10–11.

91 Sir Robert Filmer, *Patriarcha and Other Political Works,* edited by Peter Laslett (Oxford, 1949), p. 57.

92 Filmer, *Patriarcha,* pp. 60–1.

As the tell-tale phrase 'or are to be reputed' indicates, this whole edifice is clearly a mythologized version of history, and fuses uneasily the assertion of biological genealogical continuity with the persuasive metaphor of fatherly control. Filmer was not alone in his invocation of Adamic government, however, and other writers contributed to this myth of origins, according to which subordination reaches back as far as Adam and Eve, and patriarchal control begins with the beginning of the human race.[93] The king who is located within this tradition is at once the physical and the political heir of Adam; political power is associated inalienably with biological inheritance.

This reassertion of patriarchy is therefore linked with an insistence upon the absolute indefeasibility of the hereditary principle. The history of the succession in England is interpreted to show that behind the actual history there is an ideal history, a God-given line of succession which cannot be broken. John Brydall argued that the powers of the crown are essential, inherent, and cannot be transferred or delegated to others; nor can the correct line of succession be changed, either by Act of Parliament or by the action of the sovereign himself, so the statutes which gave Henry VIII the power to determine the succession (which he used to exclude the Stuarts) were null and void because they were trying to interfere with what God has ordained to be immutable.[94] As another writer explained:

> all the Human Acts and Powers in the World cannot hinder the Descent of the Crown upon the next Heir of the Blood, (I do agree they may hinder the possession, and enjoyment, and so they have often done by open Hostilities and Violence) but I say they cannot hinder the Descent. And the reason is plain, because this is a Dowry which the great King of Kings hath reserved to his own immediate Donation, and hath plac'd above the reach of a mortal Arm; and Mankind can no more hinder or intercept this Descent, than it can the Influences of the Stars, or the Heavens, upon the sublunary World, or beat down the Moon.

Any attempt which man makes to intervene in this divinely ordered succession is an offence against nature which will have to be repaired in due course if the body politic is to regain its health. States which have set aside the succession

> have always continued under Convulsion, and Disease . . . And in such Case it hath constantly far'd with those Bodies Politic, as with a Body Natural upon a Dislocation of a principal Bone; they have breathed it may be, and moved a little, but still under Langours, and Anguish, and Feavorish Habits, and Dispositions, and never well till the Bone was set again, and reduced to its right place.

---

93 *A Letter to a Friend. Shewing from Scripture, Fathers, and Reason, how false That State-Maxim is, Royal Authority is Originally and Radically in the People* (London, 1679), pp. 6–7; J. A. [John Maxwell], *Sacrosancta Regum Majestas: or the Sacred and Royal Prerogative of Christian Kings* (London, 1680), p. 132.

94 John Brydall, *Jura Coronae. His Majesties Royal Rights and Prerogatives Asserted, Against Papal Usurpations, and all other Anti-Monarchical Attempts and Practices* (London, 1680), pp. 28–31.

Nature herself will restore the correct line of succession:

> For though all human and written Laws may be worn out by Desuetude, and *tacit* Consent, yet the Institutions of Nature will never be abolish'd by the longest tracts, and courses of Time, but will always retain an *Animum revertendi*, and will certainly at length attain it.[95]

Thus the king is placed not within a history which may be shaped by human hands, but within an idealized and sacrosanct order which is outside of time and transcends the contingencies of history. It is therefore impossible for mere accident or political choice to create an interregnum, for kingship passes immediately from one monarch to his inevitable hereditary successor:

> The King of *England* is Immortal; and the young *Phoenix* stays not to rise from the spicy ashes of the old one, but the Soul of Royalty by a kind of *Metempsychosis* passes immediately out of one body into another.[96]

Therefore the coronation ceremony is not essential to the making of a king, but only a public declaration of what had already happened at the moment of his predecessor's death:

> Coronation is but a Royal Ornament, and outward Solemnization of the Discent; a Ceremony to shew the King unto the People. That is to say, Coronation is only a Ceremony, and such a Ceremony as doth not any thing, only declareth what is done.[97]

The people can have no part in the coronation except as spectators at this exhibition of royal power, a power which has already been conferred by God and which it is quite beyond their capacity to abridge or transfer.

What the coronation ceremony declares is not merely that the king is divinely appointed, but that he is sacred. According to 'W.P.':

> *Rex Angliae est persona mixta, cum sacerdote*, say our Lawyers, He is a Priest as well as a King; he is anointed with Oyl, as the Priests were at first, and afterward the Kings of *Israel*; to intimate that his Person is Sacred and Spiritual.[98]

The anointing is to 'intimate', to be a sign, that the king's person is sacred, but the anointing does not confer that sacredness. The king is not only sacred, however, he shares the attributes of God himself:

---

[95] *A Letter from a Gentleman of Quality in the Countrey, to his Friend, Upon His being Chosen a Member to serve in the Approaching Parliament* (London, 1679), pp. 3–4.

[96] John Nalson, *The Common Interest of King and People* (London, 1677), pp. 117–18. Charles II was represented as a phoenix on a medal in 1649: see Kantorowicz, *The King's Two Bodies*, fig. 23.

[97] Brydall, *Jura Coronae*, p. 29.

[98] W. P., *The Divine Right of Kings Asserted in General* (London, 1679?), p. 2; cp. Edward Pelling, *David and the Amalekite upon the Death of Saul* (London, 1683), pp. 6–7.

carrying God's stamp and mark among men, and being, as one may say, a God upon Earth, as God is a King in Heaven, in a similitudinary sort given him . . . that is to say – 1. Divine Perfection: 2. Infiniteness. 3. Majesty. 4. Sovereignty and Power. 5. Perpetuity. 6. Justice. 7. Truth. 8. Omniscience.[99]

But the status of the similitude here is unclear; W.P. evidently wishes to avoid blasphemy, but he is not content with saying simply that kings are *like* gods. Another writer seems to abandon the metaphorical for the literal when saying that the persons of kings 'are so Divine and Sacred, that they themselves are the *Angels of God, and Sons of the most high*'.[100] George Hickes was more circumspect in a sermon preached in 1682:

> Yes, Kings are petty Gods, who Govern men upon Earth as *Michael* and *Gabriel* Govern their Angels in Heaven, by immediate delegation from God. Their Soveraignty is an Image of his Soveraignty, their Majesty the Figure of his Majesty, and their Empire a similitude of his Empire, they are Supream on Earth as he is in Heaven.[101]

But Hickes's claim for kingly power as an image, figure, and similitude of divine power still inhabits a world of authoritative and authoritarian representation. The king is not simply 'like' God, he shares his power; the image is one of synecdoche, not simile, as the king partakes in that with which he is compared. There is a linguistic scandal here of a kind common in theological language, and it is appropriate to the old theology of kingship. But it is not a language which can command widespread assent in the pluralist culture of the Restoration.

Visible confirmation of the language of royal sacredness is provided by Charles's ability to heal those suffering from the King's Evil. John Browne's treatise *Charisma Basilicon* (1684) is a description of what happens at the ceremony of touching, but it is curiously defensive on two counts, anxious to persuade sceptics that the cures are genuine, and also eager to use this evidence as a testimony to the divine authority of the king. It is in the action of healing that the king 'appears as the Soul to the Body', and this happens because God has made each portion of the king's body sacred, 'guarding his Tongue, preserving his Lips, blessing his Hands with this Salutiferous Gift, and defending his Body from outward Injuries and private Plottings'. To deny the king's gift of healing is a matter not of medical scepticism but of political treachery, for 'they must needs . . . be allowed no good Subjects, who dare deny this Sanative Faculty.' The proven success of Charles's healing touch is

---

99 W.P., *The Divine Right*, p. 3.
100 *A Letter to a Friend*, p. 4.
101 George Hickes, A *Discourse of the Soveraign Power* (London, 1682), p. 7. The comparison of the king with God was developed by James I in a speech to Parliament in 1610: see *Divine Right and Democracy*, edited by David Wootton (Harmondsworth, 1986), p. 107.

evidence for his legitimacy, for Cromwell had tried it in vain, 'he having no more right to the Healing Power, than he had to the Regal Jurisdiction.' Charles has not only touched large numbers of people, but 'hath as far excelled his Predecessors in this Sanative Faculty, as King *Edward* did his Ancestors', which places him on a par with England's last royal saint.[102]

When the body of the king is held sacred, the body of the subject exists in a relation of natural subjection to royal power, and as John Brydall puts it, 'Legiance being connatural, written by the Pen of Nature in the Heart of every Subject; it is therefore indelible.'[103] Accordingly the appropriate punishment for treason is the ritual dismemberment of the traitor's body so that royal power can be both literally and metaphorically inscribed upon it. Stuart apologists feel the need to associate their description of the king's body with an account and explanation of the fate of the traitor's body:

> The judgment against a *Traytor* doth much describe the abominableness of *High Treason*; And it is this, That he shall be drawn to Execution, because he is not worthy to go upon the Earth. 2. His Privy Members shall be cut off. 3. His Bowels burnt; because the Treason was there hatcht. 4. He shall be decapitated. 5. Dismembered. And in this Judgment are Five Judgments included. 1. All his goods are Forfeited. 2. Life, and Member. 3. His Honour. 4. His *pudenda* cut off, which shews that his Issues are disinherited, and their blood corrupted. 5. The Dower of the Wife is forfeited. 1. Because he is a *Traitor* to God. 2. To the King, that is God's Vice-Gerent upon Earth. 3. To the King, and Realm. 4. To the Law. 5. To his own Allegiance.[104]

This is an appropriate fate for one who denies the power of the king's two bodies: the king's position as the head of the body politic is asserted through decapitation of the traitor, while the origin of the king's right in hereditary succession, and his patriarchal authority, are enforced through the rebel's castration.

Such symbolic disfigurement of the bodies of opponents takes other forms. During the Exclusion Crisis the bodies of the Whig leaders were subjected to ridicule by the king's poets and pamphleteers. Dryden in *Absalom and Achitophel* describes a mismatch of body and soul in Shaftesbury, who punishes

> a body which he could not please,
> Bankrupt of life, yet prodigal of ease?
> And all to leave what with his toil he won
> To that unfeathered, two-legged thing, a son:

---

[102] John Browne, *Charisma Basilicon, or, The Royal Gift of Healing Strumaes, or Kings-Evil* (London, 1684), sig. Bb3ʳ, pp. 2, 17, 82, 76.

[103] Brydall, *Jura Coronae*, p. 123.

[104] John Brydall, *Decus & Tutamen: or, a Prospect of the Laws of England* (London, 1679), pp. 2–3; cp. W. P., *The Divine Right*, p. 4.

> Got while his soul did huddled notions try,
> And born a shapeless lump, like anarchy.[105]

The man who would pervert the hereditary principle has himself produced an heir who is deformed. Titus Oates is also deformed; the opening of his portrait – 'Erect thyself thou monumental brass' – makes him a creature of alloy rather than flesh, and, by innuendo, one more given to masturbation than procreation. His face too is distorted, his features a series of signs which the poet can interpret ironically:

> Sunk were his eyes, his voice was harsh and loud,
> Sure signs he neither choleric was, nor proud:
> His long chin proved his wit, his saintlike grace
> A church vermilion and a Moses' face.[106]

In such instances Dryden is resuming control of the language in which the body politic may be represented, which involves control over the representation both of the individual subjects who are its limbs and organs, and of the monarch who is its head.

Dryden's hardest task in *Absalom and Achitophel* was to reclaim control over the representation of the king, and to retrieve the language of sacred patriarchal authority from the travesty to which it had been subjected. This he did in the opening of the poem by a masterly redeployment of the Davidic image. Charles's promiscuity is now presented as an attractively energetic sexuality which far from being tyrannical is a relic of a libertine golden age before priestly control:

> In pious times, ere priestcraft did begin,
> Before polygamy was made a sin,
> When man on many multiplied his kind,
> Ere one to one was cursedly confind;
> When nature prompted, and no law denied
> Promiscuous use of concubine and bride;
> Then Israel's monarch, after heaven's own heart,
> His vigorous warmth did variously impart
> To wives and slaves: and wide as his command
> Scattered his maker's image through the land.[107]

The scattering of God's image through the kingdom is a generous excess of patriarchy, not its perversion. Dryden seeks to recuperate this language from travesty through his own form of parody; the ironies are admitted, but not

---

105 Dryden, *Absalom and Achitophel*, ll. 167–72.
106 Dryden, *Absalom and Achitophel*, ll. 633, 646–9. For other examples of Shaftesbury and Oates being represented as physically deformed see the commentary in *Poems* i 468, 470, 506–7.
107 Dryden, *Absalom and Achitophel*, ll. 1–10.

admitted to damage the inherent authority of the king. If, like David, he is prone to sexual temptation he is also, like David, God's anointed deputy, and at the end of the poem – a thousand lines away from this playful opening – the king's voice is authenticated by a divine intervention:

> He said. Th' Almighty, nodding, gave consent,
> And peals of thunder shook the firmament.
> Henceforth a series of new time began,
> The mighty years in long procession ran;
> Once more the godlike David was restored,
> And willing nations knew their lawful lord.[108]

Nevertheless, Dryden's astute and even cheeky handling of Charles's person is a unique response to the problem of representing the king, and is quite specifically the product of his own particular cast of mind, which permitted deference and scepticism to co-exist in any consideration of authority, whether political or religious. Moreover, Dryden was fascinated by the unruliness of the human body, the mismatch between the aspirations of the spirit and the demands of the flesh, and in his translations from Lucretius, Virgil, and Homer he relished the comedy of men and gods alike being in thrall to sexual passion. *Absalom and Achitophel* is, therefore, both a shrewd and a highly idiosyncratic response to the crisis of Stuart mythology. When Dryden returned to the representation of Charles in the last months of his reign, after the opposition had been defeated, he presented in *Albion and Albanius* a celebration of Charles's deliverance from his enemies which is conservative both in its politics and its form.[109] Using the devices of the early Stuart masque, Dryden depicts the opposition either as allegorical figures – Democracy, Zelota ('Feign'd Zeal'), Tyranny and Asebia ('Atheism or Ungodliness') – or as physically distorted individuals half transmuted into emblems, as in this metamorphosis of Shaftesbury:

> *a Man with a long, lean, pale Face, with Fiends Wings, and Snakes twisted round his Body: He is incompast by several Phanatical Rebellious Heads, who suck poyson from him, which runs out of a Tap in his Side.*[110]

At the end of the play, Charles (whose name 'Albion' subsumes the nation's identity into his own) is deified, and all ends harmoniously.

---

[108] Dryden, *Absalom and Achitophel*, ll. 1026–31.
[109] See Paul Hammond, 'Dryden's *Albion and Albanius*: The Apotheosis of Charles II', in *The Court Masque*, edited by David Lindley (Manchester, 1984), pp. 169–83.
[110] *Works of John Dryden*, xv 53.

VI

Whether or not Charles and his ministers aimed at absolutism,[111] they were unable to achieve it so long as there was no possibility of imposing an absolutist discourse upon the nation. Mechanisms of censorship were inefficient, and both the political opposition and dissenting congregations maintained effective resources for printing and publishing their work. Attempts to reimpose Stuart ideology met with as much resistance as welcome. To many the person of the king could no longer be an acceptable symbol of sovereignty now that the nation had learned other ways of representing itself. Even if Charles II had been chaste, or at least discreet, the king's body could not have occupied the same place in the national discourse which it had been granted before the Civil War. The Restoration settlement, in the very act of asserting legal continuity and providential design, was an acknowledgement of discontinuity, an admission that the law was a convenient fiction. The Exclusion Crisis, which was generated by the failure of the king to produce a legitimate heir for the crown, occasioned a fundamental debate over the way subjects exist in a legal relationship with the sovereign. A literal failure of patriarchy occasioned a crisis in the constitutional system which took paternity as its practical basis and its symbolic rhetoric.

But we may also conjecture that another reason why patriarchy could not function as a completely persuasive figure of the relation between prince and people was because of contemporary social changes. We are told that relations within families were becoming less authoritarian. No doubt this was a slow and erratic process, but if it was indeed happening, and the family was looking less like an absolutist monarchy, then patriarchy was becoming less capable of acting as a structuring principle in the state by evoking a supposedly natural continuity between political and familial authority. We are also told that sexuality was becoming more private, more bourgeois. If so, was the public flaunting of promiscuous behaviour becoming less acceptable? Was predatory male sexuality more offensive in an age of increasingly affective and companionable marriage? It is clear at least that the poems which satirize Charles's sexual exploits – written, so far as we know, exclusively by men – often hover uneasily between rebuke and admiration. If their crudities and fantasies figure a crisis of royal authority, they also reveal – through their very excess, their instability of tone – a crisis of some kind in masculine sexuality, a crisis in the sway of male power over society at large.

Difficult though it is to read the underlying forces of society through such texts, it is evident that the very existence of these texts effects a shift in the

---

[111] See John Miller, 'The Potential for "Absolutism" in Later Stuart England', *History*, 69 (1984) 187–207.

power relations within society. The subject would no longer allow his body to exist in a state of subjection to royal power, permitting the king to prescribe and proscribe his speech; no longer could the king enforce his authority over his subject's body through the ostensibly benign structure of paternal power. As the subject takes command of his own body, he uses his own voice to represent the nation in his own way. This refusal of royal authority over the means of representation enables the subject to represent his king in language other than that which is prescribed by the official codes.[112] Thus the king is made subject to history, placed within narratives where he is vulnerable to contingency and to political action, and these narratives may now tell a story of immemorial political rights transgressed by upstart rulers. The king is displaced from the timeless sphere constructed for him by early Stuart mythology in which he was responsible to God alone. Though monarchy was said to be 'more ancient than story or record',[113] there proved to be more than one story.

But it is possible to place too much stress upon the radical autonomy which the Restoration inherited from the Republic. Subjects may have asserted their rights, and the immemorial monarchy may have lapsed into the contingencies of history, but the strength of the conservative reaction should not be underestimated. The divine right of kings was proclaimed all the more loudly, and this was far from being a doomed cause. The form of Whiggism which triumphed in 1689 was very different from the vigorous, sceptical republicanism voiced in the poems and pamphlets of the 1670s and the Exclusion Crisis. After the Revolution, the monarchy, reinvented once again, found the rhetoric of sanctity and of dynastic continuity invaluable, and this potent fiction has performed sterling service for subsequent rulers, from the Hanoverians to the Windsors. The second temple proved remarkably durable.

---

[112] For a general discussion of this question see Steven N. Zwicker, 'Lines of Authority: Politics and Literary Culture in the Restoration', in *Politics of Discourse: The Literature and History of Seventeenth-Century England*, edited by Kevin Sharpe and Steven N. Zwicker (Berkeley, 1987), pp. 230–70. For a discussion of the very different conditions which obtained in France see Louis Marin, *Portrait of the King* (London, 1988).

[113] Edie, 'The Popular Idea of Monarchy', p. 355.

Part II

The Making of Authors and Texts

7

The Circulation of Dryden's Poetry

I

CONTINGENCY AND THE CANON

WHEN WE read the poems of Dryden in a collected edition, it is easy to forget that this is not how his contemporaries would have encountered his work. Even if an edition arranges the poetry in the chronological order of its publication, and provides ample details about its bibliographical history, it is still difficult to make an imaginative leap back to a period before the canon was completed and ordered, before the occasional and fugitive pieces were bound up with the major public masterpieces. Modern editors cannot avoid creating an anachronistic canon by reason of their very fidelity in collecting all that was written, with an assiduity far beyond anything that Dryden himself ever envisaged. It is the purpose of this essay to attempt to recover a sense of the fragmentary, haphazard, and contingent character of the circulation of Dryden's poetry, and to suggest what a late seventeenth-century reader would have understood by the phrase 'Dryden's poems'. It will chart the pattern of publication across Dryden's career, investigating which form of publication he thought suitable for particular kinds of poems; which pieces he collected and reprinted, and which were forgotten; and which were given circulation in manuscript, either by Dryden himself, or by his readers. Building on the information presented by Hugh Macdonald and Peter Beal in their invaluable bibliographies,[1] the present essay will seek to interpret this and other evidence so as to reconstruct both Dryden's attitude to the publication of his poetry, and the extent of the opportunities available to contemporary readers who were interested in following his work.

It is an elementary fact, but one which is nevertheless both remarkable and rarely remarked upon, that Dryden did not issue collections of his work. There were no volumes from him called *Poems Written upon Several Occasions*. It was not that the Restoration publishing trade eschewed such collections: notable examples of that kind of book include Denham's *Poems and Translations*

---

[1] Macdonald, *Bibliography*; Beal, *Index*.

139

(1668), Tate's *Poems* (1677), Marvell's posthumous *Miscellaneous Poems* (1681), Oldham's *Some New Pieces* (1681) and *Poems, and Translations* (1683), and Behn's *Poems upon Several Occasions* (1684). It is clear that the collection of miscellaneous poems by a single writer was a familiar form of book in the Restoration, yet Dryden chose not to publish in this way. Virtually all his poems are occasional pieces, called forth by some public event or private obligation, and he seems to have been generally content with the form of publication which they received on the occasion for which they were designed: a prologue to a colleague's play, a prefatory poem for a friend's book, an intervention in a political crisis; moreover, many of the translations seem to have been commissioned rather than volunteered. When Dryden did gather some of his pieces together for the first of Tonson's miscellanies – the *Miscellany Poems* of 1684 – he was quite self-effacing. His name does not appear on the title page, and although the volume begins with his three most celebrated and controversial poems, *Mac Flecknoe*, *Absalom and Achitophel*, and *The Medal*, they are anonymous. Later in the volume comes a selection of Dryden's prologues and epilogues, but although most of them are attributed to him they are not marked out in any way from the miscellaneous poems by other hands which surround them. The conclusion which one draws from this is that Dryden was generally content with the contingency of publication for a specific purpose, and had no desire to assemble an œuvre under his name, as modern editors do on his behalf.

This raises the question of Dryden's use of anonymity.[2] There were good reasons why *Mac Flecknoe*, *Absalom and Achitophel*, and *The Medal* appeared anonymously. The two political poems were outspoken attacks on the Whig leaders, and violent physical retaliation was a possibility, although this was more likely in 1681–2 when they were first published than in 1684 when the political crisis was over. In fact, anonymity did not prevent the first readers of *Absalom and Achitophel* from guessing its authorship very quickly, and no one seems to have attributed it to anyone other than Dryden. Only five days after its publication one potential reader had heard of it, and wrote: 'Tis Dreydon's they say; and no doubt, upon ye presumption, somebody will fall upon him'.[3] Somebody had already fallen upon him in Rose Alley on 18 December 1679, upon the presumption that he had written the anonymous *An Essay upon Satire*, which was probably the work of the Earl of Mulgrave alone.[4] The anonymity of *Mac Flecknoe* might likewise have stemmed from a fear of retribution, but may also be attributable to a form of delicacy in not forcing an open, public breach with Shadwell. The two men had in fact been punctilious in not referring to each other by name in the critical debates which led up to the poem.

---

2 See further chapter 3.
3 Macdonald, *Bibliography*, p. 20.
4 See Edward L. Saslow, 'The Rose Alley Ambuscade', *Restoration*, 26 (2002) 27–49.

Added to this calculated anonymity is the accidental anonymity which attended the publication of many of Dryden's works. We do not know whether the prologues and epilogues which he wrote for other men's plays, or for special occasions such as a performance before the king and queen, were announced as being by Dryden when they were spoken in the theatre; they did not always carry his name when they were printed or when they circulated in manuscript. When Dryden's songs were printed in anthologies or copied in manuscript, they too were often anonymous. Doubts over authorship even attached sometimes to plays. In some cases the authorship was divided or disputed: *The Indian Queen* was probably a collaboration between Dryden and Sir Robert Howard, but was printed without any mention of Dryden in Howard's *Four New Plays* (1665).[5] *Sir Martin Mar-all* was probably written by Dryden based on some materials by the Duke of Newcastle; it was printed anonymously in 1668, but as Dryden's in 1691.[6] Pepys refers to the play as 'by my Lord Duke of Newcastle, but as everybody says corrected by Dryden': evidently in some cases one's view of a play's authorship depended on what one heard. In another instance Pepys seems to have attributed to Dryden a play which was actually by Flecknoe – a beautifully ironic misattribution.[7] Anonymity, both deliberate and accidental, concealed the authorship of many of Dryden's works from his readers.[8]

Positive misattribution, the crediting to Dryden of work which was not his, also had an effect on his reputation.[9] Even a well-intentioned deception proved unfortunate when the commendatory verses which Tonson wrote in Dryden's style for Creech's translation of Lucretius were accepted as Dryden's not only by the grateful Creech but also by the malevolent Tom Brown, who turned them into evidence of Dryden's treachery towards Creech.[10] More

---

5 Macdonald, *Bibliography*, pp. 89–91.

6 Macdonald, *Bibliography*, pp. 97–9; *Works of John Dryden*, ix 354–5, and see the facsimile of the title page (of an unidentified copy) on ix 206, which carries a manuscript note attributing the play to Newcastle.

7 *Diary of Samuel Pepys*, viii 387, ix 307.

8 The question of the anonymity of Dryden's prose lies outside the scope of this essay, but it may be mentioned that Dryden did not put his name to *Notes and Observations on the Empress of Morocco* (1674), or *His Majesties Declaration Defended* (1681): see Macdonald, *Bibliography*, pp. 166–7.

9 For a list of poems attributed to Dryden but now rejected or doubted by scholars, see *Poems of John Dryden*, v 681–9.

10 For Tonson's deception see G. Thorn-Drury, 'Some Notes on Dryden', *Review of English Studies*, 1 (1925) 197, and James A. Winn, ' "Dryden's Epistle before Creech's Lucretius": A Study in Restoration Ghostwriting', *Philological Quarterly*, 71 (1992) 47–68; for Brown, see his *The Late Converts Exposed* (London, 1690), pp. 53–4. Perhaps influenced by Brown's attribution, one reader penned the following verses at the end of the supposed Dryden poem in his copy of Creech's translation, presumably after Creech had committed suicide in 1700: 'Why Oh Unhappy Creech did'st thou not credit giue | To ye Fam'd Drydens wholsome Councells & yet liue | Then had wee All w:^th his Prophettick hopes been bless't | And seen ye Ancient

unfortunate was the misattribution of *An Essay upon Satire,* which may have been associated with Dryden by readers who knew about his authorship of *Mac Flecknoe;*[11] otherwise there was nothing in what we now perceive to be Dryden's poetic oeuvre by 1679 to suggest that he had an inclination either for verse satire or verse criticism. But misattribution can also be mischievous, and in the hands of his opponents in 1682 and 1689 Dryden's supposed authorship of the *Essay* became another charge against him.[12] Nevertheless, a significant number of satirical verses are attributed to Dryden by contemporaries from 1677 onwards, which suggests that the circulation of *Mac Flecknoe* in manuscript in 1676 may have prompted some readers to believe that Dryden had joined the semi-clandestine world in which political and literary satire circulated in handwritten copies. Amongst the satires and epigrams attributed to Dryden during his own lifetime, and excluded from modern editions, are verses on the Duchess of Portsmouth's picture (*circa* 1677);[13] a satire in 1677 on Robert Julian, the 'Secretary to the Muses' who masterminded much of the manuscript circulation of unprintable verses;[14] the lines ' On the Young Statesmen' (1680);[15] a ballad on Sir Robert Peyton (1680);[16] *An Heroic Poem* lampooning various victims (1681);[17] lines on Count Konigsmark (1682);[18] an epigram on Lawrence Hyde, Earl of Rochester (1687);[19] the anticlerical satire *The Tribe of Levi* (1691);[20] an epigram on Louis XIV (1692);[21] and a satirical epitaph on Queen Mary (1694).[22] Whether or not Dryden actually wrote any of these, the fact that contemporaries thought it likely is a significant (and now neglected) element in how his poetic canon was imagined. Of course, some of these spurious attributions may have been made mischievously or maliciously by readers who wished to cause trouble for him. There were also obviously

---

Romans in thy English Dress't' (*Titus Lucretius Carus His Six Books of Epicurean Philosophy, Done into English Verse, with Notes,* third edition (London, 1683), sig. B2ʳ; copy in the Brotherton Collection, Leeds University Library).

[11] For contemporaries' assumptions about the authorship of the *Essay upon Satire,* see *Gyldenstolpe,* pp. 350–1.

[12] Macdonald, *Bibliography,* p. 217.

[13] Attributed to Dryden in BL MS Harley 6914, and in Victoria and Albert Museum MS Dyce 43.

[14] See *POAS,* i 387–91. Four MSS attribute this poem to Dryden: see p. 477.

[15] See *POAS,* ii 339–41, 537.

[16] See *POAS,* ii 305–11. No attributions are recorded here, but the poem is attributed to Dryden in Nottingham University Library MS Portland PwV 199.

[17] See *POAS,* ii 228–34; attributed to Dryden in BL MS Harley 7317.

[18] See James M. Osborn, *John Dryden: Some Biographical Facts and Problems,* revised edition (Gainesville, Fla., 1965), pp. 269–70.

[19] 'Here lies a creature of indulgent fate' (*c.*1687) is attributed to Dryden in BL MS Harley 6914 and MS Add. 27408, and in Bodleian Library MS Firth c. 15; see also Macdonald, *Bibliography,* p. 319.

[20] Attributed to Dryden by Anthony Wood: see Macdonald, *Bibliography,* p. 269, n. 4.

[21] Attributed to Dryden in Bodleian Library MS Rawl. poet. 173.

[22] English translation attributed to Dryden in Bodleian Library MS Eng. poet. f. 13.

malevolent misattributions which were actually a form of ventriloquism, such as *The Address of John Dryden, Laureat to His Highness the Prince of Orange* (1689), and the *Satyr upon Romish Confessors* and *Satyr upon the Dutch* which were fabricated by sly editing of his genuine prologues and epilogues.[23] That readers also fathered on him several prologues, epilogues, and songs is less significant: these were forms which Dryden regularly employed, whereas the association of him with clandestine satires shows that at least some of his early readers assumed him to have quite another kind of literary role from the ones which he was prepared to claim in public. With hindsight editors can reject such accretions to and distortions of the pure, authorially based canon, but we need to remind ourselves that such purity is anachronistic, and that Dryden's contemporary readers would have known a canon and a reputation which was to some extent reworked and reimagined by others, generally for political reasons.

It is not only the public perception of Dryden's canon which was shaped by such factors: the œuvre itself, the poetry which he actually wrote and published, was also determined partly by political and economic constraints. Dryden was never in a position socially or financially to ignore the practicalities which attended the career of a professional writer. Indeed, to support himself and his family simply from the writing of poetry was not an option, at least not until the arrival of Tonson. Given the dearth of documentary evidence for the relations between Dryden and his chief publishers, Herringman and Tonson, it is difficult to assess their influence on his work, but a brief discussion must be attempted here. Dryden was probably employed by Herringman in the late 1650s and early 1660s to write prefaces for some of his publications, and no doubt to assist generally in preparing books for the press.[24] It was Herringman who entered on the Stationers' Register the volume containing Dryden's *Heroic Stanzas* on the death of Cromwell, and Herringman who published Dryden's first major poems after the Restoration, *Astraea Redux*, *To His Sacred Majesty*, *To My Lord Chancellor*, and *Annus Mirabilis*. Herringman also published two books to which Dryden contributed commendatory poems – Sir Robert Howard's *Poems* and Walter Charleton's *Chorea Gigantum*. Herringman's list provided good company for Dryden, for he was also publishing Cowley, Davenant, Denham, Killigrew, and Waller. But Herringman does not appear to have been an adventurous publisher, and it is noticeable that, particularly after 1680, he survived on classic stock rather than by breaking new ground.[25] Dryden's poems of the 1660s look entirely appropriate in a list which includes Davenant's *A Panegyrick to Generall Monck*

---

[23] Macdonald, *Bibliography*, pp. 265, 320; for other examples, see pp. 319–21.

[24] See Osborn, pp. 184–99.

[25] For Herringman's output see C. William Miller, 'Henry Herringman Imprints: A Preliminary Checklist' (mimeographed by the Bibliographical Society of the University of Virginia, University Library, Charlottesville, Va., 1949).

(1659), Cowley's *Ode, upon the Blessed Restoration* (1660), and Waller's *Instructions to a Painter* (1666), but his publications after 1680 seem to reflect the interests of a different publishing house, and almost of a different writer. The long hiatus in Dryden's publication of non-dramatic poetry between 1667 and 1680 is explicable in one way because of his concentration on drama (an economic necessity, quite apart from Dryden's artistic preferences), but it may be no coincidence that his resumption of non-dramatic poetry began soon after he met Jacob Tonson.[26] Tonson published *Troilus and Cressida* in the autumn of 1679, and *Ovid's Epistles* in the spring of 1680. We do not know who organised *Ovid's Epistles*; Dryden no doubt played a leading role, but it is worth noting that Tonson or his brother had previously published work by four of the contributors – Behn, Otway, Rymer, and Tate – so that he already had his own literary contacts. *Miscellany Poems* (1684) and *Sylvae* (1685) seem to have been put together chiefly by Tonson, with some indecision and improvisation on his part,[27] and although Dryden wrote to Tonson that for *Sylvae* he was 'resolvd we will have nothing but good, whomever we disoblige'[28] he did not see all the contributions.[29] Tonson's preface to *Examen Poeticum* (1693) indicates that he organized both that volume and the translation of Juvenal and Persius, for he recalls that 'Having formerly Printed two Parts of Miscellany Poems, they were so very kindly receiv'd, that I had long before now Endeavour'd to obtain a Third, had I not almost ever since the Publishing of the Second been Solliciting the Translating of *Juvenal,* and *Persius.* Soon after the Publishing of that Book I waited upon several Gentlemen to ask their Opinion of a Third Miscellany, who encourag'd me to endeavour it, and have considerably help'd me in it.'[30] The complete Virgil was a commission from Tonson which Dryden accepted with misgivings that grew as the project wore on. Whatever the dynamics of their relationship, it is clear at least that Tonson took a leading role in the promotion of classical translation in the 1680s and 1690s, and provided Dryden with a financial incentive to pursue that side of his interests. Moreover, the forms of publication which Tonson developed – the miscellany and the composite translation – allowed Dryden to be selective in his translating, and to concentrate on those mutually complementary and

---

[26] For Dryden and Tonson generally, see Kathleen M. Lynch, *Jacob Tonson: Kit-Cat Publisher* (Knoxville, 1971), pp. 17–30. There is a somewhat rudimentary list of Tonson's publications in G. F. Papali, *Jacob Tonson, Publisher: His Life and Work (1656–1736)* (Auckland, 1968), pp. 144–213.

[27] For a discussion of the preparation and printing of this volume, see Paul Hammond, 'The Printing of the Dryden-Tonson *Miscellany Poems* (1684) and *Sylvae* (1685)', *PBSA*, 84 (1990) 405–12.

[28] *The Letters of John Dryden*, edited by Charles E. Ward (Durham, N.C., 1942), p. 23.

[29] *Sylvae: or, The Second Part of Poetical Miscellanies* (London, 1685), sig. a8v.

[30] *Examen Poeticum: Being the Third Part of Miscellany Poems* (London, 1693), sig. B7r.

contrasting portions of the classics which appealed to his philosophical interests.[31]

II
THE OCCASIONAL POEMS 1658–1685

Most of Dryden's non-dramatic writing from the reign of Charles II is occasional, composed for a particular event or person, and published in an appropriate form for that occasion. There is a small group of political poems from the early years of the reign which were all published as separate items: *Astraea Redux* (1660) on the Restoration, *To His Sacred Majesty* (1661) on the coronation, *To My Lord Chancellor* (1662), and the more substantial *Annus Mirabilis* (1667) on the Dutch War and the Fire of London which occurred together in 1666. The separately published topical poem was a recognized contemporary form, and one which is well represented in Herringman's list.[32] A single printing of each of these poems seems to have satisfied public interest. *To His Sacred Majesty* was reprinted in 1662 in *Complementum Fortunatarum Insularum*,[33] but this was probably to help fill out a volume of 'Peeces relating to the present Times' rather than to satisfy any public clamour for more copies of Dryden's poem. *Annus Mirabilis* was pirated in 1668,[34] at a time when the handling of the Dutch War was growing increasingly controversial, and further poems on the subject – notably the *Advice to a Painter* series – were stimulating interest among readers. It is difficult to know at this distance how much respect was accorded to *Annus Mirabilis* in its own right: Pepys thought it 'a very good poem' but did not choose to keep it in his library;[35] on the other hand the poem was preserved in a verse miscellany bound up in 1667.[36] Manuscript copies of *To His Sacred Majesty* and *To My Lord Chancellor* survive in British Library MS Burney 390, but they were probably not transcribed until the mid-1670s.[37] These four poems on public occasions were reprinted

---

[31] For the philosophical interests which Dryden explored through his translations, see my *Traces*.

[32] For example, Sir William Davenant, *A Panegyrick to . . . Generall Monck* (1659), and *Poem, upon His Sacred Majesties Most Happy return* (1660); Abraham Cowley, *Ode, Upon the Blessed Restoration* (1660); Sir Thomas Higgons, *A Panegyric to the King* (1660); Edmund Waller, *To the King Upon his Majesties Happy Return* (1660).

[33] Macdonald, *Bibliography*, p. 10.

[34] Macdonald, *Bibliography*, pp. 14–15.

[35] *Diary of Samuel Pepys*, viii 40 and note.

[36] Beal, pp. 392, 398–9. This MS is now BL MS Add. 69823. It was transcribed from a copy of the second issue of the first edition of *Annus Mirabilis* (Macdonald, *Bibliography*, no. 9a ii): it has the revised text of the lines on Prince Rupert (ll. 419–20), but the unrevised text of the line on Berkeley (l. 267). It fails to take account of the errata listed in all known copies of the first edition.

[37] *To His Sacred Majesty* occurs on fols. 9ʳ–10ʳ, *To My Lord Chancellor* on fols. 11ᵛ–12ʳ, and 'To

together in 1688 as Tonson's first attempt to create a 'Collected Poems' by issuing Dryden's poems in a uniform format ready for binding together,[38] but prior to that reprint readers would have had access only to the original pamphlets, supposing they survived. It is unlikely that a reader whose interest had been caught by *Absalom and Achitophel* in 1681 would have had much success if he had enquired for Dryden's earlier poems in booksellers' shops.

However, there is one public poem from this early period which proved to be an exceptional case: the *Heroic Stanzas* on the death of Cromwell. Dryden himself prepared a fair copy of the poem,[39] perhaps for presentation to an influential politician, around the time of Cromwell's funeral in 1658: as a member of the Cromwellian civil service it might have been a useful way for him to draw attention to his talents at a time of upheavals in government. The poem was first printed in 1659 along with pieces by Waller and Sprat, and was not reissued by Dryden until 1691 or 1692 when Tonson reprinted it to add to the four titles which he had already produced in a uniform format in 1688. However, the poem was reprinted by Dryden's enemies in 1681, twice in 1682, and again in 1687, in an attempt to embarrass the Poet Laureate with his former allegiance. Moreover, fourteen other manuscript copies of the poem survive, an unusually large number for one of Dryden's poems.[40] One copy seems to date from 1667, another from 1673, and a third from 1681, while others may belong to the later 1680s and 1690s.[41] This evidence suggests that the poem retained its political sensitivity and interest right through Dryden's career, though it was brought back to public attention at a period of national crisis when his role as a Tory polemicist made this poem too much of a hostage to fortune for it to be forgotten.

There is another group of occasional pieces to be considered, those which

---

the Lady Castlemaine' on fols. 12ᵛ–13ʳ; all are attributed to Dryden. They are preceded on fols. 6ʳ–7ᵛ by Rochester's *A Satyre against Reason and Mankind*, which was probably composed in 1674, and thus provides a *terminus a quo* for the transcription of the three poems by Dryden.

38 Macdonald, *Bibliography*, p. 15.

39 BL MS Lansdowne 1045, fols. 101ʳ–103ᵛ, transcribed in *Poems of John Dryden*, i 532–8 (with an illustration of the first page as Plate 2) and discussed by Paul Hammond, 'The Autograph Manuscript of Dryden's *Heroique Stanza's* and its Implications for Editors', *PBSA*, 76 (1982) 457–70.

40 For the printed texts see Macdonald, *Bibliography*, pp. 3–7, and for the MSS see Beal, pp. 403–4.

41 The copy in BL MS Egerton 669 (which Beal dates 'late 17th century') probably dates from 1667, as a note on fol. 2ʳ indicates that the MS was bound on 16 March 1667; Dryden's poem appears along with Waller's elegy and other material from 1651–63. The copy in BL MS Add. 18220 (dated '1672–3' by Beal) was probably transcribed in the early summer of 1673, as it follows items dated March, April, and May 1673. It is possible that the copy in BL MS Harley 7315 (*c*.1703, according to Beal) may date from the Exclusion Crisis, as it follows a list of items for auction on 9 January 1680 (which probably means 1680/1). (It is also possible that it is, rather, the exemplar from which this MS derives which belongs to 1680–1.)

were written to or for fellow-writers, and published as part of the prefatory material to their books. Dryden contributed complimentary verses to Sir Robert Howard's *Poems* (1660), Walter Charleton's *Chorea Gigantum* (1663), Nathaniel Lee's *The Rival Queens* (1677), the Earl of Roscommon's *An Essay on Translated Verse* (1684), John Oldham's *Remains* (1684), and John Northleigh's *The Parallel* (1685). In addition to these there is one commendatory poem which stayed in manuscript: 'To Mr L. Maidwell on his new method' was written *circa* 1684 to promote Maidwell's Latin grammar, and survives only in one manuscript copy of that work.[42] Dryden never collected any of these pieces, and the only circulation which they had was in the books which they were designed to promote. The fact that Dryden published some of his most important reflections on the English language, translation, the classical heritage, and the role of the poet, in these occasional and uncollected pieces suggests several inferences about his self-understanding and his use of publication. First, it points to a generosity and diffidence which is content that these poems should work to promote the books of his friends. Dryden's writing *circa* 1684 is particularly concerned with the art of the poet and translator (besides the poems to Roscommon, Oldham, and Maidwell, there are the translation of Virgil's *Eclogue* IX and the Preface to *Sylvae*), but he does not build these various statements into a single volume which would carry his name and assert his status: he eschews any Jonsonian ambition to definitiveness and personal importance. This attitude seems to fit with the reticence about his authorial voice which one observes elsewhere in Dryden's work, in his liking for dialogue, allegory, and translation.[43] On the other hand, Dryden is not simply conferring favours through these commendatory poems: the gains are often reciprocal, for his association with these addressees helps to establish his own poetic status and cultural role. Though hindsight (which includes our perception of the significance of Dryden's completed œuvre compared with that of his self-important aristocratic contemporaries) may suggest that Dryden was the dominant literary figure of his age, it is important to recall his vulnerability – his financial dependence on the theatre, on the king, and on Tonson; his social need for the goodwill of aristocratic patrons; his political danger as a Tory partisan and, later, as a Catholic; and his artistic need to differentiate himself from the mass of 'holiday writers' and hacks. In such circumstances his commendation of Roscommon (like his dedication of two Horatian translations in *Sylvae* to Roscommon and Hyde) makes a self-protective social and literary claim.[44] These poems also form part of a

---

[42] See John Barnard and Paul Hammond, 'Dryden and a Poem for Lewis Maidwell', *TLS*, 25 May 1984, p. 586. The poem is printed in *Poems of John Dryden*, ii 223–7.

[43] I have discussed this extensively in *John Dryden: A Literary Life* (Basingstoke, 1991).

[44] Dryden was one of the members of the informal academy around the Earl of Roscommon (see Carl Niemeyer, 'The Earl of Roscommon's Academy', *Modern Language Notes*, 49 (1934) 432–7; and Greg Clingham, 'Roscommon's "Academy", Chetwood's Manuscript "Life of

refashioning of his poetic role for the mid-1680s after the literary battles of the Exclusion Crisis, for in the poems to Roscommon, Oldham, and Maidwell, Dryden is establishing his credentials as a classical poet and translator, both through what the poems themselves say and through the associations which they establish for him – the links to Roscommon the theorist of translation, to Oldham the successful practitioner of classical imitation, and to Maidwell the classical grammarian. But as well as helping Dryden to rework his own image and role, these poems also map out a collaborative project to promote translation, one in which Tonson was a leading figure. In this respect there is a reciprocity involved here, with Roscommon himself in his *Essay* singling out some of Tonson's translators for commendation.[45]

In the case of the major public poems of the early 1680s, the pattern of publication is relatively simple. *Absalom and Achitophel* was published in 1681 (see Plate 11) and rapidly reprinted both by Tonson and by pirates. Approximately nine editions were published in 1681–2: the number depends somewhat on how one defines 'editions', since there seems to have been some very rapid partial resetting and reprinting in the early stages,[46] but it is clear that a large number of copies were printed in the first year of the poem's life, possibly eight or nine thousand if the normal size of an edition was a thousand copies.[47] Dryden revised the poem for its first appearance in quarto format in 1681 by adding some lines to soften the portrayal of Shaftesbury and Monmouth, and some readers were evidently aware of what he had done, for one copy of the first edition has the additional lines recorded in manuscript in the margin.[48] There were also two Latin translations, which were presumably undertaken primarily to advance the translators' own careers politically, though it is possible that they were also designed as Tory propaganda for foreign readers. Thereafter the poem appeared again in *Miscellany Poems* (1684) and in 1692 in Tonson's uniform format. In this case, demand seems to have been satisfied by the printed texts without recourse to manuscript circulation. Only two manuscripts survive, and these probably testify to the prestige value of a manuscript rather than to any difficulty in obtaining a printed copy. This is not surprising,

---

Roscommon", and Dryden's Translation Project', *Restoration*, 26 (2002) 15–26). For an instance of Dryden emphasizing his aristocratic literary connections, see his account of genial evenings in the company of Sir Charles Sedley in the dedication to *The Assignation* (1673) (*Works of John Dryden*, xi 319–23).

[45] In turn, Dryden would later advise Tonson on reprinting Roscommon's *Essay on Translated Verse* (*Letters of John Dryden*, pp. 22–3).

[46] Macdonald (*Bibliography*, pp. 21–4) indicates the rapidity with which the early editions were produced, though his account is incomplete. The treatment of the printing of *Absalom and Achitophel* in *Works of John Dryden*, ii 411–13 is seriously defective. I hope to clarify this problem in a future article.

[47] Dryden recommended that Tonson print an extra thousand copies of Roscommon (*Letters of John Dryden*, pp. 22–3).

[48] Private collection.

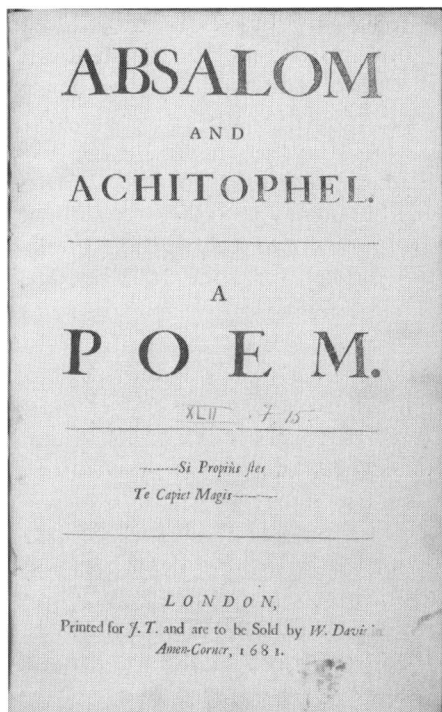

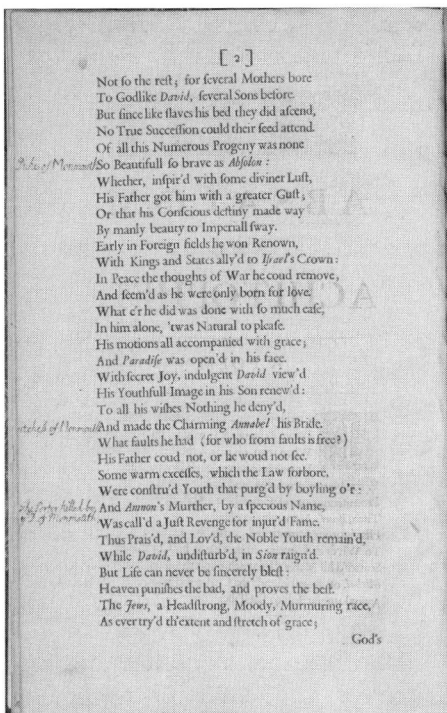

Plate 11. [John Dryden], *Absalom and Achitophel* (London, 1681), title page and p. 2. As the title page shows, the poem was originally published anonymously. This copy, like many, has manuscript marginalia which show an early reader identifying characters in the biblical allegory with contemporary political figures.

149

since it was in both the political and commercial interests of Dryden and Tonson that the poem should achieve the widest possible circulation.[49] Indeed, its publishing history shows that it probably reached a larger audience than Dryden had ever previously achieved for his poems, or would ever achieve again.

The pattern in the case of *The Medal* is similar, though less spectacular: two issues of Tonson's edition, an Edinburgh edition, and a Dublin edition; there is no complete manuscript copy. As with *Absalom and Achitophel*, republication in *Miscellany Poems* seems to have sufficed until the 1692 reprint. *Religio Laici* went through two editions in 1682, and a third in 1683, but was never subsequently reprinted in Dryden's lifetime. However, a letter from Dryden to Tonson which probably dates from August or September 1684[50] shows that at that stage he thought of including it in *Sylvae* (1685), which indicates that he had no serious theological reservations about the poem at that date. Its exclusion from the 1692 collection suggests that after his conversion Dryden wanted to suppress this embarrassing product of his Anglican years – though it is interesting that he did not feel the same way about the commitment expressed in the *Heroic Stanzas. Threnodia Augustalis*, Dryden's poem on the death of Charles II, went through three London editions and one Dublin edition in the first year, but was not reprinted subsequently. In this case the reason for its neglect is unclear: perhaps there was simply no interest in such praise of Charles once history had moved on.

In the cases discussed so far, the circulation of poems in manuscript is merely a minor adjunct to the primary mode of publication through print. But there are three poems from this period for which manuscript was the chief mode of publication because of the very nature of the poems themselves.[51] The 'Verses to her Highness the Duchess' which Dryden printed in the prefatory material to *Annus Mirabilis* had evidently circulated in manuscript in 1665, for he records criticism of them: 'Some who have seen a paper of verses which I wrote last year to her Highness the Duchess, have accused them of that only thing I could defend in them: they have said I did *humi serpere*'.[52] Perhaps a fair copy had been presented to the duchess and other copies had been passed around the coffee houses. No separate manuscript now survives. Presumably the verses 'To the Lady Castlemaine' had originally been presented to that lady in manuscript at some time around 1667. The poem first reached print in John Bulteel's *A New Collection of Poems and Songs* (1674), but since five manuscripts survive, all of which derive from a source independent of *A New*

---

[49] Tonson's political position at this date is unclear; after 1688 he certainly had Whig sympathies.

[50] *Letters*, p. 23.

[51] For a general discussion of the MS circulation of works in the seventeenth century, see Harold Love, *Scribal Publication in Seventeenth-Century England* (Oxford, 1993).

[52] *Poems of John Dryden*, i 125.

Collection, there was evidently sufficient interest in the poem (or in its addressee) for a small manuscript circulation to have been created.[53] At least three of the extant manuscript copies can be dated approximately. That in British Library MS Burney 390 fols. 12v–13r dates from the mid-1670s,[54] while the one in Bodleian Library MS Eng. poet. e. 4 was probably transcribed late in 1672.[55] The copy in Society of Antiquaries MS 330 likewise probably dates from 1672.[56] Dryden did not collect the poem himself until he included it, with some revisions to remove youthful excesses and awkwardnesses, in *Examen Poeticum* (1693). It seems likely that the poem served its purpose as a piece of flattery to the king's mistress in the late 1660s, and there was no point in Dryden reprinting it – indeed, it could have caused him embarrassment – once her liaison with the king had ended in 1670, and Dryden had become established as a dramatist. By 1693, however, it was merely of historical (perhaps even nostalgic) interest.

The most remarkable instance of a poem being published solely and deliberately in manuscript is *Mac Flecknoe.* After writing it in the summer of 1676,[57] Dryden probably released a manuscript copy into circulation in the London literary world.[58] Fifteen manuscript copies now survive,[59] which is a remarkably high number for a poem by Dryden, though not particularly unusual for a popular Restoration satire. The manuscripts are of two kinds. Some are

---

53 I have discussed the MS circulation of this poem in 'Dryden's Revision of *To the Lady Castlemain*', *PBSA*, 78 (1984) 81–90. Since then Peter Beal has discovered a fifth MS of the poem: Society of Antiquaries MS 330. The readings of this MS place it firmly within the MS tradition identified in my article, and associate it particularly closely with Bodleian Library MS Eng. poet. e. 4.

54 See p. 145 above.

55 The poem occurs on pp. 173–4. It is preceded by two datable poems: on p. 167 lines on 'Michaelmas Term 1672' and on pp. 172–3 Dryden's 'Prologue to *Albumazar*' (spoken February 1668; printed in *Covent Garden Drolery* (1672)). It is followed on p. 175 by Dryden's 'Prologue to *Wit without Money*' (spoken February 1672; printed in *Covent Garden Drolery*), on pp. 176–7 by an Oxford prologue from July 1671, and on pp. 177–8 by the prologue to *Cambyses* (1672).

56 The poem occurs on fol. 44r–v. It is preceded on fol. 42r–v by the 'Prologue to *An Evening's Love*' (spoken June 1668, printed 1671), and followed by the 'Prologue to *Wit without Money*' and the Oxford prologue of 1671.

57 The date is established by David M. Vieth, 'The Discovery of the Date of *Mac Flecknoe*' in *Evidence in Literary Scholarship*, edited by René Wellek and Alvaro Ribiero (Oxford, 1979), pp. 63–87.

58 For the MS transmission of *Mac Flecknoe*, see David M. Vieth, 'Dryden's *Mac Flecknoe*: The Case against Editorial Confusion', *Harvard Library Bulletin*, 24 (1976) 204–45; supplemented by Paul Hammond, 'The Robinson Manuscript Miscellany of Restoration Verse in the Brotherton Collection, Leeds', in *Proceedings of the Leeds Philosophical and Literary Society: Literary and Historical Section*, 18 (1982) 275–324. None of the extant MSS is particularly close to the archetype, so the evidence from the MS tradition does not allow us to connect the circulation directly with Dryden.

59 Beal lists fourteen MSS. I am informed by Professor Harold Love that a further MS exists in National Library of Ireland MS 2093.

separates – single leaves or small booklets – and it must have been in this form that the poem was originally passed from hand to hand; they generally survive now only because they have been bound up with other papers. An example is the transcript made by John Oldham (now part of Bodleian Library MS Rawl. poet. 123). The other copies are found in large manuscript miscellanies, usually along with other Restoration satires; these were either personal miscellanies compiled by individual readers, or anthologies written by a professional scribe for commercial sale. Examples of this kind of manuscript are the Gyldenstolpe and Robinson miscellanies.[60] But how popular was *Mac Flecknoe*, and how widespread a circulation did it achieve before an opportunistic pirate printed it in 1682? John Oldham's transcript is dated 1678; three of the scribally produced miscellanies can be dated to 1680.[61] These are the only four manuscripts which can certainly be shown to predate the poem's appearance in print. Six more are assigned by Peter Beal to '1678–80s,' while he assigns the remaining five simply to the late seventeenth century. But even if as many as ten of the extant manuscripts predate 1682, what does that tell us about the extent of the poem's circulation? A significant (but unquantifiable) number of copies must have perished, for David M. Vieth has established that none of the extant manuscripts was copied from any of the others; we might therefore easily double the number of extant copies to estimate the number which originally existed. Perhaps twenty or thirty were in existence before 1682, each being read by a small group of friends. However conjectural these figures may be, they suggest a relatively small readership of perhaps a hundred or two in the poem's first six years. That may have been all the attention which Dryden wanted for his poem, so long as its readers were knowledgeable and influential in the contemporary literary and theatrical world – as, indeed, they would have to be if they were to appreciate its rich allusiveness. A few allusions to and borrowings from *Mac Flecknoe* before 1682 show that the poem was known to a select group,[62] but the rarity of these allusions points to that group being small. *Mac Flecknoe* had nothing like the enormous contemporary impact of *Absalom and Achitophel* which is so evident both from its publishing history and from the number of replies and allusions which the poem generated. Moreover, not only did *Mac Flecknoe* circulate in manuscript, it circulated anonymously. Only two manuscripts attribute it to Dryden, and only one of these (Yale Osborn Collection b 105) can be dated before 1682: only the select few would know its authorship.

The pirated publication of *Mac Flecknoe* in 1682 by the mysterious 'D. Green' turned the poem from a semi-private literary satire into a public, political satire, for its new (and unauthorized) subtitle 'A Satyr upon the *True-*

---

60 See *Gyldenstolpe*; Hammond, 'The Robinson Manuscript Miscellany.' The Robinson MS is Leeds University Library Brotherton Collection MS Lt 54.

61 These are Gyldenstolpe, Robinson, and Yale University Library MS Osborn Collection b 105.

62 Examples are collected by Vieth in 'The Discovery of the Date of *Mac Flecknoe*', pp. 67–9.

Blew-Protestant Poet, T. S. By the Author of *Absalom & Achitophel'* clearly relocates the poem within the series of verse satires generated by the Exclusion Crisis, and specifically as part of the very bitter personal and political exchange between Dryden and Shadwell. This started with Shadwell's savage *The Medal of John Bayes,* which had appeared by 15 May 1682; though anonymous, it was attributed to Shadwell by some contemporaries.[63] Presumably Dryden reached the same conclusion, for he contributed the outspoken lines on Shadwell as Og to *The Second Part of Absalom and Achitophel;* the passage was probably written in May, though the poem was not published until about 10 November. Green's edition of *Mac Flecknoe* was available by 4 October. Meanwhile, Green had already published the lampoon on Dryden called the *Satyr to his Muse,* which appeared in late July. Green's publication of *Mac Flecknoe* materially altered the poem's purpose, and in so doing altered the public's conception of the kind of poet that Dryden was, thwarting any intentions which Dryden may have had of confining Shadwell's humiliation to a select audience rather than parading it before the general public. Of course, after *The Medal of John Bayes* Dryden may not have been sorry to see *Mac Flecknoe* in print, though the fact that the text of the 1682 edition derives from the manuscripts currently in circulation[64] indicates that he did not personally arrange its publication. After the deterioration in their public relationship which all this occasioned, Dryden presumably had no reason not to issue a correct text of the poem in *Miscellany Poems* in 1684 along with *Absalom and Achitophel* and *The Medal.* By that date he was clearly on the winning side of the political debate, while the literary dispute which had originally occasioned *Mac Flecknoe* (centring on Ben Jonson, the function of comedy, plagiarism, and Shadwell's classical pretensions) had lost its edge. Moreover, by printing *Mac Flecknoe, Absalom and Achitophel,* and *The Medal* in that sequence, Dryden was engaging in a retrospective revision of *Mac Flecknoe's* significance: placing it in its correct chronological order, yet acquiescing in the now prevailing association of it with the two political satires.

III

THE SONGS, PROLOGUES, AND EPILOGUES FROM THE PLAYS
1665–1685

The songs from Dryden's plays had a life which was quite independent of the plays themselves.[65] They circulated in various forms: as words only, in printed

---

63 See p. 50 above.
64 Vieth, 'Dryden's *Mac Flecknoe*'.
65 Unless separately documented, the following information about the circulation of Dryden's songs depends upon *The Songs of John Dryden,* edited by Cyrus Lawrence Day (Cambridge, Mass., 1932), for their appearance in print, and Beal, *Index,* for their circulation in MS.

miscellanies or in manuscript; and as musical settings, generally in print but sometimes also in manuscript. A fashion for printing the texts of songs in miscellanies seems to have been a particular feature of the 1670s, and there are some seventeen anthologies from this decade which include songs by Dryden. The popularity of the songs varied, but most of Dryden's songs found their way into at least one printed anthology, and many had a manuscript circulation as well. This pattern may be illustrated by a few examples.

The song 'Ah fading joy' from *The Indian Emperor* (1665) exists in three anthologies, two manuscripts, and a setting by Pelham Humphrey. 'I feed a flame' from *Secret Love* (1667) survives in one anthology and four manuscripts. One song from *Sir Martin Mar-all* (1667) is included in three anthologies and the other in two. But particularly popular were the songs from *An Evening's Love* (1668). 'After the pangs of a desperate lover' is found in five anthologies (two with music) and two manuscripts; 'Calm was the evening' in nine anthologies (three with music) and four manuscripts; and 'Celimena, of my heart' in three anthologies and two manuscripts. It is notable that only one manuscript has all three songs, which testifies to the eclecticism of those who compiled these manuscripts, particularly the personal miscellanies. The songs from *An Evening's Love* also inspired adaptations. 'Calm was the evening' acquired two extra stanzas in some texts, while five different imitations and parodies were penned.[66] 'Celimena' also prompted two parodies.[67] Similarly popular were the songs from *The Conquest of Granada* (1670–1): 'Beneath a myrtle shade' is found in five anthologies (three with music) and four manuscripts; 'Wherever I am' in seven anthologies (three with music) and five manuscripts; 'How unhappy a lover am I' in six anthologies (three with music) and five manuscripts (one with music). Rapid quotation and parody once again testify to the popularity and familiarity of these songs:[68] the first four lines of 'Wherever I am' are quoted in Joseph Kepple's novel *The Maiden head lost by Moonlight* (1672), where the context indicates that the reader was expected to recognize the song: after quoting the first four lines, the narrator says: 'Now you'l say this is very like a modern Song of ours, but I assure you what follows, could I but remember it, was not at all like it, and it was only by chance, that he thought of the first Stave, for it is certain there are common notions, which are obvious to all that make upon the same Subject'.[69] And in Edward Ravenscroft's *The Citizen Turn'd Gentleman* (1672) Mr Jordan sings

---

66 The version in *The New Academy of Compliments* (London, 1671), pp. 192–3, adds two further stanzas; the imitation 'Green was the garden and pleasant the walk' is found in the same volume, pp. 289–90; 'Fair was my mistress, and fine as a bride' is found in *Covent Garden Drolery*, pp. 38–9; 'Sharp was the air, and cold was the ground' in *Mock Songs and Joking Poems* (London, 1675), pp. 129–30; 'Bright was the morning, clear the air' in BL MS Add. 30303; and 'Serene was the air, and unpearled the fields' in *Holborn-Drollery* (London, 1673), pp. 50–3.

67 Both in *Mock Songs and Joking Poems*, pp. 107–8 and 133.

68 The following information adds to Day and Beal.

69 *Restoration Prose Fiction 1666–1700*, edited by Charles C. Mish (Lincoln, Nebr., 1970), p. 169.

an adaptation of Dryden's song, 'How happy a lover am I'. *Marriage A-la-mode* (1671) also provided a popular song, for 'Whilst Alexis lay prest' found its way into seven anthologies (two with music) and three manuscripts. Most of the songs from Dryden's subsequent plays had some afterlife in anthologies, but it is the songs from the period 1668–71 which seem to have been most successful in catching the public's attention. It is worth remarking, however, that when they were thus reprinted or transcribed, these songs almost always appeared without any attribution. Sometimes the appearance of songs in printed anthologies seems to have preceded the printing of the play itself. (It is hardly ever possible to ascertain more about the date of these anthologies than the year given on their title pages.) *An Evening's Love* was not printed until 1671, but two songs from it appear in *Merry Drollery, Complete,* whose title page is dated 1670 (as well as in *The New Academy of Compliments,* dated 1671). Songs from *The Conquest of Granada* (printed in 1672) appear in *Westminster Drollery* (1671) and *The New Academy of Compliments.* It is clear that the songs must have circulated in copies which were obtained either from the author or (whether licitly or illicitly) from the playhouse.

In the light of this evidence that Dryden's songs were well known, and sometimes parodied, it is interesting to turn to the curious case of the song 'Farewell, fair Armida,' where the evidence for Dryden's authorship rests entirely upon allusion and parody. The song appeared anonymously in four miscellanies in 1672, three more in subsequent years, and survives in two manuscripts. Edmond Malone attributed it to Dryden on the basis of references in *The Rehearsal* which associate it with Mr Bayes, who says: 'If I am to write familiar things, as Sonnets to *Armida,* and the like, I make use of Stew'd Prunes only'.[70] It was evidently a popular piece, for there is a reply 'Blame not your Armida', and no fewer than three parodies, one of which seems to refer to Dryden's mistress Anne Reeves.[71] Thus the song is associated with Dryden once through allusion and once through parody, but nowhere directly.

Dryden's prologues and epilogues also had an existence which was independent of the printed texts of the plays for which they were written. Dryden almost always composed both a prologue and an epilogue for his own plays, and these were printed with the play. It was rare for any of Dryden's prologues and epilogues to appear in printed miscellanies (other than Tonson's *Miscellany Poems* and *Examen Poeticum*). The only significant exception is *Covent Garden Drolery* (1672), which prints the Prologue to *Albumazar* (from 1668), the Prologue and Epilogue to *Marriage A-la-mode* (from 1671), the Prologue

---

[70] George Villiers, Duke of Buckingham, *The Rehearsal,* edited by D. E. L. Crane (Durham, 1976), II i 114–16.

[71] 'Farewell dear *Revechia*' appeared in *Covent Garden Drolery,* pp. 39–40; other parodies are found in *Mock Songs and Joking Poems,* pp. 79–80; BL MS Egerton 2623; *Roxburghe Ballads,* vol. 4, edited by J. W. Ebsworth (Hertford, 1881), p. 82.

and Epilogue to *Secret Love* performed by the women (1672), and the Prologue to *Wit without Money* (also 1672).[72] It is clear from the textual problems of the Prologue and Epilogue to *Marriage A-la-mode* that these texts originated in the playhouse.[73] This exceptional appearance of a group of Dryden's prologues and epilogues in a miscellany may be associated with the exceptional plight of the King's Company at this particular juncture. After the fire which destroyed their theatre they were thrown back upon improvised resources and upon the loyalty of their audience: both the Prologue to *Secret Love* and Prologue to *Wit without Money* reflect these exigencies. Perhaps the company was glad of the extra publicity which it received from the publication of these pieces in *Covent Garden Drolery*.

Dryden's prologues and epilogues may not have been published much in the printed anthologies, but beginning with the Prologue to *Albumazar* some of them enjoyed a limited circulation in manuscript. It is difficult to discern a pattern in this circulation. Two dozen manuscripts contain prologues or epilogues from the period 1668–85; most of the interest was taken in those from the years 1670–6, and, to a lesser extent, in the political prologues and epilogues from 1680–2. The prologues spoken at Oxford during the annual visit of the King's Company in July are well represented. However, because the number of extant texts is small, it is not clear whether the pattern of distribution among the surviving manuscripts provides a reliable index to the original popularity of the pieces, or is simply attributable to the chances which attend the survival or disappearance of manuscripts. The latter must surely weigh heavily. At least two of the manuscripts which include the Oxford prologues have an Oxford provenance,[74] suggesting a local source for the text. The Epilogue to *The Man of Mode* (1676) is the piece most frequently represented in the manuscripts, though even here the number of copies is only five. As with *Mac Flecknoe*, the extant manuscripts probably represent only a fraction of those which once existed, the interest taken in prologues and epilogues being to a large extent topical and ephemeral. In most cases the playhouse seems the most likely provenance for the text of these manuscript copies.

Instances of manuscript circulation for which there is no longer any direct evidence can be inferred from the papers of John Oldham. He evidently knew Dryden's 1673 'Prologue to the University of Oxford', for he echoes it in a manuscript draft from *circa* 1678;[75] the prologue did not reach print until the

---

[72] The volume also contains the 'Prologue to *Julius Caesar*' but I have argued that the attribution of this to Dryden by modern scholars is mistaken (see Paul Hammond, 'Did Dryden write the Prologue to '*Julius Caesar*'?', *English Studies*, 65 (1984), 409–19).

[73] See Paul Hammond, 'The Prologue and Epilogue to Dryden's *Marriage A-la-mode* and the Problem of *Covent Garden Drolery*', *PBSA*, 81 (1987) 155–72.

[74] Bodleian Library MS Don. f. 29 (compiled by William Doble at Trinity College *c*.1669–74); BL MS Add. 14047.

[75] *The Poems of John Oldham*, edited by Harold F. Brooks with the collaboration of Raman Selden (Oxford, 1987), p. 545.

publication of *Miscellany Poems* in 1684, several months after Oldham's death in December 1683. Oldham therefore had access to a manuscript of the poem, though none now survives amongst his papers. Indeed, since Oldham was an undergraduate at Oxford in 1673 it is quite likely that he heard the prologue spoken, and either made notes from it himself in the theatre or obtained a copy from the players. Oldham's papers furnish a second example, for in his sketches for 'A Letter from the Country' (begun in late March 1678 and finished in July) he uses an idea from Dryden's Prologue to Shadwell's *A True Widow*.[76] The play was staged in March 1678 but not printed until early 1679, after Oldham's 'Letter' was finished, so once again Oldham is recalling what he heard in the theatre, or using a manuscript copy. No manuscript of that prologue now survives. Similarly, Oldham echoes Dryden's 'To the Lady Castlemaine' in 'A Letter from the Country'[77] and therefore knew that poem either in manuscript or in John Bulteel's *A New Collection of Poems and Songs* (1674).

While the prologues and epilogues which Dryden composed for particular plays (whether his own or those of his colleagues) were almost invariably printed with those plays, the pieces which he composed for specific occasions (such as the opening of the new playhouse, or the summer visit to Oxford) were not put into print. Dryden, as a man of the theatre, seems to have thought that they served their purpose if they were successful on the occasion for which they were designed: they were not poems to be accorded the permanence of print. It was not until the prologue as a form acquired a polemical political function with the onset of the Exclusion Crisis that it became something which he thought should be printed as a poem in its own right. Previously, prologues and epilogues were part of the bantering relationship between dramatist, actors, and audience; they were written for a particular play or performance, a specific theatre with its regular audience, and they had a tone of voice which marked them out as essentially spoken pieces. The first of Dryden's prologues to be printed separately was his 'Epilogue Spoken to the King', which was performed in March 1681 during the critical session of parliament at Oxford. An ostensibly eirenical and patriotic poem, it was effectively a partisan intervention in the crisis on behalf of the king's position. It was important for the king to sway public opinion, and in this the epilogue may have had a small part to play. It was no doubt to this end that it was printed rapidly in Oxford (the lack of an imprint suggests a hasty and even a clandestine arrangement, while the subtitle 'Spoken . . . on Saturday last' indicates its immediacy), and also published in London (by Richard Royston, the royalist bookseller). Next came the printing of the 'Prologue and Epilogue Spoken at *Mithridates*', controversial pieces which were evidently being talked about around London, for both

---

[76] *Poems of John Oldham*, p. 543.
[77] *Poems of John Oldham*, p. 430.

Whig and Tory newspapers quoted them.[78] In 1682 Dryden's 'Prologue and Epilogue to *The Loyal Brother*', 'Prologue to His Royal Highness', 'Prologue to the Duchess', 'Prologue and Epilogue to the King and Queen', and 'Prologue and Epilogue to *The Duke of Guise*', were all put into print as separate pamphlets, each of them making its contribution to the management of public opinion. Each was published by Tonson.[79] These were followed by the 'Epilogue to *Constantine*', 'Prologue to *The Disappointment*', and 'Prologue and Epilogue to *Albion and Albanius*'. In the case of the politically controversial 'Epilogue to *Constantine*', Tonson's publication was a riposte to a pirated printing by 'C. Tebroc' (i.e. 'C. Corbet'), a text whose errors may have originated in a shorthand copy made during a performance.[80] The pattern of publication therefore changes as the function of prologues and epilogues alters with the political climate.

It was only after public events had conferred this significance on his prologues and epilogues that Dryden made an effort to collect them. There are nineteen prologues and epilogues included in *Miscellany Poems* (1684), arranged in a group.[81] When preparing the volume Dryden must have made a careful review of his work, for he can be seen to have followed a coherent pattern when selecting from amongst his many pieces in this genre. He did not reprint those which had already appeared with his own plays or the plays of his colleagues (except for one recent, topical piece, the 'Epilogue to *The Unhappy Favourite*'). But he did reprint all his occasional pieces, except for those prologues from the 1680s which had already appeared in pamphlet form, and with the further anomalous exception of the Oxford prologue of July 1681, which was first collected in *Examen Poeticum* in 1693. From the evidence which survives, it seems that Dryden generally did not revise these pieces, though the text of the Epilogue to Banks's *The Unhappy Favourite* as printed in *Miscellany*

---

[78] See John Harrington Smith, 'Dryden's Prologue and Epilogue to *Mithridates*, Revived', *PMLA*, 68 (1953) 251–67.

[79] Tonson and others were also printing a number of politically topical prologues and epilogues by Otway at this date: *Prologue. By Mr. Otway to his Play call'd Venice preserv'd* (A. Green, 1681); *Prologue To a New Play, called Venice Preserv'd* (A. Banks, 1682); *Epilogue to Venice Preserv'd on the Duke's coming to the Theatre* (Hindmarsh, 1682); *Prologue to the City-Heiress* (Tonson, 1682); *Epilogue to Her Royal Highness* (Tonson, 1682). For other instances of topical prologues being published in broadside form in the crisis years 1681–3, see *The Prologues and Epilogues of the Restoration 1660–1700: Part II: 1677–1690*, edited by Pierre Danchin (Nancy, 1984), pp. xviii–xx and nos. 315, 319, 320, 321, 324, 326, 328, 332, and 334.

[80] Smith, 'Dryden's Prologue and Epilogue to *Mithridates*, Revived', p. 287, n. 8. The only Corbet who is known to have been a publisher at this date is Charles Corbet, who published a poetical broadside on the Plot in 1683, and two ballads on the frost in 1683–4 (Henry R. Plomer, *A Dictionary of the Printers and Booksellers . . . from 1668 to 1725* (London, 1922), p. 81). He seems to have been just the kind of small, opportunistic operator who would have cashed in on a topical poem, while at the same time trying to conceal his identity.

[81] For this section, and the anomalous place of the 'Prologue intended for *Calisto*', see Hammond, 'Printing of the Dryden-Tonson *Miscellany Poems*'.

Poems is less colloquial than that originally printed with the play, and also tends to move the printed text away from its original theatrical occasion by substituting 'they' for 'you' in references to the audience.[82] By 1684, then, all but one of Dryden's prologues and epilogues which we now know about had been printed, either in the plays to which they refer, or as separate pieces, or in *Miscellany Poems*. In the latter volume they were printed together in a single group, offered for the first time as a coherent body of work in their own right.

IV

THE MISCELLANIES AND TRANSLATIONS 1684–1700

The publication of *Miscellany Poems* [83] in 1684 gave Dryden the opportunity to collect *Mac Flecknoe, Absalom and Achitophel,* and *The Medal* (though not *Religio Laici*, perhaps because Tonson still had copies on his hands), together with many of his prologues and epilogues. But the volume gives no special prominence to Dryden. Even if Tonson had begun by reprinting Dryden's three satires in octavo format to provide a collection of his public poems, that aim was not carried through, and *Miscellany Poems* as published has a different emphasis. Dryden is not named on the title page, and the three satires are anonymous. Indeed, it is the presence of classical translations which is given prominence, for *Miscellany Poems* seems to have been inspired by Tonson's desire to build on the success of his *Ovid's Epistles* by publishing several other collections of classical translations by various hands. The title page of the volume indicates this clearly enough: *Miscellany Poems. Containing a New Translation of Virgills Eclogues, Ovid's Love Elegies, Odes of Horace, and Other Authors; with Several Original Poems. By the most Eminent Hands.* Typographically the most striking word on the title page is 'TRANSLATION'. The same is true of the joint title page which Tonson produced for *Miscellany Poems* and its sequel *Sylvae*, which reads: *Miscellany Poems, In two Parts. Containing New Translations of Virgil's Eclogues, Ovid's Love-Elegies, Several Parts of Virgil's Aeneids, Lucretius, Theocritus, Horace, &c. With Several Original Poems, Never before Printed. By the most Eminent Hands.* The contents page of *Miscellany Poems* draws the reader's attention to the constituent parts of the volume: Dryden's three satires appear first, but without any collective heading; then come 'Several of *Ovids* Elegies' arranged in order, book by book, and occupying ninety pages; then follows a heading 'Odes of *Horace*' and a list of ten odes and one epode. Miscellaneous poems come next without any separate heading, a mixture of other classical translations (from Propertius, Petronius, Theocritus, and Virgil), with a batch of Dryden's prologues and

---

[82] *Poems of John Dryden,* i 428–32.
[83] For the preparation and printing of this volume, see Hammond, 'Printing of the Dryden-Tonson *Miscellany Poems*'.

epilogues. Finally there is another separate heading, '*Virgils* Eclogues, Translated by several Hands'; all ten eclogues are translated, with numbers II, VIII, and X being offered in two different versions. Since this section of Virgil's *Eclogues* is separately paginated and has its own title page, it seems likely that Tonson originally intended this an independent collection.

So, far from a reader of *Miscellany Poems* registering Dryden as being specially prominent in the collection, it is likely that the connoisseur of translation, at whom the volume seems to have been aimed, would have been attracted by other names whose reputation in this field had already been established. The Earl of Roscommon contributed translations of Horace's *Odes* I xx and III vi, and Virgil's *Eclogue* VI (as well as a poem in praise of *Religio Laici*). Roscommon was already presiding over an informal academy with an interest in translation, and his version of Horace's *Ars Poetica* had been published in 1680 (by Herringman, whose subsequent loss of Roscommon to Tonson is worth noting); it was reprinted in 1684, the year which also saw the publication by Tonson of his *Essay on Translated Verse*. Thomas Creech, whose translation of Lucretius had been published in 1682 and reprinted three times in 1683, contributed versions of five of Ovid's *Elegies* and two of Virgil's *Eclogues*. His complete translations of Horace and of Theocritus would appear later in 1684. Other names which might impress the potential purchaser were Sir Car Scroope, Sir Charles Sedley, the Earl of Rochester, Thomas Rymer, Nahum Tate, the Earl of Mulgrave, Richard Duke, and Thomas Otway.

While *Miscellany Poems* gave Dryden the chance to collect some fugitive pieces, and to contribute to Tonson's aim of producing more-or-less co-ordinated sets of classical translations, the second miscellany, *Sylvae* (1685), was conceived differently. Six months after the publication of *Miscellany Poems* in February 1684 Dryden was writing to Tonson about the compilation of its sequel.[84] They agreed that *Religio Laici* would not be included, and that the collection would consist wholly of new material. *Sylvae* does not attempt to offer groups of translations from a particular classical corpus, though there are small groups of translations from Theocritus, Catullus, Ovid, and Horace. The most coherent section of the volume is Dryden's opening sequence of translations from Virgil, Lucretius, Theocritus, and Horace, prefaced by a substantial critical essay; there are thematic links between the translations (notably the topics of death, sexuality, and retirement from the life of city and court), but Dryden does not attempt to draw out these connections in his preface, nor does he reprint in *Sylvae* those of his contemporary poems which have strong links with these translations, particularly 'To the Memory of Mr Oldham' and 'To the Earl of Roscommon'. Once again, it seems that Dryden is declining the opportunity to create an œuvre for himself by bringing together those poems which speak to related issues.

---

[84] *Letters of John Dryden*, p. 23.

Examen Poeticum (1693),[85] the third of the miscellanies, mixes classical translation with the rounding up of strays from earlier in Dryden's career, though in this volume the work of other named contributors dominates. Even so, Dryden's translation of the first book of Ovid's *Metamorphoses* is accorded special prominence, coming first in the volume and being given its own half-title. It is followed by other fables from books IX and XIII. There is an episode from Homer, but otherwise Dryden's activities as a translator seem to have been devoted chiefly to his versions of Juvenal and Persius, which were published separately that same year. *Examen Poeticum* reprints several pieces which had previously not been collected by Dryden: the 'Prologue to the Duchess' (separately printed in 1682); the 'Song for St Cecilia's Day' (separately printed in 1687); 'To the Lady Castlemaine', now revised; 'To the Memory of Anne Killigrew' (published in her *Poems* of 1686); and the 'Epitaph on Sir Palmes Fairborne' (printed in *Poetical Recreations* (1688)). To these Dryden added some previously unpublished items: two prologues, two songs, a hymn, and an epitaph. Once again, however, these pieces do not add up to an instalment of a 'Collected Poems', for they are scattered through the volume. Dryden's contribution to the fourth miscellany, *The Annual Miscellany for the Year 1694*, was minor in quantity though not in quality: a translation of Virgil's *Georgics* III, and 'To Sir Godfrey Kneller'. Dryden had already planned his complete translation of Virgil (he had determined upon it by December 1693) and *Georgics* III was evidently a trailer for the larger collection, however much it may have appealed to Dryden in its own right.

The major volumes of translations which were the product of Dryden's last decade – the Juvenal and Persius of 1693, the Virgil of 1697, and the *Fables* of 1700 – are relatively straightforward from the point of view of the present inquiry. The Juvenal reached a second edition in 1697, and the Virgil a second edition in 1698. Lines which Dryden translated from Juvenal's *Satire* VI but which were omitted from the printed text for reasons of decency, had a very limited circulation in manuscript, since they survive in the margins of Dryden's presentation copy of the book to Thomas Monson, and on the endpapers of two other copies.[86] A few passages from the Juvenal, Persius, and Virgil translations survive in manuscript copies,[87] but they are of minor interest. There was no reason for any circulation of the translations outside the printed editions, though some readers did transcribe passages which they considered specially fine.[88]

---

85 For the circumstances of the publication of *Examen Poeticum,* see Tonson's preface (B7ʳ–B8ʳ), partly quoted on p. 144 above.

86 *Poems of John Dryden,* iv 43 and Plate 1, reproducing MS additions on the endpaper of the Huntington Library copy. Since the publication of this volume of *Poems* in 2000, a second copy of the 1693 Juvenal with the same MS additions on the endpaper has come to light, and is now in a private collection.

87 Beal, *Index,* i 416, 422–3.

88 Beal, *Index,* i 396–7.

V

THE OCCASIONAL POEMS 1685–1700

In one respect the circulation of Dryden's poetry in the reigns of James II and William III followed a pattern which is now familiar. Dryden generally made no effort to collect the poems which he had written to or for his friends and colleagues: like the earlier poems to Roscommon, Oldham, and Maidwell, his poems introducing books by John Northleigh, Henry Higden, Thomas Southerne, William Congreve, George Granville, and Peter Motteux were left to work for the benefit of their addressees. Dryden did, however, reprint his poem on Anne Killigrew in *Examen Poeticum*, perhaps because it included his partly autobiographical regret that poets had profaned their sacred gift by writing bawdy verse. The separately published memorial poems *Eleonora* (1692) and *An Ode on the Death of Mr Henry Purcell* (1696) were not reprinted, though *Alexander's Feast* (1697) was included in *Fables* (1700).

Dryden may have regarded his verse letter to Sir George Etherege, written in 1686, as a private poem with no business in the public domain, but (along with Etherege's verse correspondence with the Earl of Middleton) it achieved a comparatively wide circulation in manuscript: eleven copies now survive, some of them quite close to the date of composition.[89] Others are assigned by Peter Beal to the period *circa* 1690, which is the point at which the poem was put into print in *The History of Adolphus* (1691) – presumably no more than an opportunistic piece of publishing which had nothing to do with Dryden himself.

But the major factor which affected the circulation of Dryden's poetry in this period was the political climate. The publication of *The Hind and the Panther* in 1687 was an event which had a considerable political importance, in that it was the first public account of his new Catholic faith by the Poet Laureate to the new Catholic king.[90] The poem went through three London editions in 1687, and was printed in the same year at Edinburgh, in Holyrood House, by James Watson, 'Printer to His Most Excellent Majesties Royal Family and Houshold'; it was also printed in 1687 in Dublin. Evidently the poem was important to the court. It was not, however, reprinted after 1687, either because there was no commercial demand, or because after the Revolution in 1688–9 it was thought too provocative to the new regime. Two

---

[89] Peter Beal dates BL MS Add. 11513 to *c.*1687, which is also a likely date for the transcription of the copy in University of Leeds Brotherton Collection MS Lt 54 (see Paul Hammond, 'Robinson Manuscript', pp. 318–19). For the circumstances in which these verse letters circulated, see Beal, *Index*, i 448.

[90] Interest in the poem is attested by the replies which it provoked (see Macdonald, *Bibliography*, pp. 253–63); see also Peter Beal, ' "The most constant and best entertainment": Sir George Etherege's Reading in Ratisbon', *The Library*, sixth series, 10 (1988) 122–44, especially pp. 131–2.

manuscripts of *The Hind and the Panther* are extant, one of which, the Traquair copy, testifies to Jacobite interest in the poem.[91]

Several of Dryden's poems from this period had a significant manuscript circulation because of their political character. 'The Lady's Song', a Jacobite piece, was not printed until after Dryden's death (in *Poetical Miscellanies: the Fifth Part* (1704)), but five manuscripts from the late seventeenth century survive.[92] In Bodleian Library MS Don. c. 55 the song is dated 1691, and that is also the probable date at which it was copied into University of Leeds Brotherton Collection MS Lt 54 (see Plate 12).[93] This particular text has been adapted to make it less Jacobite in its implications than other versions of the poem.[94] The song must have circulated in manuscript in the early 1690s amongst sympathetic readers, but was too provocative to be printed. Secondly, the 'Prologue to *The Prophetess*' included lines critical of William III's expensive preparations for war in Ireland, and was banned after the first night. Although it was printed with the play in 1690, most copies lack the separate leaf on which the prologue appeared.[95] The person who copied out the prologue for a Mr Charlett of Trinity College Oxford wrote: 'This Prologue was spoken but once & after forbid by ye Ld Chamberlain, which I suppose will encrease the value with persons of yr Curiosity'.[96] Not surprisingly, the prologue circulated widely in manuscript: seventeen copies are known.[97] All date approximately from the last decade of the seventeenth century, and the text in Brotherton Collection MS Lt 54 was almost certainly transcribed in 1691.[98] Thirdly, Dryden's lines 'Upon the Death of the Earl of Dundee', translated from the Latin verses by Dr Archibald Pitcairne, were likewise accorded an extensive circulation in manuscript. (They too were first printed in *Poetical Miscellanies* in 1704.) Nineteen manuscripts are known to survive, the largest number of extant manuscript copies of any poem by Dryden.[99] In several copies the poem is dated 1689, and most of the surviving manuscripts were apparently written in the 1690s. There is also a song with Jacobite resonances which is attributed to Dryden in one manuscript, and may be his.[100] In the last

---

91   Beal, *Index*, i 405; Richard Eversole, 'The Traquair Manuscript of Dryden's *The Hind and the Panther*', *PBSA*, 75 (1981) 179–91.

92   See Beal, *Index*, i 406; Anne Barbeau Gardiner, 'A Jacobite Song by John Dryden', *Yale University Library Gazette*, 61 (1986) 49–54; *Poems of John Dryden*, iii 244–7.

93   Hammond, 'Robinson Manuscript', p. 321; it is preceded and followed by material from 1691.

94   See *Poems of John Dryden*, iii 244–7 for the various MSS of this poem, and the political significance of their variant texts.

95   Macdonald, *Bibliography*, pp. 161–2.

96   Bodleian Library MS Ballard 47, fols. 83–4; Beal, *Index*, i 412.

97   Beal, *Index*, i 412–13.

98   Hammond, 'Robinson Manuscript', p. 323.

99   Beal, *Index*, i 421–2.

100   See Paul Hammond, 'A Song Attributed to Dryden', *The Library*, sixth series, 21 (1999) 59–66, and *Poems of John Dryden*, iv 451–3, v 682.

448

> The Queen of May:
>
> 1
>
> A grove of bright beautys in spring did appear,
> To choose a May Lady to govern the year;
> The Nymphs were in white, & the shepheards in green
> The guarland was given, & Phillis was Queen
> But Phillis refus'd it, & sighing did say,
> I'le not wear a guarland & Daphnis away.
>
> 2
>
> When ye: God of the shepheards is farr from our shore,
> The graces are banish'd, & love is no more;
> ye: soft god of pleasure that warm'd our desires,
> hath broken his bow, & extinguish't his fires,
> & vows that himself & his mother will mourn,
> till ye: God of ye: shepheards in triumph return.
>
> 3
>
> Then forbear your addresses, & court us no more,
> for wee will perform what ye: deity swore,
> But if you dare think of deserving our charms,
> away with your sheephooks, & take to your arms;
> Then myrtles & laurels your brows shall adorn,
> & I'le wear my guarland to grace his return.

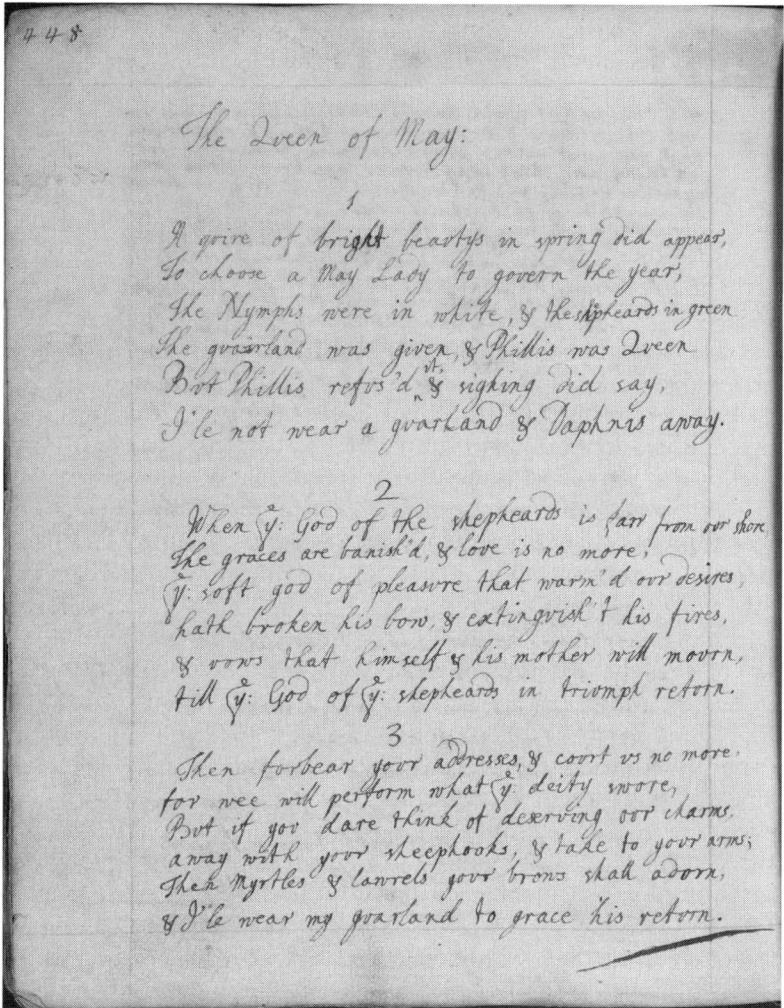

Plate 12. Brotherton Collection MS Lt 54, p. 448 (cp. Plate 7), a portion of the manuscript written in a later hand *circa* 1691, showing a text of Dryden's 'The Lady's Song', here entitled 'The Queen of May'.

This is a Jacobite poem which circulated in manuscript, and was only printed in 1704 after Dryden's death. The present text, however, has been modified to remove some of the more obviously Jacobite elements.

decade of his life, Dryden evidently found that even mildly oppositional verse could only be circulated in this clandestine manner.

VI
THE CHANGING PERCEPTION OF DRYDEN'S ŒUVRE

This essay has considered the circulation of Dryden's poetry from the point of view of the author, his publishers, and scribes. But what would his readers have had available to them at different stages in Dryden's career? Let us finally consider briefly what interested (but not especially privileged) readers of contemporary poetry might know of Dryden's work at five-year intervals.

In 1660 there would be no reason to single Dryden out from the crowd of versifiers who greeted the king's return. His *Heroic Stanzas* on the death of Cromwell had appeared in print in 1659, but a year later had probably been forgotten (albeit only temporarily). Hardly any reader in 1665 would consider asking his bookseller for poems by Dryden: the few occasional pieces from the early 1660s had probably disappeared. By 1670, however, Dryden was an established playwright. Theatre-goers would have come across Dryden's prologues, epilogues, and songs in the playhouse; they might have bought play quartos and read the poems there; they would be likely purchasers for *Covent Garden Drolery* and its rivals when they appeared in the early 1670s. *Annus Mirabilis,* along with the oppositional 'Advice to a Painter' poems which followed it, may already have been forgotten, though the compiler of MS Burney 390 in the early 1670s was sufficiently interested in Dryden's panegyrics from the early 1660s to copy them out (which may suggest that no printed copies were available at that date). Five years later, in 1675, the perception of Dryden as a poet would be much the same: almost exclusively as a successful dramatist, with a talent for songs and a pleasing line in prologues. By 1680 little would have changed, for although other writers had poured out verses on the Popish Plot and the Exclusion Crisis, Dryden was keeping a discreet distance from these political squabbles, except for some barbed references in occasional prologues and epilogues. Readers who moved in exclusive literary circles might have come across a manuscript copy of *Mac Flecknoe,* and made themselves a transcript; the wealthier ones could have commissioned a handsome manuscript anthology of unprintable poems on contemporary affairs: 1680 is the year when several of these were being produced for connoisseurs. Readers might have seen other manuscript satires attributed to Dryden, and wondered whether the attributions were correct. In 1680 one could also have purchased *Ovid's Epistles,* with its rather indifferent poems redeemed by Dryden's sharp and confident essay on translation.

By 1685 everything had changed. The publications of 1681–2 had quite suddenly revealed a remarkably diverse and astringent poetic talent, equally adept at literary demolition, political invective, and religious controversy. The prologues and epilogues had become more polemical, and had been appearing as printed leaflets as well as turning up in manuscript copies: they were now poems for the streets and the coffee houses as well as for the theatre, pieces to read as well as to hear. *Miscellany Poems* had gathered a lot of Dryden's poetry together rather conveniently, and though the major satires were still anonymous the pretence at concealment did not fool many; even so, there was no 'Collected Poems', and Dryden's early work was hard to come by (except for the maliciously reprinted *Heroic Stanzas*). The promise which had been held out by *Ovid's Epistles* that Dryden was turning his attention to translation was confirmed briefly in *Miscellany Poems* and impressively in *Sylvae*, though many of his most important statements about the writer's art and the state of contemporary language and literature had been made in passing in commendatory poems which were only accessible if one bought the books of his friends.

By 1690 everything had changed again. The flood of major publications in the early 1680s had dried up. *The Hind and the Panther* had made an impact in 1687, but the Revolution seemed to have silenced him. Soon Dryden's work would begin to be seen in surreptitious manuscript copies passed round in Jacobite circles. His position was awkward, perhaps dangerous, and it was hard to foresee what kind of role Dryden would make for himself as a writer under this new regime. Meanwhile Tonson was reprinting Dryden's earlier work in a uniform format, so that the interested reader could have the major poems bound up together: *Annus Mirabilis, To His Sacred Majesty*, and *To My Lord Chancellor* were reissued in 1688, *Heroic Stanzas* in 1691 or 1692, *Britannia Rediviva, Mac Flecknoe, Absalom and Achitophel*, and *The Medal* appeared in 1692. Sets of Dryden's poems were made available with suitable title pages.[101] Demand for Dryden's earlier work clearly continued.

By 1695 it was clear that Dryden had decided to devote himself to translation: readers had seen from *Examen Poeticum* and the Juvenal and Persius that his gifts were undiminished, and there were promises of a great literary event in the offing, the publication of Dryden's complete Virgil. By 1700, the year of Dryden's death, the Virgil of 1697 had been followed, and his career crowned, by the publication of *Fables Ancient and Modern*. After Dryden's death Tonson collected a few stray pieces in his continuing series of Miscellany Poems (which he promoted by advertising the first four parts as having been 'Published by Mr. *Dryden*'[102]); those rescued in this way included the Jacobite pieces, and some Ovidian translations left over from an attempt in the 1690s to produce a composite *Metamorphoses*.[103]

To follow the course of Dryden's career in this way is, in however summary

---

101 Macdonald, *Bibliography*, pp. 15–16.
102 Macdonald, *Bibliography*, p. 75.
103 David Hopkins, 'Dryden and the Garth-Tonson *Metamorphoses*', *Review of English Studies*, 39 (1988) 64–74.

a form, to reconstruct the contingencies of publication which our easy overview of the completed canon so often obscures. It also reminds us that Dryden was a very different kind of writer from Pope; whereas Pope paid scrupulous attention to the promotion of his work and the construction of his image from an early date, self-consciously fashioning his persona and his œuvre, Dryden left his poetry to work for itself, to fulfil the functions for which it was composed, and only sought for it to live beyond its first occasion if there was a real demand. In this attitude to his writing there is both the professionalism which we associate with him, and a modesty which the slanders of his enemies have sometimes encouraged us to forget.

8

Flecknoe and *Mac Flecknoe*

WHY DID Dryden select Richard Flecknoe as the man whose poetic kingdom Shadwell was to inherit? Although scholars have refined our understanding of the circumstances in which *Mac Flecknoe* was composed,[1] the precise point of choosing Flecknoe rather than anyone else remains obscure. It is often asserted that Flecknoe was for Dryden's contemporaries the epitome of the bad poet, and as evidence for this assumption one is referred to Marvell's satire 'Flecknoe, an English Priest at Rome'; yet this poem was not printed until 1681, five years after the composition of *Mac Flecknoe*, and seems not to have circulated in manuscript first, so that it is unlikely that Dryden and his readers would have known of Marvell's poem in the late 1670s.[2] And even if Flecknoe did have a low reputation, the link with Shadwell which this suggests is an uncharacteristically imprecise starting point for one of Dryden's most incisive satires. However there is a very specific reason for Dryden's choice of Flecknoe, and one which gives added point to the poem.

We need to begin by recalling briefly the main points at issue between Dryden and Shadwell in the debate which led up to *Mac Flecknoe*. Richard Oden summarizes the issues in this way:

> (1) their different estimates of the genius of Ben Jonson, (2) the preference of Dryden for comedy of wit and repartee and of Shadwell, the chief disciple of Jonson, for humors comedy, (3) a sharp disagreement over the true purpose of comedy, (4) contention over the value of rhymed plays, and (5) plagiarism.[3]

---

[1] For the context of *Mac Flecknoe* see David M. Vieth, 'The Discovery of the Date of *Mac Flecknoe*' in *Evidence in Literary Scholarship: Essays in Memory of James Marshall Osborn*, edited by René Wellek and Alvaro Ribero (Oxford, 1979), pp. 63–87; and *Dryden and Shadwell: The Literary Controversy and 'Mac Flecknoe' (1668–1679)*, edited by Richard L. Oden (Delmar, N.Y., 1977). Three scholars have previously explored the question of the relationship between Flecknoe and Dryden's poem: John Harrington Smith, 'Dryden and Flecknoe: A Conjecture', *Philological Quarterly*, 33 (1954) 338–41; Maximillian E. Novak, 'Dryden's "Ape of the French Eloquence" and Richard Flecknoe', *Bulletin of the New York Public Library*, 12 (1968) 499–506; and Helmut Castrop, 'Dryden and Flecknoe: A Link', *Review of English Studies*, 23 (1972) 455–8. For comprehensive annotation to *Mac Flecknoe* see *Poems of John Dryden*, i 306–36.

[2] For Marvell's poem and its context see *Poems of Andrew Marvell*, pp. 166–74.

[3] Oden, p. ix.

The ground upon which Shadwell takes his stand is that he is the true heir of Ben Jonson, and the true representative of English classicism. Shadwell's prefaces invoke Jonson as his model, and cite Horace in support of his insistence that plays should not merely entertain, but should also instruct. Shadwell is thus attempting to appropriate classical authority for his own cause, and creating an image of himself as the true heir to this tradition. Dryden's outrage with this unjustified claim finds expression in the Augustan imagery of *Mac Flecknoe*, which dresses Shadwell in precisely those robes which he had assumed, so that readers might see how uneasily they fit him. But for the image to work cogently, the transformation from Son of Ben to Son of Flecknoe has to be pointed.

When Dryden recast Shadwell's own image of himself he chose Flecknoe instead of Jonson as Shadwell's poetic father because Flecknoe too had created a Jonsonian image for himself. His *Epigrams*, which appeared in several editions in the 1660s and 1670s, are a collection of moral, pious, panegyrical, and satirical pieces which attempt to echo Jonson both in their scope and in their details. For instance, Flecknoe's lines 'On the death of *Charles* Lord *Gerard* of *Bromley*' read like a degenerate version of Jonson on William Roe. Jonson had written:

> Roe (and my ioy to name) th'art now, to goe
>   Countries, and climes, manners, and men to know,
> T' extract, and choose the best of all these knowne,
>   And those to turne to bloud, and make thine owne:[4]

Flecknoe writes:

> Who alive so far had been,
> He almost every Land had seen,
> And almost every thing did know,
> As man cou'd in this World below.
> At last his knowledge to improve,
> Is gone unto the World above.
> Where his knowledge is so much;
> And his Happiness is such,
> Twou'd Envy and not sorrow seem,
> In those too much shou'd grieve for him.

The epigram 'Of the difference of Travellers' likewise picks up Jonson's idea of travel as a contribution to the humanist's self-definition.[5] Another collection offers an array of titles which could have come straight from Jonson's *Epigrammes*: 'On Sir Querilous Coxcomb', 'On a Rich vain-glorious Miser',

4   *Ben Jonson*, edited by C. H. Herford, Percy and Evelyn Simpson, 11 vols (Oxford, 1925–52), viii 80.
5   Richard Flecknoe, *Epigrams of All Sorts. I Book* (London, 1669), pp. 4, 16.

'On Simple', 'To one Who desired him not to name him'.[6] We may also see Flecknoe's attempt to be an arbiter of the world of letters as the assumption of a Jonsonian role: his *Miscellania* (1653) includes 'A Discourse of Languages' and an essay 'Of Translation of Authors',[7] while the Horatian and Virgilian mottos which adorn many of his title pages repeat his claim to be a classical critic and poet. Unlike Jonson, however, he is liable to get his Latin wrong. The title page of *A Treatise of the Sports of Wit* (1675) carries the motto *Omne tulit punctam quae miscuit utile dulci*, which would have made both Horace and Jonson wince.

Furthermore, Flecknoe's works abound with dedications to, and complimentary verses from the Duke of Newcastle, who had been Jonson's patron and was also Shadwell's. These are, of course, the 'northern dedications' mentioned in *Mac Flecknoe*.[8] Dryden himself had dedicated *An Evening's Love* (1671) to Newcastle, and had earlier collaborated with him in adapting *Sir Martin Mar-all* (1668) from Molière; and since Dryden had, according to Professor Novak, derided Flecknoe as an 'Ape of the French Eloquence' for his attachment to farce, particularly to Molière, this may seem to be unsafe ground for Dryden to attack on. Yet Dryden's poem is directed against that misuse of classicism which unites Flecknoe and Shadwell: their nominal attachment to Horace or to Jonson or to Molière is but a travesty of true classical values and practices, and must have been particularly irritating to Dryden at a time when he was trying to fashion in his own work an art which was truly classical for his own times without being merely an aping of his predecessors.

Flecknoe's self-assumed role as heir and champion of Jonson extends also to his dramatic criticism. His own play *Loves Dominion* (1654) has a preface which speaks of the corruption of the stage, and claims that this play restores it to its original purity:

> For my part I have endeavoured here the clearing of it, and restoring it to its former splendor, and first institution; (of teaching *Virtue*, reproving *Vice*, and amendment of *Manners*.)[9]

Like Shadwell, Flecknoe insists on the drama's function of moral instruction. The subsequent editions of this play in 1664 and 1674, now entitled *Love's Kingdom*, drop this preface and add instead *A Short Discourse of the English*

---

6   Richard Flecknoe, *Epigrams of All Sorts, Made at Divers Times on Several Occasions* (London, 1670), pp. 61, 57, 60.
7   Richard Flecknoe, *Miscellania. Or, Poems of all sorts, with divers other Pieces* (London, 1653), pp. 75–117.
8   Dryden, *Mac Flecknoe*, l. 170. This connection between Flecknoe and Shadwell was noted in *Works of John Dryden*, ii 325, but it is the common link back to Jonson that gives the observation its real point.
9   Richard Flecknoe, *Loves Dominion, A Dramatique Piece, Full of Excellent Moralitie; Written as a Pattern for the Reformed Stage* (London, 1654), sig. A4ᵛ.

Stage, which contains some judicious comparative criticism of Shakespeare, Jonson, and Fletcher:

> For Playes, *Shakespear* was one of the first, who inverted the Dramatick Stile, from dull History to quick Comedy, upon whom *Johnson* refin'd ... To compare our English Dramatick Poets together (without taxing them) *Shakespear* excelled in a natural Vein, *Fletcher* in Wit, *Johnson* in Gravity and ponderousness of Style; whose onely fault was, he was too elaborate; and had he mixt less erudition with his Playes, they had been more pleasant and delightful then they are. Comparing him with *Shakespear*, you shall see the difference betwixt Nature and Art; and with *Fletcher*, the difference betwixt Wit and Judgement: Wit being an exuberant thing, like *Nilus*, never more commendable then when it overflowes; but Judgment a stayed and reposed thing, always containing it self within its bounds and limits.[10]

Though not so precise as Dryden's criticism four years later in his *Essay Of Dramatick Poesie*, Flecknoe's brief characterization of the three dramatists is not unintelligent. Unfortunately, Flecknoe allowed himself to be led from judicious criticism to injudicious satire.

An interesting development may be traced in the successive editions of Flecknoe's *Epigrams of All Sorts*. The collection first appeared in 1669, when it included an attack on Etherege: 'On the Play, of she wou'd, if she cou'd, To the Duke of *N*.' The play, says Flecknoe, offers

> ... sparks of wit, as much as you'd desire,
> But sparks alone, as far from solid fire ...
> So hard tis now for any one to write
> With *Johnson*'s fire, or *Fletcher*'s flame and spirit.
> Much less Inimitable *Shakspear*'s way
> *Promethean*-like to animate a Play.[11]

In the 1670 edition this attack on one example of the modern comedy of wit is rewritten to form an epigram 'Of the difference Betwixt the Ancient and Modern Playes', which in 1671 is retitled again, and expanded even further:

> *Former Playes and Poets vindicated*
> In former times none ever went away
> But with a glowing bosom from a Play,
> With somewhat they had heard, or seen, so fir'd,
> You'd think they were celestially inspir'd:
> Now, we have only a few light conceits,

---

[10] Richard Flecknoe, *Love's Kingdom. A Pastoral Trage-Comedy. Not as it was Acted at the Theatre near Lincolns-Inn, but as it was written, and since corrected ... With a short Treatise of the English Stage, &c. by the same Author* (London, 1664), sigs. G5ʳ–G6ʳ. The play was reissued in 1674 with a new title page, but using the sheets of the 1664 edition.

[11] Flecknoe, *Epigrams of All Sorts* (1669), pp. 10–11.

Like *Squibs* and *Crackers*, neither warms nor heats,
And sparks of *wit*, as much as you'd desire,
But nothing of a *true* and *solid fire*.
So few w'ave now a dayes know how to write
With *Johnsons* fire, and *Fletchers* flame and sprite,
Much less inimitable *Shakspears* way,
Promethian-like to animate [a] play,
Compar'd to whom, for moving *passion*,
There's none know how to do't, now they are gon;
And this for learned *Johnson* I shall say,
As few know, now he's gone, to *plot* a Play.
And though for th' *writing*, *Criticks* wont allow,
Their Times as *witty* were, as ours are now.
Yet know, who e'r thou art, dost less esteem
Of *Johnson* for the faults oth' Times, not him;
Had he writ now h'ad better writ than thee,
Hadst thou writ then, th'adst writ far worse than he;
And all in spight of *Envy* must confess,
If he be'nt worthy praise, others much less.[12]

The 1670 version of this epigram ended at line 12; the last twelve lines added in 1671 are quite clearly directed at Jonson's critics, of whom Dryden was (or was perceived to be) the chief, so that it is hard not to take the passage as being addressed particularly to him.[13] Dryden's views on Jonson had been aired in the prologue to *The Tempest* (performed 1667; printed 1670), and propounded more fully in the *Essay Of Dramatick Poesie* (1668). Shadwell replied in his preface to *The Sullen Lovers* (1668) and *The Royal Shepherdess* (1669). Dryden's critique was renewed in the preface to *An Evening's Love* (1671), to which Shadwell replied in the same year in *The Humorists*. Flecknoe's revised epigram of 1671 appears, therefore, at a point when the debate between Shadwell and Dryden is in full swing. So Flecknoe had taken up what he claimed was the cause of Ben Jonson against the modern 'wits': he was on the side of Shadwell against Dryden.

And yet the 1670 edition of Flecknoe's *Epigrams* had included some laudatory verses on Dryden:

> To Mr. *John Dreyden.*
> *DReyden* the Muses darling and delight,
> Than whom none ever flew so high a flight,
> Some have their vains so drosie, as from *earth*,
> Their Muses only seem to have tane their birth.
> Others but *Water-Poets* are, have gon

---

[12] Richard Flecknoe, *Epigrams. Of All Sorts, Made at Several Times, on Several Occasions* (London, 1671), pp. 51–2.
[13] This is noted by Macdonald, *Bibliography*, p. 191; and Novak, p. 503.

No farther than to th' *Fount of Helicon*:
And they'r but *aiery ones, whose Muse* soars up
No higher than to mount *Pernassus* top;
Whilst thou, with thine, dost seem to have mounted higher,
Then he who fetcht from *Heaven* Celestial fire:
And dost as far surpass all others, as
Fire does all other Elements surpass.[14]

Flecknoe also offers a panegyric to Davenant, saying that *The Siege of Rhodes* 'does out do | Both *Ancients* and the *Moderns* too'.[15] Perhaps these verses on Dryden and Davenant were an act of reparation on Flecknoe's part for two ill-tempered and unfunny satirical pamphlets which he had issued in 1667–8. The first was *The Life of Tomaso the Wanderer* (1667), an attack on Thomas Killigrew, the manager of the King's Company for which Dryden wrote. It is mere abuse, with no matter of literary principle at stake, and was probably occasioned simply by Flecknoe's wounded pride at having a play turned down. But the attack on Davenant was more serious.[16] Called *Sr William D'avenant's Voyage to the Other World: With His Adventures in the Poets Elizium. A Poetical Fiction* (1668), it not only attacks the man who was Dryden's collaborator in adapting *The Tempest*, but also makes charges to which Dryden himself might well feel vulnerable. When Davenant arrives in the underworld he finds

never a poet there, Antient or Modern, whom in some sort or other he had not disoblig'd by his discommendations, as Homer, Virgil, Tasso, Spencer, and especially Ben. Johnson; . . . Nay even Shakespear, whom he thought to have found his greatest Friend, was as much offended with him as any of the rest, for so spoiling and mangling of his Plays.[17]

If Davenant is to be charged with disrespect for Shakespeare and Jonson, Dryden too must be implicated. But Flecknoe does not only attack Davenant's activities as a critic and adaptor; his style is also derided:

Momus answered that he had mar'd more good Plays, than ever he had made; That all his Wit lay in Hyperbolies and Comparisons, which, when Accessory, were commendable enough, but when Principal, deserv'd no great commendations; That his Muse was none of the Nine, but onely a Mungril, or By-blow of Parnassus, and her Beauty rather sophisticate than natural.[18]

This too might well apply to the young Dryden, some of whose stylistic

---

14 Flecknoe, *Epigrams of All Sorts* (1670), p. 70.
15 Flecknoe, *Epigrams of All Sorts* (1670), p. 69.
16 See Castrop; and Novak, pp. 504–5.
17 Richard Flecknoe, *Sr William D'avenant's Voyage to the Other World: With His Adventures in the Poets Elizium. A Poetical Fiction* (London, 1668), pp. 8–9.
18 Flecknoe, *Sr William D'avenant's Voyage*, p. 11.

extravagances were ridiculed in the same year by one 'R.F.'[19] Flecknoe's pamphlet against Davenant ridiculed a friend and colleague of Dryden, and, by implication, the poetic and critical predilections which they shared.

In Richard Flecknoe we have, then, a writer who aped Ben Jonson with offensive pride and lamentable incompetence; who joined Shadwell against Dryden in the debate over what constituted true classicism; whose attacks on Killigrew, Davenant, and Etherege must have offended Dryden; and whose complimentary epigram would hardly have impressed him very much, since it was but one item from Flecknoe's cornucopia of sycophantic doggerel. Moreover, Flecknoe was a continuing irritant. H. T. Swedenberg assumed that 'by the time Dryden wrote *Mac Flecknoe*, Richard Flecknoe, who had become the symbol of bad poetry, had disappeared from the records and was presumably dead',[20] but this remark was based upon a mistaken dating of the poem to 1678; the correct dating of *Mac Flecknoe* to 1676 allows us to see that Flecknoe was both alive and active in the period preceding the poem. *Love's Kingdom* had been reissued in 1674, *Euterpe Revived* and *A Treatise of the Sports of Wit* came out in 1675, and his *Seventy-eight characters* were to appear in 1677. However, although Flecknoe was not dead, he had announced his withdrawal from public life. In 1675 he published a poem in his *Treatise of the Sports of Wit* entitled 'The Adue':

> Nothing but Storms and Tempests? then 'tis time
> To seek for shelter in some Forein Clime,
> Where I may hope to find the happiness,
> If not to live, at least to die in peace . . .
> 'Tis time to go, my singing days are done.[21]

Signed with his initials, this is a clear personal statement, and is echoed later in the same volume in the poem '*The Remembrance* or the *Petition* Renewed', where he speaks of himself as one

> Who in the late Dutchess of *Lorrains* days,
> To all their mirth, so instrumental was
> *His Majesty* never danc' d, nor *Dutchess* sung;
> But he with's *Lute* or *Viol* still was one . . .
> Now aged grown, does in some *hermitage*,
> Desire to end the *remnant* of his age.[22]

This was not the first time that Flecknoe had announced his retirement: it is also spoken of in 'L'Envoy', likewise printed in 1675, but first published two

---

19 R. F., *A Letter from a Gentleman To The Honourable Ed. Howard Esq.* (London, 1668) has sometimes been attributed to Flecknoe. Novak (pp. 503–4) convincingly argues against this attribution, but we do not know that Dryden came to the same conclusion.

20 *Works of John Dryden*, ii 308.

21 Richard Flecknoe, *A Treatise of the Sports of Wit* (London, 1675), p. 7.

22 Flecknoe, *A Treatise of the Sports of Wit*, p. 15 *bis*.

years earlier.[23] Perhaps Dryden thought that Flecknoe had announced his positively final appearance rather too often, and decided to take him at his word, for in *Mac Flecknoe* the 'aged Prince'

> Worn out with business, did at length debate
> To settle the succession of the state:[24]

The self-styled Son of Ben is retiring; who will inherit his mantle? It will be Shadwell, presented by Dryden not as the legitimate son of Jonson, but the son of Flecknoe – and the illegitimate son, too, if Flecknoe was indeed a Roman Catholic priest.[25]

The image of retirement is only one example of Flecknoe himself providing material for Dryden's poem; there are other instances, and to trace these images to their source shows that Dryden had been reading at least some parts of Flecknoe's work with attention when preparing his poem, and may also imply that it was sufficiently notorious for readers to recognize certain images as specific allusions. One of Flecknoe's works seems to have been particularly useful to Dryden: *A Relation Of ten Years Travells in Europe, Asia, Affrique, and America*. The first edition is undated, but probably appeared in 1656; it cannot have sold very well, for the 1665 edition is simply a reissue of the sheets of the first edition with a new title page. It was in this book that Dryden would have found Flecknoe's account of his visit to the King of Portugal in 1648, which is referred to in *Mac Flecknoe*:

> My warbling lute, the lute I whilom strung
> When to King John of Portugal I sung .[26]

As well as taking up Flecknoe's reminiscence in '*The Remembrance*' (quoted above) these lines allude to his account in *A Relation*, where he describes how the Portuguese Secretary of State noticed his lute and informed the king:

> He no sooner understood of my arrival, but he sent for me to Court . . . The next day he sent for me again, where after some two or three hours tryal of my skill, (especially in the composative part of Musick, in which his Majesty chiefly exceeded) I past *Court* Doctor.[27]

As this found its way into *Mac Flecknoe*, perhaps other details of Flecknoe's

---

[23] Novak (pp. 499, 506) also notes that *Mac Flecknoe* is concerned with Flecknoe's retirement, and cites 'L'Envoy'; it was first published in *Epigrams Made at Several Times Continued to the Year 1673* (London, 1673), p. 98, and reprinted in *Euterpe Revived* (London, 1675), p. 98.

[24] Dryden, *Mac Flecknoe*, ll. 7–10.

[25] Marvell's poem seems to be the chief evidence for Flecknoe being a priest, though a number of Flecknoe's epigrams and characters suggest that he was a Catholic.

[26] Dryden, *Mac Flecknoe*, ll. 35–6.

[27] Richard Flecknoe, *A Relation Of ten Years Travells in Europe, Asia, Affrique, and America* (London, [1656]), pp. 50–1.

journey also caught Dryden's eye. Dryden dresses Flecknoe in coarse drugget[28] – an odd detail, but actually a very suitable attire for this particular monarch, since he had commented on the homely dress worn by the King of Portugal:

> the *King* is an honest plain man . . . faring as homely as any *Farmer*, and going as meanly clad as any Citizen, neither did he ever make use of any of the Crown Wardrope, since he came unto the Crown.[29]

The same passage in *Mac Flecknoe* mentions a voyage on the Thames, accompanied by music and a throng of fish,[30] which may be a travesty of Flecknoe's voyage from Lisbon to Brazil:

> Our ship being all incompast with *Dorado's* or shining Fishes (somwhat like *Dolphins*) hunting the Flying Fishes, which you might see on Top of the water, fluttering to escape . . . nor wanted we Musick to our Feast, (besides an excellent set of Trumpets) the Mariners having some *Fiddles* amongst them, to which they often danc'd to delight the Passengers.[31]

But the richest contribution which Flecknoe made to *Mac Flecknoe* is the image of kingship. In presenting Flecknoe as a monarch, Dryden is taking up an image which Flecknoe himself had made public. In a letter in this same volume Flecknoe writes:

> To Madamoiselle de *Beauvais*, in Raillerie, On his being King on Twelf-night. Anno 51.
> *Madamoiselle,*
>   *Pythagoras* (or I imagin) would never have been such an Enemy to *Beans*, had he received such favours from them as I have done, who by the Suffrage of one am chosen *King* to night; Think me not now one of those who change their natural Condition, with the condition of Fortune, and wax proud with their honours. No, more I am in capacity of doing good, more I mean to do; and I promise you on my *Royal* word, my Subjects here shall all have cause to rejoice whilst I reign over them, my raign shall be nothing but one continued Feast, which they shall celebrate with joyful acclamation, nothing shall be consum'd but in the Kitchen; and nothing be exhausted but the Cellar, I will do Grace to all, and no Justice shall be done, but in drinking healths, amongst the rest Madamoiselle, yours shall not be forgot, and think but what Grace I may do you, and account it done.
>
> *Il Rey.*[32]

---

28 Dryden, *Mac Flecknoe*, ll. 33, 214.
29 Flecknoe, *A Relation Of ten Years Travells*, p. 56.
30 Dryden, *Mac Flecknoe*, ll. 38–50.
31 Flecknoe, *A Relation Of ten Years Travells*, pp. 61, 63.
32 Flecknoe, *A Relation Of ten Years Travells*, pp. 137–8. Novak mentions this Twelfth Night game in passing (p. 500*n*), but does not accord it the significance which, I think, it deserves.

Flecknoe prints the lady's reply in French ('A sa Majeste Flecknotique') and provides a translation:

> To his Flecknotique Majesty.
> Your Majesty may please to know that I rejoyce exceedingly for his happy accession to the Crown, which I easily believe will be the more happy, since Antiquity has alwayes been of opinion, that then Kingdoms would be happiest, when Philosophers were Kings, or Kings Philosophers; according to this, I esteem your Kingdom very happy, and hope your Greatnesse will not hinder you from remembring one so little as I.[33]

This image of Flecknoe as monarch was a gift which Dryden accepted gratefully, all the more so since it is so rich in allusion, not only to the monarchy of wit but also to Flecknoe's titles *Love's Dominion* and *Love's Kingdom*, and to his persistent addresses to minor European royalty in his epigrams and letters.

This is Flecknoe's major contribution to the imagery of Dryden's poem, but a few other points may be briefly noted. The 'mighty mug of potent ale'[34] which he holds instead of an orb may allude to the abundant drink which characterizes Flecknoe's reign at Twelfth Night, and to his epigram in execration of small beer,[35] as well as to Shadwell's invocation of ale at the opening of his verse letter to Wycherley:

> Inspir'd with high and mighty Ale,
> That does with stubborn Muse prevail:
> Ale, that makes Tinker mighty Witty,
> And makes him Droll out merry Ditty:[36]

Flecknoe and Shadwell are the heirs of Jonson in their drinking if not in their wit.[37] Ironically, Dryden associates Shadwell and Flecknoe by alluding to the very poem in which Shadwell had himself spoken slightingly of Flecknoe's wit:

> Critics that Damn with little Wit,
> As *Ned*, or *Fleckno* ever writ;[38]

Shadwell's empire which extends to Barbados[39] also links him with Flecknoe, since it alludes both to the setting of Dryden's version of *The Tempest*[40]

---

33 Flecknoe, *A Relation Of ten Years Travells*, pp. 138–9.
34 Dryden, *Mac Flecknoe*, l. 121.
35 Flecknoe, 'In Execration of small Beer', in *Epigrams of All Sorts* (1669), pp. 13–14.
36 'A Letter from Mr. Shadwell to Mr. Wicherley', in *The Complete Works of Thomas Shadwell*, edited by Montague Summers, 5 vols (London, 1927), v 227. Summers dates the poem to May–June 1671.
37 Dryden, *Mac Flecknoe*, ll. 193–6.
38 Shadwell, *Complete Works*, v 228.
39 Dryden, *Mac Flecknoe*, l. 140.
40 Oden, p. 240

appropriated by Shadwell for his operatic version, and also to one of Flecknoe's epigrams celebrating 'the Riches of the *Barbados*'.[41] Flecknoe's collection *A Treatise of the Sports of Wit*, which provided Dryden with the idea of Flecknoe's retirement, may also have given him a further hint. Dryden's monarch advises his heir to give up the drama 'and choose for thy command | Some peaceful province in acrostic land'.[42] This remark has not seemed hitherto to have any particular relevance to the work of Flecknoe or Shadwell, but Flecknoe's *Treatise* is in fact concerned with the word games which he has devised for the amusement of his royal patrons:

> The next Nights sport, and that of many Nights after, was the Acting of *Proverbs*, a sport of so great variety . . . some which cause laughter without any *Wit*, others more studious then delightful as *Ridles, Rebus's*, and *Anagrams*.[43]

Here the Jonsonian scourge of Restoration wit has become a maker of riddles and anagrams; moreover, he has dared to claim that this sort of activity is true wit, saying in this *Treatise* that

> *Wit* to the subject it treats of, is, as the *Soul* to the *Body*, animating it with *Life* and *Spirit*, which else were but *dead* and *dull*; it is the quintescence of *Conceit*, extracted out of *Words* and *Matter*, as the *Bee* extracts *Honey* out of *Flowers*; and as out of dull *Flint* we strike sparks of *Fire*, so out of dull *Matter* we strike sparks of *Wit*.[44]

'Out of dull *Matter* we strike sparks of *Wit*': this could be the motto for Dryden's method in *Mac Flecknoe*, which by exploiting Flecknoe's own images of himself distinguishes true from false wit.

Flecknoe's work seems to have come into Dryden's mind on two subsequent occasions when he was seeking to define false wit. In *Absalom and Achitophel* the unstable wit Zimri is described as

> Chemist, fiddler, statesman, and buffoon:[45]

a line which may have been shaped in part by a lingering echo of Flecknoe's gibe that Killigrew was 'one born to discredit all the Professions he was of; the *Traveller, Courtier, Soldier, Writer,* and the *Buffoon*'.[46] The second case is beautifully ironic. In 1665 Flecknoe published an essay *Of Raillery*, which includes this definition:

---

41 Flecknoe, 'On the Riches of the *Barbados* to Col. *Henry Drax*', in *Epigrams of All Sorts* (1669), p. 15.
42 Dryden, *Mac Flecknoe*, ll. 205–6.
43 Flecknoe, *A Treatise of the Sports of Wit*, p. 25.
44 Flecknoe, *A Treatise of the Sports of Wit*, p. 5.
45 Dryden, *Absalom and Achitophel*, l. 550.
46 Richard Flecknoe, *The Life of Tomaso the Wanderer* (London, 1667), p. 6.

There is as much difference betwixt *Raillerie* and *Satyrs, Jesting* and *Jeering,* &c, as betwixt *gallantry* and *clownishness*; or betwixt a *gentle Accost* and *rude Assault* . . . [Raillery] differs from *Gybing* as gentle smiles from scornfull laughter, and from rayling as Gentlemens playing at foyls, from Butchers and Clowns playing at Cudgels.[47]

This, surely, was transformed by Dryden into his own celebrated account of the art of satire in his *Discourse concerning Satire* (1693):

there is still a vast difference betwixt the slovenly butchering of a man, and the fineness of a stroke that separates the head from the body and leaves it standing in its place.[48]

Touché?

---

47 Richard Flecknoe, *Enigmaticall Characters, All Taken to the Life, from severall Persons Humours, & Dispositions* (London, 1658), p. 30. The essay also appears in *Sixtynine Enigmaticall Characters*, second edition (London, 1665), pp. 33–4.
48 *Poems of John Dryden*, iii 423.

9

Marvell's Coy Mistresses

I

THE CONTEMPORARY reputation of seventeenth-century poets depended much upon the mode of publication which was used for their work. In Donne's lifetime, his *Songs and Sonets* circulated in manuscript amongst a relatively privileged readership: only after his death were the erotic poems penned by the Dean of St Paul's revealed in print to a wider public. Rochester's poetry was also passed around primarily in manuscript form, becoming increasingly degenerate (textually if not morally), and with his name also being attached to all manner of illegitimate offspring. His licentious life and ostensibly pious death ensured a ready market for the printed editions which appeared within months of his final illness in 1680. Marvell's case is strikingly different: apart from the political satires associated with his name, few of his poems were published in his lifetime in either manuscript or print; and some of them must have looked decidedly old-fashioned when the posthumous folio collection of *Miscellaneous Poems. By Andrew Marvell, Esq; Late Member of the Honourable House of Commons* was published in the turbulent year of 1681, with the country gripped by the Exclusion Crisis.[1]

Amongst the poems printed for the first time in this Folio was 'To his Coy Mistress', but *circa* 1672 a shorter version of the poem had been copied into his manuscript collection of topical verse and prose by Sir William Haward, MP and Gentleman of the Privy Chamber to Charles II. This is now Bodleian Library MS Don. b. 8, and the poem is found on pages 283–4, without title or attribution.[2] In the following discussion the Folio printed text will be referred

---

[1] The text used here is that of one of the copies in the Brotherton Collection, Leeds University Library. The British Library copy (C. 59. i. 8) and some pages from the annotated Bodleian Library copy MS Eng. poet. d. 49 (which also has MS leaves supplementing the printed text) are reproduced in the Scolar Press facsimile, Andrew Marvell, *Miscellaneous Poems 1681* (Menston, 1969), with a useful bibliographical note.

[2] This text was first printed and discussed by Hilton Kelliher, 'A New Text of Marvell's "To His Coy Mistress" ', *Notes and Queries*, 215 (1970) 254–6, and a facsimile is provided in Hilton Kelliher, *Andrew Marvell: Poet & Politician 1621–78* (London, 1978) and in *Poems of Andrew Marvell*, pp. 79–80. See also Beal, *Index*, ii 23. It is not always easy to tell majuscules from minuscules in Haward's hand.

to as '*F*', and the Haward manuscript as '*H*'. The relationship between the two texts is puzzling, and raises a number of critical and editorial questions which this paper will attempt to address. The two versions are printed below in parallel columns, where for ease of comparison spacing has been introduced into the *H* text to keep the two texts aligned; there are no such gaps in the original. Substantive variants between the two texts are underlined.

F	*H*
To his Coy Mistress.	
Had <u>we</u> but World enough, and Time,	Had <u>I</u> but world enough, & tyme,
This coyness <u>Lady</u> were no crime.	This Coynesse, <u>Madam,</u> were noe Crime.
<u>We would</u> sit down, and think which way	<u>I could</u> sitt downe, & thinke, which way
To walk, and pass our long Loves Day.	To walke, & passe our long-loues day.
<u>Thou</u> by the *Indian Ganges* side 5	<u>You</u> by yᵉ Indian Ganges side 5
<u>Should'st</u> Rubies <u>find</u>: I by the Tide	<u>Should</u> Rubyes <u>seeke</u>, I by the Tide
Of *Humber* would complain. I would	Of Humber would complaine, I wo'ud
Love you ten years before the Flood:	Loue you ten yeares before yᵉ Floud,
And you should if you please refuse	And you should, if you please, refuse,
Till the Conversion of the *Jews.* 10	Till yᵉ Conuersion of the Jewes. 10
My vegetable Love should grow	My vegetable Loue should grow
Vaster then Empires, <u>and</u> more slow.	Vaster, then Empires, <u>but</u> more slow.
<u>An</u> hundred years should go to praise	<u>One</u> hundred yeares should goe, to prayse
<u>Thine Eyes</u>, and on <u>thy</u> Forehead Gaze.	<u>Your Brow</u>, and on <u>your</u> forehead gaze;
Two hundred to adore <u>each Breast</u>: 15	Two hundred to adore <u>your eyes</u>, 15
But thirty thousand to <u>the rest</u>.	But thirty thousand to <u>your Thighes</u>.
An Age at least to every part,	An age att least to euery part,
And the last Age <u>should</u> show your Heart.	And the last Age <u>to</u> shew your heart.
For <u>Lady</u> you deserve this State;	For, <u>Madam,</u> you deserue this state,
Nor <u>would</u> I love at lower rate. 20	Nor <u>can</u> I loue att lower Rate. 20
But <u>at my back I alwaies</u> hear	But <u>harke, behind meethinkes I</u> heare
Times winged Charriot hurrying near:	Tymes winged Charriot hurrying neare,
And yonder all before us <u>lye</u>	And yonder all before vs <u>lyes</u>
Desarts of vast <u>Eternity</u>.	Desarts of vast <u>Eternityes</u>.
<u>Thy</u> Beauty <u>shall no more be found</u>; 25	<u>Your</u> beauty <u>will stand neede of Salt</u>, 25
<u>Nor</u>, in <u>thy</u> marble Vault, <u>shall sound</u>	<u>For</u> in <u>the hollow</u> Marble Vault
My <u>ecchoing Song: then</u> Worms <u>shall</u> try	<u>Will</u> my <u>Songs Eccho</u>, Wormes <u>must</u> try
<u>That</u> long preserv'd Virginity:	<u>Your</u> longe preseru'd Virginity.
<u>And your quaint Honour turn to durst;</u>	
<u>And into ashes all my Lust.</u> 30	
<u>The Grave's a fine and private place.</u>	
<u>But none I think do there embrace.</u>	
Now <u>therefore, while</u> the youthful <u>hew</u>	Now <u>then whil'st</u> yᵉ youthfull <u>Glue</u>
<u>Sits</u> on <u>thy skin</u> like morning <u>glew</u>,	<u>Stickes</u> on <u>your cheeke</u>, like Morning Dew, 30
<u>And while thy willing Soul transpires</u> 35	

At every pore with instant Fires,
Now let us sport us while we may;
And now, like am'rous birds of prey,
Rather at once our Time devour,
Than languish in his slow-chapt
   pow'r.   40
Let us roll all our Strength, and all
Our sweetness, up into one Ball:
And tear our Pleasures with rough strife,
Thorough the Iron gates of Life.
Thus, though we cannot make our Sun 45
Stand still, yet we will make him run.

Or like the amorous Bird of prey,
Scorning to admit delay,
Lett vs att once our Selues deuoure,
Not linger in Tymes slow-Chop't power,

And synce Wee cannot make the Sun 35
Goe backe, nor stand, wee'l make him run.

In addition to these two texts, there is another copy of the poem, headed 'To a Coy Mistress', transcribed from *F* (as a note at the end states) in Leeds University Library MS Lt 61 fols. 24ᵛ–25ᵛ, a personal verse miscellany compiled *circa* 1715 and owned by James Gollop. It follows *F* except for reading 'pleased' for 'please' (l. 9), a grammatical improvement; 'the' for 'thy' (l. 26); and 'Through' for 'Thorough' (l. 44); while in line 30 the epigram is refined as 'The Grave's a fine, a private place'. While this manuscript has no textual value, it usefully illustrates the combination of error and revision which tends to occur in the process of transcription. More significantly, there are manuscript alterations from *circa* 1700 in the Bodleian Library copy of *F* (MS Eng. poet. d. 49; referred to hereafter as *T2*):[3] in line 24 'Desarts' has been changed to 'Deserts'; in line 33 'hew' has been changed to 'glew'; in line 34 'glew' has been changed to 'dew'; and in line 44 'gates' has been changed to 'grates'.[4]

The origin and authority of these various texts are unclear. Even their dates are doubtful: the publication of *F* in 1681 and the transcription of *H* around 1672 provide for each of those texts a *terminus ante quem*, but there is no evidence for their date of composition.[5] Nor is the hand responsible for *T2*

3   This is not an obvious *siglum*, but as it is the one used in the Oxford edition (*The Poems and Letters of Andrew Marvell*, edited by H. M. Margoliouth, third edition revised by Pierre Legouis and E. E. Duncan-Jones, 2 vols (Oxford, 1971)), it is retained here to facilitate cross-reference: for a discussion of *T2* see *Poems and Letters*, i 227, 234–5, and Beal, *Index*, ii 22–3.

4   For 'iron grates' cp. Edward Phillips, *The New World of English Words*, fifth edition (London, 1696): 'Grates, a sort of Iron Lattices, and serving instead of Windows, in Prisons and Popish Cloysters' (sig. Aaa 3ʳ); not in the fourth (1678) edition; cp. 'Upon Appleton House', ll. 103–4. The image suggests that the ecstatic physical union of the lovers will let them escape from the prison house of the body.

5   A *terminus a quo* for the *F* text is provided by the publication of Cowley's *The Mistress* (1647) and Herrick's *Hesperides* (1648), which contributed to Marvell's poem: see the notes in *Poems and Letters* for the use of Cowley, and for Herrick see Paul Hammond, 'Marvell's Sexuality', *The Seventeenth Century*, 11 (1996) 87–123, at p. 114.

easily datable. The prefatory note to the 1681 Folio, signed 'Mary Marvell', claims that 'all these Poems . . . are Printed according to the exact Copies of my late dear Husband, under his own Hand-Writing'.[6] Though one might be sceptical about the status of this supposed widow, it is difficult to dismiss out of hand the assertion that the copytext for the volume was Marvell's holograph, though that does not rule out unacknowledged editorial intervention, or compositorial error, affecting the text of *F*. Nevertheless, *F* does at least deserve *prima facie* respect. So too does the confident correcting hand *T2*, probably working from a manuscript source which he believed to be authoritative. What of *H*? Haward was a conscientious transcriber, but what is at issue here is not his own work so much as the status of the text which he received. There are several possibilities. It could represent (a) an early, rather rough draft of the poem, preceding the version found in *F*; (b) a later version than *F*'s text, perhaps adapted for a different milieu; (c) a version corrupted in transmission by copying; or (d) a version corrupted by oral transmission. It could also represent a combination of these: Hilton Kelliher suggested that it was both an early text and a memorial reconstruction.[7] It could even be an early version, reworked independently of *F*, transmitted orally, and corrupted in transcription. Let us consider in turn the characteristics of *H* which might suggest each of these origins.

The idea that it may represent an early version of the poem, before it received the final polish represented by *F*, might be supported by a number of variants which suggest deliberate revision rather than accidental corruption. 'I' for 'we' (ll. 1, 3) deliberately focuses attention on the male speaker. The variant 'Madam' for 'Lady' (ll. 2, 19) shows a change of mind over the mode of address. The variant 'find'/'seeke' also points to revision. In all these instances, however, the direction of the change is debatable. Other variants may point to *H* representing an unrefined early draft: the more blatant reading 'eyes l. . . Thighes' for 'Breast l. . . rest' (ll. 15–16), and the strikingly direct comment, 'Your beauty will stand neede of Salt' (l. 25), both lack the subtlety of *F*. The absence from *H* of some of the epigrammatic lines for which the poem is best remembered (ll. 29–32 and 41–4) might also point to its being an early version, on the grounds that few attentive readers would omit or (if memorizing the poem) forget such verses.

But some of the evidence just cited could also be enlisted in support of the hypothesis that the poem was revised away from the *F* text, perhaps for readers of broader tastes: 'Thighes' is certainly more direct than 'the rest', and might indicate a target audience with a preference for the mode of Rochester over that of Herrick, whose poem 'Upon the Nipples of *Julia's* Breast' is a possible source for that euphemism 'the rest'. 'Your beauty will stand neede of Salt' is

---

6   Andrew Marvell, *Miscellaneous Poems* (London, 1681), sig. [A2r].
7   Kelliher, 'A New Text', p. 255.

similarly unsubtle, if not downright crude. The tone of *H* seems less refined than that of *F*, as if *H* represents a man striking a Don Juan pose to a male homosocial gathering rather than choosing the best strategy to appeal to a particular woman. The prominence of 'I' rather than 'we' supports such a scenario.

As for errors of transcription, 'would'/'could' (l. 3), 'would'/'can' (l. 20), and 'An'/'One' (l. 13) are typical of the almost indifferent variant which one regularly finds in seventeenth-century manuscript verse, though these variants could be generated in either written or oral transmission. The plural 'Eternityes' (*H* l. 24) is conceptually awkward, but to mistake 'e' and 'es' at the end of a word is an easy and common error of transcription. 'Nor' and 'For' (l. 26) could be mistaken for each other, and while they introduce statements of opposite effect, both ideas are plausible, *F* meaning: 'I shall not want to court you when you are in your vault', or 'When you are in your vault you will not be able to hear my love songs'; and *H* meaning: 'If you continue to resist, I shall still be trying to court you when you are in your vault', or 'When you are in your vault, you will hear my love songs echoing around you, and regret the lost opportunity.' Again, though, *H* is cruder, so this variant may not be simple error.

Other variants seem to point to lapses of memory rather than of transcription. Complete couplets are missing from *H*, and couplets, as poor Mr Brooke found when addressing the electors of Middlemarch, are liable to slip from the memory under the influence of a glass or two of sherry. The rephrasing of lines with a new syntactical structure and the approximate rendition of striking images also points to memorial reconstruction (*H* ll. 26–7, 31–4). We know that the memory is liable to recall the unusual image but not its precise grammatical or rhetorical function: the mind behind the bad (first) Quarto of *Hamlet* recalled the phrase 'The vndiscouered country', but produced:

> The vndiscouered country, at whose sight
> The happy smile, and the accursed damn'd.[8]

with its commonplace and ungrammatical second line, rather than:

> The vndiscouer'd country, from whose borne
> No trauiler returnes.[9]

which is the reading of the good (second) Quarto. And, to cite a Restoration example, when Rochester's satire on Charles II circulated orally, being too dangerous to be frequently transcribed, some couplets dropped out, others

---

[8] William Shakespeare, *The Tragicall Historie of Hamlet, Prince of Denmarke* (London, 1603), sig. D4v.

[9] William Shakespeare, *The Tragicall Historie of Hamlet, Prince of Denmarke* (London, 1605), sig. G2r–v.

were reordered, became triplets, or had their syntax rearranged.[10] In *H* there is surely a lapse of memory between its lines 30 and 31, where the joining of the two similes 'like Morning Dew, | Or Like the amorous Bird' is grotesque. (It is just possible, however, that eye-skip could have led a copyist to move from the first 'like' to the second 'like', if working hastily and not reading the result.) The introduction of 'Thighes', 'Salt', and the rhyme on 'Vault' is not beyond the ingenuity of someone patching up a text from an imperfectly remembered version.

II

Weighing the textual variants in so short a poem cannot produce any certain conclusions, since several readings can be accounted for in more than one way. But it is possible to strengthen one of the hypotheses about the origin of *H* by considering some of the text's linguistic features. There are two such elements in *H* which suggest a different target audience from the audience envisaged for *F*, and perhaps a different date of origin. While *F* calls the coy mistress 'Lady', *H* calls her 'Madam'. The latter had become a standard polite form of address by the Restoration period, as Edward Phillips noted in 1696: '*Madam*, a Title of Honour, which is given as well in Writing as Speaking, to Women of Quality, as Princesses, Dutchesses, and others; but grown a little too common of late'.[11] Secondly, while *F* mixes 'you' and 'thou' forms, *H* uses only the 'you' form. 'In the course of the seventeenth century', writes Charles Barber, 'the *thou* forms fall into disuse, and by 1700 have disappeared from Standard English except as literary archaisms and in the special language used for liturgical purposes'.[12] If the *F* text were composed in the late 1640s or the 1650s, the mixture of 'you' and 'thou' forms would have been usual, for writers at that date might switch between them indifferently, or for grammatical ease. By the Restoration period, 'you' was standard polite usage, with 'thou' used to inferiors, to children, or 'when the emotional temperature rises'.

Etherege had a good ear for social nuances in language, and in *The Man of Mode* (1676) we find that the characters regularly address one another as 'you'. One exception is Sir Fopling Flutter, who, trying to ingratiate himself as an intimate friend of Dorimant, switches from using 'you' to Emilia to using 'thou' to Dorimant: 'Lady, your servant. – Dorimant, let me embrace thee.' Later, when Harriet turns aside to seek private support from her friend, she

10 *Works of John Wilmot*, pp. 85–90.

11 Phillips, *The New World of English Words* (1696), sig. Iii^v; not in the fourth (1678) edition. Unfortunately, nowhere else in his verse does Marvell use either 'Lady' or 'Madam' as a vocative.

12 Charles Barber, *Early Modern English*, second edition (Edinburgh, 1997), pp. 152–3; and see p. 156 for pronouns in Restoration comedy.

says, 'Dear Emilia, do thou advise me.' But moments of erotic intimacy do not seem to attract the 'thou' form, and when Dorimant and Bellinda discuss their mutual fidelity, they almost exclusively use 'you':

Bellinda.	*You* have no more power to keep the secret than I had not to trust *you* with it.
Dorimant.	By all the joys I have had, and those *you* keep in store –
Bellinda.	– *You*'ll do for my sake what *you* never did before.
Dorimant.	By that truth *thou* hast spoken, a wife shall sooner betray herself to her husband.
Bellinda.	Yet I had rather *you* should be false in this than in another thing *you* promised me.[13]

The opening and closing lines of this extract are in an idiom which soberly considers adult desire and sexual freedom; the characters use 'you'. The tone modulates into mock-seriousness in the rhyming couplet which the two characters construct, still using 'you'. Only in Dorimant's second line do we find 'thou', where he is using a now archaic biblical register to italicize wryly the seriousness of her promise. 'You' is the polite norm; 'thou' marks a move into a more intense register. Another character who uses 'thou' is Old Bellair, who says admiringly to Harriet, 'Adod, sirrah, I like thy wit well', and flirtatiously to Emilia, 'Go to, thou'rt a rogue';[14] here 'thou' seems a generational marker, part of Old Bellair's antiquated idiolect. It may be that in 1672 (if the composition of *H* is close to its date of transcription) 'thou' would have seemed dated, out of place in a poem of libertine courtship. The supposition is strengthened by a glance at Rochester's usage. His erotic poems use 'thou' when they are cast in a formal and somewhat archaic pastoral mode – 'Canst thou feele Love and yet noe pitty know?'[15] – or a religious idiom: 'If I by miracle can be | This livelong Minute true to Thee | 'Tis all that Heaven allows'.[16] He uses 'you' when addressing a woman as an autonomous sexual partner – 'You Rivall Bottle must allow | I'll suffer Rivall Fopp'[17] – or a long-suffering wife: 'I am by Fate slave to your Will'.[18] 'Thou' is used with affectionate contempt when addressing a male companion – 'Love a Woman! Th'rt an Ass'[19] – or, in mock heroic vein, a disobedient servant, in this case his own unruly penis: 'Base Recreant to thy Prince, thou durst not stand'.[20] There are significant nuances here. So in Marvell's poem the removal of 'thou' (and perhaps the substitution

13 Sir George Etherege, *The Man of Mode*, edited by John Barnard (London, 1979), III ii 133–4; V ii 38; IV ii 21–8; emphases added.
14 Etherege, *The Man of Mode*, III i 170, V ii 26.
15 Rochester, 'Dialogue', l. 2.
16 Rochester, 'Love and Life', ll. 13–15.
17 Rochester, 'To A Lady, in A Letter', ll. 7–8.
18 Rochester, 'To his more than Meritorious Wife', l. 1.
19 Rochester, 'Love to a Woman', l. 1.
20 Rochester, 'The Imperfect Enjoyment', l. 61.

of 'Madam' for 'Lady'), along with the introduction of salt and thighs, suggest that the text has been slightly modernized, and angled towards the libertine taste and idiom of court or coffee-house wits.

III

Though the origin of *H* is uncertain, there is one point in the poem where *H* may be able to clarify a crux,[21] the much-debated rhyme in lines 33–4, where the various witnesses read:

> Now therefore, while the youthful hew
> Sits on thy skin like morning glew, (*F*)

> Now therefore, while the youthful glew
> Sits on thy skin like morning dew, (*T2*)

> Now then whil'st ye youthfull Glue
> Stickes on your cheeke, like Morning Dew, (*H*)

H supports the correction made by *T2*. Since *H* and *T2* are almost certainly independent of each other, they are witnesses to the fact that 'glew/dew' was the rhyme in their common ancestor. While it is possible that this ancestor was itself corrupt at this point, it is also possible (and on the principle of *lectio difficilior* probable) that 'glew/dew' is the rhyme which stood in Marvell's original manuscript. If so, then 'hew/glew' is an alteration made by the editor or compositor of *F*. At this point in the argument, textual probabilities need to be supported by critical exegesis. What do the two pairs of rhymes mean? The originator of the 'hew/glew' rhyme seems to have imagined the mistress's youthful colour ('hew' being 'hue' in modern spelling) being like the rosy colour of the morning sky ('glew' being 'glow' in modern spelling).[22] The originator of the 'glew/dew' rhyme seems to have imagined the mistress's perspiration being like the morning dew. Here 'glew' may mean (a) 'glow', in the sense 'heat'[23] or even 'sweat';[24] and also (b) 'glow' in the associated metonymic sense

---

[21] For an extensive (and somewhat opaque) discussion of this crux see Thomas Clayton, ' "Morning Glew" and Other Sweat Leaves in the Folio text of Andrew Marvell's Major Pre-Restoration Poems', *English Literary Renaissance*, 2 (1972) 356–75.

[22] Cp. Milton, *Paradise Lost* viii 612. The *OED* lists 'glew' and 'glewe' as seventeenth-century spellings of the verb 'glow'; I assume that the same spellings were available for the noun, though discussions of the crux have disputed this, and no example has been produced. Helge Kökeritz asserted (without citing evidence) that 'glew' must have been a northern dialect form of 'glow', which Marvell, as a Yorkshireman, would have known (quoted in Andrew Marvell, *Complete Poetry*, edited by George deF. Lord (London, 1984), p. 24).

[23] *OED* glow sb. lb, first example 1793; but glow *v.*1 5 has the same meaning from 1386.

[24] Not in *OED*, but certainly a modern usage; how far back does it go?

'ardour',[25] implicitly sexual ardour;[26] or (c) 'glue' in the sense 'sweat';[27] or (d) 'glue' in the sense 'gum', which was applied to a perfumed excretion.[28] The primary sense is probably either (a) or (c), 'sweat', each implying (b), 'ardour', with (d) 'perfume' as a punning additional conceit. The idea that the lady is perspiring with incipient erotic pleasure is extended in the following couplet: 'And while thy willing Soul transpires | At every pore with instant Fires' (ll. 36–7). Besides, the verb 'sits' seems more appropriate for moisture than for colour. Textually and rhetorically the reading of *T2* seems preferable to that of *F*, which is by comparison a commonplace image. The reading of *H* ('Glue') clearly takes 'glew' to mean 'glue' rather than 'glow', as its verb 'Stickes' confirms.

The editor of a single text of the poem based upon *F* has to choose between the *F* rhymes and the *T2* rhymes, since each presents a clear and coherent, but different, simile. The editor might reasonably choose *T2* ('glew/dew'): textually on the principle of *lectio difficilior* and the support of *H*, and critically on the basis of the rhetorical coherence of the passage and the productive Marvellian ambiguities which the reading offers.[29] This would assume that *F* on the one hand, and *T2* and *H* on the other, are witnesses to a common original which was corrupted and simplified into the *F* reading by someone other than Marvell. But an editor might also choose *F*,[30] on the grounds that its reading could have been Marvell's own work, perhaps a revision made in order to remove an indecorous reference to the lady's perspiration. Whatever its status, the *F* reading does seem to be a change: for the reading of *T2* and *H* to be a textual corruption, one would have to posit a common ancestor which

---

25 *OED* glow *sb.* 3, first example 1748, but glow *v.*[1] 6 has the same meaning from 1649.

26 'A moist hand argues an amorous nature' (Morris Palmer Tilley, *A Dictionary of the Proverbs in England in the Sixteenth and Seventeenth Centuries* (Ann Arbor, 1950), H 86); cp. *Othello* III iv 39, *Antony and Cleopatra* I ii 52–3.

27 This sense is not recorded in the *OED*, but Thomas Blount glosses 'glutinosity' as 'gluiness, clamminess', showing that 'glue' might be thought of as clamminess or moisture, not only as a sticky substance (Thomas Blount, *Glossographia* (London, 1656), sig. S4ʳ). Nicholas Hookes plays comically on the two senses 'sweat' and 'glue' in his poem 'A Sacrifice to *Amanda*': 'I'd rather foot it twenty miles, | Then kisse a lasse whose moisture reeks, | Lest in her clammie glew-pie cheeks | I leave my beard behinde' (*Amanda: A Sacrifice to an Unknown Goddesse* (London, 1653), pp. 16–17). The *OED* records 'glew' and 'glewe' as seventeenth-century spellings of the noun 'glue'.

28 *OED* glue *sb.* 3b, *OED* gum *sb.*[2] 2; cp. *Paradise Lost* xi 327.

29 Nigel Smith follows *T2/H* in *Poems of Andrew Marvell*, p. 83. Elizabeth Story Donno also followed the reading of *T2/H* in her Penguin edition (Andrew Marvell, *The Complete Poems*, edited by Elizabeth Story Donno (Harmondsworth, 1972), p. 51). However, her apparatus quotes the reading of *F* in modernized spelling as 'hue' and 'glue' which is misleading. She glosses 'glue' only by means of a quotation from William Baldwin (1547): 'Life is nothing else but as it were a glue, which in man fasteneth the soul and body together', which may resonate with other poems by Marvell but is insufficiently precise as an explanation of this particular image.

30 George deF. Lord followed *F* in his edition (p. 24).

had turned a simple reading into a difficult one before the stemma branched and the *H* text was damaged and adapted, which is theoretically possible, but complex. What an editor should not do is to conflate *F* and *T2* as the Oxford editors did, choosing one word from each and printing 'youthful hew / . . . like morning dew', which compares a colour with a liquid.[31] This creates a reading for which there is no seventeenth-century evidence, and removes the one word ('glew') which all witnesses agree is one of the rhymes.

In conclusion, the stemma looks something like this:

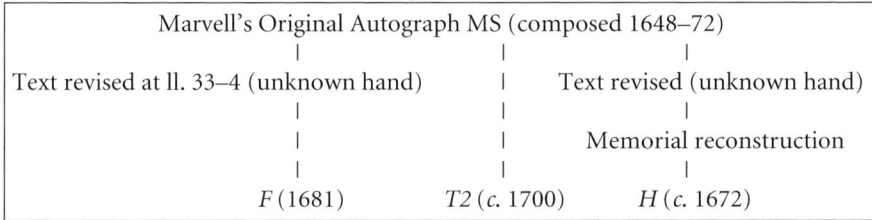

Marvell's Original Autograph MS (composed 1648–72)		
Text revised at ll. 33–4 (unknown hand)		Text revised (unknown hand)
		Memorial reconstruction
F (1681)	*T2* (*c*. 1700)	*H* (*c*. 1672)

Where does this leave us? It leaves us, I think, with two coy mistresses. The text in *F* is presumably close to a Marvellian holograph, but will require emendation from *T2* and *H* at ll. 33–4 if we think that the 'hew/glew' rhyme was generated by a simplifying editor or printer; but *F* can stand without emendation if we hold the poet himself responsible for the change. The text in *H* is certainly corrupt (though at exactly which points is far from certain), having passed through scribal and probably also memorial transmission. It may represent an early version of the poem, though there seem to be no features which suggest this which cannot equally be explained by corruption, or by the hypothesis that an Interregnum poem was adapted for a Restoration audience with less refined sensibilities. It deserves to stand in its own right, perhaps as an example of a communally crafted coffee house text, but perhaps as an instance of Marvell himself trying to demonstrate his heterosexual credentials. For this text, with its raunchier style and its dramatization of the sexually demanding 'I', reached Haward in the very year, 1672, in which Marvell was being derided in print for his homosexual interests.[32]

---

[31] *Poems and Letters*, i 28.
[32] For these attacks on Marvell see Hammond, 'Marvell's Sexuality', p. 115.

10

Rochester and his Editors

He takes me in his Coach, and as wee goe
Pulls out a Libell, of a Sheete or Two;
Insipid as the Praise, of Pious Queenes,
Or Shadwells, unassisted former Scenes;
Which he admir'd, and prais'd at evr'y Line,
At last, it was soe sharpe, it must be mine.
I vow'd, I was noe more a Witt than he,
Unpractic'd, and unblest in Poetry:
A Song to Phillis, I perhaps might make,
But never Rhym'd but for my Pintles sake;
I envy'd noe Mans Fortune, nor his Fame,
Nor ever thought of a Revenge soe tame.
He knew my Stile (he swore) and twas in vaine
Thus to deny, the Issue of my Braine.
Choakt with his flatt'ry I noe answer make,
But silent leave him to his deare mistake.
Which he, by this, has spread o're the whole Town,
And me, with an officious Lye, undone.[1]

IN THIS passage Rochester recounts the experience of being accosted by an
admirer who has come across an anonymous satire and recognized it as his
by its style. Though Rochester denies authorship, the admirer refuses to
believe him, and circulates the poem through the town with this erroneous
attribution. It is a vivid example of the way poetry circulated in the period, and
of the hazards of attribution, especially when a major name like Rochester's is
speculatively attached to all manner of verses. Except that this is not Rochester
speaking: it is the persona of Timon in a satire modelled on Boileau's adaptation of Horace,[2] and so the voice is both a fictional Restoration voice and one
which echoes the complaints of French and Roman poets. All too often editors
and critics have assimilated the voice in Rochester's poems to that of the

---

[1] 'Satyr. [Timon]', ll. 13–30, from Harold Love's text in *Works of John Wilmot*, pp. 258–9.
[2] It is an imitation of *Satire* III by Nicolas Boileau-Despréaux, which in turn is modelled on
Horace's *Sermones* III viii.

historical John Wilmot, regardless of the games which are played with voice and role right across his œuvre. Moreover, this poem, though it appears in every twentieth-century edition of his work, may not even have been written by Rochester. As Harold Love explains:

> The poem is attributed to Rochester in three manuscripts only, in one of which his name has been deleted and replaced by Sedley's. Two other manuscripts attribute the poem to Sedley, and four give no author. The printed sources (some of which attribute the poem, or a share in it, to Buckingham) are of no authority.[3]

So much for recognizing a poet by his style.

During his lifetime, and in the decades after his death when his canon was being formed, Rochester's texts were subjected to myriad alterations by scribes and printers; attributions were attached to works which were not his, and detached from works which were; genuine poems were shuffled in amongst others which might pad out a saleable volume. He was presented in some contexts as the writer of graceful songs, for besides poems which appeared in some printed song books in the 1670s, it appears that manuscript collections of his songs were made, perhaps at his instigation;[4] other readers would have encountered – or sought out – his libertine and pornographic writings, which were available in connoisseurs' manuscript anthologies; serious-minded readers copied and replied to his philosophical satires, such as the *Satyre against Reason and Mankind*.[5] But twentieth-century editions have also presented readers with a variety of Rochesters, in terms of text, canon, and authorial persona.[6]

The story of Rochester's treatment at the hands of modern editors begins in 1926 with the publication of a limited edition, printed on fine paper, and edited by John Hayward, the friend of T. S. Eliot.[7] Though rightly criticized since for his indiscriminate gathering of poems on the basis of sometimes very dubious attributions, his ignorance of manuscripts, and his lack of interest in the principles of textual editing (all rather surprising in the age of E. K. Chambers, Herbert Grierson, and Geoffrey Keynes), Hayward nevertheless made available work which had previously been hard to find, so that readers did at

3   *Works of John Wilmot*, p. 482.
4   Harold Love, 'The Scribal Transmission of Rochester's Songs', *Bibliographical Society of Australia and New Zealand Bulletin*, 20 (1996) 161–80; Nicholas Fisher, 'Love in the Ayre: Rochester's Songs and their Music', in *That Second Bottle: Essays on John Wilmot, Earl of Rochester*, edited by Nicholas Fisher (Manchester, 2000), pp. 63–80; *Songs to Phillis: A Performing Edition of the Early Settings of Poems by the Earl of Rochester*, edited by Steven Devine and Nicholas Fisher (Huntingdon, 1999).
5   Fisher, 'Publication', pp. 58–84.
6   Love has a judicious and generous account of his predecessors' work in *Works of John Wilmot*, pp. xv–xvi, xxxviii–xlii.
7   *Collected Works of John Wilmot Earl of Rochester*, edited by John Hayward (London, 1926).

least have usable texts of many of the poems, together with a good deal of Rochesteriana – albeit of indeterminable status.[8] But it was the edition published by Vivian de Sola Pinto in 1953[9] which placed Rochester in the canon of English poetry for the student and the educated general reader. The series in which it appeared, the Muses' Library, was published by a respectable press, Routledge and Kegan Paul, with a reputation for scholarly publishing in literature and philosophy, and was produced in a pocket format with good quality paper and binding. Rochester thus joined Sir Thomas Wyatt, Sir Walter Ralegh, Ben Jonson, and Andrew Marvell in their list of impeccable sixteenth- and seventeenth-century poets. A biographical and textual introduction was followed by an anthology of critical opinion from readers as diverse as Marvell, Pope, Johnson, and Leavis. (Pinto even sportingly included Leavis's tart rejoinder to Pinto's own observation that Rochester is the period's 'great poet of unbelief' – 'Rochester is not a great poet of any kind'.)

Pinto was constrained by the obscenity laws then in force to omit two poems, 'The Imperfect Enjoyment' and 'A Ramble in St. *James's Park*' because the publisher feared prosecution. His volume was in some respects an echo of that produced by Tonson in 1691, an elegant book which was designed to take Rochester out of the twilight world of manuscript satire and pornography and scruffy illicit editions, and into the mainstream English canon, and Pinto not surprisingly took Tonson's 1691 edition as the copy-text for most of the poems which Tonson included, supplementing that canon with some additional material from the 1680 edition and selected manuscripts. Since Tonson's edition tidied up Rochester's texts, and is now known to have bowdlerized some poems at a late stage in the printing process when sheets had already been run off, necessitating the insertion of cancel pages,[10] Pinto's edition to some extent took over the respectable version of Rochester which Tonson had promoted. But Pinto knew that bawdier versions of some of the poems in *1691* existed in other sources, and he supplied readers with some of this material in his notes, adding Rochester's manuscript draft of 'How perfect Cloris, and how free' (with its reference to 'The juice of Lusty Men' which Tonson's readers were spared, or deprived of); the final stanza of '*Faire Cloris* in a pigsty lay' in which the girl wakes and masturbates; and the final stanza of 'Love a Woman! Th'rt an Ass' with its thoughts of sex with the speaker's pageboy. Readers of Pinto's edition thus had in front of them most of the major variations in the texts of the songs, along with some of the principal variant readings in the satires. But what readers could not work out from Pinto's presentation

---

8   There was subsequently an equally elegant but less scholarly limited edition: *The Poetical Works of John Wilmot Earl of Rochester*, edited by Quilter Johns ([London], 1933).

9   *Poems by John Wilmot Earl of Rochester*, edited by Vivian de Sola Pinto (London, 1953; second edition, London, 1964).

10 David M. Vieth, 'An Unsuspected Cancel in Tonson's 1691 "Rochester" ', *PBSA*, 55 (1961) 130–3.

of this material – and what Pinto himself would not have been able to establish in the then prevailing state of knowledge – was the relationship between these variant readings, and the status and authority of their respective texts. For example, it is impossible to know from this edition whether the editor of *1691* censored an erotic song, or the compiler of a manuscript added a bawdy conclusion to what had left Rochester's hands as a chaste lyric. And this means that readers could not determine what kind of poet Rochester was: what was his sense of decorum, what was his aesthetic.

A breakthrough in the understanding of Rochester's text was effected by David M. Vieth, first in his substantial study *Attribution in Restoration Poetry* (1963),[11] and then in his edition of 1968.[12] Vieth's *Attribution* was a magisterial analysis of the textual tradition behind the 1680 *Poems on Several Occasions By the Right Honourable, the E. of R– – –*, and for the first time directed scholars' attention to the importance of scriptorium manuscripts. His scrupulous evaluation of the competing attributions found in manuscript and printed texts formed the basis for the radical pruning of the canon which resulted in his edition in 1968, a modernized text which controversially attempted for the first time to arrange the poems in chronological order. As various scholars have pointed out, this arrangement was unduly speculative, since there is little or no evidence for the date of many poems, and there is certainly not sufficient basis for the fine-grained dating which is needed if one is to arrange the poems in chronological order within what was a relatively brief writing career.[13]

Moreover, Vieth divided Rochester's career into periods which he labelled 'Prentice Work (1665–1671)', 'Early Maturity (1672–1673)', 'Tragic Maturity (1674–1675)', and 'Disillusionment and Death (1676–1680)'. This was ill-advised on a number of counts. First, it made a clear – indeed, a naïve – link between the poet and the poems, turning the work into simple biographical evidence, and, more seriously in its implications for the way we read Rochester's verse, turning the first person singular voice into a simple authorial utterance. Since so many of Rochester's poems play games with personae, and his contemporaries were intrigued and puzzled by the Rochester phenomenon to the point of imitating his personae and devising new ones for him, this was a distinctly unhelpful simplification to have enshrined in an edition. Even if we just look at Vieth's labels, it is far from clear that they work as descriptions of Rochester's life, let alone the poems which are gathered under each of these headings. Vieth's trajectory for Rochester's life is a tragic one, ending in disillusionment and death. But where are the qualities for which he was, and is,

---

[11] David M. Vieth, *Attribution in Restoration Poetry: A Study of Rochester's 'Poems' of 1680* (New Haven, 1963).

[12] *The Complete Poems of John Wilmot, Earl of Rochester*, edited by David M. Vieth (New Haven, 1968).

[13] For a recent chronology of Rochester's poems see Nicholas Fisher, 'A New Dating of Rochester's *Artemiza to Chlöe*', *English Manuscript Studies 1100–1700*, 8 (2000) 300–19, at pp. 304–8.

most admired: where is the exuberance, the wit, the panache? What was tragic about Rochester's maturity, especially if it included (as Vieth believes) the poised, complex wit of 'Upon his Leaving his Mistress', the confident literary satire of *An Allusion to Horace*, and the teasing philosophical paradoxes of the *Satyre against Reason and Mankind*? To place his translation from Seneca's *Troades* ('After Death nothing is, and nothing, Death') as the final poem in the section headed 'Disillusionment and Death' is rhetorically effective, but on the biographical level it ignores Rochester's deathbed conversion, and on the literary level it obscures the fact that the poem was sent by Rochester to Charles Blount some time before 7 February 1680, months before Rochester's death on 26 July.[14] We have no right to regard it as his final poem, let alone his final view of life. Moreover, as a translation from Seneca it is far from being a simple autobiographical utterance.

Vieth's text was based upon a wide-ranging study of the surviving manuscript copies, but he did not report his collations, stemmata, or arguments in his apparatus, leaving readers of his edition almost as much in the dark as readers of Pinto's as to the significance of the manuscript tradition. Indeed, in one respect Vieth's readers know less than Pinto's, for while Vieth lists the manuscripts which he has collated, he only records variants from his chosen copy-text, but not the source of those readings. Nor do we get any glimpse of the rejected manuscript variations. The next scholarly edition, that by Keith Walker, published in 1984, rectified that omission and was the first edition of Rochester to print a collation of variants for most of the poems.[15] There are problems, however. Walker did not collate all the manuscripts which were then available even in major repositories such as the Bodleian, and tended not to record the presence of a poem in the 1691 edition if he was not using that edition as copy-text, so the unwary reader might infer from these silences that Tonson omitted the poem in question. He did not provide stemmata, or any other account of the interrelation of the witnesses, or any explanation for his own choice of copy-text,[16] so the reader is somewhat at a loss as to how to use the extensive (but not very accurate) collations. But his collations did provide the reader for the first time with a view of the range of variants in Rochester's text, from which it was possible to comprehend the scale of the corruption, censorship, and rewriting which went on, and to see scribes struggling with the paradoxes of poems such as 'Upon Nothing' and the *Satyre against Reason and*

---

14 In 'The Dating of Three Poems by Rochester from the Evidence of Bodleian MS Don. b. 8', *Bodleian Library Record*, 11 (1982) 58–9, I argued for a date *c.* 1674, but Harold Love is right to object (*Works of John Wilmot*, pp. 370–1) that this 'rests on the assumption that Haward [the transcriber of the MS] was entering material on receipt, rather than (say) retrospectively from a roughly ordered collection of separates'.

15 *The Poems of John Wilmot, Earl of Rochester*, edited by Keith Walker (Oxford, 1984). Some of the points in the following discussion of Walker's edition were originally made in my review in *The Review of English Studies*, 37 (1986) 263–5.

Mankind. Walker also offered much more extensive explanatory annotation than Vieth. Sensibly, he did not attempt to follow Vieth's method of arranging the poems, and instead presented them by genre: 'Juvenilia', 'Love Poems', 'Translations', 'Prologues and Epilogues', 'Satires and Lampoons', 'Poems to Mulgrave and Scroope', 'Epigrams, Impromptus, *Jeux d'Esprit,* etc.' and 'Poems possibly by Rochester'. This makes good sense, and although not all the categories map precisely on to Restoration genres, they do correspond approximately to the groupings which contemporary readers would have encountered.

Another respect in which Walker's edition varies significantly from Vieth's, is that whereas Vieth modernized the spelling, punctuation, capitals, and italics of his chosen copy-texts, Walker did not. This is an important and controversial matter. The debate between proponents of modernized and of old-spelling texts is often intemperate, and usually futile, for in truth both ways of editing have their advantages and their disadvantages.[17] In the case of Rochester, a modernized text gives readers the impression of contemporaneity, and when Vieth's text appeared in 1968, complete with previously unobtainable bawdy poems printed in modern American spelling, Rochester's voice must often have sounded more alternative than canonical:

> Naked she lay, clasped in my longing arms . . .
>
> who fucks who, and who does worse . . .
>
> And then to cunt again.[18]

But modernization of spelling may destroy rhymes and puns, and modernization of punctuation replaces the predominantly rhetorical pointing of seventeenth-century texts, intended to point up emphasis and to aid reading aloud, with the predominantly grammatical punctuation used today, which may deaden the spontaneity of what is often a colloquial rather than a formal syntax. Yet by preserving the accidentals of his copy-texts, Walker risks causing unnecessary problems for the reader. When the reader comes across the phrase 'Persuaded Art', it takes a moment to realize that the capitalized

---

[16] He simply says (p. xiv) that he has followed Vieth's method of determining an appropriate copy-text and has generally arrived at the same choice.

[17] Interested readers may wish to consult the case for modernizing Dryden's texts as set out by Paul Hammond in the Introduction to *Poems of John Dryden*, i xvi–xxi, and by David Hopkins in 'Editing, Authenticity, and Translation: Re-presenting Dryden's Poetry in 2000', in *John Dryden: Tercentenary Essays*, edited by Paul Hammond and David Hopkins (Oxford, 2000), pp. 330–57; and the case against, cogently argued by Phillip Harth in a review of *Poems of John Dryden*, vols i–ii: 'The Text of Dryden's Poetry', in *John Dryden: A Tercentenary Miscellany*, edited by Susan Green and Steven N. Zwicker (San Marino, Calif., 2001), pp. 227–44; the book was also issued as vol. 63 nos 1–2 of *The Huntington Library Quarterly*.

[18] Vieth, pp. 37, 40, 53.

'Art' is a verb, not a noun, since to capitalize verbs is rare even in seventeenth-century printing, particlarly such an insignificant one as 'Art'.[19] The phrase 'a Cast of Spavin'd Horse' requires Walker to add a gloss explaining that 'Cast of' is 'cast-off', which is itself a perfectly good seventeenth-century spelling, and one found at this point in several manuscripts of the poem.[20] Some punctuation taken over from the copy-texts is confusingly heavy:

> But thoughts, are giv'n, for Actions government[21]

where the two commas are impediments to the sense, while in other cases the pointing is too light, as in:

> I'le nere recant defend him if you can[22]

which needs at least a comma after 'recant'. What is at issue here is not simply that the modern reader is unused to Restoration punctuation; rather, that the pointing of early printed texts and manuscripts is erratic and often downright counterproductive. In Walker's edition in the line:

> Some Fopp, or other fond, to be thought lewd[23]

the commas tell us that 'Fopp' and 'fond' are nouns, the latter meaning 'foolish person' (*OED n.*[2] B). Not so; the sense, as other witnesses make clear, is: 'Some fop or other, fond to be thought lewd', 'fond' meaning 'eager' (*OED adj.* 7). Of course, this is not just a problem with Walker's edition, as some lines in the passage quoted at the beginning of this chapter from Harold Love's edition will illustrate:

> Insipid as the Praise, of Pious Queenes,
> Or Shadwells, unassisted former Scenes;

where the two medial commas trip up the reader.

As an example of the various problems which can occur when reading a sustained passage in old spelling, here is part of the *Satyre against Reason and Mankind*, where Walker's copy-text is the 1680 edition:

> *Reason*, an *Ignis fatuus*, in the *Mind*,   12
> Which leaving light of *Nature*, sense behind;
> Pathless and dang'rous wandring ways it takes,   14
> Through errors Fenny – *Boggs*, and Thorny *Brakes*;
> Whilst the misguided follower, climbs with pain,   16

---

19 Walker, p. 73, l. 153.
20 Walker, p. 73, l. 169.
21 Walker, p. 94, l. 94.
22 Walker, p. 94, l. 113.
23 Walker, p. 88, l. 182.

Mountains of Whimseys, heap'd in his own *Brain*:
Stumbling from thought to thought, falls headlong down,   18
Into doubts boundless Sea, where like to drown,
Books bear him up awhile, and make him try,   20
To swim with Bladders of *Philosophy*;
In hopes still t'oretake th'escaping light,   22
The *Vapour* dances in his dazling sight,
Till spent, it leaves him to eternal Night.[24]   24

This is a difficult passage at the best of times, but the seventeenth-century accidentals – which are the spellings, italics, capitals, and punctuation of the compositor, not the poet – create many problems for the modern reader. The printer has chosen to italicize some key concepts, '*Reason*', '*Mind*', '*Nature*', '*Philosophy*' – but not others, such as 'thought', 'doubts', and 'errors'. 'Night' is capitalized, but not 'light'. Some of these key terms are both capitalized and italicized, including '*Reason*', but also, oddly, '*Boggs*'. To capitalize the principal abstract nouns might be helpful, but not if our eye is also caught by the capitalization of 'Fenny' and 'Bladders'. Punctuation should help us through the argument of the passage, but even when we make allowances for the fact that seventeenth-century punctuation was more rhetorical than grammatical, the pointing of this passage causes difficulty. The opening line of the quotation has a misleading comma: Rochester is saying that reason is an *ignis fatuus* (Will-o'-the-wisp) in the mind, not that reason (an *ignis fatuus*) is in the mind, as the *1680* punctuation has it. In line 13, 'sense' is an explanation of 'light of *Nature*', and therefore we need a comma after that word. The semicolon at the end of line 13 stops the argument, but in fact we discover that the sense continues into line 14, where the main verb 'takes' is found. Line 15 ('Through errors Fenny – *Boggs*, and Thorny *Brakes*;') creates multiple problems. Is 'errors' plural? Through fenny errors, through bogs, and through brakes? No: 'errors' is the singular possessive, for Reason leads man through the figurative bogs and brakes of Error (the latter is an abstract noun and should probably have been capitalized in this schema). Then how do we read 'Fenny – *Boggs*'? The en-rule set spaced[25] is normally read as a dash, so the reader infers that the meaning is: 'through fenny errors, that is, bogs and thorny brakes'. But this will not do: the en-rule must be a hyphen, and these are fenny-bogs, though it is not clear why 'Fenny' should be linked to its noun with a hyphen while 'Thorny' is not. In line 16 a comma in 'follower, climbs' separates the subject from its verb. Terminal commas at the end of lines 14, 16, and 20 break up the sense and interrupt what should be enjambement. We pause over whether

---

[24] Walker, p. 92. He has made three emendations to the *1680* text here: 15 errors *Walker*; errors, *1680*; 19 drown, *Walker*; drown. *1680*; 20 make *Walker*; makes *1680*.

[25] The problem is created by Walker's edition, since in *1680* the en-rule is set close, and so is unambiguously a hyphen.

'doubts' is plural or a singular possessive without its apostrophe. In line 22 the spelling 't'oretake' wrecks the metre, which requires 'to' to be pronounced rather than elided:

```
   x    /  | x  / | x  / |   x / | x  /  |  |
In hopes | still to | o'ertake | th' esca | ping light |
```

(Even though one might also want to stress 'still', the line nevertheless requires ten syllables.) The semicolon at the end of line 21 isolates the ensuing triplet grammatically and makes 'Vapour' the subject of line 22; but it is not the vapour which has hopes to overtake the escaping light, because the vapour *is* the escaping light; it is still the 'follower' who is the subject of this sentence, swimming in an effort to pursue the light which always eludes him.[26]

Here now is the passage in Vieth's edition:

> Reason, an *ignis fatuus* in the mind,
> Which, leaving light of nature, sense, behind,
> Pathless and dangerous wandering ways it takes
> Through error's fenny bogs and thorny brakes;
> Whilst the misguided follower climbs with pain
> Mountains of whimseys, heaped in his own brain;
> Stumbling from thought to thought, falls headlong down
> Into doubt's boundless sea, where, like to drown,
> Books bear him up awhile, and make him try
> To swim with bladders of philosophy;
> In hopes still to o'ertake th' escaping light,
> The vapor dances in his dazzling sight
> Till, spent, it leaves him to eternal night.[27]

There are problems here too. Not all readers will want Rochester in modern American spelling (as in 'vapor'). And the complete removal of capitals from the abstract nouns diminishes the impression that this is a dramatic narrative involving powerful, almost personified, entities (Reason, Sense, Nature, Error) which are engaged in a form of psychomachia. Vieth's consistently lower-case text has lost contact with the allegorical thinking which the passage shares with Spenser and Bunyan. This loss is felt even more keenly in the subsequent lines, where, despite the vivid personification provided by the image 'hand in hand', Vieth prints:

> Then old age and experience, hand in hand,
> Lead him to death, and make him understand . . .

---

26 However, the punctuation of all the editions which I have consulted makes 'vapour' the subject of l. 22, except Lyons's, which places semicolons at the end of both ll. 21 and 22, making l. 22 an isolated grammatical unit, which I do not understand. Admittedly, Rochester's syntax in this poem is rather loose.

27 Vieth, p. 95.

Walker, following *1680* in capitalizing only one of the three abstract nouns, has:

> Then Old Age, and experience, hand in hand,
> Lead him to death, and make him understand . . .

Harold Love, taking his old-spelling text from a manuscript, capitalizes two out of three abstractions:

> Then old Age and Experience hand in hand,
> Lead him to death, and make him understand . . .[28]

Surely what the reader needs is something like this:

> Then Old Age and Experience, hand in hand,
> Lead him to Death, and make him understand . . .[29]

There is no right way to handle the accidentals: original spelling preserves certain kinds of evidence for those who want it – evidence for a particular scribe or compositor's preferences, for their perception of the grammatical and rhetorical structure of a passage, and their recognition of what constitute its key words; and beyond that, sometimes valuable indications of contemporary pronunciation. But inconsistent and downright erroneous accidentals risk creating the wrong meanings. Modern spelling clarifies the thoughts, but risks abolishing puns, spoiling rhymes, and desensitizing the modern reader to the conceptual nuances of the language with its implication (particularly insidious for being nowhere signalled) that words such as 'sense', 'reason', or even 'love' had the same lexical meanings and cultural resonances then as now.

After Walker's edition, two paperback editions primarily for a student market were produced by Paddy Lyons and Frank H. Ellis,[30] but the next substantial edition was Harold Love's magisterial work which appeared in 1999. The fragile manuscript separates and scruffy little printed volumes in which Rochester's verse met its first readers are a world away from this 760-page Oxford English Texts edition. Love's work builds on Walker's to provide an old-spelling text with extensive collations, but for the first time readers were presented with an account of the editor's choice of copy-text and

---

[28] *Works of John Wilmot*, p. 58.

[29] But I confess that when I edited the poem for a student edition in 1982 I printed the same lower-case text as Vieth here (*Selected Poems of John Wilmot, Earl of Rochester*, edited by Paul Hammond (Bristol, 1982), p. 59).

[30] *Rochester: Complete Poems and Plays*, edited by Paddy Lyons (London, 1993), and John Wilmot, Earl of Rochester, *The Complete Works*, edited by Frank H. Ellis (Harmondsworth, 1994). Lyons's edition was the first to include *Sodom* in a commercially available volume. Both Lyons and Ellis turn the clock back textually by their adherence to printed editions, which they sometimes patch up from manuscripts.

variant readings, not in the form of a stemma, but as a descriptive analysis which generally sorts manuscripts into groups and signals the dependence of one witness on another where this can be established. This heroic work, carefully and judiciously executed, provides all that a scholarly reader could reasonably expect, and more. This Rochester is presented primarily as a writer for the court[31] (which of course included different groups with their own political, literary, and sexual interests, and their personal and factional rivalries), from which the poems were transmitted to wider circles of readers, some of whom did not always like or understand what they read, as one can see from the many textual variants. As Love himself observes, some of the surviving personal miscellanies can be traced to identifiable owners, so that we can associate one manuscript with an Oxford don, another with a Cambridge vicar, another with a courtier, another with a lady at the Charterhouse.[32]

The question which Love's edition repeatedly prompts is what kind of poet Rochester was: how political? how colloquial? how shocking? In the case of the lyrics, two aesthetic questions suggest themselves: how attentive to metre was Rochester? and how often did his smooth lyrics end with a sting? Take the opening stanza of 'Upon his leaving his Mistresse':

> Tis not that I am weary growne,
> Of being yours, and yours alone;
> But with what face can I design
> To damn you to be only mine?
> You whom some kinder Pow'r did fashion   5
> By merrit, or by inclination,
> The joy at least of one whole Nation.[33]

Thus Love, following Yale MS Osborn b 105. The metre is regularly iambic except for the startlingly reversed foot which opens line 5, with its emphasis on 'You':

> /   x   l   x   / l x   /   l x   / l x
> You whom l some kin l der Pow'r l did fash l ion

And the triplet which closes the stanza has a hypermetrical extra syllable at the close of each line. The metrical regularity seems necessary if we are to be surprised in line 5 by the unexpected stress on 'You', and if we are to appreciate the witty analogy between the excess syllables and the excess sexuality in the triplet which describes the woman's promiscuity. But other editors hear the opening line differently, with a trochaic metre: not

---

[31] *Works of John Wilmot*, p. xvi.
[32] *Works of John Wilmot*, pp. xxxii, xli.
[33] *Works of John Wilmot*, p. 17.

<pre>
    x / | x / | x   / | x   /
'Tis not | that I | am wea | ry grown
</pre>

but

<pre>
   / x | /   x | / x | /
'Tis not | that I'm | weary | grown[34]
</pre>

is the more colloquial opening in Walker's edition (following *1680*) and in Pinto's (following *1691*).[35] Here the stress falls not on 'I', but on 'weary', so that there are two versions of the line with rather different emphases:

Tis not that **I** am weary growne,

and

'Tis not that I'm **weary** grown

The logic of the poem requires the former, the emphasis on 'I' (with secondary emphases on 'not' and 'weary') since the argument runs: 'It is not that *I* am weary of being faithful to you, but how can I require *you* to be faithful to me?' Harold Love would likewise have printed 'I'm' if he had followed his copy-text, but here he has emended it, drawing 'I am' from a group of six manuscripts, two of which (Longleat House, Thynne Papers, vol. XXVII, the 'Harbin' manuscript, and Yale MS Osborn b 334, the 'Hartwell' manuscript) he has identified as having a close relationship with the Rochester family.[36] It seems that the colloquial version of the opening line was a scribal corruption. The same two manuscripts provide the otherwise unattested reading 'design' in line 3: prior to Love's edition, all modern readers of this poem have known the line as: 'But with what face can I incline'.[37] If this is a scribal corruption, it might have been generated by a recollection of Edward Sherburne's poem on a similar theme, 'Change defended':

> Then if my Heart, which long serv'd thee,
>   Will to *Carimtha* now encline,
> Why term'd inconstant should it be,
>   For bowing 'fore a richer shrine?[38]

---

34 Walker, p. 37.

35 Vieth prints ''Tis not that I am weary grown' (p. 81) and says (p. 196) that he is following *1680* and its cognate Yale MS Osborn b 105, but he has silently emended 'I'm' to 'I am'; Ellis and Lyons likewise follow *1680* but silently emend.

36 *Works of John Wilmot*, p. xxxvii, and 'Rochester: A Tale of Two Manuscripts', *Yale University Library Gazette*, 72 (1997) 41–53.

37 Vieth, p. 81, emphasis added.

38 Edward Sherburne, *Salmacis, Lyrian & Sylvia . . . With Severall other Poems and Translations* (London, 1651), p. 109.

But these two manuscripts used by Love are not impeccable witnesses, as we can see from variant readings which he rejects elsewhere in the same poem. Where *1680* and all other known sources read

> To damn you to be only mine?

these two manuscripts read 'make you ever' in place of 'damn you to be', and in the later line

> Let meaner Spirits of your Sex

they have 'beauties' instead of 'Spirits'. It looks as if the compiler of the version preserved in these two sources thought that the religious language in 'damn' and (to some eyes) in 'Spirits' was unacceptable. So several forms of contemporary response reveal themselves if one works though Love's collation for this poem: the text in some hands becomes a touch coarser, more colloquial, in the first line; it becomes more commonplace when the conventional 'incline' displaces 'design'; and in other hands it is made blander by the removal of the possibly blasphemous implications. If the text as reconstructed by Love is indeed more or less as Rochester wrote it, he emerges as a poet with a precise ear for metre and its disturbance, and one who precisely calculated the disturbance to be caused by unexpected vocabulary.

The problem of decorum raised by the text of this lyric reappears in several other poems which combine lyric grace with bawdy vocabulary. 'Nestor' (also known as 'Upon his Drinking a Bowl') is a graceful drinking song with a problematic final stanza. Does the poem end like this:

> *Cupid* and *Bacchus* my Saints are;
>   May Drink and Love still reign:
> With Wine I wash away my Cares,
>   And then to Love again.[39]

as Pinto prints it, following *1691*? Or perhaps like this:

> *Cupid*, and *Bacchus*, my Saints are,
>   May drink, and Love, still reign,
> With *Wine*, I wash away my cares,
>   And then to *Cunt* again.[40]

which is how it appears in Walker's edition, based upon *1680*. (Vieth prints a modernized version of the same source.) Love wryly comments that Walker, 'when given a choice between an obscene word and a euphemism, seems nearly always to use the obscene word.' He continues:

---

39 Pinto, p. 29.
40 Walker, p. 38.

This is not done from what Greg called 'a superfluity of naughtiness' but from an honest conviction that the direct colloquial term is the one Rochester would have preferred; and yet it may be that this judgment has led to some coarsening of the poet's effects. Rochester . . . has left us a number of charming, gentle songs and love poems that would never offend a soul. He could also do exactly the reverse – writing specifically to shock and disgust. But his favorite stratagem was to set up an illusion or expectation of refinement and then unexpectedly puncture it with an indecency: or vice versa – suddenly to modulate from indecency into delicacy and tenderness. In other words the effect often stems from the unexpected switch between registers. An editor needs to consider the aesthetic effect aimed at in the particular context.[41]

This is well said, but the problem remains how the editor decides on authorial intention when the only evidence which he has is of scribal or compositorial intention. In this particular case, an editor who, like Vieth, had discovered that *1691* at several points bowdlerized a text which is preserved in its rawer form in *1680*, might well assume that in this case too *1680* prints the obscenity with which Rochester shockingly changed the register in the final line of his poem, and for which Tonson's editor substituted a softer term. To readers of Vieth and Walker, their decision seemed justified by such reasoning (though such reasoning was never actually presented). Love's further researches, however, led him in another direction, and he prints the final stanza as follows:

> *Cupid* and *Bacchus* my Saints are:
>   May Drink and Love still Reign:
> With wine I wash away my cares
>   And then to *Phill:* again.[42]

'Phill'? This seems to be a shortened form of the girl's name Phillis, used elsewhere in Rochester ('A Song to Phillis, I perhaps might make', says Timon) – though it might also be short for 'Philip', which would leave in play the homoerotic implications generated in the previous stanza:

> But Carve thereon a spreading vine
>   Then add Two lovely Boyes;
> Their Limbs in amorous folds entwine,
>   The Type of Future Joyes.[43]

According to Love's interpretation of the textual evidence,[44] what Rochester originally wrote evoked a return to Phillis after his drinking session; then 'cunt' was substituted by a scribe who did not realize that the poem ended with

---

41 *Works of John Wilmot*, p. xlii, quoting his own article, 'Refining Rochester: Private Texts and Public Readers', *Harvard Library Bulletin*, 7 (1996) 40–9, at p. 48.

42 *Works of John Wilmot*, p. 42.

43 *Works of John Wilmot*, p. 41.

44 *Works of John Wilmot*, p. 366.

a proper name, and this in turn was replaced with 'love' by another scribe who could not tolerate the word 'cunt'. So we have two redactors with radically different understandings of Rochester's aesthetic – one who knew that Rochester liked to mix the graceful and the shocking, and another who preferred (or knew that his employer required) the inoffensive lyric manner. But there is another possibility: two manuscripts reported by Love[45] read 'fill'. This may simply be a misreading of 'Phill:' but it could be an inspired one: 'fill' means 'fill up the glass' but also 'have intercourse with, make pregnant'.[46] Was this a Rochesterian pun, uniting the two pleasures which the song celebrates, or an editorial pun based on certain assumptions about Rochester's aesthetics?

Let us turn now to the strange and rather moving poem, 'A Song of a Young Lady to her Ancient Lover', which reads as follows in *1691*, which was the only early text known to Pinto, Vieth, and Walker:

A SONG of a young
LADY.
To her Ancient Lover.

1.

Ancient Person, for whom I,
All the flattering Youth defy;
Long be it e're thou grow Old,
Aking, shaking, Crazy Cold.
But still continue as thou art,   5
Ancient Person of my Heart.

2.
On thy withered Lips and dry,
Which like barren Furrows lye;
Brooding Kisses I will pour,
Shall thy youthful Heart restore.   10
Such kind Show'rs in Autumn fall,
And a second Spring recall:
Nor from thee will ever part,
Antient Person of my Heart.

3.
Thy Nobler part, which but to name   15
In our Sex wou'd be counted shame,
By Ages frozen grasp possest,
From their Ice shall be releast:

---

45   *Works of John Wilmot*, p. 536.
46   Gordon Williams, *A Glossary of Shakespeare's Sexual Language* (London, 1997), p. 124; *OED* fill *v.* 2.

And, sooth'd by my reviving hand,
In former Warmth and Vigor stand.　　　　　　　　　　20
All a Lover's wish can reach,
For thy Joy my Love shall teach:
And for thy Pleasure shall improve,
All that Art can add to Love.
Yet still I love thee without Art,　　　　　　　　　　25
Antient Person of my Heart.[47]

The first thing which strikes the reader who opens Love's edition is that the poem is in four stanzas rather than three. Pinto, Vieth, and Walker all follow *1691* and print one six-line stanza, one eight-line stanza, and one twelve-line stanza, each ending with the refrain 'Ancient Person of my Heart'; and as many readers have realized, the tumescence of the stanzas matches the lady's promise that her lover's 'part' will 'in former Warmth and Vigor stand'. But Love prints a stanza break at line 20, dividing what had previously been thought of as one final, swelling stanza into two, the first of which now breaks the form of the poem by having no refrain:

Thy nobler parts which but to name
In our Sex would be Counted shame,
By ages frozen grasp possest
From their Ice shall be releast
And sooth'd by my revieing hand
In former warmth and Vigour stand.

All a Lovers wish can reach
For thy Joy my Love shall teach
And for thy pleasure shall improve
All that Art can add to Love;
Yet still I'le Love thee without art
Antient person of my heart.[48]

In a poem which is partly about art and artlessness, we need to be specially aware of the poet's artistry. It is hard to see any aesthetic reason why Rochester should write one stanza of six lines, one of eight, and two of six, and supply a refrain to only three of the four. This peculiar text arises because apart from *1691* there is only one other witness, Yale MS Osborn b 334 (the Hartwell manuscript), which is the source that Love follows.[49] He notes that 'both Harbin and Hartwell draw on a source that was also available to Tonson when he was editing the 1691 edition, and which appears to have come down

---

[47] *Poems, &c. On Several Occasions: with Valentinian, a Tragedy.* Written by the Right Honourable John Late Earl of Rochester (London, 1691), pp. 32–3; line numbers added.

[48] *Works of John Wilmot*, p. 30.

[49] The closely related Harbin MS (Longleat House, Thynne Papers, vol. XXVII) gives only the first four lines of this poem (*Works of John Wimot*, p. 529).

through Rochester's extended family'.[50] But an inattentive scribe can introduce an inappropriate stanza break, however good the textual tradition which
he inherits.

Besides the poem's form, there are also some verbal variants to consider.
There appears to be a grammatical mismatch in *1691*'s third stanza:

> Thy Nobler <u>part</u>, which but to name
> In our Sex wou'd be counted shame,
> By Ages frozen grasp possest,
> From <u>their</u> Ice shall be releast:

What has happened here? Does the problem lie with 'part', singular, which
should be plural? Pinto emends to 'Part<s>'. Love also prints 'parts', following
his manuscript. But is this manuscript preserving a correct original reading or
devising a plausible emendation? For, not to go into too much anatomical
detail, it is clear that the man's 'part' might be 'sooth'd' and then 'stand', but
would 'parts' 'stand'? Or is the problem with 'their'? Perhaps whoever created
this text thought that 'their' referred back to 'Ages', which he understood as a
plural instead of (as it probably should be construed) the possessive form of a
personification: 'Age's frozen grasp'. If so, one might emend 'their' to 'his' as
Vieth and Walker do.[51] In line 10, Vieth emended *1691*'s 'Heart' to 'heat'.[52]
Love also prints 'heat', following Osborn b 334. But 'Heart' is not obviously
wrong (it did not trouble Pinto); on the principle of *lectio difficilior*, it is
perhaps the more attractive reading, and 'heat' the more banal. What is the
basis on which one might choose between Osborn b 334 and *1691*? In line 2 an
unexpected variant emerges in Love's edition which had not been available to
earlier editors: for 'flattering' he reads 'Flutt'ring', which is the reading of both
manuscripts (the Longleat MS has just the first four lines, so is available here).
Are the youths who are rejected by the lady merely flattering her (whereas she
receives the truth from the old man), or are they merely insubstantial butter-
flies unlike the solid, dependable ancient lover? Here the simpler word is surely
'flattering'; 'Flutt'ring' evokes Etherege's Sir Fopling Flutter in *The Man of
Mode* (1676), and the sense is *OED v.* 3: 'To move about aimlessly, restlessly,
sportively, or ostentatiously; to flit, hover'.[53] At some points in this poem the
manuscript seems preferable (probably 'Flutt'ring', and perhaps also 'heat'), at
others the printed text ('part' seems preferable, and the three-stanza form
must be right). But what about the lady's last words? Are they:

---

50 *Works of John Wilmot*, p. xxxvii.
51 See Vieth's discussion of the crux, p. 199. Walker does not credit Vieth with this emendation.
52 Again followed by Walker, again without acknowledgement.
53 The *OED*'s first example in this sense comes from 1694 in a translation from Milton's state
    correspondence, so it was perhaps a modish word rather earlier in the Restoration – unnoticed
    by the *OED* – which passed later into ordinary usage.

Yet still **I** love thee without Art,

as in *1691*, or

Yet still **I'le** Love thee without art

as in Osborn 334b? Present, or future? Is the lady saying that she does love him, or that she will love him? And does 'still' mean 'nevertheless' (in spite of everything I do/will love you) or does 'still' mean 'ever' (I do/will always love you)? This poignant poem has, it seems, two alternative endings, poised between present and future in a way which Rochester might have appreciated, but could not have intended. This variant seems impossible to determine.

Beyond these local questions about what Rochester actually wrote, and therefore what kind of artist he was, lies the larger question of the canon. Hayward's rather indiscriminate collection printed 120 poems as Rochester's; Pinto printed 67, with a further 21 in an appendix of 'Some Poems Ascribed to Rochester on Doubtful Authority'. Vieth printed 75 poems in his main section, with another 8 'Poems Possibly by Rochester'; Walker 83 with 5 'Poems Possibly by Rochester'; Lyons 105, and Ellis 92. Love cautiously calls his main section 'Poems probably by Rochester', which includes 75 pieces; then follow an intriguing section reporting five lost works, five 'Disputed Works', and an 'Appendix Roffensis' of a further 36 poems which have been attributed to or associated with Rochester at some stage and are collected for the convenience of scholars. The variation in numbers is accounted for partly by how one treats fragments and variant versions, but nevertheless indicates considerable disagreement as to the boundaries of the canon. Rochester's principal editors have shown proper caution in sifting the often indiscriminate attributions which have accrued over the years, but even so there remain some familiar poems whose claims for inclusion in the canon are more precarious than is generally realized. *Timon*, as noted at the beginning of this chapter, is attributed in the early sources to Rochester, to Sedley, and to Buckingham, and Love consigns it to his section of disputed works. Another satire which should perhaps have joined it there is *Tunbridge Wells*, which is 'solidly attributed to Rochester in the manuscript sources', as Love says,[54] yet computational analysis by Love's collaborator John Burrows places *Tunbridge Wells* (and to a lesser degree *Timon*) stylistically outside the Rochester canon.[55] Some lyrics are also problematic. 'The Platonic Lady' was first printed by Hayward from

---

[54] *Works of John Wilmot*, p. 373.

[55] *Works of John Wilmot*, p. 686, 697–8, 703. Pope thought that *Tunbridge Wells* was not by Rochester. Pope knew a good deal about Restoration poetry, and was in touch with some survivors from Rochester's generation, so he may have been well informed. For Pope's annotations correcting attributions of several Restoration poems in his copy of *Poems relating to State Affairs* (1705) see Maynard Mack, *Collected in Himself: Essays Critical, Biographical, and Bibliographical on Pope and Some of his Contemporaries* (Newark, N.J., 1982), pp. 434–6.

Bodleian MS Add. A 301, where it is attributed to Rochester. There is another text, not attributed, in Bodleian MS Rawl. D 361, a closely related manuscript. Both belong to the early eighteenth century.[56] Whether Rawl. D 361 is the ancestor or descendant of Add. A 301, or independently descended from a common source,[57] the fact that only one of these closely related manuscripts attributes the poem to Rochester is disquieting. Whether the attribution was added when Add. A 301 was copied, or removed when Rawl. D 361 was copied, its status is thrown into doubt. Moreover, this is the only poem within the Rochester canon (broadly conceived) which appears in either manuscript, so this poem has a textual tradition quite separate from the transmission of most of Rochester's lyrics. Put simply, there is no obvious reason to trust Add. A 301. Pinto cautiously consigned the poem to his appendix, but it has, rather too hastily, been added to the central canon by Vieth, Walker, and Love.[58] The status of 'Against Constancy' is also precarious. Like 'The Platonic Lady', this poem is not transmitted in the usual manuscript sources for Rochester's songs, and is attributed to him only in Bodleian MS Don. b. 8. This is a large miscellany compiled by Sir William Haward, a courtier who was in a position to know a good deal about the poetry which was passed around in such circles, but again one needs to be cautious. It *sounds* like Rochester, but is that because we have been reading it since Vieth first included it in his edition of 1968 as part of the Rochester corpus?

The problem of Rochester's voice links all these individual cases. Though there is a distinctive Rochesterian manner, described by Love, which disconcerts the reader by changes of register, many of the songs attributed to him are simple in form and diction, while many of the satires and lampoons are rough in manner: such pieces are not inimitable. Contemporaries whose ears were attuned to current idiom often made attributions which we now question. Moreover, many poems in the Rochester corpus are impersonations: monologues or dialogues which experiment with different voices. Besides the pastoral dialogues, there are the female voices of the 'Young Lady to her Ancient Lover' and perhaps 'The Platonic Lady', as well as the verse letter 'Artemiza to Chloe'. There is Rochester's conversation with the postboy, which ends with him asking the boy the readiest way to hell, with the boy replying:

The Readyest Way, my Lord's by Rochester.[59]

Several manuscripts drop the last two words on to a new line ranged right, punningly implying an attribution as well as an ending. Is this Rochester

---

56 Beal, *Index*, ii 259.

57 Walker (p. 156) changed his mind about which MS was copied from which, while Love (p. 531) suggested that they could have a common source.

58 'The Platonic Lady' appears in both MSS in couplet form, but was divided, without warrant, by Vieth and Walker into stanzas.

59 *Works of John Wilmot*, p. 43.

denouncing his own way of life, or one of his associates impersonating the great impersonator? Pinto puts it in his appendix, Vieth in his main text (in the section 'Disillusionment and Death'), Walker amongst the canonical satires and lampoons (presumably as self-satire). Love also prints it as a canonical poem, but notes that the fact that Rochester was the speaker has led to some ambiguity in the manuscripts as to whether an attribution is also intended, and he even suggests Marvell as a possible author.[60]

Another question which arises is that of Rochester's politics. The reader of Hayward's and Pinto's editions would have found several pieces which suggested that Rochester had an active interest in politics. Pinto includes 'The History of *Insipids*. A LAMPOON 1676', which begins:

> Chast, pious, prudent, C[*harls*] the Second,
> The Miracle of thy Restauration,
> May like to that of *Quails* be reckon'd
> Rain'd on the Israelitick Nation;
> The wisht for Blessing from Heav'n sent,
> Became their Curse and Punishment.[61]

Pinto's source is *A Second Collection of the Newest and Most Ingenious Poems, Satyrs, Songs &c Against Popery and Tyranny, Relating to the Times* (London, 1689), specifically a copy in the British Library which has 'By John Earl of Rochester' added in a late seventeenth-century hand.[62] Subsequent editors have contested the attribution (which appears also in other printed texts and manuscripts), and it is no longer found in editions of Rochester.[63] But it is worth noting that after the Revolution of 1688–9, when the Whig satirical canon was being assembled, some people thought that this was the kind of poem which Rochester would or should have written. Pinto also prints as canonical the anti-Catholic verses 'On Rome's Pardons', and as doubtful 'Rochester's Farewell', a satire on the corruptions of court life under Charles II. Vieth, Walker, and Love all print 'On Rome's Pardons' in their sections of doubtful poems, but exclude 'Rochester's Farewell'.[64] Vieth's edition conveyed little impression that Rochester was politically engaged, at least in the medium of poetry, but in Love's edition there is a good deal more material which prompts a reconsideration. He may not print 'The History of Insipids', but he does include a substantial selection of no fewer than five variant versions of the notorious satire on the king, which show through their very differences that

---

60 *Works of John Wilmot*, p. 367.
61 Pinto, p. 107.
62 Pinto, p. 206.
63 For discussions of 'The History of Insipids' see Vieth, p. 225; *POAS*, i 243; Walker, p. xvii, who suggests that the attribution to Rochester deserves consideration, but also suggests Marvell as a possible author.
64 For discussions of 'Rochester's Farewell' see *Gyldenstolpe*, pp. 361–5; *POAS*, ii 217–18.

the verses were widely distributed, memorized, and adapted. Then there is a set of verses on the conversion of James, Duke of York, consigned to the 'Appendix Roffensis',[65] but nevertheless a valuable addition to the collection of political pieces which contemporaries associated with Rochester (probably, in this case, after 1688).

Love also includes for the first time a manuscript prose satire 'To the Reader' ostensibly intended as the preface to an edition of the *Satyre against Reason and Mankind*, which comments on one of the key words of Restoration politics, 'liberty'. The speaker is apparently an honest countryman:

> Commeing to Towne in Jully, and findeing the Tavernes and Coffee houses strew'd with Libells against God and the Government, and the streets Echoeing with the Cryes of Pamphlets seditious, profane, scandalous rebellious, Atheisticall, and Blasphemous (besides nonsensicall the most greivous of all) I Reflected vpon that guilded Idoll Lyberty I had soe Long held in the highest Veneration, and began to question my self whither indeed it were not fitter to be pray'd against than fought for, and might not better be added to the Lytannys of the Church of England Than stand A motto upon the sheild of any True serious Englishman; Since the meere shaddow of Lyberty, I meane this of the Press had allready introduced the most abject slavery subjecting us to the Tyrany one of another, by allowing our Insolent equalls or envious Inferiours the ridiculous prerogative of defameing and Vilifying our persons, Lives; Laws; and Religion and all that is nearest and dearest to vs without Lett or Controule. If this be Lyberty what slaves are such Freemen for to be Lawless is true Vassalage: this was not the Lyberty of Brutus, 'tis the Lyberty of Brutes; and a state to make men in Love ev'n with Tyrany, The better evill of the Two, if there be a choice of Evills.[66]

Attributed in the manuscript to a Devon clergyman, William Lovesey, this is interpreted by Love as a parody by Rochester of conservative outrage at the results of a free press; but how many readers would have taken this eloquent attack on the confusion of liberty with licence at face value? And is Love's reading right?

Also included within this prose work is the poem from 1679 beginning 'The freeborn English Generous and wise | Hate chains but do not government despise', which also circulated separately, and is included by Love in his section of disputed works, not having been printed by previous editors.[67] Here the poet argues that Englishmen respect law and reject tyranny and government imposed by force; this is a land in which arbitrary government cannot thrive. There is advice here for kings, for

> The surest way to Reigne is to protect.
> Kings are least safe in their unbounded will

---

[65] *Works of John Wilmot*, pp. 265–6.
[66] *Works of John Wilmot*, p. 54.
[67] *Works of John Wilmot*, pp. 257–8.

Joyn'd with the wretched pow'r of doing ill.
Forsaken most when they'r most absolute
Laws guard the Man and only bind the Brute.

No sensible king would become a tyrant, and often arbitrary rule is attributable to an over-mighty minister who wrongs both king and people:

Tis rather some base favourites vile pretence
To Tyrannize at the wrong'd kings expence.

Here, with paradoxes (and rhymes) reminiscent of the *Satyre against Reason and Mankind*, we hear a Whiggish voice, detesting tyranny but reluctant to blame the king himself. If this is Rochester, it is a Rochester who is more politically engaged as a poet than we had previously appreciated.

All these editorial labours have been devoted to creation of a canon around a single author, and it may seem ironic that the increasingly sophisticated analysis of manuscripts and the deployment of computer-assisted techniques of stylistic analysis should be applied to these works in order to determine the boundaries of one writer's canon at just the time when literary theorists have been asking us to think in subtler ways about the problems of invoking authorial intention, the complex ways in which authors are fashioned through the media in which they publish, and the creation of authorial personae in the texts themselves. But in fact the evidence which is gradually unfolded in these editions provides rich materials for us to contemplate exactly these questions. We can see how frequently scribal intervention or inattention, and the commercial requirements of the press, overrode any authorial intention in matters of metre, verse form, diction, decorum, and on a larger scale reconfigured the authorial persona and the associated canon. Timon's admirer undid his reputation 'with an officious Lye'; Rochester's modern editors have attempted to repair the damage wrought by those early readers, scribes, and printers, but lurking within their editions is the occasional 'deare mistake' which reminds us that their versions of Rochester are also recompositions of his text and canon.

BIBLIOGRAPHY

Primary Sources

Printed works which are cited or discussed are listed here, but books merely alluded to in passing are not included. Manuscripts are listed when they have been used at first hand, but those whose readings are cited (especially in chapters 2 and 10) from printed sources are not listed.

Manuscripts

Bodleian Library Oxford
    MS Don. b. 8 (miscellany compiled by Sir William Haward)
    MS Don. c. 55 (verse miscellany)
    MS Don. f. 29 (notebook of William Doble)
    MS Eng. poet. d. 49 (poems by Andrew Marvell)
    MS Eng. poet. e. 4 (verse miscellany)
    MS Eng. poet. f. 13 (verse miscellany)
    MS Firth c. 15 (verse miscellany)
    MS Rawl. poet. 123 (papers of John Oldham)
    MS Rawl. poet. 173 (verse miscellany)
British Library
    MS Add. 14047 (verse miscellany)
    MS Add. 18220 (verse miscellany)
    MS Add. 23722 (verse miscellany)
    MS Add. 27408 (verse miscellany)
    MS Add. 69823 (transcript of *Annus Mirabilis*)
    MS Add. 73540 (verse miscellany)
    MS Burney 390 (verse miscellany)
    MS Egerton 669 (verse miscellany)
    MS Egerton 2623 (verse miscellany)
    MS Harley 6914 (verse miscellany)
    MS Harley 7315 (verse miscellany)
    MS Harley 7317 (verse miscellany)
    MS Lansdowne 1045 (Dryden's autograph MS of *Heroic Stanzas*)
Leeds University Library Brotherton Collection
    MS Lt 54 (verse miscellany)
    MS Lt 55 (verse miscellany)
    MS Lt 87 (verse miscellany)
    MS Lt 110 (verse miscellany)
    MS Lt q 5 (poems by Henry Hall)
    MS Lt q 52 (collection of separates)

Nottingham University Library
   MS Portland PwV 31 (autograph poems by Rochester)
Trinity College Cambridge
   MS O. 10A. 33 (James Duport's rules for students)

Printed Books

A Letter from a Gentleman of Quality in the Countrey, to his Friend, Upon His being Chosen a Member to serve in the Approaching Parliament (London, 1679)

A Letter to a Friend. Shewing from Scripture, Fathers, and Reason, how false That State-Maxim is, Royal Authority is Originally and Radically in the People (London, 1679)

A., J., [John Maxwell], *Sacrosancta Regum Majestas: or the Sacred and Royal Prerogative of Christian Kings* (London, 1680)

Address of John Dryden, Laureat to His Highness the Prince of Orange (London, 1689)

An Exact and Faithful Narrative of the Horrid Conspiracy of Thomas Knox, William Osborne, and John Lane (London, 1680)

Behn, Aphra, *The Works of Aphra Behn*, edited by Janet Todd, 7 vols (London, 1992–6)

Blount, Thomas, *Glossographia* (London, 1656)

Brown, Tom, *The Late Converts Exposed* (London, 1690)

Browne, John, *Charisma Basilicon, or, The Royal Gift of Healing Strumaes, or Kings-Evil* (London, 1684)

Brydall, John, *Decus & Tutamen: or, a Prospect of the Laws of England* (London, 1679)

———, *Jura Coronae. His Majesties Royal Rights and Prerogatives Asserted, Against Papal Usurpations, and all other Anti-Monarchical Attempts and Practices* (London, 1680)

Buckingham, George Villiers, Duke of, *The Rehearsal*, edited by D. E. L. Crane (Durham, 1976)

Clarendon, Edward Hyde, Earl of, *The Life of Edward Earl of Clarendon . . . written by himself*, 3 vols (Oxford, 1759)

Covent Garden Drolery (1672)

Carne-Ross, D. S., and Kenneth Haynes (editors), *Horace in English* (Harmondsworth, 1996)

Creech, Thomas, *T. Lucretius Carus the Epicurean philosopher, his six books De natura rerum done into English verse, with notes* (Oxford, 1682)

———, *Titus Lucretius Carus His Six Books of Epicurean Philosophy, Done into English Verse, with Notes*, third edition (London, 1683)

Danchin, Pierre (editor), *The Prologues and Epilogues of the Restoration 1660–1700: Part II: 1677–1690* (Nancy, 1984)

Danielsson, Bror, and David M. Vieth (editors), *The Gyldenstolpe Manuscript Miscellany of Poems by John Wilmot, Earl of Rochester, and other Restoration Authors*, Stockholm Studies in English 17 (Stockholm, 1967)

Denham, Sir John, *The Poetical Works of Sir John Denham*, edited by Theodore Howard Banks, second edition (n.p., 1969)

Donne, John, *The Epithalamions, Anniversaries, and Epicedes*, edited by W. Milgate (Oxford, 1978)

Dryden, John, *Absalom and Achitophel: A Poem* (London, 1681)

———, *Fables Ancient and Modern* (London, 1700)

———, *Mac Flecknoe or a Satyr upon the True-Blew-Protestant Poet, T. S. By the Author of Absalom & Achitophel* (London, 1682)

———, *Poems on Various Occasions; and Translations from Several Authors* (London, 1701)

———, *The Letters of John Dryden*, edited by Charles E. Ward (Durham, N.C., 1941)

———, *The Poems of John Dryden*, edited by Paul Hammond and David Hopkins, 5 vols (London, 1995–2005)

———, *The Songs of John Dryden*, edited by Cyrus Lawrence Day (Cambridge, Mass., 1932)

———, *The Works of John Dryden*, edited by H. T. Swedenberg et al., 20 vols (Berkeley, 1956–2000)

———, *The Works of Virgil* (London, 1697)

Ebsworth, J. W. (editor), *The Roxburghe Ballads*, vols 4–5 (Hertford, 1881–5)

Etherege, Sir George, *The Man of Mode*, edited by John Barnard (London, 1979)

Evelyn, John, *The Diary of John Evelyn*, edited by E. S. de Beer (Oxford, 1959)

Examen Poeticum: Being the Third Part of Miscellany Poems (London, 1693)

F., R., *A Letter from a Gentleman To The Honourable Ed. Howard Esq.* (London, 1668)

Farley-Hills, David (editor), *Rochester: The Critical Heritage* (London, 1972)

Filmer, Sir Robert, *Patriarcha and Other Political Works*, edited by Peter Laslett (Oxford, 1949)

Flecknoe, Richard, *A Relation Of ten Years Travells in Europe, Asia, Affrique, and America* (London, [1656])

———, *A Treatise of the Sports of Wit* (London, 1675)

———, *Epigrams Made at Several Times Continued to the Year 1673* (London, 1673)

———, *Epigrams of All Sorts. I Book* (London, 1669)

———, *Epigrams of All Sorts, Made at Divers Times on Several Occasions* (London, 1670)

———, *Epigrams. Of All Sorts, Made at Several Times, on Several Occasions* (London, 1671)

———, *Euterpe Revived* (London, 1675)

———, *Loves Dominion, A Dramatique Piece, Full of Excellent Moralitie; Written as a Pattern for the Reformed Stage* (London, 1654)

———, *Love's Kingdom. A Pastoral Trage-Comedy. Not as it was Acted at the Theatre near Lincolns-Inn, but as it was written, and since corrected . . . With a short Treatise of the English Stage, &c. by the same Author* (London, 1664)

———, *Miscellania. Or, Poems of all sorts, with divers other Pieces* (London, 1653)

———, *Sʳ William D'avenant's Voyage to the Other World: With His Adventures in the Poets Elizium. A Poetical Fiction* (London, 1668)

Fowler, Alastair (editor), *The Country House Poem* (Edinburgh, 1994)

Hammond, Paul (editor), *Restoration Literature: An Anthology* (Oxford, 2002)

Hickes, George, *A Discourse of the Soveraign Power* (London, 1682)

Hobbes, Thomas, *Behemoth, or The Long Parliament*, edited by Ferdinand Tönnies (London, 1889)

Holborn-Drollery (London, 1673)

Hookes, Nicholas, *Amanda: A Sacrifice to an Unknown Goddesse* (London, 1653)

Hoole, Charles, *A New Discovery of the Old Art of Teaching Schoole* (London, 1660)

Horace, *In Horatium Flaccum, Dionysii Lambini . . . Commentarius locupletissimus* (Geneva, 1605)

Jonson, Ben, *Ben Jonson*, edited by C. H. Herford, Percy and Evelyn Simpson, 11 vols (Oxford, 1925–52)

Marvell, Andrew, *Complete Poetry*, edited by George deF. Lord (London, 1984)

———, *Miscellaneous Poems By Andrew Marvell, Esq; Late Member of the Honourable House of Commons* (London, 1681)

———, *Miscellaneous Poems 1681* (Menston, 1969) [facsimile of the previous item]

———, *The Complete Poems*, edited by Elizabeth Story Donno (Harmondsworth, 1972)

———, *The Poems and Letters of Andrew Marvell*, edited by H. M. Margoliouth, third edition revised by Pierre Legouis and E. E. Duncan-Jones, 2 vols (Oxford, 1971)

———, *The Poems of Andrew Marvell*, edited by Nigel Smith (London, 2003)

Milton, John, *Paradise Lost*, edited by Alastair Fowler, second edition (London, 1998)

———, *The Complete Prose Works of John Milton*, edited by Don M. Wolfe et al., 8 vols (New Haven, 1953–82)

Miscellany Poems (London, 1684)

Mish, Charles C. (editor), *Restoration Prose Fiction 1666–1700* (Lincoln, Nebr., 1970)

Mock Songs and Joking Poems (London, 1675)

Nalson, John, *The Common Interest of King and People* (London, 1677)

Oden, Richard L. (editor), *Dryden and Shadwell: The Literary Controversy and 'Mac Flecknoe' (1668–1679)* (Delmar, N.Y., 1977)

Ogilby, John, *The Entertainment of His Most Excellent Majestie Charles II, in His Passage through the City of London to his Coronation* (London, 1662)

Oldham, John, *Garnets Ghost, Addressing to the Jesuits, met in private Caball, just after the Murther of Sir Edmund-Bury Godfrey* [London, 1679]

———, *Poems, and Translations* (London, 1683)

———, *Remains of Mr. John Oldham in Verse and Prose* (London, 1684)

———, *Satyrs upon the Jesuits* (London, 1681)

———, *Some New Pieces* (London, 1681)

———, *The Poems of John Oldham*, edited by Harold F. Brooks and Raman Selden (Oxford, 1987)

Ovid's Epistles (London, 1680)

P., W., *The Divine Right of Kings Asserted in General* (London, 1679?)

Pelling, Edward, *David and the Amalekite upon the Death of Saul* (London, 1683)

Pepys, Samuel, *The Diary of Samuel Pepys*, edited by Robert Latham and William Matthews, 11 vols (London, 1970–83)

Philips, Katherine, *Poems. By the Incomparable, Mrs. K. P.* (London, 1664)

———, *Poems By the most deservedly Admired Mrs. Katherine Philips The matchless Orinda* (London, 1667)

———, *The Collected Works of Katherine Philips The Matchless Orinda*, edited by Patrick Thomas, G. Greer, and R. Little, 3 vols (Stump Cross, 1990–3)

Phillips, Edward, *The New World of English Words*, fifth edition (London, 1696)

Poems on Affairs of State (London, 1697)

Poems on Affairs of State, edited by George deF. Lord et al., 7 vols (New Haven, 1963–75)

Pope, Alexander, *The Twickenham Edition of the Poems of Alexander Pope*, edited by John Butt et al., 10 vols (London, 1938–67)

Prior, Matthew, *The Literary Works of Matthew Prior*, edited by H. Bunker Wright and Monroe K. Spears, 2 vols (Oxford, 1971)

Rochester, John Wilmot, Earl of, *Collected Works of John Wilmot Earl of Rochester*, edited by John Hayward (London, 1926)

————, *Poems by John Wilmot Earl of Rochester*, edited by Vivian de Sola Pinto (London, 1953; second edition, London, 1964)

————, *Poems, &c. on Several Occasions: with Valentinian, a Tragedy. Written by the Right Honourable John Late Earl of Rochester* (London, 1691)

————, *Poems on Several Occasions by the Right Honourable, The E. of R— — — (Antwerp, 1680)*

————, *Rochester: Complete Poems and Plays*, edited by Paddy Lyons (London, 1993)

————, *Rochester's Poems on Several Occasions*, edited by James Thorpe (Princeton, 1950)

————, *Selected Poems of John Wilmot, Earl of Rochester*, edited by Paul Hammond (Bristol, 1982)

————, *Songs to Phillis: A Performing Edition of the Early Settings of Poems by the Earl of Rochester*, edited by Steven Devine and Nicholas Fisher (Huntingdon, 1999)

————, *The Complete Poems of John Wilmot, Earl of Rochester*, edited by David M. Vieth (New Haven, 1968)

————, *The Complete Works*, edited by Frank H. Ellis (Harmondsworth, 1994)

————, *The Poems of John Wilmot, Earl of Rochester*, edited by Keith Walker (Oxford, 1984)

————, *The Poetical Works of John Wilmot Earl of Rochester*, edited by Quilter Johns ([London], 1933)

————, *The Works of John Wilmot, Earl of Rochester*, edited by Harold Love (Oxford, 1999)

S., G., *Britains Triumph* (London, 1660)

Shadwell, Thomas, *The Complete Works of Thomas Shadwell*, edited by Montague Summers, 5 vols (London, 1927)

Shaftesbury, Anthony Ashley Cooper, Earl of, *A Letter from a Person of Quality, to his Friend in the Country* (London, 1675)

Shakespeare, William, *The Tragicall Historie of Hamlet, Prince of Denmarke* (London, 1603)

————, *The Tragicall Historie of Hamlet, Prince of Denmarke* (London, 1605)

Sherburne, Edward, *Salmacis, Lyrian & Sylvia . . . With Severall other Poems and Translations* (London, 1651)

Stepney, George, *A Poem Dedicated to the Blessed Memory of her late Gracious Majesty Queen Mary* (London, 1695)

Sylvae: or, the Second Part of Poetical Miscellanies (London, 1685)

The New Academy of Compliments (London, 1671)

The Nine Muses (London, 1700)

Thorn Drury, G. (editor), *Covent Garden Drollery* (London, 1928)

Two Speeches. I. The Earl of Shaftsbury's Speech in the House of Lords, the 20th of October, 1675 . . . (Amsterdam, 1675)

Waller, Edmund, *The Poems of Edmund Waller*, edited by G. Thorn Drury, 2 vols (London, 1901)

Wilmot: see Rochester

Wilson, John Harold (editor), *Court Satires of the Restoration* (Columbus, Ohio, 1976)

Wood, Thomas, *Juvenalis Redivivus, or the First Satyr of Juvenal Taught to Speak Plain English* (London, 1683)

Wootton, David (editor), *Divine Right and Democracy* (Harmondsworth, 1986)

Secondary Sources

Achinstein, Sharon, *Milton and the Revolutionary Reader* (Princeton, 1994)

Armitage, David, Armand Himy, and Quentin Skinner (editors), *Milton and Republicanism* (Cambridge, 1995)

Ashcraft, Richard, *Revolutionary Politics and Locke's 'Two Treatises of Government'* (Princeton, 1986)

Axton, Marie, *The Queen's Two Bodies: Drama and the Elizabethan Succession* (London, 1977)

Barber, Charles, *Early Modern English*, second edition (Edinburgh, 1997)

Barnard, John, 'Dryden, Tonson, and Subscriptions for the 1697 *Virgil*', *PBSA*, 57 (1963) 129–51

———, 'Dryden, Tonson, and the Patrons of *The Works of Virgil* (1697)' in Hammond and Hopkins, pp. 174–239

———, and D. F. McKenzie, with the assistance of Maureen Bell (editors), *The Cambridge History of the Book in Britain: Volume IV: 1557–1695* (Cambridge, 2002)

———, and Paul Hammond, 'Dryden and a Poem for Lewis Maidwell', *TLS*, 25 May 1984, p. 586

Barthes, Roland, *Œuvres complètes*, 5 vols (Paris, 2002)

Beal, Peter, *In Praise of Scribes: Manuscripts and their Makers in Seventeenth-century England* (Oxford, 1998)

———, *Index of English Literary Manuscripts*, vol. 2, parts i–ii (London, 1987–93)

———, ' "The most constant and best entertainment": Sir George Etherege's Reading in Ratisbon', *The Library*, sixth series, 10 (1988) 122–44

Berry, Philippa, *Of Chastity and Power: Elizabethan Literature and the Unmarried Queen* (London, 1989)

Bottkol, J. McG., 'Dryden's Latin Scholarship', *Modern Philology*, 40 (1943) 214–54

Brennan, Michael, and Paul Hammond, 'The Badminton Manuscript: A New Miscellany of Restoration Verse', *English Manuscript Studies 1100–1700*, 5 (1995) 171–207

Brooks, Harold F., 'A Bibliography of John Oldham the Restoration Satirist', *Oxford Bibliographical Society Proceedings and Papers*, 5 (1936–9) 1–38

Brower, Reuben Arthur, *Alexander Pope: The Poetry of Allusion* (Oxford, 1959)

Cameron, W. J., 'Miscellany Poems 1684–1716', unpublished PhD thesis, University of Reading, 1957

Castrop, Helmut, 'Dryden and Flecknoe: A Link', *Review of English Studies*, 23 (1972) 455–8.

Catalogue of the Pamphlets, Books, Newspapers, and Manuscripts Relating to the Civil War, the Commonwealth, and Restoration, Collected by George Thomason, 1640–1661, 2 vols (London, 1908)

Clayton, Thomas, ' "Morning Glew" and Other Sweat Leaves in the Folio text of Andrew Marvell's Major Pre-Restoration Poems', *English Literary Renaissance*, 2 (1972) 356–75

Clingham, Greg, 'Roscommon's "Academy", Chetwood's Manuscript "Life of Roscommon", and Dryden's Translation Project', *Restoration*, 26 (2002) 15–26

Coolidge, J. S., 'Marvell and Horace', *Modern Philology*, 63 (1965) 111–20

Corns, Thomas N. (editor), *The Royal Image: Representations of Charles I* (Cambridge, 1999)

Crist, Timothy, 'Government Control of the Press after the Expiration of the Printing Act in 1679', *Publishing History*, 5 (1979) 49–77

Derrida, Jacques, *L'Écriture et la différence* (Paris, 1967; new edition 1994)

Dobranski, Stephen B., *Milton, Authorship, and the Book Trade* (Cambridge, 1999)

Edie, Caroline, 'Right Rejoicing: Sermons on the Occasion of the Stuart Restoration, 1660', *Bulletin of the John Rylands University Library of Manchester*, 62 (1979–80) 61–86

———, 'The Popular Idea of Monarchy on the Eve of the Stuart Restoration', *Huntington Library Quarterly*, 39 (1975–6) 343–73

Erskine-Hill, Howard, *The Augustan Idea in English Literature* (London, 1983)

Eversole, Richard, 'The Traquair Manuscript of Dryden's *The Hind and the Panther*', *PBSA*, 75 (1981) 179–91

Fisher, Nicholas, 'A New Dating of Rochester's *Artemiza to Chlöe*', *English Manuscript Studies 1100–1700*, 8 (2000) 300–19

——— (editor), *That Second Bottle: Essays on John Wilmot, Earl of Rochester* (Manchester, 2000)

———, 'The Publication of the Earl of Rochester's Works, 1660–1779', unpublished PhD thesis, University of Leeds, 2004

Foucault, Michel, 'Qu'est-ce qu'un auteur?' in *Dits et Ecrits 1954–1988: I: 1954–1969* (Paris, 1994), pp. 789–821

Gardiner, Anne Barbeau, 'A Jacobite Song by John Dryden', *Yale University Library Gazette*, 61 (1986) 49–54

Genette, Gérard, *Palimpsestes: la littérature au second degré* (Paris, 1982)

George, M. D., *English Political Caricature to 1792* (Oxford, 1959)

Greaves, Richard L., *Deliver Us from Evil: The Radical Underground in Britain, 1660–1663* (New York, 1986)

Green, Susan, and Steven N. Zwicker (editors), *John Dryden: A Tercentenary Miscellany* (San Marino, Calif., 2001); also issued as vol. 63 nos 1–2 of *The Huntington Library Quarterly*

Griffin, Dustin, 'Dryden's "Oldham" and the Perils of Writing', *Modern Language Quarterly*, 37 (1976) 133–50

Hageman, Elizabeth H., and Andrea Sununu, 'New Manuscript Texts of Katherine Philips, the "matchless Orinda" ', *English Manuscript Studies*, 4 (1993) 174–219

———, ' "More copies of it abroad than I could have imagin'd": Further Manuscript Texts of Katherine Philips, "the matchless Orinda" ', *English Manuscript Studies*, 5 (1995) 127–69

Hammond, Paul, 'A Song Attributed to Dryden', *The Library*, sixth series, 21 (1999) 59–66

———, 'Did Dryden write the *Prologue to 'Julius Caesar'*?', *English Studies*, 65 (1984) 409–19

———, *Dryden and the Traces of Classical Rome* (Oxford, 1999)

———, 'Dryden's *Albion and Albanius*: The Apotheosis of Charles II', in *The Court Masque*, edited by David Lindley (Manchester, 1984), pp. 169–83

———, 'Dryden's Revision of *To the Lady Castlemain*', *PBSA*, 78 (1984) 81–90

———, 'Figures of Horace in Dryden's Literary Criticism', in Martindale and Hopkins, pp. 127–47

————, *Figuring Sex between Men from Shakespeare to Rochester* (Oxford, 2002)

————, *John Dryden: A Literary Life* (Basingstoke, 1991)

————, *John Oldham and the Renewal of Classical Culture* (Cambridge, 1983)

————, 'Marvell's Pronouns', *Essays in Criticism*, 53 (2003) 225–40

————, 'Marvell's Sexuality', *The Seventeenth Century*, 11 (1996) 87–123, revised and reprinted in *Figuring Sex between Men*, pp. 186–225

————, 'Milton, Dryden, and Lucretius', *The Seventeenth Century*, 16 (2001) 158–76

————, 'Rochester's Homoeroticism', in Fisher (editor), *That Second Bottle*, pp. 46–72, revised and reprinted in *Figuring Sex between Men*, pp. 226–54

————, 'Sir Philip Wodehouse's Pantheon of Renaissance Poets', *The Seventeenth Century*, 18 (2003) 54–60

————, 'Some Contemporary References to Dryden', in Hammond and Hopkins, pp. 359–400

————, 'The Autograph Manuscript of Dryden's *Heroique Stanza's* and its Implications for Editors', *PBSA*, 76 (1982) 457–70

————, 'The Dating of Three Poems by Rochester from the Evidence of Bodleian MS Don. b. 8', *Bodleian Library Record*, 11 (1982) 58–9

————, 'The Interplay of Past and Present in Dryden's "Palamon and Arcite" ', in *The Age of Projects*, edited by Maximillian E. Novak (Toronto, forthcoming)

————, 'The Janus Poet: Dryden's Critique of Shakespeare', in *John Dryden (1631–1700): His Politics, His Plays, and His Poets*, edited by Claude Rawson and Aaron Santesso (Newark, N.J., 2004), pp. 158–79

————, ' "The Miseries of Visits": An Addition to the Literature on Robert Julian, Secretary to the Muses', *The Seventeenth Century*, 8 (1993) 161–3

————, 'The Printing of the Dryden-Tonson *Miscellany Poems* (1684) and *Sylvae* (1685)', *PBSA*, 84 (1990) 405–12

————, 'The Prologue and Epilogue to Dryden's *Marriage A-la-Mode* and the problem of *Covent Garden Drolery*', *PBSA*, 81 (1987) 155–72

————, 'The Robinson Manuscript Miscellany of Restoration Verse in the Brotherton Collection, Leeds', *Proceedings of the Leeds Philosophical and Literary Society, Literary and Historical Section*, 18 (1982) 275–324

————, 'Two Echoes of Rochester's *A Satire Against Reason and Mankind* in Dryden', *Notes and Queries*, 233 (1988) 170–1

————, and David Hopkins (editors), *John Dryden: Tercentenary Essays* (Oxford, 2000)

Harris, Brice, 'Captain Robert Julian, Secretary to the Muses', *ELH*, 10 (1943) 294–309

Harris, Tim, *London Crowds in the Reign of Charles II: Propaganda and Politics from the Restoration until the Exclusion Crisis* (Cambridge, 1987)

Harrison, J. P., and Peter Laslett, *The Library of John Locke*, second edition (Oxford, 1971)

Harth, Phillip, *Pen for a Party: Dryden's Tory Propaganda in its Contexts* (Princeton, 1993)

————, 'The Text of Dryden's Poetry', in Green and Zwicker, pp. 227–44

Helgerson, Richard, 'The Land Speaks: Cartography, Chorography, and Subversion in Renaissance England', *Representations*, 16 (1986) 51–85

Hopkins, David, 'Dryden and the Garth-Tonson *Metamorphoses*', *Review of English Studies*, n.s. 39 (1988) 64–74

————, 'Editing, Authenticity, and Translation: Re-presenting Dryden's Poetry in 2000', in Hammond and Hopkins, pp. 330–57

Horden, John, *Francis Quarles (1592–1644): A Bibliography of his Works to the Year 1800* (Oxford, 1953)

Hughes, Derek, *Dryden's Heroic Plays* (Basingstoke, 1981)

————, 'Naming and Entitlement in Wycherley, Etherege, and Dryden', *Comparative Drama*, 21 (1987) 259–89

Hume, Robert D., *The Development of English Drama in the Late Seventeenth Century* (Oxford, 1976)

Jose, Nicholas, *Ideas of the Restoration in English Literature, 1660–71* (Basingstoke, 1984)

Kantorowicz, Ernst H., *The King's Two Bodies: A Study in Medieval Political Theology* (Princeton, 1957)

Keeble, N. H., *The Literary Culture of Nonconformity in Later Seventeenth-Century England* (Leicester, 1987)

Kelliher, Hilton, 'A New Text of Marvell's "To His Coy Mistress" ', *Notes and Queries*, 215 (1970) 254–6

————, *Andrew Marvell: Poet & Politician 1621–78* (London, 1978)

King, John N., *Tudor Royal Iconography: Literature and Art in an Age of Religious Crisis* (Princeton, 1989)

King, Kathryn R., *Jane Barker, Exile: A Literary Career 1675–1725* (Oxford, 2000)

————, *The Poems of Jane Barker: The Magdalen Manuscript*, Magdalen College Occasional Paper 3 (Oxford, 1998)

Kitchin, George, *Sir Roger L'Estrange: A Contribution to the History of the Press in the Seventeenth Century* (London, 1913)

Knoppers, Laura Lunger, *Constructing Cromwell: Ceremony, Portrait, and Print, 1645–1661* (Cambridge, 2000)

Love, Harold, 'Dryden, Rochester, and the Invention of the "Town" ', in *John Dryden (1631–1700): His Politics, His Plays, and His Poets*, edited by Claude Rawson and Aaron Santesso (Newark, N.J., 2004), pp. 36–51

————, *English Clandestine Satire 1660–1702* (Oxford, 2004)

————, 'Oral and Scribal Texts in Early Modern England' in Barnard and McKenzie, pp. 97–121

————, 'Refining Rochester: Private Texts and Public Readers', *Harvard Library Bulletin*, n.s. 7 (1996) 40–9

————, 'Rochester: A Tale of Two Manuscripts', *Yale University Library Gazette*, 72 (1997) 41–53

————, 'Rochester's "I' th' isle of Britain": decoding a textual tradition', *English Manuscript Studies 1100–1700*, 6 (1997) 175–223

————, *Scribal Publication in Seventeenth-Century England* (Oxford, 1993)

————, 'Scribal Texts and Literary Communities: The Rochester Circle and Osborn b. 105', *Studies in Bibliography*, 42 (1989) 219–35

————, 'The Scribal Transmission of Rochester's Songs', *Bibliographical Society of Australia and New Zealand Bulletin*, 20 (1996) 161–80

Lynch, Kathleen M., *Jacob Tonson, Kit-Cat Publisher* (Knoxville, Tenn., 1971)

Macdonald, Hugh, *John Dryden: A Bibliography of Early Editions and of Drydeniana* (Oxford, 1939)

Macgillivray, Royce, *Restoration Historians and the Civil War* (The Hague, 1974)

Mack, Maynard, *Collected in Himself: Essays Critical, Biographical, and Bibliographical on Pope and Some of his Contemporaries* (Newark, N.J., 1982)

McKeon, Michael, *Politics and Poetry in Restoration England: The Case of Dryden's 'Annus Mirabilis'* (Cambridge, Mass., 1975)

McRae, Andrew, *Literature, Satire and the Early Stuart State* (Cambridge, 2004)

Manning, Gillian, 'Some Quotations from Rochester in Charles Blount's *Philostratus*', *Notes and Queries*, 231 (1986) 38–40

Marin, Louis, *Portrait of the King* (London, 1988)

Martindale, Charles, and David Hopkins (editors), *Horace Made New: Horatian Influences on British Writing from the Renaissance to the Twentieth Century* (Cambridge, 1993)

Mason, H. A., 'The Dream of Happiness', *The Cambridge Quarterly*, 8 (1978) 11–55 and 9 (1980) 218–71

———, *To Homer through Pope* (London, 1972)

Mason, J. R., 'To Milton through Dryden and Pope', unpublished PhD thesis, University of Cambridge, 1987

Mendelson, Sara Heller, *The Mental World of Stuart Women* (Brighton, 1987)

Miller, John, 'The Potential for "Absolutism" in Later Stuart England', *History*, 69 (1984) 187–207

Miller, C. W., *Henry Herringman Imprints: A Preliminary Checklist* (Charlottesville, Va., 1949)

Morris, Brian, *John Cleveland (1613–1658): A Bibliography of his Poems* (London, 1967)

Mowl, Timothy, and Brian Earnshaw, *Architecture without Kings* (Manchester, 1995)

Mullan, John, 'Dryden's Anonymity', in *The Cambridge Companion to John Dryden*, edited by Steven N. Zwicker (Cambridge, 2004), pp. 156–80

Niemeyer, Carl, 'The Earl of Roscommon's Academy', *Modern Language Notes*, 49 (1934) 432–7

Norbrook, David, *Writing the English Republic: Poetry, Rhetoric and Politics 1627–1660* (Cambridge, 1999)

Novak, Maximillian E., 'Dryden's "Ape of the French Eloquence" and Richard Flecknoe', *Bulletin of the New York Public Library*, 12 (1968) 499–506

O'Neill, J. H., 'Oldham's "Sardanapalus": a Restoration Mock-encomium and its Topical Implications', *Clio*, 5 (1976) 193–210

Osborn, James M., *John Dryden: Some Biographical Facts and Problems*, revised edition (Gainesville, Fla., 1965)

Owen, Susan J., *Restoration Theatre and Crisis* (Oxford, 1996)

Papali, G. F., *Jacob Tonson, Publisher* (Auckland, 1968)

Parry, Graham, *The Golden Age Restor'd: The Culture of the Stuart Court, 1603–42* (Manchester, 1981)

Patterson, John D., 'Another Text of Rochester's "To the Post Boy" ', *Restoration*, 4 (1980) 14–16

Pickering, Oliver, 'Henry Hall of Hereford's Poetical Tributes to Henry Purcell', *The Library*, 16 (1994) 18–29

Plomer, Henry R., *A Dictionary of the Printers and Booksellers . . . from 1668 to 1725* (London, 1922)

Rahn, B. J., '*A Ra-ree Show* – A Rare Cartoon: Revolutionary Propaganda in the Treason Trial of Stephen College' in *Studies in Change and Revolution: Aspects of*

English Intellectual History 1640–1800, edited by Paul J. Korshin (Menston, 1972), pp. 77–98

Raylor, Timothy, *Cavaliers, Clubs, and Literary Culture* (Newark, N.J., 1994)

———, 'Reading Machiavelli; Writing Cromwell', *Turnbull Library Record*, 35 (2002) 9–32

———, 'Waller's Machiavellian Cromwell: The Imperial Argument of *A Panegyrick to My Lord Protector*', *Review of English Studies*, 56 (2005) 386–411

Raymond, Joad, 'Milton', in Barnard and McKenzie, pp. 376–87

Reedy, Gerard, 'Mystical Politics: The Imagery of Charles II's Coronation', in *Studies in Change and Revolution: Aspects of English Intellectual History 1640–1800*, edited by Paul J. Korshin (Menston, 1972), pp. 19–42

Reverand, Cedric D., 'The Final "Memorial of my own Principles": Dryden's Alter Egos in his Later Career', in Hammond and Hopkins, pp. 282–307

Richards, J., ' "His Nowe Majestie" and the English Monarchy: the Kingship of Charles I before 1640', *Past and Present*, 113 (1986) 70–96

Ricks, Christopher, *Allusion to the Poets* (Oxford, 2002)

Robertson, Randy, 'The Delicate Art of Anonymity; The Case of *Absalom and Achitophel*', *Restoration*, 27 (2003) 41–60

Roper, Alan, 'Who's Who in *Absalom and Achitophel*?', in Green and Zwicker, pp. 98–138.

Røstvig, Maren-Sofie, *The Happy Man: Studies in the Metamorphoses of a Classical Ideal*, second edition (Oslo, 1962)

Saslow, Edward L., 'The Rose Alley Ambuscade', *Restoration*, 26 (2002) 27–49

Sensabaugh, George F., *That Grand Whig Milton* (Stanford, Calif., 1952)

Sherbo, Arthur C., 'Dryden as a Cambridge Editor, *Studies in Bibliography*, 38 (1985) 251–61

———, 'The Dryden-Cambridge Translation of Plutarch's Lives', *Études Anglaises*, 32 (1979) 177–84

Simonsuuri, Kirsti, *Homer's Original Genius* (Cambridge, 1979)

Smith, John Harrington, 'Dryden and Flecknoe: A Conjecture', *Philological Quarterly*, 33 (1954) 338–41

———, 'Dryden's Prologue and Epilogue to *Mithridates*, Revived', *PMLA*, 68 (1953) 251–67

Smyth, Adam, 'Printed Miscellanies in England, 1640–1682: "store-house[s] of wit." ', *Criticism*, 42 (2000) 151–84

Stack, Frank, *Pope and Horace* (Cambridge, 1985)

Staves, Susan, *Players' Scepters: Fictions of Authority in the Restoration* (Lincoln, Nebr., 1979)

Swedenberg, H. P., 'England's Joy: *Astraea Redux* in its Setting', *Studies in Philology*, 50 (1953) 30–44

The Library of John R. B. Brett-Smith: London Thursday 27 May 2004 (London, 2004)

Thorn-Drury, G., 'Some Notes on Dryden', *Review of English Studies*, 1 (1925) 187–97

Tilley, Morris Palmer, *A Dictionary of the Proverbs in England in the Sixteenth and Seventeenth Centuries* (Ann Arbor, 1950)

Turner, James Grantham, *Libertines and Radicals in Early Modern London: Sexuality, Politics and Literary Culture, 1630–1685* (Cambridge, 2002)

Vaisey, D. G., 'Anthony Stephens: The Rise and Fall of an Oxford Bookseller', in *Studies in the Book Trade in Honour of Graham Pollard* (Oxford, 1975), pp. 91–117

Venuti, Lawrence, '*The Destruction of Troy*: Translation and Royalist Cultural Politics in the Interregnum', *Journal of Medieval and Renaissance Studies*, 23 (1993) 197–219

Vieth, David M., 'A Textual Paradox: Rochester's "To a lady in a letter" ', *PBSA*, 54 (1960) 147–62 and 55 (1961) 130–3

———, 'An Unsuspected Cancel in Tonson's 1691 "Rochester" ', *PBSA*, 55 (1961) 130–3

———, *Attribution in Restoration Poetry: A Study of Rochester's 'Poems' of 1680* (New Haven, 1963)

———, 'Dryden's *Mac Flecknoe*: The Case against Editorial Confusion', *Harvard Library Bulletin*, 24 (1976) 204–45

———, 'The Discovery of the Date of *Mac Flecknoe*' in *Evidence in Literary Scholarship*, edited by René Wellek and Alvaro Ribiero (Oxford, 1979), pp. 63–87

von Maltzahn, Nicholas, 'Marvell's Ghost', in *Marvell and Liberty*, edited by Warren Chernaik and Martin Dzelzainis (Basingstoke, 1999), pp. 50–74

———, 'The First Reception of *Paradise Lost* (1667)', *Review of English Studies*, n.s. 47 (1996) 479–99

Weber, Harold, 'Representations of the King: Charles II and his Escape from Worcester', *Studies in Philology*, 85 (1988) 489–509

Williams, Gordon, *A Glossary of Shakespeare's Sexual Language* (London, 1997)

Wilson, A. J. N., 'Andrew Marvell: *An Horatian Ode Upon Cromwell's Return from Ireland*: The Thread of the Poem and its Use of Classical Allusion', *Critical Quarterly*, 11 (1969) 325–41

Winn, James Anderson, ' "Dryden's Epistle before Creech's Lucretius": A Study in Restoration Ghostwriting', *Philological Quarterly*, 71 (1992) 47–68

———, *John Dryden and his World* (New Haven, 1987)

———, *"When Beauty Fires the Blood": Love and the Arts in the Age of Dryden* (Ann Arbor, 1992)

Yates, Frances, *Astraea: The Imperial Theme in the Sixteenth Century* (London, 1975)

Zwicker, Steven N., *Dryden's Political Poetry: The Typology of King and Nation* (Providence, R.I., 1972)

———, 'Lines of Authority: Politics and Literary Culture in the Restoration', in *Politics of Discourse: The Literature and History of Seventeenth-Century England*, edited by Kevin Sharpe and Steven N. Zwicker (Berkeley, 1987), pp. 230–70

INDEX

Footnotes are indexed only when significant information about seventeenth-century writers or books would not otherwise be found. The names of modern scholars are not indexed when they occur only in the footnotes, but are included when they appear in the main text. Noblemen are indexed under their titles, not their surnames.

Index

Studies in Renaissance Literature

Volume 1: *The Theology of John Donne*
Jeffrey Johnson

Volume 2: *Doctrine and Devotion in Seventeenth-Century Poetry*
Studies in Donne, Herbert, Crashaw and Vaughan
R. V. Young

Volume 3: *The Song of Songs in English Renaissance Literature*
Kisses of their Mouths
Noam Flinker

Volume 4: *King James I and the Religious Culture of England*
James Doelman

Volume 5: *Neo-historicism: Studies in Renaissance Literature,*
History and Politics
edited by Robin Headlam Wells, Glenn Burgess
and Rowland Wymer

Volume 6: *The Uncertain World of Samson Agonistes*
John T. Shawcross

Volume 7: *Milton and the Terms of Liberty*
edited by Graham Parry and Joad Raymond

Volume 8: *George Sandys: Travel, Colonialism and Tolerance*
in the Seventeenth Century
James Ellison

Volume 9: *Shakespeare and Machiavelli*
John Roe

Volume 10: *John Donne's Professional Lives*
edited by David Colclough

Volume 11: *Chivalry and Romance in the English Renaissance*
Alex Davis

Volume 12: *Shakespearean Tragedy as Chivalric Romance:*
Rethinking Macbeth, Hamlet, Othello, and King Lear
Michael L. Hays